Scrapbooking
YOUR FAVORITE
Family Memories

MEMORY
MAKERS
BOOKS

DENVER, COLORADO

Table *of* Contents

Introduction

Lovers of scrapbooking, this book is for you.

Whether you are just entering the world of scrapbooking or have been involved with this art for many years, this book has plenty to get you inspired. Learn unique ways to creatively save your old photographs. Crop photographs so that they beautifully adorn every page. Artistically capture the joyous moments of your baby's life. Document the challenges and successes of your child's school days.

We've compiled a huge selection of ideas and projects—over 500 pages of instruction and inspiration—in four scrapbooking areas: basic scrapbooking, photo cropping, baby scrapbooks and school days scrapbooks. Within **Scrapbooking Your Favorite Family Memories**, you will not only find project ideas, but also basic materials, techniques and personal stories from other scrapbookers. Check out the Table of Contents at the beginning of each section for creative project ideas and the resource page at the back of each section for help finding materials. So gather up your family photos and start scrapbooking today!

INTRODUCING!

BAYLESS FARMS
organically grown

FIVE MAGIC BEANS
NET WT 10 g

MAY FLOWERS
FILL YOUR HEART
WITH A FRESH
PERSPECTIVE
AND NEW LIFE!

OUR FAMILY HAS
GROWN...
AND WE HAVE A NEW
SPROUT!

JACK CONNOR
WeGe BAYLESS

SPROUTED
MAY 5, 1999
9:55 AM
HT. 23 1/2 INCHES
WT. 10LBS. 3 OZS.

PROUD PARENTS

SCOTT AND KATY
BAYLESS

Magic Beans   (HYBRED)

Children are like seeds, in each
there is a promise of the future.
Nurture them with love.

type	inches	grows best	days to germinate
annual	23½"	full sun	280

PLANTING INSTRUCTIONS

Sow in fertile soil giving lots of love
and affection. Water and feed often.
After becoming well established,
harvest after 18-21 years. Comes
from good stock.

A YEAR IN THE LIFE OF JR

Terri Robichon
Plymouth, Minnesota

STARTING OUT

APRIL 1999

Chris-Craft

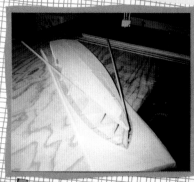

NOW IT'S

MAY '99

MEMORY
M A K E R S

Michele Gerbrandt's

Scrapbook BASICS

**The Complete
Guide to Preserving
Your Memories**

**MEMORY
MAKERS
BOOKS**

DENVER, COLORADO

Contents

20

45

61

84

117

THE GERBRANDT'S

OUR FAMILY

DANIEL, AGE 7
MICHELE, AGE 36
SASHA, AGE 9½
RON, AGE 38
ANNA, AGE 12

2002

Introduction

Welcome to the world of creative scrapbooking! There seems to be at least one person in each family who always has a camera in hand. She's the one recording the three-legged races at Fourth of July picnics and that special moment when birthday wishes are made and candles blown out. She understands that the rich and most rewarding moments in our lives are worth reliving through photos, carefully preserved in albums. If you are holding this book in your hands, chances are that we are describing you.

Contemporary scrapbooking is the art of arranging photos and journaling in a photo-safe environment. Scrapbook pages can be simple or complex. They may include memorabilia such as movie ticket stubs, theater programs or sports tickets. Pages can be decorated with stickers, pens, embossed designs and much, much more. With the wide and growing range of products available, only time and imagination limit today's scrapbooker.

If you are new to the art of scrapbooking, you may be confused about where and how to begin. This book has been created to set you on the path to a lifetime of scrapping enjoyment. We will address questions such as: What do I need to get started? How do I find supplies? What does "photo safe" mean and how do I identify safe albums and products? What should I include in my journaling? There are instructional pages that will guide you through the process of sorting and organizing photos and laying out beautiful scrapbook pages. Both new and seasoned scrapbookers will draw inspiration from the page ideas of *Memory Makers* readers and our talented staff.

Creating an album can be a very rewarding experience. I discovered contemporary scrapbooking in 1992 and it has changed my life, opening up new worlds of possibilities. I continue to learn and grow as a scrapbooker day by day and year by year. I am so pleased that you have decided to join me on this journey. Enjoy creating your albums. You have so many special memories to preserve and stories that are just waiting to be told.

> SCRAPBOOKING BONDS, TRANS-FORMS AND CAN HELP HEAL PEOPLE.
> —*Michele*

Michele

Michele Gerbrandt

Founder of *Memory Makers*® magazine

The history of scrapbooking

A scrapbook is magic. It captures and cradles life's most precious moments. Through photographs, memorabilia, journaled thoughts and stories, scrapbooks evoke our fondest memories and allow us to relive daily and once-in-a-lifetime experiences.

While the earliest forms of scrapbooking can be traced back to the 16th century, modern scrapbooking really began with the invention of photography in 1826. That's when a Frenchman by the name of Nicéphore Niépce first captured an image on a sheet of metal. Thirteen years later the first camera became available to the public. In the mid-1800s, the popularity of portrait photography received an infusion when a method was discovered which made it possible to make multiple prints. Today's scrapbookers are walking in the well-tread footsteps of photography's Golden Age, set down more than one hundred years ago!

LOOKING BACK

1598 An author refers to gathering "words and approved phrases...to make use as it were a common place booke [sic]."

1709 John Locke, a philosopher, publishes his *New Method of Making Common-place Books*.

1769 William Granger introduces a book that includes extra blank pages. It starts a hobby known as "extra illustrating" books.

1798 Lithography, a printing technique which fixes images on a stone or metal plate using ink-absorbent and ink-repellent vehicles, is invented.

1800s Young women keep friendship albums filled with hair weavings and writings.

1837 Godefroye Englemann invents chromolithography, a process of lithography in colors from a series of plates.

1859 Card photographs known as cartes de visite come to the United States.

1860s Mass production of advertising cards for companies and products begins.

1867 John Jerrard of London calls himself a dealer in photographs and scrap prints of every description for albums and scrapbooks.

My Nana's Wedding portrait Ann M. Baron June 18th, 1938 Chester, PA.

Preserving beloved wedding photos, whether they are contemporary photos or heritage photos, is a common thread that often brings people to scrapbooking.

I modeled my wedding flowers after Nana's.

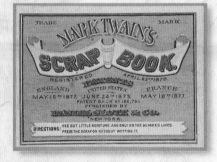

1872 Mark Twain markets his self-pasting scrapbook.

1880 E.W. Gurley publishes *Scrapbooks and How to Make Them.*

1888 George Eastman sells the Kodak camera for amateur photographers under the slogan, "You push the button, we do the rest."

1945 Prizes offered for children's scrapbooks.

1970s Alex Haley's *Roots* spurs a resurgence of interest in family history.

1996 *Memory Makers®* magazine begins publication.

Scrapbooking today

Scrapbookers know the value of preserving memories. They understand that the pages they create are, and will be, cherished. By using carefully selected products, they ensure their albums will survive and become heirlooms. Future generations will open the scrapbooks and hear the voices of their creators. In learning about us, they will have a better understanding of themselves.

Modern scrapbooking has evolved as an understanding of those elements damaging to photos and memorabilia has emerged. Only in recent years have the terms "archival quality," "photo-safe," "lignin- and acid-free," and "buffered paper" become household words. Today's scrapbookers look for products bearing these labels, knowing the use of these products will create a safer environment and better preserve album contents. As scrapbooking has grown in popularity, more supplies and products have become available. Today, shoppers can choose from thousands of products, including stickers, stamps, papers, die cuts and pens, which open windows of creative opportunity.

SAFER SCRAPBOOKING PRODUCTS

- PVC-free plastic page protectors and memorabilia keepers: PVC releases fumes that destroy photos and paper.

- Permanent pigment inks: Other inks fade, bleed and spread.

- Photo-safe and acid-free adhesives: Other adhesives can damage photos.

- Acid- and lignin-free album pages and paper products: Acid and lignin cause photos and paper to degrade and discolor.

- Buffered paper: Buffered products help act as a barrier to prevent chemicals from contaminating paper and damaging photos and pages.

REMOVE PHOTOS FROM MAGNETIC ALBUMS

Sandwiched between the self-adhesive pages and plastic overlays, your photos will discolor, become brittle and deteriorate. Here are ways to remove photos safely:

- Remove photos by slipping a slender knife or dental floss beneath a corner to loosen it.

- To loosen photos that are firmly stuck to the page, try a commercial adhesive remover such as un-du's PhotoCare™ Solution. It removes smudges and adhesive residue safely from photos.

- If the album's plastic overlay is stuck to your photos, consult a conservator.

- Never force a photo from a page. If photos are truly stuck, consider investing in reprints rather than attempting to remove.

- Never use heat to loosen photos from a page.

Why do we scrapbook?

There are as many reasons to scrapbook as there are scrapbookers. Your reason for scrapbooking is as personal and unique as the album you are about to create. On the pages that follow, you will find a number of scenarios that bring people just like you to the rewarding hobby of scrapbooking.

1. DOCUMENT FAMILY HISTORY

Photos are a great way to document important family events as they unfold. Displayed within a scrapbook, they can be enjoyed each time the book is opened. Long after those in the images are gone, their faces remain familiar and journaled pages give voice to their hopes, dreams, fears and foibles.

2. TELL A STORY

Pictures tell stories that can be expanded upon through creative and concise journaling. Using photos as springboards, scrapbookers then fill in important information such as when and where a picture was taken and who appears in the image. But they can do much more. By recording snippets of conversation, jokes and contemplations, journaling can recreate the mood of events and bring the stories back to life.

Recipients of heritage photos and those fond of genealogical research often turn to scrapbooking because it provides the perfect harbor for preserving images and hard-found documentation together.

Bonnie Peacock, Sevierville, Tennessee

3. MAKE A GIFT

Show those you love how important they are and what their presence has meant in your life with a gift album. Gift albums may include photos of special times you have shared or may pay tribute to the scrapbook's recipient. Either way, a gift album is sure to be a cherished treasure.

4. GET PHOTOS ORGANIZED

If you're like most people, there's a box or drawer somewhere in your home devoted to a mess of random photos. Tucked away in that desk or dresser, or hidden in boxes under beds and in closets, they are all but forgotten. Creating a scrapbook is a great motivator to finally pull out your photos and put them in order.

5. ENJOY SOMETHING CREATIVE

Break out the scissors. Wade through reams of colored paper. Make a scrapbook that is fun, creative and uniquely your own. Scrapbooking lets your imagination run wild. You're preserving memories and at the same time stretching your artistic side. The sense of accomplishment you gain will be long lasting.

At one time or another, we all have a stockpile of unorganized photos just begging to be put in a scrapbook album to have their stories told.

6. HELP HEAL

A tragedy, whether it is suffering personal illness or the loss of a loved one, can leave you staggering with grief. When the pain has subsided, you may wish to scrapbook about your experience, your thoughts and feelings. Scrapbooking is a wonderful tool for reliving the good times and moving past those that are difficult. It can be extremely therapeutic.

Baby's first year bustles with rapid growth and change. Few parents can resist capturing those sweet little grins and miraculous "firsts" in a baby scrapbook album.

7. START A BABY ALBUM

The first tooth, the first word, the first step. Those baby days go by in a flash and you'll want to record all those special "firsts" in an album. A scrapbook featuring your children will bring back the smell of baby powder and the sound of "patty cake" hands. Later, your children will revel in their earliest adventures (and misadventures!).

8. MAKE NEW FRIENDS

New people are discovering scrapbooking daily. Scrapbookers gather at quilting-bee-like events called "crops." They attend large conventions and small workshops, gather in mountain and lakeside resorts and on cruise ships, and chat online. Wherever they meet, scrapbookers make new friends with whom they share their love of scrapbooking.

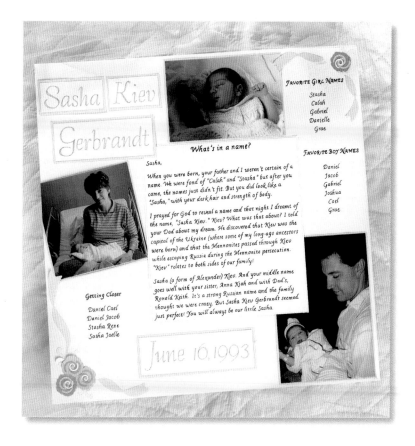

The future of scrapbooking

A handful of years ago creative scrapbooking was in its infancy. In intervening years, it has grown, matured, and gained in popularity. Today, more than 20 percent of American households have members who scrapbook and the hobby is gaining popularity worldwide.

Where once it was difficult to find scrapbook tools and supplies, now more and more stores are dedicating whole sections to meeting the needs of this craft audience. Across the nation, scrapbook stores are popping up, catering exclusively to scrapbookers' needs. Today's scrapbookers continue to push the envelope, exploring new ways to use the growing variety of available products and tools. You are part of this great movement to preserve life's memories. And your efforts will help define the future of this wonderful art form.

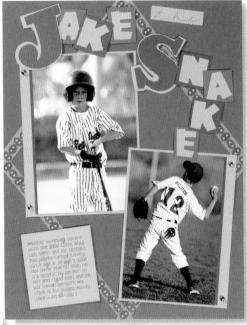

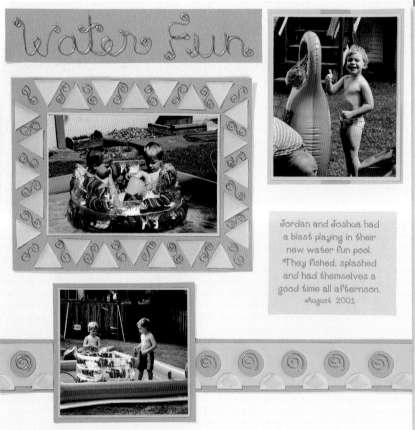

More and more scrapbookers are adding hardware to their scrapbook pages. Metal fasteners and eyelets are the latest craze to hit scrapbooking.

Photos MaryJo Regier, Littleton, Colorado

Wire is adding a new twist to scrapbooks with its hand-shaped versatility and its many colors.

Alexandra Bleicher, Chilliwack, BC, Canada

One of the most fun trends to come to scrapbooking is creative photo cropping. Silhouette cropping is just one of the many simple cropping techniques that can bring visual impact to your scrapbook pages.

Photos Tiare Smith Woods, Evanston, Illinois

the first American Whitcomb

Mary Irene became a citizen January 3, 1916

Baubles, in the form of buttons, and organic materials such as raffia are increasingly finding their way into scrapbook albums when a homespun look is desired. Beads and embroidery stitching are also perfectly at home on scrapbook pages.

Erikia Ghumm, Denver, Colorado
Photos Pennie Stutzman, Broomfield, Colorado

Creative photo cropping takes on many artistic forms—in this case a mosaic—which allows you to use many photos on one scrapbook page.

Veronique Grasset, Montreau, France

Heat embossed rubber stamping continues to grow in popularity with the increasing numbers of gorgeous stamp designs in countless themes and pigment inks and embossing powders in dazzling colors.

Joyce Schweitzer
Greensboro, North Carolina

From every human being there rises a light that reaches straight to heaven, and when two souls that are destined to be together find each other, the streams of light flow together, and a single, brighter light goes forth from that united being.

AS YOU WISH

For Sasha's 9th Birthday, we had a Ceramics party at As You Wish in Boulder, Colorado. Sasha received a Birthday plate, that we now use for each family member's Birthday!   June 15, 2001

Tools & supplies

Most experienced scrapbookers feel like kids in a candy shop when visiting their local scrapbook or hobby store. But newcomers to the hobby can easily be overwhelmed, even intimidated, by the plethora of scrapbook supply choices available. If you've never been in a scrapbook store or the scrapbook section of a hobby store, prepare yourself to see shelves and shelves filled with adhesives, albums, die cuts, papers, pens, punches, stamps, stickers, templates and more. Some shoppers give in to temptation and scoop up goodies by the basketful, while others flee out the door as empty-handed as when they arrived.

Successful shopping for supplies involves planning and an understanding of your personal scrapbooking needs. In the following pages you'll learn how to select the tools and products needed to create lasting books. You'll discover ways to organize and care for your materials so they'll continue to perform year after year.

PURCHASING SUPPLIES IS JUST LIKE GOING TO THE GROCERY STORE. IT'S BEST TO START OUT WITH A LIST

–Michele

Building a scrapbook toolbox

You are probably wondering what you need to get started. Beginning any new hobby requires an investment. Scrapbooking is no different. While you may find some useful tools in your home utility drawer (see page 23), you will most likely need to purchase some basic supplies in order to begin creating albums.

CONSUMABLE SUPPLIES VS. NON-CONSUMABLE TOOLS

Consumable supplies are those products that will be used up and need to replenished over time. Non-consumable supplies are those tools that keep on giving and giving until they eventually break or wear out. With proper care, most non-consumable tools will last indefinitely! As you become more involved with scrapbooking, you will note a distinct difference between the two.

CONSUMABLE SUPPLIES

Adhesive remover

Die cuts

Ink pads

Photo-safe adhesives

Pigment pens and markers

Solid and patterned papers

Stickers

NON-CONSUMABLE TOOLS

Craft knife

Cutting mat (not shown)

Paper crimpers

Paper trimmer (not shown)

Punches

Rulers

Scissors

Shape cutters

Stamps

Templates

Tools you may already have

The majority of hobbyists who come to scrapbooking already have some basic craft tools they use regularly for other hobbies. Many of the supplies you will find useful in scrapbooking are already close at hand, such as a sturdy, sharp pair of scissors and a metal straightedge ruler. Before you go shopping for new items, check around the house for any of the following supplies to add to your beginner's toolbox.

TOOLS YOU MAY OWN

Adhesive remover
Craft knife and extra blades
Cutting mat
Graphing or grid ruler
Metal straightedge ruler
Photo-safe adhesives
Regular scissors
Removable artists tape
Small, sharp scissors
Tweezers

Tools you'll need

As your interest in scrapbooking grows, and as you are ready to explore new artistic challenges, you can slowly add to your scrapbooking toolbox. Let's take a look at the various tools and supplies that eventually end up in a scrapbooker's arsenal, starting with the most basic needs of any beginner.

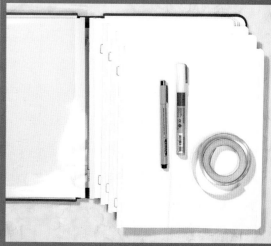

THE BEGINNER'S TOOLBOX
Album
Album pages
Black pigment pen
Page protectors
Photo-safe adhesive

INTERMEDIATE ADD-ONS
Colored paper
Corner rounder punch
Decorative rulers
Decorative scissors
Fancy and colored pens
Personal paper trimmer
Scrapbook magazines and
    idea books
Simple shape templates

COST-SAVING TIPS

BECOME A PREFERRED CUSTOMER Frequent shoppers may be rewarded with discounts. Some scrapbooking stores have punch cards that add up to steep savings based on the amount of goods purchased.

BUY IN BULK Many retailers offer quantity discounts on items such as paper, stickers and page protectors. Consider splitting the supplies with friends.

COMPARE PRICES Shop around, search catalogs and watch for sales in order to get the best bargains.

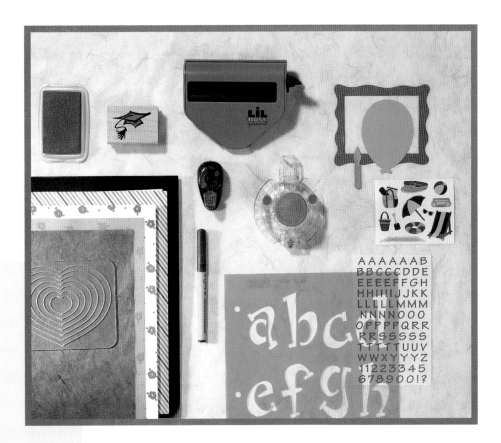

SUGGESTIONS FOR
THE EXPERIENCED

Alphabet and decorative
   stickers

Die cuts

Lettering and nested
   templates

Paper crimper

Patterned paper

Punches

Shape cutters

Stamps and ink pads

Vanishing ink pen

Vellum, mulberry, and
   other specialty papers

KEEP IT SIMPLE Great layouts aren't necessarily busy. A lot of imagination and a few products can create stunning pages.

MAKE A WISH LIST *(see page 43)* Before a gift-giving holiday, supply those who love you with a list of products you would like to receive. Be specific about manufacturers, colors, sizes and styles.

SHARE OR RENT TOOLS Rent tools from your local store, or crop with friends and share tools, conversation and laughter.

SWAP SUPPLIES Collect tools and supplies you no longer want and swap them with friends for products you need.

USE COUPONS Stores provide discount coupons in ads and fliers, which may cut the cost of your purchases by up to 50 percent.

USE YOUR COMPUTER Download free fonts and clip art or order supplies online at discount prices.

USE YOUR LOCAL LIBRARY Borrow books on art design or scrapbooking from your local library.

Using your tools & supplies

It's time to shop! But before you get started, take a few minutes to learn more about the scrapbook supplies and tools that are on the market. Understanding the products and their uses will make it easier for you to select precisely the items that will best suit your needs. Remember that all supplies you purchase should be safe for use with your photos and memorabilia (see page 14). Keep those archival issues in mind as your interest in scrapbooking and your number of tools and supplies grow.

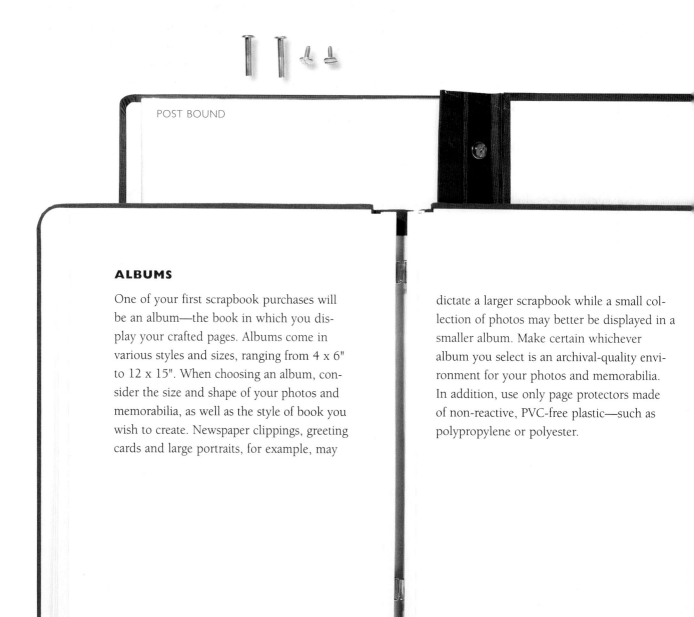

POST BOUND

STRAP STYLE

ALBUMS

One of your first scrapbook purchases will be an album—the book in which you display your crafted pages. Albums come in various styles and sizes, ranging from 4 x 6" to 12 x 15". When choosing an album, consider the size and shape of your photos and memorabilia, as well as the style of book you wish to create. Newspaper clippings, greeting cards and large portraits, for example, may dictate a larger scrapbook while a small collection of photos may better be displayed in a smaller album. Make certain whichever album you select is an archival-quality environment for your photos and memorabilia. In addition, use only page protectors made of non-reactive, PVC-free plastic—such as polypropylene or polyester.

POST BOUND This album type features post screws in the album's binding that allow you to add or rearrange pages. Extension posts may also be purchased for further expansion. Most post-bound albums include a starter set of pages with refill pages and page protectors available separately. Some post-bound albums bind the page protectors into the album's posts rather than the page.

STRAP STYLE A strap-style album uses plastic straps woven through sturdy staples attached to pages or page protectors. The albums lie flat when opened, and facing pages lie close together, hiding the binding. Like three-ring and post-bound albums, this style lets you add or rearrange pages.

THREE-RING BINDER This style of album is expandable to the width of its spine. Its pages generally slide in and out of top loading page protectors mounted on the binder rings. Using separate sheets of paper for the front and back of each scrapbook page, you can easily change the order of the pages in the album. Look for cloth binders with acid-free cores and nonreactive adhesives.

SPIRAL A spiral-bound album is great for finite projects such as gift albums. They come with pages already bound in to them. If you have an ongoing project, however, look for a more expandable album style.

THREE-RING BINDER

SPIRAL

PAPER

Paper, an essential ingredient in creative scrapbooking, comes in hundreds of colors, patterns, textures and weights. To be photo-safe, paper should be pH neutral (acid-free) and lignin-free. Many varieties of paper are also buffered, which is preferable for scrapbooking projects. Not all vellums, mulberry, metallic or handmade papers are archivally safe and, as such, should not be allowed to directly touch photos and memorabilia. Paper is sold in single sheets, packets and booklets. Mix and match both to create a one-of-a-kind look in your album. Create punch art and select die cuts and stickers that work well with the colors of your papers and the themes of your photos.

TYPES OF PAPER

DECORATIVE OR PATTERNED PAPER Multi use paper that can tie pages together and support theme layouts; available in hundreds of different designs and patterns.

SOLID-COLORED PAPER Basic solid papers, available in hundreds of colors and a variety of weights, can be used alone or with decorative or patterned paper.

CARDSTOCK Sturdier paper that is available in a multitude of colors and patterns; especially useful for matting photos and making die cuts. Used as a base for pages in top-loading albums.

VELLUM Transparent paper great for decorative elements; can be drawn or printed upon and laid over pages for sheer effects.

SUEDE A leathery-looking paper available in a number of colors; useful for adding texture to pages that have hair, clothing, or animal themes.

MULBERRY Papers with a heavy look of wood fiber; useful for pages calling for a natural, outdoorsy feel.

HANDMADE Reminiscent of old-fashioned, rough-textured paper, its fibers, confetti and other elements are visible; great for heritage pages and poetic layouts.

METALLIC Shiny, metallic papers—some holographic—available in many colors; useful for replicating page accents of metallic objects such as jewelry, eyeglasses, picture frames, candlesticks, cars, etc.

PENS

A pen is more than just a writing implement. It is an important scrapbooking tool. Only pigment pens should be used in scrapbooks. Pigment ink is lightfast, fade-resistant, waterproof and colorfast. The right pen can make writing a pleasure. The wrong pen can ruin a pretty page. So, before you buy your scrapbook pens, consider your writing style and project needs. Remember that getting used to any pen takes practice. If, after some time, you still don't feel comfortable with the tool, set it aside and move on. Eventually you'll find the pen that works best for you. To every person there is a pen and a tip for every purpose under the sun.

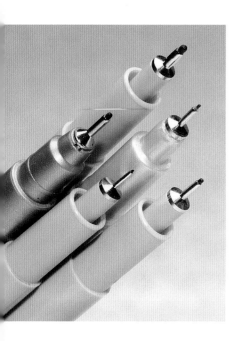

JOURNALING PENS Your first scrapbook pen should be a basic black pigment pen for journaling. These pens come with delicate, fine points as well as thicker point sizes. The best way to choose a journaling pen is to experiment. If your store has testers, try them. See how a pen feels in your hand. Try to buy an individual pen rather than a large set. Take it home. Get used to it and, if it feels as though it is right for you, invest in others that are similar.

DECORATIVE PENS When you're ready to experiment with more creative lettering, you'll want to invest in special decorative pens. These writing tools come in a variety of tips, from brush to bullet and calligraphy to chisel. Each decorative pen creates a different look. Experts advise beginners to stick to the bullet tip, a general-use pen that is good for a variety of decorative purposes.

PEN TYPE AND USES

SMALL BRUSH
Decorative lettering, creating thick and thin lines

SMALL CALLIGRAPHY
Decorative lettering, pen work, journaling

BULLET
Journaling, bold lettering, drawing and coloring in

SCROLL
Fancy letters, pen work, not for extensive journaling

CHISEL
Decorative lettering and embellishments

FINE POINT DRAWING AND WRITING
Journaling, detailed pen work

LARGE BRUSH
Decorative lettering, pen work, coloring in

LARGE CALLIGRAPHY
Decorative lettering, embellishments

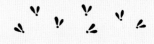 

 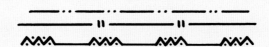

 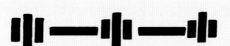 

Lettering created by Carol Snyder for EK Success

ADHESIVES

The word "adhesives" conjures visions of kindergarten class and white-paste projects. However, today's scrapbook adhesives are nothing like the goopy glues of the past. Modern scrapbookers have access to a wide range of glues and tapes that make it quick and easy to attach photos and memorabilia to pages. While the choice of adhesive often boils down to personal preference, scrapbookers should be certain to select products that are photo-safe and acid-free. Unsafe adhesives can damage photos, causing deterioration.

Adhesives are considered either "wet" or "dry". Each is right for different tasks. Because different adhesives require different types of application, it may take some experimentation to find the one that suits your needs.

HOW TO USE ADHESIVES

BOTTLED GLUE Bottled glue is more fluid than other scrapbook adhesives, and requires careful application. It dries slowly, but creates a strong bond between photo and paper. Overuse can buckle some types of paper; test it on a sample scrap first. This type of adhesive works well on small embellishments and three-dimensional objects such as buttons and sequins.

GLUE STICKS Glue sticks contain a thick, pasty adhesive that dries quickly and will not buckle paper. The sticks come in a variety of sizes. Consider using these to mount photos and large pieces of paper, journaling blocks and titles, as well as die cuts.

LIQUID GLUE PENS Glue pens come in a variety of pen tips. The pens dispense glue when pressed against paper. The pens are especially useful for adhering tiny pieces, such as punched shapes and hand-cut lettering, to a scrapbook page.

PHOTO SPLITS Photo splits are double-sided tape, precut into tiny pieces. Some splits are packaged inside of applicators. Other types of splits are sold in a roll with protective backing that must be peeled off before applying them to the page. Splits are especially useful for adding photo mosaics, photos, blocks of journaling or titles and paper embellishments to your scrapbook pages.

PHOTO TAPE Photo tape is two-sided tape that comes on a roll. Unlike splits, the tape is not pre-sectioned and therefore the scrapper may cut pieces of any size as needed. The tape comes with a protective backing that must be peeled away. Photo tape makes it easy to attach pocket pages and other large decorative elements or photos to your pages.

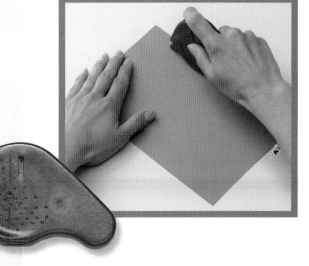

SELF-ADHESIVE FOAM SPACERS
These double-sided adhesives come in a variety of sizes and thicknesses and can be cut to add dimension to even the tiniest page accent.

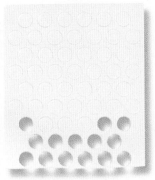

TAPE ROLLERS Tape rollers are applicators that allow you to roll double-sided adhesive on paper. They are similar to photo tape, however they do not require you to strip off a protective backing. The most versatile of all adhesives, tape rollers can be used to mount photos, journaling blocks and titles, die cuts and paper embellishments. To dispense the adhesive, you roll the applicator across a page.

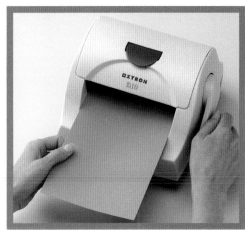

XYRON™ ADHESIVE APPLICATION MACHINE The Xyron is a machine through which you send your photos or paper and they become stickers with a peel-away backing. The Xyron works especially well for adhering vellum and punched pieces. Thermo-Web is another adhesive application product. It does not require the use of a machine.

CUTTING TOOLS

Cutting tools are an important part of any scrapbook toolbox. They are used for everything from creating mats and borders to cropping photos. The right cutting tool can make a job easier for tentative croppers. Every scrapbooker should own a pair of large and small straightedged scissors for general-purpose cutting. There are a number of other exceptional cutting tools on the market that will make cropping and creating even more fun.

DECORATIVE SCISSORS Decorative scissors come in many patterns and depths of cut. Some scissors have shallow teeth for creating tighter, smaller pattern cuts. Others have deep teeth for carving more extended, flowing designs. It may take practice to learn to successfully use decorative scissors, but it's worth the effort.

HOW TO USE DECORATIVE SCISSORS

- Draw a guideline on your paper where you plan to cut.

- Line up your blade slightly to the left of the penciled line so no markings will be visible (or on the line, if you use a vanishing ink pen).

- Steady your cutting arm by anchoring the elbow to your side. Use the other hand to turn the paper or photo as you cut. Do not turn the scissors.

- Starting halfway from the base of the blade, begin your cut.

- Use the longest strokes possible. Short, choppy strokes interrupt the scissors' pattern.

- Stop cutting before you reach the end of the blade.

- Flip the scissors over to achieve a varied scissor pattern.

- To create an uninterrupted pattern, carefully realign the blade after each cut, matching a portion of the cut pattern with the design on the blade.

- Use decorative scissors to create mats, decorative elements, crop photos, or make borders.

Felice Family Picnic
Sept. 16th, 2001
Beech Woods Park, Southfield MI.

Valerie Brincheck for Fiskars, Inc.

PERSONAL PAPER TRIMMERS Paper trimmers are perfect for making straight cuts and 90-degree angles. They come in a variety of sizes.

HOW TO USE A PAPER TRIMMER

- Place your index finger and thumb (or your entire hand) firmly on the photo or paper you wish to trim. With your other hand, bring down the handle, or slide down the blade, quickly and smoothly.

- Use smaller paper trimmers to cut mats or cleanly crop photos.

- Use larger trimmers such as a rotary disk trimmer for cutting photo enlargements, scrapbook papers, cardstock and corrugated paper.

SHAPE CUTTERS Shape blade cutters and nested templates are manufactured by a number of companies. They are useful when cropping photos, mats and journaling blocks into perfect shapes. Shape cutters can cut circles, ovals and many other simple shapes.

Photos Cheryl Rooney, Lakewood, Colorado

HOW TO USE A SHAPE CUTTER

- Determine the size of the circle you wish to cut and set the blade accordingly.

- Place the cutter so the center pin sits in the middle of the photo you wish to cut. Press the pin down firmly with one finger. With the other hand, guide the extension bar around in a circle. Apply even pressure until you have completed the revolution.

- Use a nested template such as a Colluzzle® to inexpensively cut a variety of shapes. Nested templates are transparent templates that can be placed over photos or paper. While firmly holding down the item you wish to cut, slip the blade tool into the narrow cutting channel. Allow the channel to guide your slice as you complete the pattern.

- Use shape cutters to crop photos or decorative elements such as die cuts or journaling palates.

TEMPLATES

Templates are stencil-like patterns made of plastic, sturdy paper or cardboard. They can be homemade or purchased and have a multitude of uses.

Templates come in a variety of sizes, shapes and themes including hearts, animals, simple geometric patterns, page borders and photo frames. With templates in hand, anyone can turn boxy, rectangular photos and mats into something special.

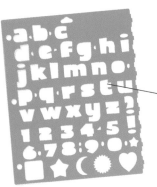

JOURNALING TEMPLATES
The circular coil of this journaling template makes it easy to follow the lines when adding words to the page.

LETTER TEMPLATES
A chunky-style letter template adds energy to a go-getting page title.

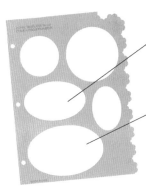

SHAPE TEMPLATES
Two different sizes of oval templates were used to crop these photos.

DECORATIVE RULER
Decorative rulers help to create fast and easy page borders.

HOW TO USE TEMPLATES

- Press the template firmly against the paper with one hand. Use your other hand to trace inside or around the template shape with disappearing ink or a pencil. Lift the template and cut out the traced shape.

- Create page titles by matting template-traced and cut letters with colored paper so they visually pop off the page.

- Use templates to create perfect mats and borders.

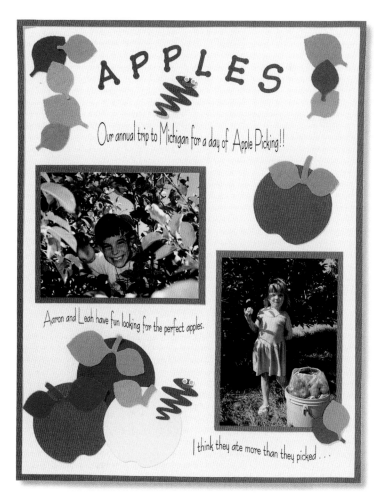

Cathy Booth for Emagination Crafts

For fresh, innovative and inspiring punch art ideas, see Memory Makers Punch Your Art Out Volumes 1, 2 and 3 *(ordering information on page 130).*

PUNCHES

Punches are rugged little tools into which you insert a piece of paper, press on a button, and out pops a perfectly punched shape. Punches are available in hundreds of sizes, shapes and designs, including geometric patterns, letters and numbers. Some punches are designed to extend deep into the middle of a piece of paper, allowing you to punch shapes inches from your paper edge.

HOW TO USE PUNCHES

• To create perfect punched shapes, insert a piece of paper into the punch. Hold the paper firmly while pressing down on the button with your other hand. Carefully remove the paper and punched shape.

• Punch patterns into die cuts and then layer the die cuts over contrasting paper.

• Use the tiny punched shapes to decorate pages or mats.

• Place punched shapes close together to create page borders.

• Layer the punched shapes to "build"—make animals, vehicles, flowers and more.

• Combine punched shapes into "quilt" patterns for mats or borders.

• Use punched letters to create page titles.

STICKERS

Stickers are one of the easiest ways to jazz up scrapbook pages. There are thousands to choose from in a multitude of colors, themes and styles—including letter and number, border, journaling and design element stickers. Stickers add such easy visual impact to a page that it is tempting to use them excessively, which can result in pages that appear disorganized or cluttered. Get the most impact from your stickers by using them selectively.

HOW TO USE STICKERS

- Draw a guideline for letter and border sticker placement. Use a template as a pattern, if needed.

- If stickers are misplaced, use adhesive remover to help lift them from the page.

- Large stickers can stand on their own, but smaller stickers have more impact when grouped together.

- Combine stickers with other page elements like photos or die cuts.

- Use stickers to frame photos by clustering them at the corners of the pictures or stringing them along the photo's sides.

- Accent titles with stickers.

- Use theme-related stickers to create "mini scenes."

- Use stickers to create page borders or to visually tie spreads together.

Andrea Grossman for Mrs. Grossman's Paper Company;
Photos Mary Liz Curtin

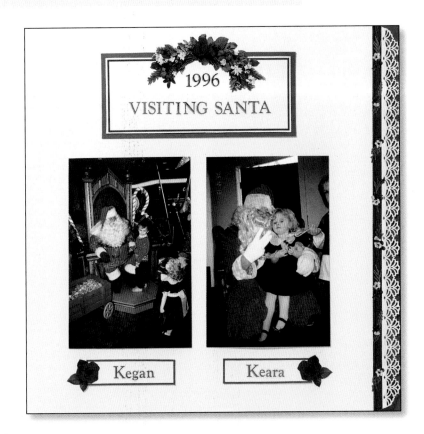

STAMPS

How can something so simple create such gorgeous and impressive results? That's the beauty of rubber stamps. With just a few stamps and an inkpad, you can make delicate borders, lacy photo corners, stamped backgrounds, eye-catching photo mats, dressed-up die cuts and jazzy page accents. With the amazing array of stamp designs and inkpad colors available, it is easy to coordinate stamped images with any page design.

Pam Hornschu for Stampendous!® Inc.

HOW TO USE STAMPS

- Evenly apply ink to the rubber stamp pad. Tap the stamp against the pad to remove excess ink.

- Apply steady pressure (don't rock the stamp) when transferring the ink to your paper.

- Allow sufficient dry time. Dye pad ink dries quickly but pigment inks (preferable) take up to 24 hours. Shorten the drying time by holding stamped paper near a heat source for several minutes.

- Customize your stamped image by coloring within the border.

- Seal a stamped image with embossing powder, which raises the design, giving it additional dimension.

- Stamp mats, page borders, frames and titles.

- Add dimension to stamped images by cropping out tiny parts of the stamped image and adding colored paper to the back.

DIE CUTS

Die cuts are pre-cut paper shapes that come in both printed and solid colors. These decorative elements are great for adding theme accents to a page. Die cuts are sold individually and in packages. Increasing numbers of scrapbook and craft stores have centers where customers can cut their own die cuts for a small fee. Some shop owners may allow you to cut die cuts for free if you use paper purchased at their store. As with all paper and paper products, make sure your die cuts are acid- and lignin-free.

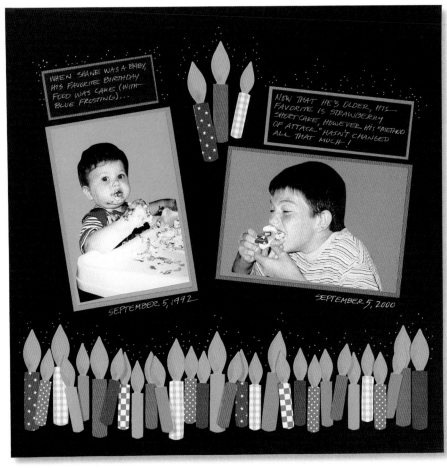

Sandi Genovese for Ellison Craft and Design
Photos Kevin Corcoran and Helen Jones

HOW TO USE DIE CUTS

- Apply adhesive to the back of your die cut and press firmly on your page. For self-adhesive die cuts, peel off the backing, and stick.

- Journal on the die cut.

- Use a die cut as a photo mat.

- Embellish die cuts with stickers or stamps. Add penned details.

- Use a punch to punch shapes into die cuts.

- Link several same-shaped die cuts together to form a paper chain border.

- Silhouette-crop photos of people and tuck them behind the windows of car-, bus-, and house-shaped die cuts.

Tool organization & care

Like most hobbies, scrapbooking involves a good number of tools and supplies. If you are like many scrapbookers, your stash of new products will seem to grow every time you turn around. Organization is the key to keeping your materials available and in good shape for scrapbooking ease. The following tips will help.

① COLLECT YOUR SCRAPBOOK TOOLS AND SUPPLIES

Empty your storage areas, bins, drawers and other nooks and crannies, where you may have stuck scissors or conveniently stashed punches.

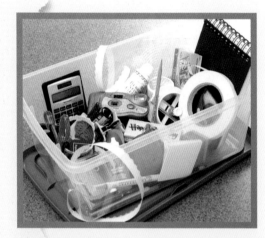

② SORT YOUR TOOLS AND SUPPLIES

Sort items into piles such as "scissors", "pens", "stamps", "punches", "adhesives," etc. Set aside any damaged or unwanted items. Later you can give them away, host a swap night with scrapbooking friends or swap them on-line in one of the many chat groups devoted to scrapbooking. Sort paper by color. Separate scraps of paper from full sheets. Divide patterned paper, die cuts and stickers into piles defined either by color or by theme.

③ CLEAN AND LABEL YOUR TOOLS AND SUPPLIES

Before storing, replace cutter blades, clean tracing marks from templates, sharpen punches with aluminum foil, clean ink residue from stamps, test pens. Label tools with your name or initials to help identify them at crops. Create an inventory supplies checklist using the work sheet on page 49 while you have everything sorted. From that list, compile an ongoing shopping/wish list to avoid duplicate purchases, to share during gift-giving holidays or when you get that discount coupon from your local craft store.

4 **STORE YOUR SUPPLIES**

Protect your scrapbook investments by storing your freshly cleaned and organized tools and supplies in storage containers that will keep items dry, dust-free and easily accessible. Keep your supplies and workspace options in mind when shopping for storage containers. When storing supplies, the materials you use the most should be the easiest to access. Time spent on getting organized and money spent on storage containers will reward you with quick-and-easy scrapbooking!

HOW TO STORE AND CARE FOR YOUR TOOLS

- Store albums in an upright position. Allow sufficient room to avoid pressing tightly against other albums.

- Paper and paper supplies should be stored in a clean, dry place, out of direct sunlight. If possible, store paper horizontally.

- Pens must be tightly capped to prevent drying and stored away from heat. Some pigment pens are best stored on their side rather than upright.

- Adhesives should be stored out of the sun and away from direct heat.

- Stamps must be cleaned after each use with stamp cleaner solvent or warm, soapy water. Dry completely. Store in a dust-free environment.

- Punches must be stored in a dry, dust-free place to prevent rusting. Sharpen punches by punching through heavy aluminum foil or very fine grade sandpaper. Punch through wax paper to lubricate sticky punches.

- Cutter blades should be changed regularly when used often.

- Templates and rulers should be cleaned with warm, soapy water to remove ink, chalk residue and adhesive. Store templates inside three-ring binders.

- Store die cuts and stickers within page protectors inside of binders. CD jewel cases and videocassette cases make acceptable, inexpensive storage containers.

- Cutting mats should be cleaned, as needed, to remove adhesive residue.

Supplies checklist & wishlist

Keep in mind that you do not need everything listed here to get started; just start with the basics and build your supplies as your budget allows. Use one copy of this list to keep track of the supplies that you already have. Use a second copy of this checklist for a shopping list. Take both lists with you when shopping to avoid any unnecessary spending. Update both lists regularly to stay well-stocked and ready to crop while working toward your album goals.

ORGANIZATIONAL SUPPLIES
- [ ] *Photo box(es)*
- [ ] *Negative sleeves*
- [ ] *Photo envelopes*
- [ ] *Self-stick notes*
- [ ] *Memorabilia keepers*
- [ ] *Storage containers*

ALBUM TYPES
- [ ] *Strap*
- [ ] *Post bound*
- [ ] *Spiral*
- [ ] *3-ring binder*
- [ ] *Mini*
- [ ] *Other*
- _____
- _____

Preferred brand(s)
- _____
- _____

ALBUM SIZES
- [ ] *4 x 6"*
- [ ] *5 x 7"*
- [ ] *8½ x 11"*
- [ ] *12 x 12"*
- [ ] *12 x 15"*
- [ ] *Other*
- _____
- _____

Preferred brand(s)
- _____
- _____

ALBUM FILLER PAGES
- [ ] *4 x 6"*
- [ ] *5 x 7"*
- [ ] *8½ x 11"*
- [ ] *12 x 12"*
- [ ] *12 x 15"*
- [ ] *Other*
- _____
- _____

Preferred brand(s)
- _____
- _____

ALBUM PAGE PROTECTORS
- [ ] *4 x 6"*
- [ ] *5 x 7"*
- [ ] *8½ x 11"*
- [ ] *12 x 12"*
- [ ] *12 x 15"*
- _____
- _____

Preferred brand(s)
- _____
- _____

ARCHIVAL QUALITY ADHESIVES
- [ ] *Photo splits*
- [ ] *Double-sided photo tape*
- [ ] *Tape roller*
- [ ] *Liquid glue pen*
- [ ] *Glue stick*
- [ ] *Bottled glue*
- [ ] *Self-adhesive foam spacers*
- [ ] *Adhesive application machine*
- [ ] *Adhesive application machine cartridge*
- [ ] *Adhesive remover*
- [ ] *Other*
- _____
- _____

Preferred brand(s)
- _____
- _____

SCISSORS & CUTTERS
- [ ] *Small scissors*
- [ ] *Regular scissors*
- [ ] *Decorative scissors*
- [ ] *Paper trimmer*
- [ ] *Shape cropper(s)*
- [ ] *Craft knife*

PENCILS, PENS, MARKERS
- [ ] *Pigment pen(s)*
- [ ] *Photo-safe pencil*
- [ ] *Vanishing ink pen*

RULERS & TEMPLATES
- [ ] *Metal straightedge ruler*
- [ ] *Grid ruler*
- [ ] *Decorative ruler(s)*
- [ ] *Journaling template(s)*
- [ ] *Shape template(s)*
- [ ] *Letter template(s)*
- [ ] *Nested template(s)*

ACID- AND LIGNIN-FREE PAPER
- [ ] *Red*
- [ ] *Orange*
- [ ] *Yellow*
- [ ] *Brown*
- [ ] *Green*
- [ ] *Blue*
- [ ] *Purple*
- [ ] *Pink*
- [ ] *Black*
- [ ] *White*
- [ ] *Patterns*
- _____
- _____
- [ ] *Themes*
- _____
- _____
- [ ] *Vellum color(s)*
- _____
- _____
- _____
- [ ] *Mulberry color(s)*
- _____
- _____
- [ ] *Specialty paper(s)*
- _____
- _____
- [ ] *Other*
- _____
- _____

Preferred brand(s)
- _____
- _____

STICKERS
Themes or types
- _____
- _____
- _____
- _____
- _____
- _____

DIE CUTS
Themes or types
- _____
- _____
- _____
- _____
- _____
- _____

PUNCHES
- [ ] *Corner rounder*
- [ ] *Hand punch(es)*
- [ ] *Border(s)*
- [ ] *Decorative corner(s)*
- [ ] *Photo mounting*
- [ ] *Shape(s)*
- _____
- _____
- [ ] *Tweezers*
- [ ] *Wax paper*
- [ ] *Aluminum foil*

RUBBER STAMPS
Themes or types
- _____
- _____
- _____
- _____
- [ ] *Ink pad(s)*
- [ ] *Embossing powder(s)*
- [ ] *Stamp cleaner*

Our Wedding
June 25th 1989

With my parents
Connie Baron, Greg Baron
Our Wedding party

Organizing photos & memorabilia

GETTING STARTED
IS THE HARDEST
PART. SOMETIMES
YOU JUST HAVE TO
CLOSE YOUR EYES,
TAKE A DEEP
BREATH AND GO!

-Michele

As long as you continue to take pictures, you will continue to face the challenge of organizing your photos. Sorting and storing those shots and related memorabilia may seem intimidating. The key to success is finding a system that works for you. Take into consideration your personal accounting style. Are you the sort who updates and balances her checkbook regularly or are you more likely to toss receipts into a box and straighten out your accounts every few months? On the following pages, we'll show you two basic ways to organize your photos— chronologically and by theme. Both your personality and the scrapbook project may dictate which of these two options you can best employ.

While the process of sorting and storing your photos may seem overwhelming at first, I promise that the effort will make future scrapbooking projects easier and more enjoyable. As with most challenging endeavors, the first step is often the most difficult. I encourage you to dive in and get started.

Sorting a lifetime of photos

All serious scrapbookers eventually have to face "the drawer," where throughout the years photos have been tossed and tossed and tossed. There they reside, in a hodge-podge jumble, waiting for you to have the time and the courage to organize them. With a bit of direction and the work sheet provided (see page 49), you will find the task easier than you might think. This process works great for sorting a lifetime of photos chronologically. If you are interested in doing theme albums, you can always pull the theme photos out later and they'll already be in chronological order!

(see page 49)

A Decade of Memories

It took a week and a whole room to start the sorting process.

These sheets are what made the whole process even possible.

WHAT YOU WILL NEED:

- Archival-quality photo boxes
- Photo-safe envelopes
- Archival-quality box for memorabilia
- Journaling pen
- Blank sticky notes
- Work sheet from page 49

Michele stayed true to her belief that "you just have to take a deep breath and go!" when she recently organized ten years of photos.

1 Start by photocopying the work sheet on page 49. Make a separate copy for each year or decade of photos represented. Date each form with an appropriate year or decade. Then focus your attention on one work sheet at a time.

2 Notice that the work sheet is divided into boxes which are labeled with the months of the year. If working with decades, cross out the "month" and insert "years". Within each box write down major events that occurred within that time period. Include such things as family birthdays (and the ages they achieved), when children began the school year (and the name of the school and grade attended), and when and where you vacationed. Use old journals, calendars and date books to supplement your information.

3 As you complete one work sheet, move on to the next. Spread out finished work sheets on a large surface. Begin matching photos to the events noted on the work sheets. Continue until all photos have been sorted. Store the newly created groupings in photo-safe envelopes inside archival-quality boxes until you are ready to scrapbook.

I'm getting closer!

A lot of detective work went into getting pictures in the right year. Ahh! feels so good to be finished!

It took Michele and a scrapbooking friend a week to organize more than a thousand photos. After being sorted, the pictures were stored in photo-safe envelopes, within archival-quality boxes. Now that her photos are organized, Michele finds it much easier to move forward with her scrapbooking projects. "It was an enormous job, and I could never have done it without my friend's help," Michele recalls. "But in the end, the work was definitely worth it!"

Work sheet to sort photos

JANUARY	JULY
FEBRUARY	AUGUST
MARCH	SEPTEMBER
APRIL	OCTOBER
MAY	NOVEMBER
JUNE	DECEMBER

Source: Barbara Tolopilo, Family Treasures, Inc.

Sorting photos chronologically

Like many scrapbookers, you may find it easiest to begin organizing your most recent photos and memorabilia first. Those are the pictures and stories about which you will remember the most. Find a space out of direct sunlight where photos may be left spread out for a long period of time if needed. Follow these four simple steps for sorting photos from the current year in chronological order.

WHAT YOU WILL NEED:

- 1 or 2 archival-quality photo boxes
- Photo-safe envelopes
- Archival-quality box for memorabilia
- Journaling pen
- Blank sticky notes

PLAYING DETECTIVE

Identifying and dating unlabeled photos requires a bit of sleuthing. If friends or family can't help, study the photos for clues.

- Fashions change frequently and provide strong clues for dating photos. Pick up a book on fashion trends at your library or bookstore for help.

- Hairstyles change as often as fashions. Ask a local hairdresser about the styles.

- Children's looks change radically from year to year. When trying to date a photo, study the children in the images. Their height, weight, and the number of teeth they have will speak volumes.

- Makes and models of cars change over time. The appearance of the automobiles in photos can narrow down the year.

- Signs and billboards may offer clues as to when and where the pictures were taken.

- The location where the photo was shot—whether a neighborhood or vacation spot—can offer important clues.

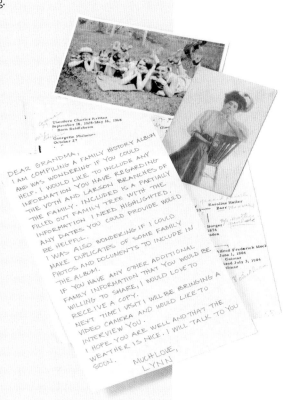

1 Gather all your photos and memorabilia from the current year. If the photos are still in their original envelopes with the negatives, transfer them to photo-safe envelopes. We'll deal with storing negatives later in this chapter.

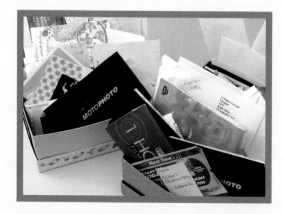

2 Label the contents of each photo envelope, or label the dividers in the photo-safe boxes. Include a "best guess" date as to when the pictures were taken. If there is related memorabilia, note it with a star next to the date. Jot down and store with the photos any information you may want to include when journaling.

3 Sort the envelopes by date. Assign each envelope a number which will assist you in filing them in consecutive order. Place them in the box.

4 Sort your memorabilia by category such as "tickets," "journals," or "brochures." Place the items in a labeled and dated memorabilia box. If you have kept an annual journal or calendar, this is a good place to store it.

Sorting photos by theme

Sorting photos and memorabilia by theme works particularly well if you are planning wedding, anniversary or vacation albums. You may also wish to use this method for creating scrapbooks featuring family events such as daily life, school days, celebrations, holidays, etc. We will examine theme albums in more detail later. But for now, follow the steps given to organize your photos by theme.

WHAT YOU WILL NEED:

- 1 or 2 archival-quality photo boxes

- Photo-safe envelopes

- Archival-quality box for memorabilia

- Journaling pen

- Blank sticky notes

MAKING JOURNALING NOTES

Journaling is an important part of preserving memories. Keep a pad of paper nearby when sorting and cataloging your photos and memorabilia. As you organize your pictures, take time to jot down any information that comes to mind. Include details such as the names of those in the images, the date the photos were taken, the location of the events and any thoughts or feelings you may have related to the pictures.

My Wedding Day
- I had to wake up at 5:30 AM to get ready. When I got in the shower there was no hot water! I was almost late getting to the church.
- The ceremony was perfect just as I always dreamed it would be.
- During our formal photos after the ceremony part of the arbor fell down and hit Grandma Jane on the head! Fortunatly, she was all right.
- Our photos turned out great! I really love the photos of Jeff and I in front of the church.

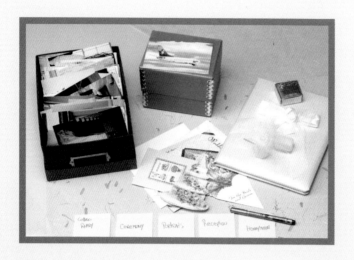

1 Collect your photos and memorabilia. On sticky notes, write down the categories pertinent to your current project. If, for example, you are working on a wedding album, you may wish to sort the photos into groups such as Getting Ready, Ceremony, Portraits, Reception, and Honeymoon. Categories for a holiday album might include Easter, Fourth of July, or Christmas. Spread the labeled sticky notes on a large work surface that is out of direct sunlight.

2 Sort your photos by category into piles near the appropriate sticky notes.

3 Re-sort the photos in each pile so they fall in logical order. This is, most often, the sequence in which you hope to place the photos in your album. Place the sorted piles in labeled, photo-safe envelopes and acid-free boxes, storing them until you are ready to scrapbook.

Storing photos & negatives

While the look of a storage container doesn't matter, making sure you've got the right container and are storing your keepsakes in the correct environment will save your photos and negatives from damage. There are numerous photo-safe storage containers available. When selecting one, make sure it is the right size to house your pictures, and the right shape to store on your shelves.

STORING PHOTOS

Store photos in photo-safe envelopes and containers in a dark, dry place or within page protectors in a scrapbook album. While some cardboard boxes are acid-free, most are not. And since most cardboard boxes are prone to collapse and won't protect photos from environmental hazards, use them only for temporary storage. If buying a plastic storage system, choose one made of either acrylic, polypropylene, polyethylene or polyester. Store at temperatures between 65-70 degrees and with 30-50 percent humidity.

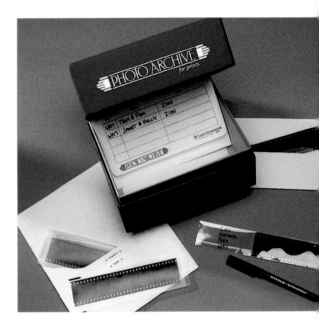

A well-organized negative storage system not only protects a critical backup but also makes it easy to order reprints and enlargements. When using an envelope system, place individual negatives in paper or plastic sleeves. Then insert your sleeved negatives in labeled archival envelopes organized in an acid-free, lignin-free box. For backup, store your photos and negatives in separate places. If disaster strikes, one or the other is likely to survive.

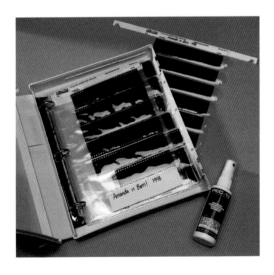

STORING NEGATIVES

Before storing dirty negatives, clean them with a commercial negative cleaner. Store negatives in negative sleeves, storage binders or storage boxes. The storage vehicles should be 100 percent acid-, lignin-, and PVC-free. If storing negatives in acid-free envelopes, separate strips with acid-free paper to prevent sticking. Keep negatives away from dust, bright light, excessive heat, and high humidity. Store at temperatures between 65-70 degrees and with 30-50 percent humidity.

HOW TO SCAN PHOTOS

A scanner takes a photo and translates the image into a digital format that can be read by, stored in, displayed on and printed from a computer. The scanner breaks an image into units of measure called "pixels" (picture elements) or "dpi" (dots per inch). To scan a standard photo at home, use the best possible original. When scanning and printing an image for a scrapbook page, use a resolution of 150-300 dpi (72 dpi for Web site images). Scale the photo to the desired size, select the type of image (grayscale for black-and-white; millions of colors for color photos), and save as a TIFF file for long-term computer storage (or JPEG if you intend to e-mail the photo or place it on a Web site). The quality of your printed photo depends on the quality of your scanner, scanning software, printer and the paper on which you print.

If do-it-yourself scanning is not for you, get high-quality photo scans put on a CD at a camera store, mini lab or professional lab. To print images from a CD, a high-quality color printer and photo-quality printer paper will give the best color results.

Photos Orealys Hernandez
Holly Springs, North Carolina

DIGITAL PHOTO STORAGE

Increasing numbers of today's scrapbookers are storing their regular and digital photos on CDs. Unlike negatives, the images saved to CDs do not wear out; with proper care they can last 100 years or more! Sealed in plastic and metal, they are more immune to every-day mishaps such as scratches, spills and accidental bending. Experts recommend storing photo CDs individually in acrylic jewel cases, not in soft plastic sleeves which may adhere to the disc upon exposure to heat and humidity.

Store jewel cases in a closed box, drawer or cabinet to protect them from sunlight, dust and climate changes. Storage temperatures should be between 50-77 degrees with 20-50 percent relative humidity. CDs should also be protected from sharp objects such as pens and pencils, solvents and fingerprints. If needed, clean discs with a lens tissue, gently wiping from the center of the disc in a radial direction toward the outside edge of the disc. Some manufacturers also produce lens cleaner that is safe to use on CDs, but it is wise to check with the product manufacturer before applying any chemicals.

Photos Becky Baanhofman
Littleton, Colorado

White Fence Farm

April 2001

Celebrating Easter and sneaking in some family photos.

Lakewood, Colorado

Sasha age 8

Anna age 11

Making your first page

It is time to take a breath and make the leap, time to start working on your first scrapbook page! Sometimes that blank scrapbook page can be a little intimidating. Put away any preconceptions you may have about how your page should look. Remember that there is no "right" or "wrong" way when it comes to creating pages. Each spread is a unique reflection of its creator. As you grow as a scrapbooker, you will define your own personal style. Your pages will go through a style evolution as you master new scrapbook techniques.

In this chapter, we will introduce you to design basics, different methods of photo cropping, how to create a pleasing photo mat, mounting photos and much more. We encourage you to draw inspiration from these pages and from the pages of those around you. Pick up a magazine or book about scrapbooking for more ideas. Enjoy experimenting. Enjoy telling your story.

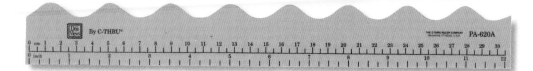

An overview of the page-making process

Making pages is easier when you break down and order the process. Take your time and enjoy each step of the way. In scrapbooking, as in many things, the journey is just as important as the destination. Here is a simple overview of the page-making process. We will examine it in more detail on the following pages.

① SELECT PHOTOS

Photos are one of the most important elements on your scrapbook pages. Spend time selecting the perfect shots for each spread. Consider the mood and intent of the page. Find pictures that carry your message.

② SELECT PAPER COLORS

Color selection can make the difference between a great and not-so-great scrapbook page. The paper colors that you choose to help showcase your photos will affect the way you and others feel when looking at the finished album. Pick colors that convey the right emotion and complement your photos.

③ LAYOUT AND DESIGN

Before adhering anything to a page, take the time to move your photos around. Experiment with different positions. Try overlapping pictures. Drag some to the page edge. Tip them. Turn them. Find a placement that looks balanced and draws focus to your best shots.

4 CROP PHOTOS

Cropping, or cutting photos, enhances the image and eliminates unwanted portions of the shot. Through cropping, you can focus the viewer's eye on a particular element of the picture and remove extraneous portions that detract from its impact.

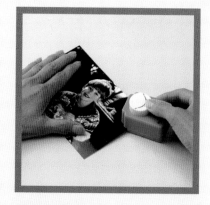

5 MAT PHOTOS

A mat goes beneath the photo and helps visually "pop" the picture off the page. Mats can also help protect photos by forming a barrier between them and unsafe embellishments or memorabilia.

6 MOUNT PAGE ELEMENTS

Mounting is the process of attaching matted photos and memorabilia on your scrapbook album pages with photo-safe adhesives. Some nonpermanent mounting techniques allow easy removal of photos and documents for copying or restoration.

7 ADD TITLE, JOURNALING AND ACCESSORIES

Page titles and journaling are the voices that bring your photos to life. They record information that may seem obvious at the present, but can be lost over time. A title should capture the essence of the page. Journal the facts, such as when and where the photo was taken. Accessorize the page with punch art, stickers and die cuts. Do so sparingly to keep the focus on the photos and their stories.

Select photos

Scrapbookers love their photos and many are determined to find room on their pages for every single picture. This is not always a good idea. Overcrowded pages do a disservice to the truly wonderful shots. In order to create good pages you must cull photos. Begin by spreading your pictures on a table and examining them. Choose the photos that truly speak to you and are of highest quality. The 3-5 pictures you select to feature on each album page should work well together, complementing each other's colors, composition and content.

To select photos, spread them all out on a table and examine them. Which photos really speak to you? Which do you notice first? Are they high quality? Do they have good color? Are they in focus? These are the photos you scrapbook.

WHAT TO DO WITH EXTRA PHOTOS

You can always save and store extra photos to use in future albums. Or put those extra pictures to use right now!

• Cut the faces from extra pictures to use as page decorations. Tuck them in the middle of a flower die cut, on an Easter egg or on a Christmas decoration.

• Use them in "star pupil" displays for your child's special day at school.

• Incorporate extra pictures in other craft projects such as when you're making greeting cards, calendars, gift tags and collages.

• Punch shapes from the photos, cut letters for page titles and other embellishments to use on your scrapbook pages.

• Give your children photos to practice their own cutting and cropping skills.

• Trade extra photos with family members who may have photos you've been coveting.

GETTING PHOTOS FROM RELATIVES

Most scrapbookers find it distressing when a particular family photo seems beyond reach. But with tenderness and tenacity there are often ways to include those treasures in your books. Many relatives are more likely to share their pictures when they better understand why you need them and exactly what you plan to do with them. Sharing this information, as well as your excitement, may inspire them to give you the pictures you desire. Promise not to use any pictures they may deem embarrassing, and to credit the photo's owner for each picture you do include. If the owner of the pictures is afraid to release them for fear they may be damaged or lost, invite her to accompany you to have the photos copied. If she lives a distance away, pay for all reproduction fees and shipping costs. Above all, promise to treat the photos with respect and care. Copy the pages on which you feature the borrowed pictures and present your relative with an album of her own as a thank-you gift.

HOW TO TAKE BETTER PHOTOS

- Keep a camera nearby to capture that unexpected but to-die-for shot.

- Use the right speed of film.

- Get close in order to better see your subject and eliminate extraneous backgrounds.

- Keep the background simple.

- Frame the subject off-center.

- Include some foreground to help put the picture in perspective.

- Watch your lighting. Bright overhead light creates unattractive shadows and is unflattering to your subject.

- Hold steady. Movement can blur pictures.

Photo Mary Jo Regier, Littleton, Colorado

Select paper colors

Color affects our thoughts and emotions as well as our physiology. Looking at certain colors increases or decreases the heart rate and blood pressure. Some colors (red) inspire energetic feelings while others (green) are calming. When selecting colors for your scrapbook pages, choose shades that are consistent with the mood of the spread.

Draw colors from your photos. You may wish to pick up on the blue in the background sky, or the green of grass, the color of an outfit or the hue of a person's eyes. Once having determined a primary color, choose other colors that complement your primary choice.

If you aren't confident about choosing colors, consider buying papers in presorted packages. These packets come with corresponding, coordinating papers in color and theme variations. Prepackaged papers help take the guesswork out of paper selection.

Can't figure out what colors to use? Pick up a color wheel at your local art or craft store. A color wheel has a rotating dial that helps users choose colors that work together harmoniously. The wheel shows complementary colors (colors that fall directly opposite each other on the wheel, such as green and red), and other combinations. There are dozens of ways to use the color wheel when scrapbooking.

HOW PAPER COLOR SETS A MOOD

Color helps sets a mood on both these scrapbook pages. The cool blues and greens used on the page to the right reflect and convey the peaceful calm of a child's lazy afternoon swing. The page below captures the glow of a southwest sunset by playing on the glowing orange shades in the sun-drenched rock formations in the background.

Ron Gerbrandt, Denver, Colorado
Photo Tonya Jeppson, Boise, Idaho

Photo Jeff Derksen, Denver, Colorado

HOW PAPER COLOR SHOWS CONTRAST

In the example below, the background color swallows up the photos. Generally, photos with a light background will get lost on a light-colored background page. Note how these same photos "pop" off the page when a darker background is used.

Layout and design

A good scrapbook page draws in the viewer. It is a comfortable place, an interesting place for her to rest her eyes. While the quality of the photos and color choices affect the success of the page, equally important to its impact is its layout and design.

A well-designed page has a strong focal point. This may be a photo, title or other element that draws the eye. Good pages also have a sense of balance. A substantial photo in one corner, for example, can be balanced by a heavy photo in its opposite corner. On the other hand, the scrapbooker may use several smaller elements grouped together to balance the visually heavier piece. Some artists ensure symmetry on a spread by mirroring the layout on the left page with the one on the right. On page 67, we have provided a few samples of simple layouts that work well.

When designing your page, make sure design elements support, rather than compete with, the photos, journaling and memorabilia. Use them sparingly and remember that white space is an important part of good design.

Move your photos around on the background pages, arranging and rearranging until you have a visually appealing layout that looks balanced.

BEFORE AND AFTER SCRAPBOOK PAGES

Simply by rearranging the same five photo elements and journaling, the scrapbook artist has turned a badly-designed page into one that is pleasing to the eye.

POOR LAYOUT AND DESIGN

- The top of the page is photo-heavy, unbalancing the layout.

- Layered photos seem to have been placed at random.

- The top edges of the layered photos create a senseless, jagged stair step.

- The silhouetted photo is "floating" and needs to be anchored.

- The photo in the top right corner is too close to the border.

- Photos seem to be grouped arbitrarily.

- Photos are tilted in different directions.

- White space is unevenly distributed.

- Journaling is clumped and difficult to read.

- The title doesn't pop.

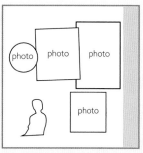

POOR COMPOSITION

Celebrating Easter and sneaking in some family photos.

Daniel age 6

Sasha age 8

Anna age 11

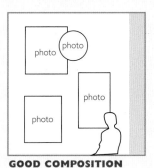

GOOD COMPOSITION

GOOD LAYOUT AND DESIGN

- The top and bottom of the page are now equally weighted.

- Photos featuring the same subject have been grouped together.

- The silhouetted photo is anchored to the bottom of the page.

- Journaling is spread out, making it easier to read.

- White space is evenly distributed.

- The page title is prominent.

Scrapbook page design work sheet

It is simple to create well-balanced page layouts. Below are just a few samples of quick-and-easy page designs to get you started. As you become more involved in the hobby, you may find page designs that you really like in scrapbooking magazines or idea books. We've left some blank pages on this work sheet so that you can sketch your own quick-and-easy page designs for future reference.

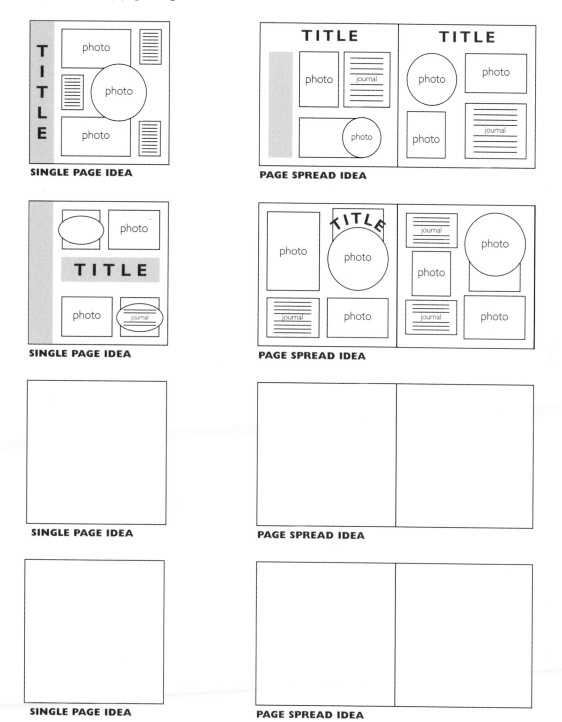

Crop photos

People often boil down the act and art of scrapbooking to one word "crop." Those who work on scrapbooks are "croppers." When they are "cropping" in groups it is called a "crop." To crop means to trim a photo in order to enhance it, or draw attention to the main subject.

Cutting pictures into hearts, circles, stars and other shapes is so much fun that people can forget the big picture. While cropping isn't the sole focus of scrapbooking, the more you know about when, why and how to crop, the better prepared you'll be to design your pages.

WHEN TO CROP AND WHEN NOT TO CROP

- Crop in order to add style and variety to your page.
- Crop to eliminate unwanted portions of the picture including photo blemishes, strangers in your pictures, lab printing errors and out-of-focus elements.
- Crop to draw emphasis to important portions of the picture such as a child's face.
- Crop to create a new piece of art.
- You may crop Polaroid peel-apart photos because the final print is separated from the reactive chemicals. Other Polaroid products may release harmful chemicals if cropped.
- Never crop original, historical or one-of-a-kind photos; you will lose valuable background information. Have reprints made if you wish to crop them.

CROPPING STRAIGHT LINES

Straight cropping can be done with a personal paper trimmer (see page 35). Paper trimmers ensure perfectly straight cuts and are great for making 90 degree angles. When you feel more comfortable with cropping photos, try using a craft knife and a metal straightedge ruler. Hold the photo and ruler down tightly to avoid slippage.

CROPPING CORNERS

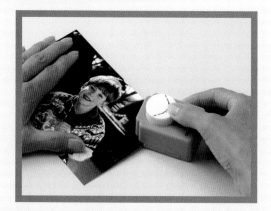

Corner cropping softens the look of a photo by removing small amounts from the photo's corners. Corner rounder punches are the perfect tool to accomplish this effect. Simply slide the punch onto the photo's corner and firmly push down on the button. Repeat on all four corners.

CROPPING WITH DECORATIVE SCISSORS

1 Before cutting with your decorative scissors, use a wax pencil and metal straightedge ruler to create guidelines for your incision.

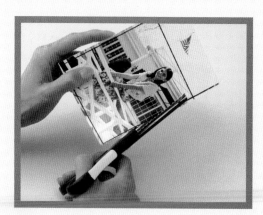

2 Use decorative scissors to cut just a bit to the outside of the cutting line. Wipe remaining pencil marks away with a dry, soft cloth.

CROPPING SHAPES

While standard square and rectangular photos suit many scrapbook spreads, there are times when a page just screams for a photo of a different shape. Use a template or shape cutter to crop your pictures into circles, hearts, animals or other shapes.

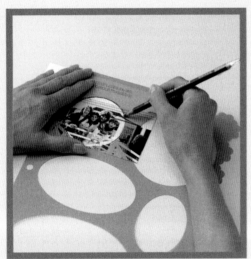

1 Place the template over your photo and trace with a wax pencil, or for mark-free cropping, trace the shape with an embossing stylus or knitting needle.

2 Cut out the shape, staying inside the line so markings will not show on your final image or wipe remaining pencil marks away with a soft, dry cloth.

CROPPING SILHOUETTES

Silhouette cropping entails trimming around the contours of the subject in your photos. Silhouetting allows you to remove unnecessary backgrounds and direct visual focus to the important portions of a picture. With less extraneous image, you can also use more photos on a scrapbook page. Use small, sharp scissors to silhouette crop around people in photos. Cut slowly, following each person's outline. Be especially careful when cutting around hair and facial features.

CROPPING PARTIAL SILHOUETTES

When silhouette cropping, pick and choose the portions of the photo you wish to remove. There may be times when you would like to leave the sides or lower edge of a picture intact and remove just the upper portion of the photo. What and how much of the photo is cut away is totally up to you. Use a sharp craft knife to crop around the tiny parts of each photo that are not accessible with small scissors.

Mat photos

Matting is one of the easiest ways to emphasize a photo. One creatively matted photo can become the focal point on a page, or several matted photos can tie together different page elements. Mats add color and contrast to monotone photos that might otherwise disappear into the background. Matting helps establish the color theme for a page and should work well with other paper and decorative elements. Freehand cut, or use a template or shape cutter, to create a mat. Accent mats with stickers, punched shapes or stamped images.

Use a template or shape cutter to create a mat for your cropped photo by cutting the mat ⅛" or larger than your photo. You can also free-hand cut a mat. Here are more simple ideas for creating photo mats.

Cut two mats the same size, center the photo on one and mount the second mat askew.

For a perfectly shaped mat for photos that are silhouetted or partially silhouetted, use a Magic Matter™ to trace around the photo on paper of choice. Then cut out the mat.

Trim the edges of photos and mats
with decorative scissors and punches.

Use a corner slot punch (or photo mounting
punch) to create a mat into which you slip the
corners of your photo.

Use mats for journaling by writing directly
on the mat around the photo.

Vary the shape of photos and mats.
You may wish, for example, to place
a round photo on a square mat, or
do just the opposite.

Experiment with double- and triple-matting photos
in different colored papers.

Mount page elements

Mounting photos or memorabilia is the process of attaching them to an album page. You may choose to put them in your album in a way that ensures they will be a part of the page permanently. Or, you may wish to place them in the album so that they can be removed at a later date.

PERMANENT MOUNTING

Permanent mounting requires the application of adhesive to the back of a photo or mat. Photo splits and tape rollers do the job neatly. Avoid liquid glues that may buckle the photo. Apply adhesive to all four corners of your image and again in the center. You may wish to add additional adhesive to ensure bonding.

NONPERMANENT MOUNTING

Nonpermanent mounting allows you to attach your items to a page and still have the option of easily moving them. This method is especially beneficial when placing materials in your scrapbook that you may wish to have duplicated someday. The easiest way to temporarily mount items is to use self-adhesive photo corners. These paper or plastic triangular pockets are applied to the album page. The photo's corners are then inserted into each pocket.

Add title, journaling & accessories

The last step to completing your scrapbook page is adding a title, journaling, and any embellishments you have selected. You'll find more about journaling and titles in the last chapter. Remember, any decorative touches you add to your finished page should support, rather than detract, from your photos.

TITLE

A title, whether created freehand, with stickers, punched or stamped shapes, or computer-generated fonts, sums up the page's content and theme. It gives readers a "heads-up" so they can be better prepared for the material to come.

JOURNALING

A picture may speak a thousand words, but words do something photos cannot. They record important information such as the names of those in photos as well as when, where and why the picture was shot. They are the vehicle for sharing insights and stories that make pages unique. That's why good journaling is an important part of good scrapbook pages.

Reluctant journalers often fear their handwriting is not attractive, their spelling is bad or they cannot express themselves succinctly. If you share these concerns, try writing on separate pieces of paper, cutting them out and applying them to your pages rather than writing directly on the page. Or use a computer to help write and check your spelling. However you journal, let your personality flow with the ink and your pages will come alive.

ACCESSORIES

Adhere design elements—borders, stickers, punch art, die cuts and stamped images— to finish the page, remembering that sometimes "less is more."

The complete page

A successful scrapbook page tells a story with photos, memorabilia and journaling. It is well-balanced and pleasing to look at. The colors help convey the mood and message of the page. Accents add that special zing. A successful scrapbook page is more than just a display of photos. It is a work of art.

Donna Leicht, Appleton, Wisconsin

Lisa Jackson, San Antonio, Texas

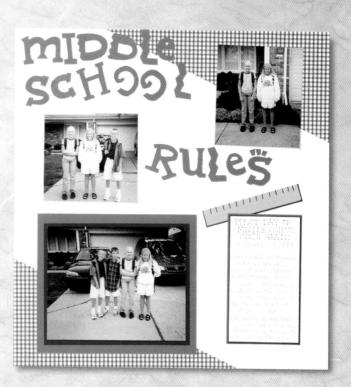

Creating page continuity

Two is often better than one, especially with scrapbook pages. Sometimes you just have too many great photos to fit on just one page. For page continuity, the key is to unify two pages to read as one, so your story can flow from page to page harmoniously. Here are some ideas to help you make your double-page spreads come together.

USE A BORDER Visually connect a double-page spread by using a border that runs across both pages. The border can extend around all four sides of the layout or simply run across the upper and lower edges.

Sandi Parrish, Grand Rapids, Michigan

USE THE SAME BACKGROUND PAPER This is the easiest way to keep your eyes flowing across both pages and eliminate the perception of delineation.

Cindy Mandernach, Grand Blanc, Michigan

COORDINATE COLORS Coordinate your page décor for an ensemble look. Use different, yet matching, paper for your second page to pull the look together.

CREATE MOVEMENT Pop-ups, peek-a-boos and moving parts can extend across two pages and add interest.

SPLIT PHOTOS OR DESIGN ELEMENTS
Consider cutting photos in half and placing each section on either side of the gutter close to the seam. This works especially well with panoramic scenery shots and photo enlargements.

MIRROR A DESIGN Repeat the same layout on both sides of the spread, or create a reverse mirror by flipping the layout upside down on the opposite page. Keep shapes and matting identical.

RUN A TITLE ACROSS THE SPREAD Running a title across the spread draws the viewer's eye from one side to the next. Titles can also be butted up against the gutter seam, diagonally across the spread or on the side borders of both pages.

ALLOW CONTACT When photos touch, your eyes follow them along the sequence. Allow the pictures to flow across the gutter of two pages.

REPEAT A DESIGN ELEMENT Place similar embellishments on both pages such as punch art, stickers, die cuts or stamps.

ZOO CREW

OUR VISIT
TO CHEYENNE
MOUNTAIN ZOO IN
COLORADO SPRINGS
DURING SPRING
BREAK MARCH
2001. THIS WAS
THE FIRST TIME
WE VISITED THIS
ZOO.

SASHA'S FAVORITES
WERE THE WOLVES.
DANIEL'S FAVORITES
WERE THE LIONS.
AND VULTURES.
ANNA'S FAVORITES
WAS THE GORILLAS.
ANNA 11   DANIEL 6
SASHA 8

Making your first album

IF YOU'RE LIKE ME,
YOU WILL WANT TO
DO 'THIS' TYPE OF
ALBUM AND THEN
'THAT' TYPE OF
ALBUM ALL AT THE
SAME TIME—AND
THEN FIT ANOTHER
ONE IN BETWEEN.
I SAY GO FOR IT!
THERE'S NO REASON
TO LIMIT YOURSELF.

—Michele

Congratulations! You have finished that first page! Now it's time to focus on the bigger picture—the creation of an album. Some believe that an album is simply a collection of individual pages, but it is much more. A successful album is cohesive and organized. When possible, the design flows from spread to spread. A good album is a substantial package that is both beautiful and informative.

Just as there are two basic methods for organizing photos and memorabilia, there are two basic types of scrapbooks. The first type displays the photos in chronological order so the pictures follow a time line. The second type of scrapbook is a theme album in which the scrapbooker pulls together and displays photos and memorabilia surrounding a particular topic or theme. Many scrapbookers keep both chronological and theme albums. Once you begin thinking of the number of ways you can present your photos, you'll find your ideas multiplying and your creative dreams becoming reality.

Chronological albums

In a chronological or on going album, a scrapbooker organizes the photos sequentially, displaying the pictures in the order in which events happened. Some scrapbookers choose to dedicate one album to each month or calendar year. Others may create an album for each child or family member and then order the pages within that book chronologically. A chronological album is a wonderful way to ensure that future generations will have a true grasp on how and when events unfolded.

Oksanna Pope, of Los Gatos California, is making a chronological, on going album that cleverly does two things: it preserves special memories for her son and it documents Royce's annual milestones of age progression.

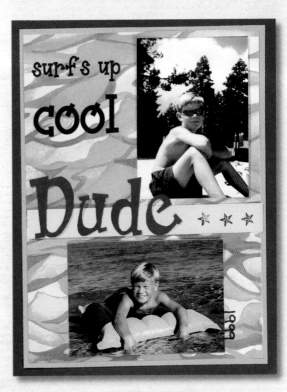

With her use of close-up, single subject photos and very simple page designs and embellishments, Oksanna is able to keep the focus of her album on one thing—her son!

Kelly Angard, of Highlands Ranch, Colorado, is typical of many scrapbookers in that she faithfully keeps up with her scrapbooking as she gets photos back from the photo lab. In doing so, she has a consistent chronology of her family's life, including day-to-day events as well as special occasions and celebrations.

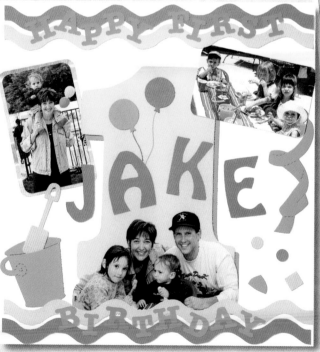

The hallmark of great chronological-order albums is the documentation of dates and the ages of those shown in the photos. By providing these details through journaling, viewers get a good glimpse of a family's progression over the course of time.

Theme albums

A theme album is limited to a single topic and may feature activities in which you are involved repeatedly over the course of years. It may also focus on a single event such as a wedding, vacation or hobby. Good theme albums owe their success to the consistent use of paper colors, patterns, journaling and decorative elements. On page 91 you will find a work sheet on which to note ideas for future theme album projects. Once you finish a theme album you'll undoubtedly look forward to beginning another.

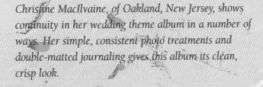

Christine MacIlvaine, of Oakland, New Jersey, shows continuity in her wedding theme album in a number of ways. Her simple, consistent photo treatments and double-matted journaling gives this album its clean, crisp look.

Doris Lemert, Fort Wayne, Indiana

ABC ALBUM ABC albums are a fun alternative to a chronologically ordered theme album, and you can make an ABC album for just about any theme! Each page or layout features photos, memorabilia and page accents that relate to a certain letter of the alphabet. Enhance an ABC album by journaling with words that start with each letter of the alphabet and that apply to the album's theme or its photos.

BABY ALBUM A baby album is a record of the milestones of pregnancy, the wonder of birth and those awesome "firsts"—from a child's first smile to the first toddling steps. The album can include photos, sonograms, notes from birth preparation classes, hospital brochures, birth announcements, congratulatory cards, scraps of wrapping paper and clips of downy hair from a child's first haircut.

HOBBY ALBUM Whether your passion is piano or soccer, building model cars or racing dune buggies, you'll want to record your pleasure and progress in a hobby album. Have someone take pictures of you participating in your favorite activity. If you are creating something, whether in clay, stone, fabric or another medium, take step-by-step photos that show the progress of your work. Purchase or buy pockets in which to store small awards or objects such as coins, flat seashells and collectible cards. Or photocopy these items as well as embroidery or other stitched works for inclusion in the album.

Terri Robichon
Plymouth, Minnesota

NEW HOME Remember the excitement of moving into a new home with photos of the construction, loading and unloading of the van, picture hanging afternoons, the unpacking of boxes, copies of mortgage papers and floor plans, journaled first impressions of neighbors, paint chips and wallpaper and fabric samples. Long after you've settled in and your house becomes a home, you'll look back through this album with triumph.

Melanie Duffy, Costa Mesa, California

PET ALBUM Pets add so much to our lives and ask for so little in return. Capture the essence of your pets and the loving relationship you share by preserving photos of daily antics and portraits, memorial tributes and labels from favorite food products. Don't forget to preserve locks of fur, feathers and I.D. tags in memorabilia keepers. Add photocopies of registered documents and certificates, too.

SEASON ALBUM The nip of fall air, the woody smell of winter, the colors of spring and the sounds of summer all evoke memories of special activities and events related to the changing seasons. Capture the moments in a seasonal album filled with photos, keepsakes, poems and journaling as you mark the passage of time.

Kristi Hazelrigg
Washington, Oklahoma

The buildings in Downtown Denver were just amazing. The picture above captures the Hyatt Regency track in the reflection of a neighboring high rise. We enjoyed the skyline throughout the day, but it was spectacular in the early morning sun and at sunset.

Joellyn Borke-Johnston
Des Moines, Iowa

TRAVEL ALBUM Whether you find adventure around the block or around the world, it's worth recording. Travel albums capture the excitement of those trips to the local park, to Granny's house in Texas, or to museums throughout Europe. Include special souvenirs and memorabilia such as maps, brochures, receipts, ticket stubs, train and plane tickets, itineraries, menus and pressed flowers—anything you collect on your journey.

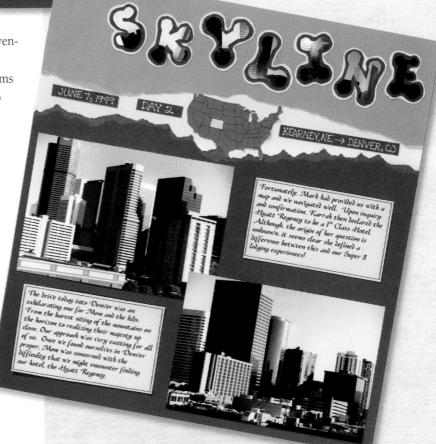

JUNE 7, 1999   DAY 2

KEARNEY, NE → DENVER, CO

Fortunately, Mark had provided us with a map and we navigated well. Upon inquiry and confirmation, Karrah then declared the Hyatt Regency to be a 1st Class Hotel. Although the origin of her question is unknown, it seems clear she defined a difference between this and our Super 8 lodging experiences!

The drive today into Denver was an exhilarating one for Mom and the kids. From the barest sitting of the mountains on the horizon to realizing their majesty up close, our approach was very exciting for all of us. Once we found ourselves in Denver proper, Mom was concerned with the difficulty that we might encounter finding our hotel, the Hyatt Regency.

Album goals work sheet

As you organize your photos and memorabilia, you are likely to come across specific albums you would like to create for yourself or for others. Use this work sheet to help you determine and define the albums you may wish to create over the course of time.

ALBUM TYPE (spiral, strap, mini, etc.)	ALBUM THEME	ALBUM FOR?	PHOTOS & MEMORABILIA ORGANIZED?	PRODUCTS TO PURCHASE	DATE STARTED	FINISH ALBUM BY?	NOTES
	Baby						
	Child						
	Family						
	Friendship						
	Heritage						
	Hobby or Career						
	Holiday						
	Portrait						
	School Days						
	The Seasons						
	Traditions						
	Travel						
	Tribute						
	Wedding						

An overview of the album-making process

The idea of creating an entire album can seem overwhelming. But with organization and planning, your album can easily take shape. Don't hurry the process. Remember, this is not a race, so take the time to enjoy the planning and the construction of each page and spread.

① ORGANIZE PHOTOS

Your photos have already been sorted by either date or theme and stored in photo-safe containers. Now it's time to pull them out and re-sort them into smaller categories or groupings, as shown. Decide which photos you wish to feature on the pages of your current album project—in this case, a college theme album. Set them aside and put away the others.

② LAY OUT PAGES

Determine what photos will appear on which pages using the worksheet on page 100. (If necessary refer to your sketches on the page design orksheet on page 67.) These rough sketches represent the pages of your scrapbook and act as a preliminary blueprint for the placement of your photos. When using the sketches to plan your layout, make sure to leave room for journaling. Build in extra room for the display of photos you wish to have enlarged. The number and sizes of photos you are going to use will determine the size of the album you need to purchase and the number of pages you will create.

③ PURCHASE AN ALBUM

Take your photos and sketched layouts with you to the store to purchase an album, refill pages and page protectors. When selecting the album, consider the size and shape of the items you will be displaying. Consider purchasing extra pages so that you can spread your layouts if you find your photos look too crowded. You can always return unopened packages of pages and page protectors if you find you do not need them. Put photos inside page protectors to "hold" space on those spreads as shown.

④ PURCHASE PAPER AND ACCESSORIES

With your new album and photos in hand, you will find it much easier to select paper colors and page accessories—stickers, die cuts, stamps, pen colors and more. Select papers and a few simple design elements based on your primary color scheme and carry the theme, color and style throughout your book to help tie your pages together and create a feeling of unity.

Creating album continuity

Just as the consistent use of colored paper and page accessories tie spreads together, they are imperative for creating a cohesive look and feel for theme albums. Borders can act as bookends, visually embracing sections of your scrapbook. The same title and cropping treatments further unite pages. The journaling "voice" and presentation are equally important in creating a tightly woven scrapbook. On the following pages you'll find examples of scrapbooks that have it all— cohesion, clarity, continuity and creativity.

The selection of black pages for this leather album is a good choice, as black is one of the University's official colors.

COLLEGE ALBUM While the University of Missouri alum that created this album had no control over the colors appearing in the photos, she could control other colors within the scrapbook. Her paper choice reflects the University's official colors: black and gold. The patterned border recalls the college mascot—a tiger. Through consistent use of these colors and embellishments, she created a cohesive look.

Repetitive use of one simple design element—a free-hand-cut paper pennant bearing the college moniker—helps carry this album's theme throughout its pages.

Journaling in the same gold pen on every page ties the pages together and creates a feeling of consistency.

Photos Kimberly Ball, Denver, Colorado

SPORTS ALBUM It is hard to strike out when you tie your album pages together with style. These baseball pages hit a design home run. Consistent paper colors unite each spread. If you plan to create a sports album that encompasses different sports and different sport seasons, consider using a new paper choice for each to help differentiate them.

BASEBALL BUILDS CHARACTER

2001

11 and 12 year old
Fayetteville
All Star
Team

Coaches: Todd Gaskill, Monty Hall, Scotty St
Players: Clay Gill, Tyler Shelton, Blake Dorris, Cody Gasl
Brandon Netherland, Chris Mitchell, Rob Gray, Matth
Barnes, Chris Shelton, Antwon Brown, Freddi

Handmade especially for you by C. Gray — Character Quality Own

We're a Team!

FAITH VS PRESUMPTION
Confidence that actions
rooted in good character will
yield the best outcome, even
when I cannot see how.

HUMILITY VS PRIDE
ACKNOWLEDGING THAT
ACHIEVEMENT RESULTS
FROM THE INVESTMENT OF
God and others in my life.

Honor   Humility   Initiative

Repetitive use of matted page titles, computer fonts and pen stroke stitching on the journaling blocks further support this album's continuation of theme and design.

Cathy Gray, Fayetteville, Tennessee

Baseball is...

A game of Adversity.

Baseball is a game of adversity, bad hops, bad breaks, bad calls, error, golfer balls, and swings and misses, slumps, benching, and demotion. They are all part of the game. When adversity hits, a player is faced with a choice to pout or push on.
— Busch

"Failure is part of the long path to success."
Kopp

Don't let your mistakes get you down.
While playing third base for the Giants in 1962, Ehalo Brenly made four errors in the fourth inning. Then he hit a home run in the fifth. In the seventh, he made a single that sent two runners home. In the bottom of the ninth, he stepped up to the plate and hit the game winning home run. ~Walley

Don't give up five minutes before the Miracle—have Faith.
~price

Alertness   Availability   Boldness   Compassion   Cautiousness   Contentment

*Consistent photo treatments and patterned paper
border along the pages' lower edges give this album
its crisp, clean, "pulled together" look.*

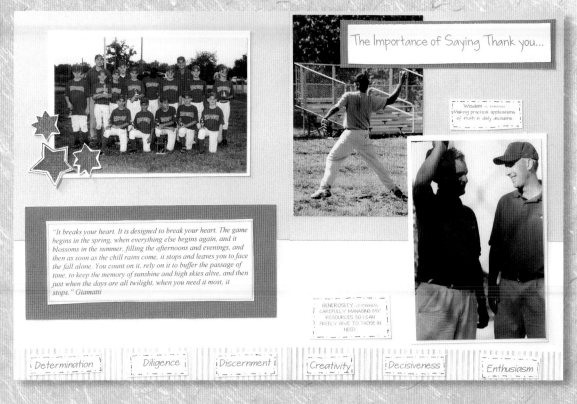

The Importance of Saying Thank you...

Wisdom vs. foolishness
Making practical applications of truth in daily decisions

"It breaks your heart. It is designed to break your heart. The game begins in the spring, when everything else begins again, and it blossoms in the summer, filling the afternoons and evenings, and then as soon as the chill rains come, it stops and leaves you to face the fall alone. You count on it, rely on it to buffer the passage of time, to keep the memory of sunshine and high skies alive, and then just when the days are all twilight, when you need it most, it stops." Giamatti

GENEROSITY vs. stinginess
CAREFULLY MANAGING MY RESOURCES SO I CAN FREELY GIVE TO THOSE IN NEED.

Determination   Diligence   Discernment   Creativity   Decisiveness   Enthusiasm

HERITAGE ALBUM These heritage photos are united on pages that share unique design elements. While the market offers an amazing array of gorgeous heritage-themed papers and accessories, beautiful pages can also be created with the paper you may already own and a few simple accessories.

Note that many of the photos are not cropped, allowing important details in the backgrounds to be included. Other photos are cropped and matted in oval shapes, lending a locket-like appearance with old-fashioned appeal.

"Remember the Ladies"

These pages successfully carry the theme and look of antique quilts. Pen stroke stitching, done in black ink, details and supports the quilted backdrops on which the photos are displayed.

Debra Fee, Broomfield, Colorado

Hatch

Etta

Ina

Maud

Edna

daughters of
Nora Ella
and
David

Friends

The following pages contain a sampling of the many photographs my grandmother treasured over the years. They were never labeled, because the names that went with these faces were etched in her heart. I have included them here because they reflect a time and culture that should never be forgotten.

Charlie Rogers   Elmer Hatch

Thumbnail sketches work sheet

Thumbnail sketches, which are nothing more than mini versions of pages in the album, can help you visualize the number of album pages you have to fill. Use this work sheet to help plan the order of your scrapbook. Begin by photocopying this page. Then group the photos and memorabilia you plan to place on each page. Order the groupings as you would have them appear in the album, beginning with the first page or spread and moving toward the back of the book. Once you're satisfied with the album's layout, write or draw in the page progression on the work sheet below.

TITLE PAGE

ENDING PAGE

Including memorabilia in your album

Memorabilia is often as important to scrapbookers as their photos. However, including those news-paper clippings, old documents and certificates, maps, postcards, letters, invitations, coins, pressed flowers, locks of hair and other keepsakes in albums poses some challenges. A lot of memorabilia is acidic and, as such, is not photo-safe. But with a little ingenuity, planning and the right supplies, photos and memorabilia can live happily side by side within your album.

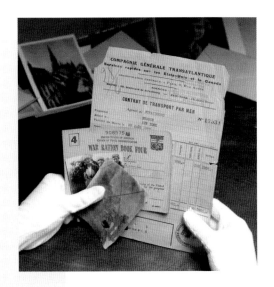

MEMORABILIA PRESERVATION TIPS

- Photocopy old documents, certificates, and newspaper clippings onto acid- and lignin-free paper. Use the copies in your album. Store additional memorabilia in an archival-quality memorabilia box.

- Encapsulate deacidified or fragile memorabilia items.

- Never allow memorabilia and photos to touch.

- When placing photos and memorabilia in close proximity, create barriers between the two. Mats help keep acids in memorabilia from migrating to photos.

- Photograph bulky memorabilia such as trophies or corsages and include the pictures in your album.

- Place memorabilia in archival-quality envelopes and attach the envelopes directly to your page.

- Mount memorabilia with nonpermanent techniques such as self-adhesive photo corners so that you can easily remove the pieces to view or copy later.

- When handling old documents, wear cotton gloves to prevent damage from skin oils and dirt.

To neutralize (de-acidify) the acids in paper such as newspaper, certificates or cards, spray with a buffering spritz. To treat paper with Archival Mist™, shake the bottle vigorously and follow the pumping directions on the container. Apply spray lightly and evenly 6" from the paper's surface on both sides of the paper and allow to dry before adhering. When treating papers containing chalk or pastels, spray the reverse side only.

Memorabilia encapsulation methods

There are a number of convenient ways to encapsulate memorabilia so it can be safely displayed in your scrapbook. Encapsulation makes it possible to include photos and memorabilia on the same pages without damaging the photos. Encapsulation systems come in a variety of sizes and include transparent plastic sleeves, keepers and pockets. Make sure the product you choose is PVC-free and made from polyethylene, polypropylene or polyester.

Plastic keepers, available in different shapes, are good for storing 3-D memorabilia, such as coins and lockets of hair.

Pam Klassen, Denver Colorado

ENCAPSULATION TIPS

- Use memorabilia keepers, sleeves or envelopes to encapsulate organic items such as pressed flowers, leaves, sand and tiny shells.

- Use encapsulation systems to display metallic items such as coins and keys. Metallic items generally do not pose a chemical risk to scrapbooks unless they contain iron. Copper also has a tendency to corrode.

- Use pockets or envelopes to encapsulate hair, fur, feathers or other similar items.

- Use sleeves to display and protect paper memorabilia such as de-acidified birth certificates, postcards or recipe cards.

- Use sleeves and pockets to encapsulate maps, playbills and other bulky pieces of paper memorabilia.

HOW TO MAKE A POCKET PAGE

Pocket pages are easy to make and provide a safe environment for flat memorabilia such as certificates, cards, schedules and other documents. You can use decorative rulers or scissors to make different cuts along the top of the pocket. Decorate with stickers, die cuts, stamps or punch art that relate to the theme of the pocket's contents.

1 *Use a decorative ruler and a pencil to draw a line across the center of a sheet of cardstock. The cardstock should be the same size as the paper used for the page background. Cut along line with scissors to create piece for "pocket."*

2 *Attach double-sided tape adhesive to the back of the "pocket" along the two sides and the lower edge, keeping the upper edge of the pocket adhesive-free.*

3 *Mount pocket onto scrapbook page along lower edge and sides. Accent as desired and fill with memorabilia.*

Special Christmas

Memories

2001

Each year before we open gifts at Grandma and Grandpa Gerbrandt's we read the Christmas story from the Bible (Luke). Now that all three kids are old enough they all want to get a piece of the action. This was Daniel's first year to read. He is doing so amazing with his reading.

Grandpa Gordon   Anna   Sasha   Daniel
        67   11   9   6

Journaling

It is the combination of words and pictures that give scrapbooks long-lasting value. I learned the importance of journaling the hard way…by looking back at my early books and realizing I simply had not included enough information. I found myself wondering who the people in the pictures were and where the photos had been taken.

While some scrapbookers are as comfortable putting words on paper as they are pictures and embellishments, others have to learn the art of journaling. Often, that means ridding themselves of preconceptions about what constitutes good writing. Scrapbook journaling isn't about dotting your "I's" and crossing your "T's." Nor is it about sentence structure or perfect paragraphs. It is about sharing important information and special stories.

I've heard every excuse in the book from those who do not journal. This chapter will address them and offer ways to work through your concerns. So pick up your pen and get ready to learn to write right!

LIKE MANY SCRAPBOOKERS, I FIRST FELL IN LOVE WITH THE ART OF PAGE DESIGN. IT HAS TAKEN SOME TIME, BUT THROUGH THE YEARS I'VE TRAINED MYSELF TO BECOME A COMPETENT JOURNALER.

–Michele

What to say

Scrapbook journaling isn't about how much you write. It is about the quality of information you share. Well-journaled scrapbook pages include information that reinforces the visuals by "telling" rather than "showing" what is displayed on the page.

While you may wish to include journaled jokes, stories and insights, you must also include some basic information such as what is happening in the pictures, who appears, and where, and when the event unfolded. How extensively you address these questions is up to you, but the bare facts are imperative. Well-journaled pages are like well-written storybooks. They leave the reader feeling content, as though all the pieces fell into place and the package was tied up with a tidy bow.

MAKE IT YOUR OWN

- Include the basic facts: what, when, who and where.

- Use your journaling to tell "the rest of the story."

- Describe how you felt and the mood of the occasion.

- Add a poem, quote or saying that illustrates the page's theme.

- Include the thoughts, feelings and words of those who shared the event.

- Share snippets of conversation or jokes.

INSUFFICIENT JOURNALING

WHAT?

What is going on in the pictures? What event is taking place? What was being said? What happened before and after the shot was taken? What inspired the expressions?

WHEN?

What day, month and year were these photos taken? Was this a special holiday or celebration?

WHO?

Who are the people in the photos? What are their names? Are they friends or relatives? Who was at the event who didn't get included in the photos?

WHERE?

Where did the event take place? Why was this location important? How was it chosen?

EFFECTIVE JOURNALING

A well-journaled page will be as pertinent to readers decades from now as it is in the present. They will be able to enjoy the pages more because the questions they might raise have been answered. They are able to see the scrapbooked events in a context that makes the page more compelling.

Sasha's 8th Birthday

June 16, 2000 We celebrated Sasha's birthday at Bana and Pop-Pop's new home. Bana, Sasha, Anna, Daniel, Katie & Pop Pop.

We had fun playing games, then opened many wonderful presents and had cake and ice cream. One of her favorite cousins, Katie Blessing was able to stay with us the whole weekend to help us celebrate.

Getting the facts

Before you begin to write, you need to know what to write. Sometimes the information is readily available. Other times you may feel as though you're trying to spin words from air because the facts have blurred in your memory. Or, perhaps you simply never knew the facts. This is especially true when working on projects such as a heritage album. There are many ways to claim the information you need. The Internet is a terrific resource and there are dozens of books that can guide you through the process of uncovering family history. Through the creation of your scrapbooks you are answering the questions that may be so important to future generations.

KEEP A JOURNAL

The human mind too often resembles a sieve. Names, dates, jokes, quotes, facts and figures run out and away almost as quickly as they are inputted. And no matter how often you tell yourself, "Oh, I'll certainly remember THAT," you just don't. Which is why it's a good idea to keep a small journal and pencil in your purse or car whenever you step out. Start making a point to jot down notes each time you pull out your camera. Include adjectives that will help you remember sights, sounds, smells and tastes. Include the date so you can later match journaled information to your pictures. If you don't keep a daily journal, holding on to your kitchen calendars can also help you "fill in the blanks" where photo information is concerned.

WHERE TO TURN FOR HISTORICAL INFORMATION

- Ask family members and friends about their memories.

- Look in family Bibles in which dates of weddings, births and deaths may be noted.

- Read old family letters and diaries.

- Visit cemeteries in which family members were buried.

- Search newspapers for references to family members.

- Find school yearbooks. If you don't have a copy, contact the school.

- Ferret out family papers such as wedding and death certificates, mortgage papers, portfolios, military commendations, household accounts, receipts, income tax statements and driver's licenses.

- Talk to religious leaders in communities in which family members lived.

- Contact and join a genealogical or historical society in the area in which you are interested.

- Use U.S. census information. Pick up a genealogy book in order to find out how to access it.

- Search county courthouse records for information about weddings, divorces, property records, wills and deeds.

INTERVIEWING

Helping others open the doors to their memories can be a challenge, but once you've mastered the technique you'll have friends and relatives sharing their most cherished stories. Brainstorm a list of questions before the interview. Include more than you may need so you can skip those that seem less pertinent while conducting the interview. Good interviewers never ask questions that can be answered with a simple "yes" or "no." Instead, they ask leading questions that begin with words such as, "why" and "how" (example: Why did you decide to move to Texas? How did you feel about the move?). While conducting the interview, focus your attention on your subject. Respond to answers by nodding, adding verbal affirmations, and laughing if something is funny. Be sure to give your subject adequate time to reply. Keep note taking to a minimum, writing down "memory joggers" and facts such as dates and names. You may wish to use a tape recorder. End the session when your subject tires.

QUESTIONS TO GET THEM TALKING

- What is your favorite song or poem and why?

- How did you feel when you found out you were going to be a parent?

- How did your family celebrate holidays?

- How do you want to be remembered?

- How would you describe yourself?

- How would you like others to describe you?

- If you could talk to your descendants 100 years from now, what would you tell them?

- Of what are you most proud and why?

- What was your childhood like?

    - What world event stands out most strongly in your memory?

    - What life choice would you change if you knew then what you know now?

    - What have been the happiest and saddest events in your life?

    - If you could spend the evening with one famous person—past or present—who would it be and why would you choose him?

Overcoming journaling fears

Many people suffer from journaling jitters. Some find themselves pulling a complete blank when they look at an empty page. Others develop sweaty palms and shaking hands the minute they pick up a pen. Many jittery writers have been sent, at some time in their lives, the message that their writing isn't up to par. Years later, they are still afraid to put words on paper for fear they won't say the right thing or won't say it the right way. If this describes you, it is time to put aside your concerns and move forward. Here are some tips and tricks to turn timid journalers into pros.

I HATE MY HANDWRITING

Handwriting is as individual as the person writing the words. It says a lot about the times in which we live. Different periods throughout history have placed more importance on penmanship than others, and popular styles of penmanship have been embraced over the years.

There is something compelling about old letters handwritten by long-gone family members. The rigid formality of some, the uneven swoops and swirls of others, and the ink splotches and doodles say as much about the writer as the letter's content.

For these reasons, many scrapbooking experts advocate journaling with a pen, rather than a computer. But if you simply can't live comfortably with your handwriting, invest in one of the many font CDs on the market. They allow you to select from a library of fonts, change their colors, sizes and even fill pattern. Print your message on photo-safe paper and apply to your page.

MISTAKE FIXERS

- Wite Out® over the mistake. Rewrite directly on top of the Wite Out.

- Cover the mistake with another piece of paper cut or punched into a decorative shape.

- Cut or tear paper into shapes. Layer the pieces to create design elements that can cover mistakes.

- Save scraps from cropped pictures. Use the pieces to patch problem areas.

- Use stickers, die cuts and shapes punched from photo scraps to cover mistakes.

HELP FOR MESSY JOURNALING

Clean and pleasant-looking journaling is often the result of planning. It is best to place your photos and decorative elements on your scrapbook page before you begin to write. Then, using a ruler, draw straight guidelines along which you can journal. Journaling templates are also wonderful tools that help prevent words from weaving and wandering arbitrarily across a page. Try templates with waves, spirals and zigzag lines to break up linear text. Simply align the template on your page or paper and trace the lines in ink or vanishing ink. Add your journaling along the lines.

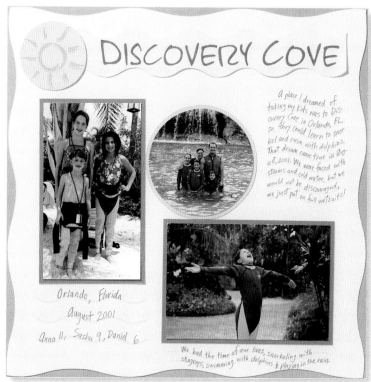

Journaling templates are a dream come true for scrapbookers. They provide guidelines which the writer can follow to ensure tidy journaling.

ADD ZING TO YOUR WORDS

- Turn certain letters into tiny illustrations. If you are writing about pizza, for example, turn the letter "A" into a mini slice. Or turn the "O" in the word "balloon" into a balloon.

- Write text and then embellish the dots above the letter "i" with stickers. Add stickers to the ends of sentences instead of periods.

- Write the first letter in a block of text larger than the rest of the text.

- Emphasize key words in sentences by making them bigger, bolder, or by changing their color.

- Write your messages on pretty journaling stickers, or use journaling stickers with pre-printed messages.

Journaling stickers and cutouts are printed with or without lines upon which you can journal. These are available in a variety of styles, sizes and themes. Some stickers are pre-printed with messages.

Types of journaling

There are many different ways to present journaling on your scrapbook pages. Some methods are direct and to the point. Others are more free flowing and creative. The type of journaling you select will be determined by a number of factors including your level of comfort with the written word and the theme and mood of your page. It will also be impacted by the amount you want to say, and the amount of room you have to say it in. On the following pages you'll find ideas for ways to include journaling in your album. Remember that journaling is a part of your page design and how you present it can be as important as what you say.

BULLET JOURNALING

Bullet journaling is a quick-and-easy way to address the facts without having to wrap text in sentences and paragraphs. Bullets supply basic information such as who, what, when and where the photos were taken.

KID CONVERSATION STARTERS

Bullet-style journaling is the perfect way to add charm to a Father's Day (or Mother's Day) gift album. The album can be illustrated with casual photos, formal portraits, children's artwork, stickers and more. Some of the conversation starters used to inspire the children's comments in the journaled page below include:

- Daddy and I are different because...
- Daddy and I are the same because...
- Daddy and I like to sing and our favorite song is...
- Daddy is like [name an animal] because...
- Daddy is silly when he...
- Daddy likes it when...
- I love Daddy as much as...
- I wish Daddy would...
- My favorite time with Daddy was...
- Our favorite thing Daddy does with us is...
- We have most fun as a family when...
- We like it when...
- What Daddy does at work is...
- What I do when Daddy is at work is...

Laurie Connolly, Mukilteo, Washington

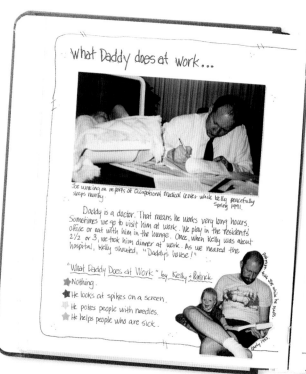

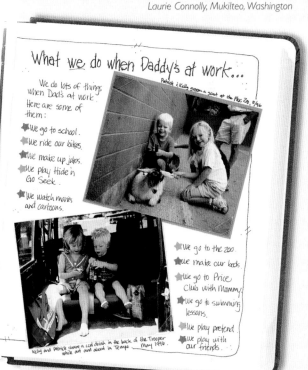

SHORT CAPTION JOURNALING

So much can be conveyed in so few words! Short caption journaling is a way of telling the story briefly and concisely. Include in the captions those basic facts about who, where, what and when and then add a few interesting details. Don't feel like you need to go to town constructing elaborate tomes. Just say what you need to say and move on.

Lifelong friendships and the shared experience of braces prompted this snapshot. Its short caption quickly hits upon what's going on in the photos without sacrificing too much detail.

Karen Regep Glover
Grosse Pointe Woods, Michigan

PERSPECTIVE JOURNALING

Perspective journaling reflects not just the memories, thoughts and feelings of the scrapbooker, but also the impressions of others. Begin adding perspective journaling to your albums by asking family members and friends to write about their thoughts on momentous occasions. If they prefer, they may wish to dictate to you. Do not feel as though you need pages of reflections from each person; a few sentences will do just fine. The more perspectives you include, the more "voices" you add to your album.

Siblings are famous for having very different memories of certain events as documented by this page featuring three sisters who clearly remember different things about Christmases past.

Photos Deborah Mock, Denver, Colorado

POETIC JOURNALING

Poetic journaling utilizes published songs, book titles, poems, stories, quotes, sayings and Bible verses. Or you can write your own poems that reflect the sentiment depicted on a scrapbook page. It can rhyme or be free verse. Poetic journaling is a natural choice for historical, holiday, wedding, anniversary, travel and children's theme albums.

Poetic journaling can be as simple as a sentimental saying.

Photos Ken Trujillo

BRING YOUR JOURNALING ALIVE

Use descriptive words that help capture the mood. A dictionary or thesaurus will offer even more great adjectives.

Adventuresome	Fragrant	Keen	Parched	Unassuming
Artistic	Frosty	Knobby	Pungent	Uncanny
Beautiful	Gooey	Legendary	Quick	Valorous
Bitter	Graceful	Loving	Quiet	Velvety
Creative	Happy-go-lucky	Magical	Restless	Waterlogged
Crisp	Homespun	Musty	Rousing	Wayward
Delectable	Icy	Naughty	Scraggly	Yippy
Downy	Irresistible	Nimble	Smooth	Yummy
Edgy	Jaunty	Original	Testy	Zingy
Elegant	Jolly	Outgoing	Trendy	Zippy

Poetry made simple work sheet

If you can't find a poem that says it all, write one yourself. These simple, fill-in-the-blank formulas—one a sentimental poem, the other, a lighter limerick—will give your pages poetic justice in no time!

SENTIMENTAL POEM EXAMPLE

My Beautiful One
By Susan Smith

Rose
Giggly, curious, dreamy, musical
Loves dancing, spinning and whirling
Hates math, cruelty, repetition
Yearns for adventure, love and fame
Shares with the world laughter and hope
Will certainly follow her heart
Without whom I would fade away
Rose
My lovely daughter.

Title of Poem _____

Author's Name _____

_____ (a person's name)

_____ , _____ , _____ , _____
(four words that describe the person's character)

Loves _____ , _____ and _____

Hates _____ , _____ , _____

Yearns for _____ , _____ and _____

Shares with the world _____ and _____

Will certainly_____

Without whom I _____

_____ (the person's name again)

My _____

LIGHTER LIMERICK POEM EXAMPLE

A limerick is a five-lined verse. The limerick is structured so that lines one, two and five all rhyme. Lines three and four rhyme. A limerick rocks along like a cantering horse with a da-da-DUM rhythm. Each of these da-da-DUM patterns is called a metric foot. Lines one, two and five of the limerick must have exactly three metric feet. Lines three and four must have exactly two metric feet. The first foot of each line may just start out with a da-DUM rather than a da-da-DUM. Good limericks have a final line that is especially clever.

There ONCE was a DOG known as RO-ver
Who RAN out to PLAY in the CLO-ver
Though once COV-ered with SPOTS—
He got BURNED 'tween the DOTS—
And NOW he looks SUN-tanned all OVER.

_____
_____
_____
_____
_____

_____
_____
_____
_____
_____

STORYTELLING JOURNALING

Storytelling journaling steps beyond the basic information and delves into the history behind pictures and memorabilia. It tends to take on a narrative voice that involves the reader, much like a novel. Similar to a novel, storytelling journaling often calls on the senses of sight, smell, sound and touch to establish and carry a mood. Text from storytelling tends to be a bit longer and descriptions are more intricate.

A Gift for Max

Zachary wanted to get his brother a gift for Maxwell's 3rd. Birthday. Zach picked out two gifts. A Blue's Clues drawing tablet and two toy Monster trucks. Grandma Landis made this a big deal with Zachary. So, before the birthday party on 6/5/99 Grandma and Zach wrapped the gifts. Zach was so proud. But, Mommy and Grandma I think were the most proud. What a wonderful thing to think of others in such a loving way. Max loves his gifts, and Zach reminds Max all the time that he got those for him.

Accented with just a silhouette-cropped and matted photo and a simple stamped border, the story of a giving soul is captured.

Michele Rank
Cerritos, California

GOOD STORYTELLING TIPS

- Write like you speak.

- Tape record the story as you tell it to a friend or family member. Transcribe it later.

- Remember that all good stories have a beginning, middle and end.

- Choose a story beginning that sets the mood and captures the reader's attention.

- Allow the story's middle to move the plot forward logically.

- Make sure the end of the story wraps up the tale and leaves the reader feeling content.

- Use powerful adjectives and strong verbs and adverbs.

- Most good stories (like the *Wizard of Oz*) have a heroine/hero who wants or needs something. On her way to achieving it she runs into obstacles. Through wit and bravery she overcomes them and gets her reward. Consider building your journaled story using the same format.

- Don't be afraid to include the good, the bad and the ugly in your story.

REBUS JOURNALING

Rebus journaling involves using both words and tiny pictures in a sentence. The pictures can either replace a word or reinforce it. For example, the letter "I" at the beginning of a phrase may be replaced with a picture of a human eye. The word "love" may be replaced with a heart. Or, you may wish to write the word "love" and place a tiny heart just after it, as an illustration. Rebus journaling takes some time and thought, but pays off in truly unique pages.

A form of rebus storytelling (pictures within journaling) helps to preserve this birthday story.

Julie Labuszewski, Littleton, Colorado

Making room for journaling

Journaling is as important to a successful scrapbook page as photos and memorabilia, but too many scrapbookers fail to consider journaling space when designing their spreads. Only after their photos and decorative items have been adhered do they realize that there is simply no room left on the page for writing. Do not get caught in this bind. Plan ahead and remember that journaling can run across the top or bottom of the page, down the sides in columns, or flow around photos. It may sit atop die cuts or be written on a separate sheet of paper and tucked behind photo mats. With a little ingenuity you can find the means and the space to add a few well-chosen words to even crowded pages.

Stacey Shigaya, Denver, Colorado

Vellum is an ideal material for creating overlays for journaling. The translucent quality of vellum allows you to place your journaling directly over a photo. Sketch the basic layout of your page on a sheet of vellum. Add journaling and then slip the overlay into an empty page protector and insert it in front of the corresponding page.

GO AROUND IT

Journal around photos, directly on the scrapbook page or on the photo mats. Journaling around photo mats is a simple solution for adding words when it seems like there is really no room for them.

Photos Sally Scamfer, Bellvue, Nebraska

EXTEND IT

Page extenders, sold in a number of different styles by different manufacturers, supply additional room on which to journal. Some extenders are conjoined page protectors. When closing your album you simply fold the extended page or pages back into the book.

Creative titles and lettering

Every successful scrapbook page must have a title. Like the headline on the front page of a newspaper, the title loudly declares what has taken place and prepares the reader for the material that will follow. Subsequent titles help steer the reader from one topic to another. The title is often placed on the top of a page like a banner, but may also run down the side or sit in the middle of a page. The title can be straight forward or catchy. From a design perspective, the title should coordinate with the other visual elements on the page. Titles can be created with computer fonts or drawn freehand. They can also be made with stickers, punches or stamps.

CREATIVE LETTERING IDEAS

When the urge hits and the page calls for it, put down the pen and pick up these tools and supplies in order to create dynamic titles.

PUNCHES & SMALL DIE CUTS Lettering punches and small die cuts are available in upper- and lowercase and various styles.

STICKERS Stickers come in a plethora of shapes and colors and are available in multiple fonts and themes.

STAMPS Letter stamps are available in upper- and lowercase and in a multitude of fonts. Personalize stamped letters by filling them in with different colors or embossing over them.

TEMPLATES Lettering templates help you create jumbo or mini letters in styles that run from whimsical to elegant.

COMPUTER FONTS Today's computer-savvy scrapbooker can choose from a number of commercial software programs that offer designer fonts with varying degrees of manipulation.

MIX AND MATCH FOR A ONE-OF-A-KIND TITLE LOOK

Let these titles jump-start your imagination. Make them your own by creatively combining different tools, papers and colors in one page title.

BEST FRIENDS *combines letter stickers and letters traced with a template.*

SUMMER DAYS *is made up of photo die cuts and stamped letters.*

HAPPY BIRTHDAY *is layered with tiny punched letters atop letter stickers.*

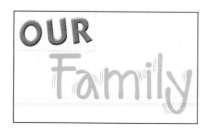

OUR LOVE UNITES US *mixes stamped letters with letter fonts.*

OUR FAMILY *was made with letter stickers and a journaling font.*

TERRIFIC TITLE IDEAS

BABY
Born to Be Wild
Cute as a Button
Diaper Daze
Special Delivery
Sugar and Spice and
 Everything Nice

CAREER
For It's Work All Day
 For the Sugar in Your Tea
Happiness Comes From a Job
 Well Done
Takin' Care of Business
Whistle While You Work
Workin' For a Living

CELEBRATIONS
Celebrate Good Times,
 Come On, Celebrate!
Happy Birthday
Party Down
The More the Merrier
We're All Together Again

COLLEGE
Goin' Places
Got Computer, Will Travel
I've Got Class
Party Animal
Student on Bored

FRIENDS
Family and Friends Are
 Life's Gifts
Friends Forever
Kindred Spirits
When Friends Meet,
 Hearts Warm
You Make My Heart Smile

HERITAGE
From Strong Roots Grow
 Lovely Branches
It's All Relative
Our Family Tree is Full of Nuts
Through the Ages
We Honor the Past

HOBBY
An Artist is Born
Better Sorry Than Safe
Craftaholic in Residence
I Am Creative, Not Tidy!
If It Does Not Move, Paint It

HOLIDAY
A Cause for Celebration
Kick Up Your Heels
Merry Christmas
Rejoice
Santa's Little Helpers

PETS
A Real Stable Pony
Fish Tales
For the Birds
It is the Cats Meow
Love Some Bunny
There is a Mouse in the House
To Err is Human,
 To Forgive, Canine

SCHOOL DAYS
Best Buddies 4 Ever
Hard at Work
Mad Science
Just a Swingin'
Kids Do the Darndest Things

SEASONS
April Showers Bring
 May Flowers
Fall Forward
Leaf the Raking to Dad
Let It Snow!
Sizzlin' Summertime Fun
Welcome Winter
You Are My Sunshine

SPORTS
Bad Losers Good Winners
Have a Ball
If First You Don't Succeed
 Try, Try Again
Kickin'
My Special Hotshot

TODDLER
Here Comes Trouble
I Spy
Make A Wish
No! No! No!
Preschool Daze
Warning, Kids At Play

TRAVEL
Destination Relaxation
Get Out the Map
If You Come to a Fork
 in the Road, Take It
The Journey Not the
 Destination, Matters
What a Wonderful World
Wish You Were Here

WEDDING
Fairy Tale Romance
Happily Ever After
I Do
On the Wings of Love
We Unite With Joyful Hearts

Where to go from here

You have come to the end of a new adventure—the creation of your first precious album and the conclusion of this book. But you are just beginning your journey as a lifelong scrapbooker. Along the way you'll meet many people who share your hobby. They will also share ideas and information that will help you grow as a preserver of memories. Enjoy making new friends as you join the worldwide community of scrapbookers.

CLASSES

Find out about scrapbooking classes by visiting your local craft or scrapbook store. Additional information can be found on numerous scrapbooking Web sites. Most stores hosting classes charge a nominal fee. Call or stop by to find out what scrapbooking topic they have planned. Classes fill up quickly; be sure to preregister.

COMPUTER

Your computer is one of your most valuable assets. Use it for genealogy research; visit the countless scrapbook product Web sites to comparison shop or locate hard-to-find items, scan, manipulate and print images; download free fonts and clip art for pages. Chat online with other scrapbookers willing to share similar concerns and to exchange ideas and tips. Use these keywords for successful searching: scrapbook, scrapbooking, scrapbook consultants, genealogy and free downloads.

CONVENTIONS

Scrapbook conventions are a great place to learn new techniques from scrapbook professionals and to pick up tips from fellow classmates. Most fill quickly, though, so be sure to preregister. Many activities are listed in scrapbooking magazines, including *Memory Makers*.

All My Memories, Llittleton, Colorado

CRAFT AND SCRAPBOOK STORES

Besides attending classes and crops, you will want to visit these to stay stocked up for scrapbooking and to keep posted on the latest and greatest products, tools, tips and techniques. Sometimes there is no better motivator to get scrapbooking than visiting a scrapbook store!

CROPS

Many craft and scrapbook stores host crops. Or form your own crop club to make new scrapping friends by running an ad in your local or school paper. You can also post a "Scrappers Wanted" notice on the bulletin board of your local scrapbooking store letting others know that you are looking to meet fellow scrapbookers to share ideas and swap tools and supplies.

LIBRARY OR BOOKSTORE

If you like to browse before you buy, visit your local public library or bookstore to check out the many inspiring scrapbook-related magazines and books on the market. If your library does not carry such publications, a few customer requests for them may prompt the library to obtain them.

Illustrated glossary of scrapbook terms and techniques

ACCESSORIES

Page accents that you can make or buy. Can include stickers, die cuts, stamped images and punch art. May also include baubles (beads, buttons, rhinestones, sequins), colorants (pens, chalk, inkpads), metallics (charms, wire, jewelry-making components, eyelets, fasteners), textiles (ribbon, embroidery floss, thread), or organics (raffia, pressed flowers and leaves, tiny shells, sand). With all of the latter, small and flat are best. See pages 59 and 75.

ACID-FREE

Look for scrapbook products—particularly pages, paper, adhesives and inks—that are free from harmful acids that can eat away at the emulsion on your photos. Harmful acids can occur in the manufacturing process. Check labels for "acid-free" and "photo-safe." See pages 14 and 28.

ADHESIVES

Products used to adhere or attach photos, accessories and memorabilia to scrapbook pages. Buy and use only acid-free and photo-safe adhesives in a scrapbook. See pages 32-33.

ALBUM

The archival-quality book in which you place your finished scrapbook pages for posterity and for safekeeping. Magnetic albums can destroy photos and memorabilia; remove items and place in safer albums. See pages 14 and 26-27.

ARCHIVAL QUALITY

A nontechnical term suggesting that a substance is chemically stable, durable and permanent. For archival qualities related to specific materials see page 14.

BALANCE

A harmonious or satisfying arrangement or proportion of photos and elements on a scrapbook page. See pages 58 and 64-67.

BORDER

The upper, lower and side edges or margins of a scrapbook page. Sometimes refers to a border design that is handmade or manufactured and attached to a page. See page 78.

BUFFERED PAPER

Paper in which certain alkaline substances have been added during the manufacturing process to prevent acids from forming in the future due to chemical reactions. See pages 14 and 28.

CARDSTOCK

The heaviest of scrapbook papers; can be solid-colored or patterned. Best for page backgrounds and pocket pages. See pages 28 and 103.

CD-ROM

A compact disc that can store large amounts of digitized photos and data files. In scrapbooking, font and lettering CDs as well as scrapbook software CDs can be helpful in the page-making process. See pages 55 and 110.

CHRONOLOGICAL

Arranged in order of time of occurrence as it pertains to the sorting and organizing of photos and memorabilia or the order in which photos and memorabilia appear in an album. See pages 82-85.

CONTINUITY

The state or quality of being continuous or a sense of that which is uninterrupted as in continuous or uninterrupted flow of pages in an album. See pages 78-79 and 94-99.

CROP

An event attended by scrapbookers for the purpose of scrapbooking, sharing ideas and tools and swapping products; held at conventions, craft and scrapbook stores and in private homes. See page 123.

CROPPING

The act of cutting or trimming photos to enhance the image, eliminate unnecessary backgrounds or turn the photos into unique works of art. See pages 59 and 68-72.

DE-ACIDIFY

To chemically treat paper memorabilia to neutralize acids while applying an alkaline buffer to discourage further acid migration from damaging photos. See page 101.

DECORATIVE SCISSORS

Scissors with special-cut blades or teeth that provide a wide array of cut patterns and designs, available in various cutting depths. Flipping decorative scissors over will result in a varied cutting pattern. See page 34.

DESIGN

A visual composition or pattern of photos, journaling and accessories that ultimately become a finished scrapbook page. See pages 58 and 64-67.

DIE CUTS

The resulting paper or photograph letter or shape cut with a die that is rolled through a die-cut machine; a page accessory. See page 40.

DIGITAL

A computer-related term for the process of using numerical digits to create uniform photographic images as shot with a digital camera or scanned into a computer with a scanner and saved on and retrieved from a CD-ROM. See page 55.

ENCAPSULATE

To encase paper or three-dimensional memorabilia in PVC-free plastic sleeves, envelopes and keepers for its own preservation and the protection of your photos. See page 102.

JOURNALING

Refers to handwritten, handmade or computer-generated text that provides pertinent details about what is taking place in photographs. See pages 105-121.

LAYOUT

To put or spread out photos and memorabilia in readiness for scrapbooking or a sketch of a scrapbook page design. See pages 58 and 64-67.

LETTERING

The act of forming or creating letters to use in scrapbook page titles and journaling. Lettering can include freehand cut or drawn, sticker, die-cut, template-cut, stamped or punched letters. See pages 120-121.

LIGNIN-FREE

Paper and paper products that are void of the material (sap) that holds wood fibers together as a tree grows. Most paper is lignin-free except for newsprint, which yellows and becomes brittle with age. Check product labels to be on the safe side. See pages 14 and 28.

MATTING

The act of attaching paper, generally cropped in the shape of a photo, behind the photo to separate it from the scrapbook page's background paper. See pages 59 and 72-73.

MEMORABILIA

Mementos and souvenirs saved from travel, school and life's special events—things that are worthy of remembrance. See pages 101-103

MOUNTING

The process of attaching photos or memorabilia to an album page. Permanent mounting requires the application of adhesive to the back of a photo or mat. Nonpermanent mounting allows you to attach your items to a page and still have the option of easily removing them. See pages 59 and 74.

ORGANIZATION

The act of having pulled or put together ordered photos and memorabilia for the purpose of scrapbooking. Organization of the scrapbook tools and supplies provides for maximum scrapbooking efficiency. See pages 41-42 and 45-55.

PAGE

One side of a scrapbook album—the surface on which you mount photos and memorabilia. Some albums come with pages; some pages are sold separately; some are colored cardstock slipped into a top loader. Buffered, acid- and lignin-free pages are best. See pages 57-79.

PAGE PROTECTORS

Plastic sleeves or pockets that encase finished scrapbook pages for protection. Use only PVC-free protectors. See pages 26-27.

PAGE TITLE

A general or descriptive heading put on a scrapbook page that sums up the theme or essence. Conversely, a "title page" is the first page at the front of the scrapbook, often decorated and embellished (without photos), that describes the book's content. See pages 59, 75 and title page sample on page 121.

PHOTO-SAFE

A term used by companies to indicate that they feel their products are safe to use with photos in a scrapbook album. For archival qualities related to specific materials see page 14.

PIGMENT INK

Pigment inks are water-insoluble and do not penetrate the paper surface. Instead, they adhere to the surface, providing better contrast and clarity. For journaling pens and inkpads,  look for "acid-free" and "photo-safe" on the label. See pages 30 and 39.

POCKET PAGE

A scrapbook page that has been transformed by the addition of a second sheet of cropped paper adhered to the surface, forming a "pocket" in which to place paper memorabilia. See page 103.

PRESERVATION

The act of stabilizing an item from deterioration through the use of proper methods and materials that maintain the conditions and longevity of the item. See pages 101-102.

PUNCHES

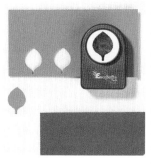

Rugged little tools in which you insert a piece of paper, press on the button and out pops a punched shape or design. Punches come in hundreds of shapes and designs and in many sizes. See page 37.

PVC OR POLYVINYL CHLORIDE

A plastic that should not be used in a scrapbook, it emits gases that cause damage to photos. Use only PVC-free plastic page protectors and memorabilia keepers. Safe plastics include polypropylene, polyethylene and polyester. See page 14.

SHAPE CUTTERS

Shape blade cutters are made by a number of different companies. They are great for cropping photos, photo mats and journaling blocks into perfect shapes. Shape cutters can cut in circles, ovals and a few other simple shapes. See page 35.

SILHOUETTE

Silhouette cropping entails trimming around the contours of the subject in your photos. When a portion of a silhouette-cropped photo's edges have been left intact, it's called a partial silhouette. See page 71.

STAMPS

A wood and rubber tool used to impress a design on paper or cloth; used with a stamp pad or inkpad. With just a few stamps and an inkpad, you can make delicate borders, lacy photo corners, stamped backgrounds, eye-catching photo mats, dressed-up die cuts and jazzy page accents. See page 39.

STICKERS

Gummed with adhesive on one side and a design or pattern on the other, stickers are one of the easiest ways to jazz up scrapbook pages. There are thousands of designs to choose from in a multitude of colors, themes and styles—including letter and number, border, journaling and design element stickers. See pages 38 and 111.

TEMPLATES

Templates are stencil-like patterns made of plastic, sturdy paper or cardboard. They can be homemade or purchased and have a multitude of uses. See pages 36 and 111.

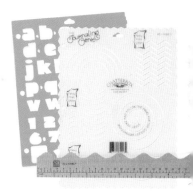

THEME

A theme is the specific subject or topic to which a scrapbook page or an entire scrapbook album is devoted. See pages 86-91.

Additional instructions & credits

Michele Gerbrandt pages featured throughout book:

PAGE 10 THE GERBRANDTS
Decorative scissors (Carl, Platte Productions), sticker letters (Making Memories), punches (Family Treasures). Photos Brenda Martinez

PAGE 13 MY NANA'S WEDDING
Background paper (Anna Griffin), journaling blocks (Anna Griffin), corner punch (Family Treasures), journaling font (Quark/Bickley Script).

PAGE 17 DANIEL
Pastel papers (Canson). Photo Joyce Feil, Golden, Colorado

PAGE 17 SASHA KIEV GERBRANDT
Swirl border punch #2 (Family Treasures).

PAGE 20 AS YOU WISH
Papers (Hot Off The Press, Rocky Mountain Scrapbook Co.), decorative ruler (C-Thru Ruler Co.), punches (Family Treasures, HyGlo/American Pin), decorative scissors (Fiskars), die cuts (Handmade Scraps), journaling template (EK Success), letter stickers (Bo-Bunny Press), pen (EK Success).

PAGE 36 LET THE GOOD TIMES ROLL
Oval template and decorative ruler (C-Thru Ruler Co.), letter template (Frances Meyer), journaling template (EK Success).

PAGE 44 OUR WEDDING
Border stickers (Mrs. Grossman's Paper Co.). Photos Greg Baron, Broomhall, Pennsylvania

PAGE 46, 48 A DECADE OF MEMORIES
Papers (Making Memories).

PAGE 56 WHITE FENCE FARM
Patterned paper (Scrappin' Dreams), decorative scissors (Paper Adventures), corner punch (McGill), decorative ruler (C-Thru Ruler Co.).

PAGE 63 GREAT SAND DUNES

PAGES 80-81 ZOO CREW, THE GERBRANDT FAMILY
Paper (Making Memories, The Paper Patch), border stickers (Mrs. Grossman's Paper Co.), journaling font on title page (Bermuda LP Squiggle).

PAGE 102 TRIP TO FRANCE
Punches (Carl, Family Treasures), memorabilia pockets (3L Corp.).

PAGE 104 SPECIAL CHRISTMAS MEMORIES
Punches (EK Success), letter stickers (Me & My Big Ideas).

PAGES 106-107 SASHA'S BIRTHDAY

PAGE 111 DISCOVERY COVE
Title template (EK Success), Bassoon font (DJ Inkers), stamp (Stampendous!), journaling templates (C-Thru Ruler Co., EK Success, Staedtler).

PAGE 119 DANIEL'S BIRTHDAY
Patterned paper (Paper Adventures), "happy birthday" confetti (Amscan), border stickers (Mrs. Grossman's Paper Co.), title letters (The Crafter's Workshop).

Other pages, products and photos featured in this book:

PAGE 29 AMANDA
Papers (Bo-Bunny Press, Club Scrap, The Crafter's Workshop, Ever After, Keeping Memories Alive, Lasting Impressions, Making Memories, Paper Fever, Provo Craft, Scrapbook Sally, Scrappin' Dreams).

PAGE 35 FALL INTO AUTUMN
Patterned paper (Hot Off The Press), NT Circle Cutter (Lion Office Products), journaling template (EK Success), Coluzzle® Nested™ Template (Provo Craft).

PAGE 37 APPLES

Punches used: super jumbo circle, jumbo impatiens leaf, large impatiens leaf, ribbon punches #61001 and #61002, allegro punch (all Emagination Crafts).

PAGE 39 MATTY'S 5TH BIRTHDAY

Stamps: birthday couleur, mon cadeau, patisserie, petite soiree, beaucoup de celebration, imagine circle, breezy birthday, small happy birthday (all Stampendous!) Designs© 2002 Stampendous, Inc.® Rubber Stamps. Brilliance™ (Tsukineko®) inkpad colors: pearlescent lavendar, pearlescent sky blue, pearlescent lime.

PAGE 40 SHANE'S BIRTHDAY

Paper (Canson, The Paper Patch), die cuts (Ellison), silver pen (Sakura).

PAGE 42

12 x 12" paper storage container (Caren's Crafts).

PAGE 52-53

Photos Susan English Photography, Denver, Colorado

PAGES 93-95 MIZZOU

Patterned paper (Embossing Arts), pennant font (Varsity).

PAGE 110

PD fonts (DJ Inkers).

PAGE 111

Journaling stickers (Mrs. Grossman's Paper Co., Sandylion).

PAGE 113 HEAVY METAL GANG

Tooth die cuts (Ellison).

PAGE 116 A GIFT FOR MAX

Patterned paper and stamp (Close To My Heart).

PAGE 120

Left to right: stickers (Making Memories, Westrim Crafts, Mrs. Grossman's Paper Co., S.R.M. Press, K & Co., Sandylion, C-Thru Ruler Co.); templates (Alpha Doodles, C-Thru Ruler Co., C-Thru Ruler Co., EK Success, Frances Meyer, EK Success, The Crafter's Workshop); punches and die cuts (AlphaPics, Accu-Cut, Family Treasures, Creative Trends, Ellison, Westrim Crafts, Deluxe Designs Little Darlings); stamps (Hero Arts, Stampin' Up!, All Night Media, Stampin' Up!, Hero Arts, All Night Media, Rubber Stampede); computer fonts (Comic Sans MS, Juicerman LET, Helvetica, Party LET, PZZ Victorian Swash, Eclectic-1, Hoefler Text).

PAGE 121

Best Friends (Frances Meyer template, Making Memories stickers); Summer Days (AlphaPics die cuts, Hero Arts stamps); Happy Birthday (Family Treasures punches, Sandylion stickers); Our Love Unites Us (PZZ Victorian Swash font, Stampin' Up! Stamps); Our Family (K & Co. stickers, Provo Craft font).

Sources

The following companies manufacture products featured in this book. The companies listed represent a few of the companies that manufacture scrapbook-related products. Please check your local retailers to find these materials. We have made every attempt to properly credit the trademarks and brand names of the items mentioned in this book. We apologize to any company that we have listed or sourced incorrectly.

3L CORP.
1-800-828-3130
www.3lcorp.com

3M®
1-800-364-3577
www.3m.com

ACCU-CUT®
1-800-288-1670
www.accucut.com

ALPHAPICS™
1-508-822-7799
AlphaPics@egroups.com

AMERICAN CRAFTS
1-800-879-5185
www.ultimatepens.com

AMERICAN TOMBOW INC.
1-800-835-3232
www.tombowusa.com

AMSCAN, INC.
1-800-444-8887

ANNA GRIFFIN, INC.
1-888-817-8170

**THE BEADERY®
/GREENE PLASTICS CORP.**
1-401-539-2432

BO-BUNNY PRESS
(WHOLESALE ONLY)
1-801-771-4010
www.bobunny.com

CANSON, INC.®
(WHOLESALE ONLY)
800-628-9283
www.canson-us.com

CAREN'S CRAFTS
1-805-520-9635

CARL MFG. USA, INC.
1-800-257-4771
www.carl-products.com

CAROLEE'S CREATIONS®
1-435-563-1100

CLOSE TO MY HEART®
1-888-655-6552
www.closetomyheart.com

CLUB SCRAP™
1-888-634-9100
www.clubscrap.com

CRAF-T PRODUCTS
1-507-235-3996

THE CRAFTER'S WORKSHOP
1-914-345-2838
www.thecraftersworkshop.com

COLORBÖK™
1-800-366-4660
www.colorbok.com

CREATIVE TRENDS
1-877-253-7687
alfsoup@aol.com

THE C-THRU® RULER COMPANY
1-800-243-8419
www.cthruruler.com

CURRENT®, INC.
1-800-848-2848
www.currentinc.com

CUT-IT-UP™
1-530-389-2233
www.cut-it-up.com

DELUXE DESIGNS
1-480-497-9005
www.deluxecuts.com

DESIGN ORIGINALS
1-800-877-7820
www.d-originals.com

D.J. INKERS™
1-800-325-4890
www.djinkers.com

DMD INDUSTRIES, INC.
1-800-805-9890
www.dmdind.com

EK SUCCESS™
1-800-524-1349
www.eksuccess.com

ELLISON® CRAFT & DESIGN
1-800-253-2238
www.ellison.com

EMAGINATION CRAFTS, INC.
1-630-833-9521
www.emaginationcrafts.com

EMBOSSING ARTS COMPANY
1-800-662-7955
www.embossingarts.com

EVER AFTER SCRAPBOOK CO.
(WHOLESALE ONLY)
1-800-646-0010

EZ2CUT
1-260-489-9212
www.ez2cut.com

FAMILY TREASURES, INC.®
1-800-413-2645
www.familytreasures.com

FISKARS, INC.
1-800-950-0203
www.fiskars.com

FRANCES MEYER, INC.®
1-800-372-6237
www.francesmeyer.com

More scrapbook inspiration from Memory Makers Books—home of Memory Makers magazine
1-800-366-6465

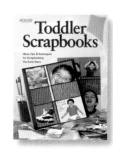

THE GIFTED LINE
1-800-533-7263

HANDMADE SCRAPS, INC.
1-801-641-4448
www.handmadescraps.com

HERO ARTS® RUBBER STAMPS, INC.
1-800-822-4376
www.heroarts.com

HOT OFF THE PRESS, INC.
1-800-227-9595
www.paperpizzaz.com

HYGLO®/AMERICANPIN
1-800-821-7125

K & COMPANY
1-888-244-2083
www.kandcompany.com

KEEPING MEMORIES ALIVE™
1-800-419-4949
www.scrapbooks.com

**LASTING IMPRESSIONS
FOR PAPER, INC.**
1-800-936-2677

LION OFFICE PRODUCTS
1-800-421-1848

MAKING MEMORIES
1-800-286-5263
www.makingmemories.com

MARVY® UCHIDA
1-800-541-5877
www.uchida.com

MCGILL INC.
1-800-982-9884
www.mcgillinc.com

ME & MY BIG IDEAS
(WHOLESALE ONLY)
1-949-589-4607
www.meandmybigideas.com

MRS. GROSSMAN'S PAPER CO.
1-800-429-4549
www.mrsgrossmans.com

NORTHERN SPY
1-530-620-7430
www.northernspy.com

NRN DESIGNS
1-800-421-6958
www.nrndesigns.com

PAPER ADVENTURES®
1-800-727-0699
www.paperadventures.com

PAPER FEVER, INC.
1-801-412-0495

THE PAPER PATCH®
(WHOLESALE ONLY)
1-801-253-3018
www.paperpatch.com

**PLAID ENTERPRISES, INC.
/ ALL NIGHT MEDIA® INC.**
1-800-842-4197
www.plaidenterprises.com

**PLATTE PRODUCTIONS
(CROP IN STYLE)**
1-888-700-2202

**PRESERVATION TECHNOLOGIES, L.P.
(ARCHIVAL MIST™)**
1-800-416-2665

PROVO CRAFT®
1-888-577-3545
www.provocraft.com

PSX DESIGN™
1-800-782-6748
www.psxdesign.com

THE PUNCH BUNCH
1-254-791-4209
www.thepunchbunch.com

PUZZLE MATES™
1-888-595-2887
www.puzzlemates.com

RANGER INDUSTRIES, INC.
1-800-244-2211

ROCKY MOUNTAIN SCRAPBOOK CO.
1-801-796-1471

RUBBER STAMPEDE
1-800-423-4135
www.rubberstampede.com

RUPERT, GIBBON & SPIDER INC.
1-800-442-0455

SAKURA OF AMERICA
1-800-776-6257
www.sakuraofamerica.com

SANDYLION STICKER DESIGNS
1-800-387-4215
www.sandylion.com

SCRAPBOOK SALLY
1-509-329-1591
www.scrapbooksally.com

SCRAPPIN' DREAMS
1-417-831-1882
www.scrappindreams.com

SRM PRESS
1-800-323-9589

STAEDTLER® INC.
1-800-927-7723
ww.staedtler-usa.com

**STAMPENDOUS!/
MARK ENTERPRISES**
1-800-869-0474
www.stampendous.com

STAMPIN' UP!®
1-800-782-6787
www.stampinup.com

STARRY NIGHT CREATIONS™
1-763-420-2411
www.starrynightcreations.com

STENSOURCE® INTERNATIONAL, INC.
1-800-642-9293
generalinfo@stensource.com

STICKOPOTAMUS®
1-888-270-4443
www.stickopotamus.com

SUZY'S ZOO®
1-800-777-4846

TSUKINEKO®, INC.
1-800-769-6633
www.tsukineko.com

UN-DU® PRODUCTS, INC.
1-888-289-8638
www.un-du.com

WESTRIM® CRAFTS
1-800-727-2727
www.westrimcrafts.com

WÜBIE PRINTS
1-888-256-0107
www.wubieprints.com

XYRON™, INC.
1-800-793-3523
www.westrimcrafts.com

 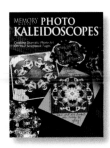 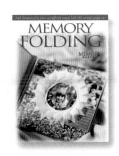  

MEMORY
MAKERS

creative

Photo
cropping

for scrapbooks

steps for turning your photos into works of art

**MEMORY
MAKERS
BOOKS**

DENVER, COLORADO

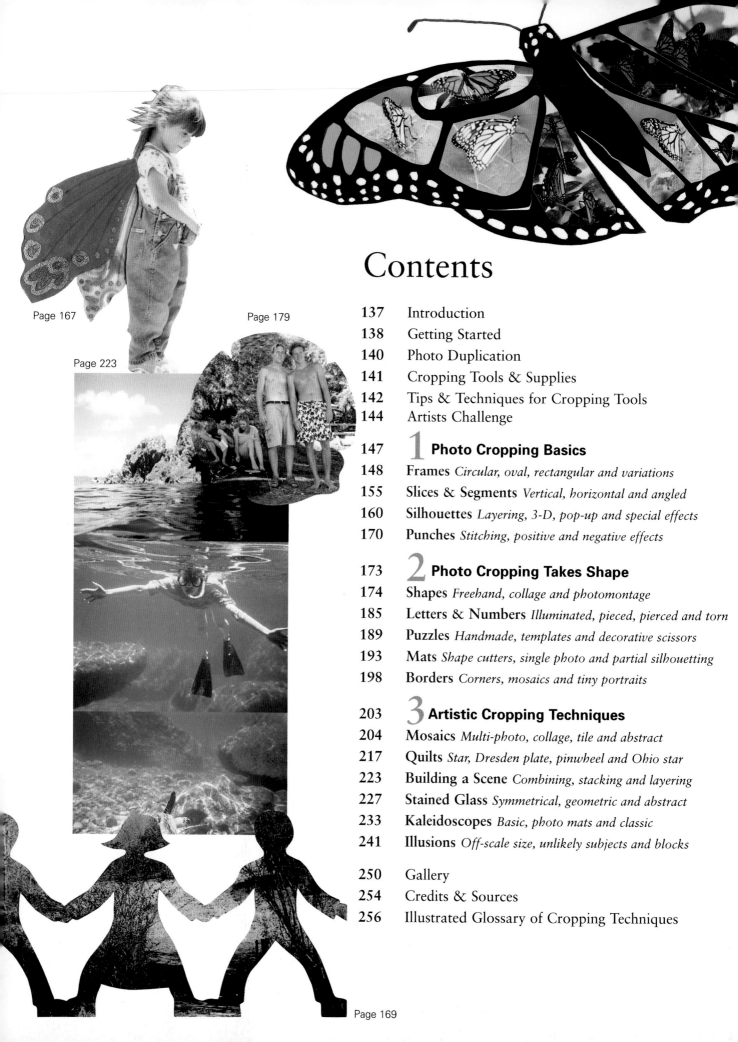

Contents

Imagination gives you Wings

ENJOYING GOD'S BEAUTY

OUR SUMMER VACATION IN ESTES PARK, COLORADO

AUGUST 2000

RON, MICHELE, ANNA, SASHA AND DANIEL

Photo Weaving technique
See page 254 for instructions.

Introduction

LITTLE DID I KNOW THAT A CLASS taken in college called "Photo Manipulation" would have such a profound influence. I had been cutting and playing with photos years before I started scrapbooking and before cropping photos became acceptable. I loved to take photos and experiment with them.

As I stand with one of my college projects, I recall being influenced by Claude Monet's series of cathedral paintings, which served as a study in light at different times of the day. I took two photos of a cathedral, one in the morning and one at dusk. Then, I cropped the photos into strips and wove them together. To the left, I recently tried weaving a color photo with a black-and-white version of the same photo. Both examples provide unique pieces of photo art made only with my pictures.

My goals with this book are to help you become comfortable with cropping your photos and to show you how to transform everyday pictures into works of art for your own scrapbook pages. Through creative cropping, you can improve a photo's focus, add inexpensive decorative elements to your page or even make up for a poorly taken photo.

I would like to note however, that from a conservator's viewpoint, creative photo cropping is not considered "long-term photo preservation" because you are manipulating the photo from its original state. Therefore, I recommend that you work with duplicates and not your original photos. Or, at least, have a negative on file for backup. I also suggest the use of photo-safe supplies for anything that comes in contact with your photos. This will help ensure the longevity of your art. You will find a list of tools and supplies on page 141.

In this book, we begin by adding several new twists to basic cropping techniques. We then move on to offer more challenging ideas by showing you how to crop photos into shapes for a wide variety of photo effects. Finally, we lead you toward more intriguing and innovative techniques. Each section provides a project with step-by-step instructions, followed by an exciting array of fun and beautiful ideas for you to try.

Whichever cropping techniques you choose, I hope to capture your imagination and inspire you to experience the "shear" fun and enjoyment of cropping and arranging your photos. Each page will be uniquely yours because it is created with your photos. Send me a picture of what you create; I'd love to see what you come up with.

Michele

Michele Gerbrandt
Founder of
***Memory Makers* magazine**

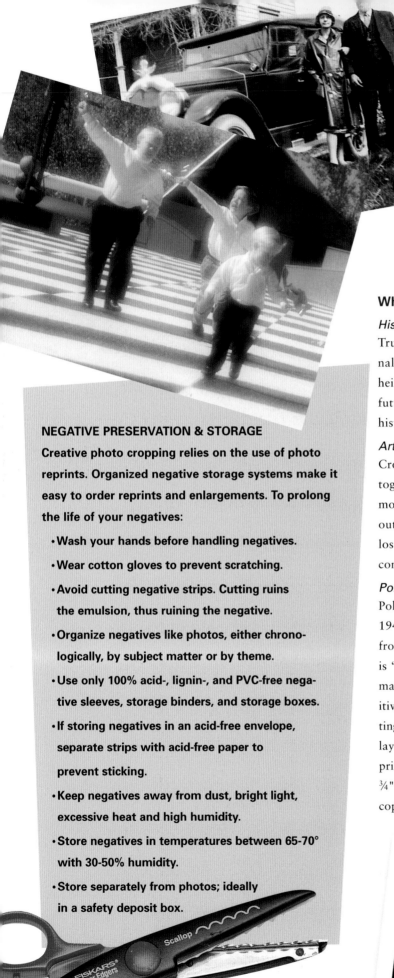

Getting Started

CREATIVE PHOTO CROPPING, the process of cutting photos to enhance the image or eliminating portions of the shot, is a fun way to turn your photos into unique works of art. There are times, however, to crop and not to crop your photos. Here are a few guidelines to follow:

When Not to Crop

Historic Photos

Truly preserving a photograph means leaving it in its original state. It's not recommended to cut one-of-a-kind family heirlooms or other old photographs. Consider the value to future generations if they are left intact. Cut duplicates of historic photos instead of the originals.

Artistic Composition

Cropping can also detract from the artistic value of a photograph. Was the photographer trying to convey a certain mood by leaving extra space around the subject? Does the out-of-focus foreground lend a perspective that would be lost if you cut it out? When cropping, take it slowly while considering the drama of a photo's imagery.

Polaroids

Polaroid "peel apart" photos (lower left), first introduced in 1948, are safe to cut because the final print is separated from the reactive chemicals and the negative when the photo is "peeled apart." Polaroid "integral" prints (lower right), manufactured since 1972, should not be cut because the positive and negative stay together, and cutting the print would expose the chemical layers. Instead of cutting an integral print, noted for its thickness and ¾" white bottom border, use a color copy of the print for cropping.

NEGATIVE PRESERVATION & STORAGE

Creative photo cropping relies on the use of photo reprints. Organized negative storage systems make it easy to order reprints and enlargements. To prolong the life of your negatives:

- Wash your hands before handling negatives.
- Wear cotton gloves to prevent scratching.
- Avoid cutting negative strips. Cutting ruins the emulsion, thus ruining the negative.
- Organize negatives like photos, either chronologically, by subject matter or by theme.
- Use only 100% acid-, lignin-, and PVC-free negative sleeves, storage binders, and storage boxes.
- If storing negatives in an acid-free envelope, separate strips with acid-free paper to prevent sticking.
- Keep negatives away from dust, bright light, excessive heat and high humidity.
- Store negatives in temperatures between 65-70° with 30-50% humidity.
- Store separately from photos; ideally in a safety deposit box.

When to Crop

Any photo can be cropped. Cropping can be as simple as trimming a photo's corners or as elaborate as cutting and reassembling a photo into a mosaic. Working with photo reprints gives you great artistic freedom. In addition, certain characteristics of a photo can dictate the best way to use cropping to enhance the image. Some basic reasons for cropping a photo are to:

Focus Attention by Removing Busy Backgrounds

Busy photos, with lots of people and unnecessary background, take attention away from the photos' subjects. Framing and silhouetting can isolate and focus attention on your subject.

Remedy Blemishes

Cropping allows you to remove photo blemishes, such as flare from flashes, closed eyes, strangers in your pictures, out of focus elements, lab printing errors and more.

Add Style and Variety

Add style and variety to your page by cropping your photos into a shape. There are many shapes to experiment with, and changing the shape will also change the final effect. Give your cropped photo breathing room, however, so that the photo's content is not lost.

Create a New Piece of Art

Herein lies the reason behind this book and the allure of creative photo cropping—the "shear" fun and enjoyment of taking a photo and creating a new piece of art with it.

SAVE CROPPED PHOTO SCRAPS & SNIPPETS
Photo cropping "leftovers" can be punched into shapes for added interest (page 170), placed in lettering (page 185), used to create borders (page 198) and mosaics (page 204), or pieced together in photo quilts (page 217) and mini kaleidoscopes (page 239).

Photo Duplication

THE EASIEST WAY TO DUPLICATE your photos is by having reprints or enlargements made from your negatives. However, we often have photos for which we have no negatives. Fortunately, there are ways to duplicate photos without the use of negatives.

Take a Picture of a Picture

The biggest benefit of this method is that it creates negatives for your photos. A manual 35mm SLR camera (with an inexpensive close-up or macro lens set), or a point-and-shoot camera (with a macro lens), works great. Simply place your photo on a flat surface or tape to a wall in bright, even light, focus and snap!

Color Copy Machines

The least expensive duplicating option is to use a laser color copier, which is sensitive to the different shades in photographs. Color copiers allow you to change the size of the image. For preservation purposes, use acid-free, 28-pound or heavier, smooth white paper. Color photocopy toner is known to be more stable than inkjet dyes, so choose color copying over printing with an inkjet printer when possible. In addition, use a mat or other barrier between layered photos and color copies of photos when possible.

Scanning

To scan your photos at home, use the TIFF file format for high-resolution images. The quality of your duplicated

photos will depend on the quality of your scanner, scanning software, printer and the paper you print on. If do-it-yourself scanning is not for you, get high-quality photo scans put on a CD at a camera store, mini lab or professional lab. To print images from a CD, a high-quality color printer and photo-quality printer paper will give the best color results.

Digital Photo Machines

Digital, print-to-print photocopy machines are user-friendly, self-service machines that can be found at your local discount, photography, drug store or supermarket. Some popular standard features include the ability to make enlargements and reductions, custom cropping, rotating and zooming in, and the ability to sharpen and adjust color and brightness of images. Some allow you to convert a color print to a black-and-white or sepia-toned photo. Many digital photo machines have the ability to write images to floppy disks and print from CDs.

Professional Photo Duplication & Restoration Services

Some specialty photography labs will make a digital copy for about the same price it costs to use a self-service digital photo machine. Some labs will charge separate prices to make the negative and print to your desired size, which could be more than double the cost of one photo machine use. Although these services can be expensive, they are worth it, particularly for reproducing valuable heirloom photos and repairing seriously damaged photographs.

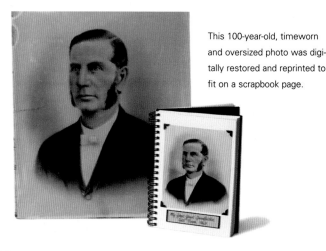

This 100-year-old, timeworn and oversized photo was digitally restored and reprinted to fit on a scrapbook page.

Cropping Tools & Supplies

USE THIS LIST OF TOOLS AND SUPPLIES to help you get started in creative photo cropping. Tips and techniques for using these tools follow on pages 142 and 143.

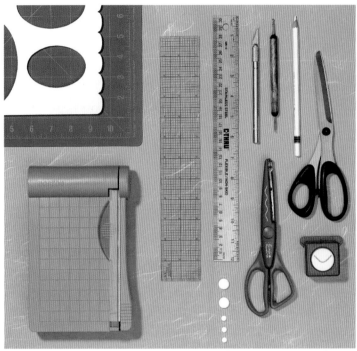

Optional Tools

Aluminum foil and waxed paper
Clear dies used for making die cuts
Clear plastic triangles
Decorative rulers
Graduated templates
Lubricating oil
Optical cleaning cloth and lint-free gloves
Shape cutters

Essential Tools

Corner rounder/punches
Craft knife
Cutting mat
Decorative scissors
Embossing stylus
Foam spacers
Rulers
 • Graphing
 • Metal straightedge

Paper trimmer
Photo-safe wax pencil
Shape templates
Straight scissors

MOUNTING YOUR PHOTO ART
We recommend the use of acid- and lignin-free albums and paper products, archival-quality adhesives, PVC-free plastics and pigment inks for journaling.

Tips & Techniques for Cropping Tools

THESE ILLUSTRATED TIPS and techniques will help you achieve the best results from your cropping tools and supplies.

Begin with a work surface that is clean and protected by a cutting mat. Make sure your tools are clean, dry and sharp before you begin cropping photos.

Clear Dies Place photo face down on foam side of die, centering in see-through area. Place die foam side up on die tray; roll through machine. Push finger through hole to push photo back out of die.

Clear Plastic Triangles Various sizes of triangles can be used to make photo kaleidoscopes, with 30° and 45° angles being the most common. Clear triangles also allow for easy viewing of photos beneath.

Craft Knife & Cutting Mat A cutting mat will protect your work surface. For straight cuts, hold the craft knife against the edge of a ruler. Use a craft knife to crop in tiny areas where scissors cannot reach.

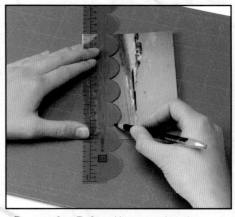

Decorative Rulers Use an embossing stylus or photo-safe wax pencil and decorative ruler on front of photos to mark cropping lines. Cut a little on the inside of the cropping line so that no markings remain.

Decorative Scissors Starting ¼" in from the base of the blade, cut using the longest stroke possible. Short, choppy strokes interrupt the scissors' pattern. Flip the scissors over to achieve a varied scissor pattern.

Foam Spacers For a three-dimensional effect, place foam spacers on the back of cropped photos prior to layering and mounting on a page.

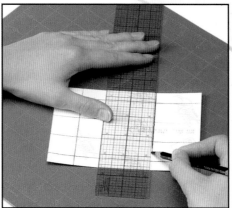

Graphing Ruler A graphing ruler can be used with a photo-safe pencil to mark grids and/or cropping lines on the back of photos when making photo mosaics. See page 204 for more on making mosaics.

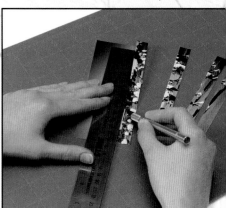

Metal Straightedge Ruler When using a craft knife to cut a line, cut against a metal straightedge ruler instead of a plastic ruler, which the knife will cut into. Hold photo and ruler firmly to prevent slipping.

Optical Cleaning Cloth and Gloves
Remove crop lines and fingerprints from photos with an optical cleaning cloth. Wear lint-free gloves when handling negatives to prevent scratches on negatives.

Paper Trimmers Paper trimmers come in many sizes and are great for straight cuts and 90° angles. Place your index finger and thumb firmly on the photo, then bring or slide the blade down quickly and smoothly.

Punches, Corner Rounder Corner rounder punches are simple to use for softening the look of a photo's corners.

Punches Flip the punch over for easier photo movement inside the punch and accurate placement of photo before punching.

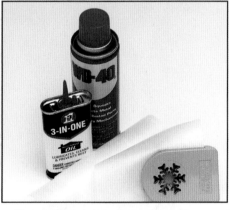

Punch Care Lubricate punches with sewing machine oil, WD-40® or punch through wax paper a few times. Clean excess oil before using punch. To sharpen punches, punch through aluminum foil.

A firm hold on both photos and cropping tools will ensure precision cutting and accuracy. To improve the cutting quality of most cropping tools, simply cut through wax paper or aluminum foil several times. Remember to save your photo scraps and snippets for use in creating even more cropped photo art.

Shape Cutters Practice using these tools first on paper or unwanted photos. Place shape cutters or croppers directly on photo and adjust to the desired size. Hold photo and cutter firmly to ensure precision.

Shape Templates Position template over your photo and use a photo-safe wax pencil or an embossing stylus to trace the outline onto the photograph. Cut the shape inside the cropping line so no markings are visible.

Straight Scissors Scissors should be clean and sharp. For precision, small scissors work best when silhouette cropping. Use long strokes with larger scissors to ensure a smooth cut line.

Artists Challenge

PHOTOGRAPHS CAN BE CROPPED a number of different ways to achieve unique results, providing infinite scrapbook page possibilities. This is why we thought it would be fun to challenge four scrapbook artists to take the same set of photos and show us their photo cropping pizazz. The result is six very different pages that will inspire you to move past the fear of cropping photos to create your own uniquely cropped photo art.

These five photos were used in the Artists Challenge. Photos Jennifer Blackham (West Jordan, UT)

Pam Friis

Hexagon Puzzle Frames For this 8½ x 11" scrapbook page, Pam Friis (Castle Rock, CO) showcases the photos on this puzzle page. Photos were first positioned on the page to determine placement. "Puzzle pages make it easy to rearrange photos to find the look that I like best," says Pam. To achieve a framing effect within the page, varied channels of a Coluzzle® Nested™ Hexagon template (Provo Craft) were used to crop photos. A Coluzzle® Waves Border template (Provo Craft) was used to create the border. To enhance her design, Pam put photo scraps to good use by filling up white space within the design and around the borders. Journaling was added in one of the hexagon frames to complete the page.

Dedicated to creative photo cropping, Sandra de St. Croix (St. Albert, Alberta, Canada), was inspired to submit three different 12 x 12" scrapbook pages using the same set of photos.

Sandra de St. Croix

Texas Star Photo Quilt Using a diamond template, 24 photo diamonds were cropped and pieced together to form a quilt. A metal ruler and pen were used to draw stitches. Journaling was added around outer edges and alphabet stickers (Creative Memories) were placed in the center for the title. "It's a spectacular effect with a little patience," says Sandra.

Layered Silhouette Collage Regular reprints and reverse-image reprints make up this layered silhouette collage. The photo tops were partially silhouetted, while the lower portions were trimmed with decorative scissors (Fiskars®). Foam spacers were added during layering for depth and dimension. Hand-lettered journaling completes the design.

Multi-Photo Mosaic Sandra cut all five photos into 1" squares and reassembled the majority of them into "one large mosaic overview of the day!" She used the "old quilter's trick" of squinting to make sure there was a balanced blend of light and dark tiles. Alphabet stickers (Creative Memories) title the page.

Matt Corwin

Memory Folding With Mosaic Border Matt
Corwin's (Ridge Manor, FL) creative, 12 x 12" page
began as a simple cardstock background and
bloomed into a folded photo showcase. A circle,
cropped from an enlarged photo of trees, was
mounted in the center and layered with a silhouette-
cropped photo of the boy. Using the circle's outer
edges as a guideline, Matt then folded and mounted
triangular cropped, wallet-sized photos to form a
frame. "Folding is a fun way to make artwork out of
your photos," says Matt. Photo scraps were put to
good use as a mosaic border, while journaling and
additional photos were added to finish the design.

Bobbi Clarke

Shape Cropping Based on Photo Theme
Bobbi Clarke (Middleburg, FL) elected to let
the photo subjects dictate her 12 x 15" page
design. "The dragonfly and water lilies char-
acterize these summer swimming scenes for
me," says Bobbi, who created her own shape
patterns and cropped photos to fit the
shapes. Photo scraps were used to create an
abstract photo mosaic for the dragonfly's
body. Its wings were stamped with silver ink,
mounted on navy paper, and trimmed with
decorative scissors (Fiskars®). An oval template was used to crop the photo of the boy,
which was then placed within a chalked
water lily to help form its flower. Green photo
scraps add dimension to the water lilies,
while journaling, punched insects and
a tiny punched frog (all McGill) complete the
waterside theme.

1
PHOTO CROPPING BASICS

BASIC PHOTO CROPPING TAKES ON many forms well beyond simply trimming a photo's corners and edges. In this section, you will learn how to:
• create partial, circular, oval, square and rectangular frames • use framing variations for unique results • reassemble cropped photo slices and segments to make interesting visual effects • use partial silhouetting to bring a subject into the foreground • use silhouette cropped photos in distinctive ways • and create fun photo art using a corner rounder and shape punches.

Mastering these basic photo cropping techniques will provide a solid foundation on which to push your cropping talents to a higher level of creativity.

Frames

CROPPING FRAMES INTO PHOTOS is an easy way to add class to your photos without taking attention away from the subject. By experimenting with a craft knife and metal ruler, various shape cutters, or graduated templates, you can achieve a wide array of interesting framing effects that will add visual impact to your scrapbook page.

Mix Framing Variations on One Page
For an engaging effect, experiment by mixing an array of framing variations on one scrapbook page, as shown on the page at right. Turn to page 150 to learn how to crop these types of frames.
Photos Kelli Noto (Aurora, CO)

Give A ROAR!

Kevin's 4

We celebrated Kevin's 4TH with a Dinosaur Party

Grandpa Ernie

Janine

1998

Food & Fun!

Eric's turn at the piñata

Framing Variations

It is easy to mix several different framing variations on one page without detracting attention from the photos themselves. Partial frames are made when one photo partially frames another. Circle and oval frames are the perfect accents for informal photos and portraits of people.

Making Partial Frames

1 *Start by placing a graduated circle template over your photo and trace with a photo-safe wax pencil (Figure 1). Then, cut out photo, staying inside the cropping lines so no marks are visible.*

2 *Using the next larger circle on the template, trace shape onto second photo that will form the partial frame on the page layout (Figure 2). Cut out shape on second photo; discard remnant.*

3 *Mount circular photo in place, within circular shape cut from second photo, to form partial frame (Figure 3).*

Making Circular and Oval Frames

1 *Place cutter on photo. Adjust blade to desired cutting diameter to create the innermost, smaller circle first, then cut (Figure 1).*

2 *Without lifting cutter from photo, adjust blade one to two sizes larger and make another cut (Figure 2). Repeat for outside of circle.*

Practice using shape cutters on paper before cropping your photos. For the best results, hold the photo firmly with one hand (or tape to mat with artist's tape) and the cutter with the other hand to prevent slipping.

Making Rectangular and Square Frames

Rectangular and square frames are a natural complement to almost any horizontal or vertical photo. You can make rectangular and square frames using a craft knife and a metal straight-edge ruler or with graduated templates. The steps below illustrate a third way to create a rectangular photo frame.

1 *Begin with one 4 x 6" photo and two rectangles (one 3½ x 5½" and one 3 x 5") hand cut from stencil film (Graphix). First, center the larger 3½ x 5½" rectangle stencil over photo and use a photo-safe wax pencil to trace cropping lines around pattern (Figure 1).*

2 *Using a craft knife and metal ruler for precision, cut on marked cropping lines (Figure 2) and set resulting frame aside. Repeat this step with the 3 x 5" stencil pattern centered over photo and trace second cropping line.*

3 *Again, using a craft knife and metal ruler, cut second set of marked cropping lines (Figure 3) and set resulting frame aside.*

4 *Mount center image, placing the outer frame around the image with an equal distance around all edges (Figure 4), removing the inner frame.*

While we used specific tools and methods to crop these frames, other cropping tools and/or methods can be used to achieve the same effect. Simply use the tool and/or method with which you feel most comfortable.

Interlock Frames For framing variation, snip the center frame. Interlock it with the four corner frames, hiding the snip under one of the corner frames. Use a lettering template (The Crafter's Workshop) to cut letters from a photo to fill one frame and mount remaining photos in place. Idea and Photos Shelley Littlefield (East Taunton, MA)

This page was made using a Coluzzle® Nested™ template (Provo Craft), a great tool for making photo frames. Simply place template over photo and insert the swivel knife blade into the appropriate template channel. Hold the knife vertically and push down firmly until you hear it pierce the photo surface. Pull the blade downward with consistent pressure, allowing the blade to steer itself through the channel.

Frame Within a Panorama
A Coluzzle® template (Provo Craft), used at an angle, helps crop a pleasing frame into Debbie Kelly's (Carl Junction, MO) peaceful panoramic photo. Her addition of a circular cropped photo provides a visually appealing design element.

Create Focus Cropping a tiny frame into a photo with a distant subject helps to focus attention on the subject. Photo Maura McDonald (Midland, MI)

Soften With Decorative Scissors After cropping photo frames using a rectangular template, Stacy Carriere (Fargo, ND) successfully softened the edges by cutting the photos and frames with deckle scissors.

More Framing Variations Three of the numerous framing variations are shown below. Experiment with your own shape cutters, graduated templates and/or metal ruler and craft knife to see what unique framing combinations you can come up with. Photos Lora Mason (Winter Park, FL)

1 *A center square is cut using a metal ruler and craft knife. After measuring ¼" out from the center square, another square cut is made. When reassembled, the square photo remnant is mounted askew instead of being discarded (Figure 1).*

2 *A circle cutter is used to cut out the center of the photo. A metal ruler and craft knife are then used to cut out a square. The inside piece is discarded upon reassembly (Figure 2).*

3 *The subject in the photo is cropped into a rectangle using a metal ruler and craft knife. Then, the remainder of the photo is taped down, and five more consecutive rectangles are cut ⅛" apart from each other and fanned out during reassembly (Figure 3).*

Use Color in Negative Spaces Try adding colored cardstock behind frames to fill in negative spaces, as Patt Kleit (Winnipeg, Manitoba, Canada) has done. First, use a metal ruler and a craft knife to make the first cut lines to form the center photos. Then, measure ¼" out from center photos' edges, make a second cut and remove resulting remnants. Mount frames and center photos on colored cardstock to finish.

Make a Mini Photo Frame To frame a tiny photo with another photo, crop a 4 x 6" photo to 4" square. Use a craft knife and ruler or a template to crop angled, 1¾" square in center. Crop second photo to 1½" square and mount in center of first photo.

Inset Oval Frames Background photos look great when framed by inset photos cropped specifically to accommodate a certain shape. In this case, six background photos were layered on a page and cropped as needed to achieve a ¼" space between all photos. Photos were tacked down with removable artist's tape to hold them in place. A graduated oval template was then used to crop two more photos. Oval photos were then placed atop background photos and moved around to determine the most pleasing placement. A graduated oval template, ¼" larger than the first oval template, was traced onto background photos to produce the oval cuts that accommodate the oval cropped photos. Experiment with this interesting framing effect using any of the available graduated shape templates. Church photos Audrey Henley (New Market, AL), Floral photos Deborah Knapp (Lorton, VA)

Slices & Segments

CROPPING A PHOTO INTO slices adds fresh perspective to page design. Slices can be cut evenly, asymmetrically, vertically, horizontally or even at an angle. After cropping, you can reassemble the photo slices and segments in countless ways for added impact.

Soften the Slices Soften a sliced photo by rounding the corners. Jill Rife (Soldotna, AK) matted photo slices on each side of her centered photo, giving primary focus to her subject while grouping the slices together on a color that complements the flower at the center.

Slice Shape Definition A shape-cropped photo can become more interesting when sliced to enhance the shape's definition. Joanne Bigelow (Lansing, MI) cropped photos into pumpkin shapes, then cut the pumpkins into slices and matted them with orange paper to mimic a pumpkin's shape.

Slice Dimension and Design
Diagonally sliced photos, matted with complementary-colored paper, jump off the page with newfound dimension and design. Idea Kelly Thompson (Ferndale, MI), photo Terry Goodman (Waccabuc, NY)

Slice Photos to Form Frames
Focus on a segment of your photo by slicing the picture's edges randomly. In the art above, Rosemary Roseo (Westchester, PA) sliced off photo edges and then left space when mounting between the slices.

Another option is to crop slices at offset angles on each corner, shown at the left, for an energetic framing effect. Photo MaryJo Regier

Grow a Photo With Stair-Stepped Slices Extend a scenic panoramic photo by slicing off the photo ends at ½" intervals. Tammy Watson (Maple Ridge, British Columbia, Canada) "stair steps" her sliced pieces, adding unique design and dimension.

Slice Horizontal Bars Pam Bailey (Thornton, CO) supported her musically themed photo by slicing the photo into evenly spaced, horizontal bars and adding a treble clef die cut (Ellison), effectively mimicking a music bar.

Slice Two Photos to Look Like One Achieve a panoramic illusion using Patti Holland's (San Jose, CA) two-photo trick. Intermittently slice two photos of the same subject into strips; mount on page leaving an equal amount of space between each slice.

For variation, experiment by slicing a panoramic photo that was photographed vertically, instead of horizontally. Some photo subjects that would work well photographed and sliced vertically are skyscrapers, long waterfalls and tall windmills. To elongate your panoramic view even more, sit on the ground and photograph up at your subject.

Slice the Action Ashley Langford (Gonzales, LA) creates a unique playing field by slicing an action-filled photo vertically and mounting on a green paper field. Note how the 50-yard line gives focus to the action with the widest sliced piece in the center, while slices gradually get narrower on each side.

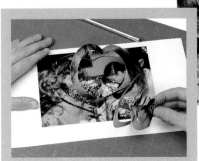

Slice to Conceal a Photo Gently lift the pull tab on Dawn Mabe's (Broomfield, CO) page to reveal a hidden photo. To make a concealed photo, you need two equal sized photos. Photo themes such as "before and after" or "then and now" work well for this project. Enlarge or reduce the heart pattern on page 254 to fit your photo size and transfer to top photo with photo-safe wax pencil. Cut photo on cropping lines. Mount top photo on bottom photo around edges. Adhere a foam spacer behind center of heart on top photo to create a lift for the pull tab.

Slice for Whimsy Surround water babies in a perfectly pictured environment by cropping photos in wavy, freehand shapes and adding water strips, cut from photo scraps, to complete the design. Idea Marie Kittle (Honolulu, HI), photo Lora Mason

Crop Movement With Dimensional Slices Decorative scissors are an effective tool for slicing motion into a photo when the photo's subject matter is begging for movement. Try this with photos of kite flying, hot air ballooning, sailing, flag waving and good, old-fashioned laundry on the line. Idea Barb Lashua (Fiskars®), photo Loralee Dischner (Westminster, CO)

Slice Random Segments and Scraps Take slicing to extremes by cropping sharp geometric shapes and angles and mounting with free-form placement. Thirteen-year-old Joshua Mayo (Indianapolis, IN) echoes his aggressive skating style, above, by slicing photo backgrounds at random while keeping the focus on his free-form style.

Likewise, action shots jump from Donna Leicht's (Appleton, WI) layout, shown at left, after slicing photo scraps into strips and triangles and randomly layering on the page.

Silhouettes

ONE OF THE MOST POPULAR cropping techniques, silhouetting requires you to trim around the contours of the figures in your photos. Photos with unnecessary backgrounds and "extra" photos are great candidates for silhouette cropping. This technique also allows you to use many photos on a scrapbook page. Cut slowly, using small scissors, staying true to the outline to ensure accuracy. While a slip of the scissors can make someone appear thinner, a slip around delicate areas of the head will lob off hair, ears and even noses. There are so many fun uses for silhouette-cropped photos, including the ability to place your subjects in all kinds of scenarios for interesting, often comical effects. You can also layer silhouetted photos on top of other photos using self-adhesive foam spacers for depth. For added impact, experiment with partial silhouetting to bring subjects into the foreground of your scrapbook page.

Fill a Fun House With Silhouettes What a fun way to house many silhouetted photos of family and friends. For this project, we supply the house pattern on page 162. Re-create the house using decorative papers for a personalized color scheme. Then, simply add your own silhouette cropped photos and watch the party unfold! Photos Tiare Smith Woods (Evanston, IL)

Winged photo (top)
Cheri O'Donnell

FAMiLY GatHeRiNG iN MiLWAUKee, WiSCONSiN

WOODS/AMBRose

AUGUSt 2000

Fun House Silhouettes

After copying and enlarging pattern, cut out and transfer pattern pieces to your paper of choice by tracing around outlines. Cut out individual house pieces. Reassemble house onto scrapbook page, using background of choice and foam spacers to add dimension. Add grass, cut with a template (Accu-Cut), on both sides of the porch, if desired.

Then, select photos and determine if you need reprints. In some cases, you might find it necessary to have enlarged or reduced reprints made to fit the size and scale of the house's windows. Once you have all of your photos together, use the tips below to complete the design.

Copy pattern at 180% on white paper, taping two sheets together lengthwise to make a 12 x 12" page pattern.

1 Use small, sharp scissors to silhouette crop around people in photos. Cut slowly, following each person's outline, and be careful around hair and facial features.

2 Use a sharp craft knife to crop around the tiny parts of each photo that are not accessible with small scissors.

3 Apply an adhesive that is flexible enough to use on tiny areas of silhouetted photos to ensure adherence prior to mounting on house or tucking inside windows.

Layer Silhouettes in a Collage
Layered silhouettes depict Catherine Hilger's (Littleton, CO) daughter growing through the years. Catherine silhouetted 28 photos of her daughter at various ages and layered the images into a collage before matting with cardstock. This is a great technique for using many extra photos of the same person, or different people, on one scrapbook page.

Silhouette for Whimsy Focusing on her favorite subject was easy for Cheri O'Donnell (Orange, CA) by simply silhouetting images of her daughter learning to crawl. Careful cropping around the baby's tiny ponytail adds whimsical detail to her page.

Capture Activity With Silhouettes
Re-create a ton of fun by silhouette cropping numerous related images and layering them among large, free-hand-cut letters. Barbara Wegener (Huntington Beach, CA) found a way to use many "old photos from the 70s" on a page by silhouetting numerous images of her kids' summer activities.

Come little leaves said the wind one Day...
come over the meadow with me and play!
put on your dresses of red and gold...
for Summer has gone and the Days grow cold.
GEORGE COOPER

Anna Grace Toner   fall 96
20 mos.

Partial Silhouetting The simplicity of partial silhouetting can add drama to your photo subject. This enlarged photo, taken by Lisa Toner (Grand Island, NE), was partially silhouetted at the top and bottom edges to highlight her daughter nestled among colorful fallen leaves.

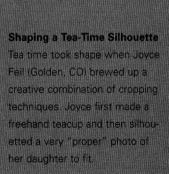

Rianne's 1st Christmas Concert

Shaping a Tea-Time Silhouette
Tea time took shape when Joyce Feil (Golden, CO) brewed up a creative combination of cropping techniques. Joyce first made a freehand teacup and then silhouetted a very "proper" photo of her daughter to fit.

Use Partial Silhouetting to Bring the Subject Into the Foreground Cathie Allan (Edmonton, Alberta, Canada) brings dimension to her page with partial silhouettes. She partially silhouetted her granddaughter's limbs, slipped them over stamped wreaths (Darcie's Country Folk) and added foam spacers to bring her granddaughter into the page's foreground.

Silhouette a Progressive Border Utilize all of those extra photos that you cannot bear to part with as a progressive photo border. Karen James (Waipio, HI) silhouetted eight progressive playtime photos of her son to create a colorful cascading border.

HEY GUYS! WHAT'S SO FUNNY?

Silhouette the Emotion By layering silhouetted images across a page, Chitchi Tabora (San Francisco, CA) captures the emotion-in-action while invoking a comical element to this simple headliner page.

Rolling, Rolling, Rolling May 1999
I sat on a ladder for 30 minutes and took pictures of James move around this carpet (3 rolls of film)!! It was hard, dizzying work!!
It is astonishing how he learns how to move himself around!
He is able to move in a general direction now, and is getting faster.
Seymour watches the action with interest.

Silhouette the Movement Show movement on your page by silhouetting multiple images of progressive action. Perched atop a ladder, Rachel Smith (Vancouver, British Columbia, Canada) captured her son's favorite method of moving from one place to another in pictures. She then used one complete photo of baby and rug (the photo at far left) for a base on which to adhere five additional silhouetted photos of her son to give the appearance of him rolling across the rug.

Silhouette a Winged Fantasy Turn silhouette cropped people photos into delightful creatures with a little paper and some fancy pen work. Silhouette photo subject and layer over handmade or vellum die cut wings (DMD Industries). This fun photo cropping technique is a great way to use extra photos of people of any age. Winged photos provided by (clockwise) Randi Green (Woodland Hills, CA), Chrissie Tepe, Lora Mason (twice), Nicole La Cour (Denver, CO)

Layer Silhouettes for Contrast For visual contrast, try layering partially silhouetted, color photos atop black and white reprints of the same photo. Cut letter photos using lettering template (The Crafter's Workshop) to complete the design. Photos Chrissie Tepe (Lancaster, CA)

Silhouette 3-D Movement Duplicate a silhouette and offset the images with foam spacers to show movement. Using three identical photos, silhouette crop the subject in two photos. Mount offset by ⅛" to ¼" on the base photo, depending on where you want the movement to be. Photo Elizabeth Wallis (San Ramon, CA)

Silhouette a Scene Set the stage and create a scene
by combining various silhouettes of a single subject. L. Nicole
Gartland (Portland, OR) wanted to "capture the chaos" of life
with a newly mobile infant, so she silhouette cropped several
photos of her daughter and mounted them in a comical scene.

Silhouette an Adventure Take silhouetting to new heights by
layering closely cropped photos and background paper images
to create a new scene. Joyce Schweitzer (Greensboro, NC)
detailed the adventure of river tubing by silhouetting images
with decorative scissors, which enhanced the rippling water
effect to give the illusion of a very bumpy ride!

Silhouette a Movable Self-Portrait

Display your self-expression with a movable self-portrait made up of silhouetted and pieced photos that are held together with grommets or brads, at arm, leg and neck joints. The body can be made either with photos that reflect your lifestyle and hobbies, or various photo scraps for a more abstract visual. Clothing can be cropped from photos or patterned paper, using the doll's body for size. Try making paper dolls of your children and loved ones, too! Photos Sarah Fishburn (Fort Collins, CO)

Stage a Scene With Silhouettes Few scrapbookers can resist taking photos simply to create a scene. Planning and simple costuming was all it took for Charla Campbell (Springfield, MO) to create a scene of her mischievous "mice." Her silhouetted photos, combined with enlarged, silhouetted photos of pantry items, work together to create an Anne Geddes®-style scene.

Silhouette a Photo Doll Chain Enlarge or reduce the pattern on page 254 to fit any size photo. Trace pattern onto photo(s) and cut out. Repeat as needed to make chain length desired. Connect cropped photos together to create photo doll chain. Idea and photos Sarah Fishburn

Silhouette a Layered Pop-Up Bring city streets to life by silhouetting building outlines and mounting on a pop-up template (Design Originals). Debby Schuh (Williamsville, NY) created a 3-D city scene by silhouette cropping 4 x 6" and panoramic photos of amazing architecture. The silhouetted photos were overlapped on the pop-up, giving a great view of European city life. Try this with your travel photos.

Punches

A corner rounder punch can soften photo edges, while a jumbo punch makes a great template, and shape punches complement similar photo subjects. Push the cropping potential of border, decorative corner and silhouette punches for your own creative results.

THERE IS NOTHING BETTER THAN FALL RIDING, EXCEPT...

Punch Photo Scraps Punched leaf photo scraps, when combined with layered and silhouetted photos, make great page embellishments, as Trish Tilden (Westmont, IL) and Tina Weatherhead (Woodridge, IL) discovered on the page shown at right.

You can also punch photo scraps with like-subject punch shapes, as Nikki Patrick (Westminster, CO) demonstrates below. She punched sky photo scraps with a cloud punch, tree photo scraps with a tree punch, and water photo scraps with a teardrop extension punch to form raindrops.

Ashton·Lake Tahoe·August 1997

Punch Drama Into Photos Darla Traynor (Star Prairie, WI) "bit" a watermelon-sliced photo with a large scallop punch. Try this technique with food photos such as cookies, fruits and crackers.

Another dramatic effect occurs when you punch upper and lower portions of photos with a large oak leaf punch, as Steve Pohl (Prescott, WI) did, leaving photo side edges intact for visual contrast. Add punched cardstock leaves for even more drama.

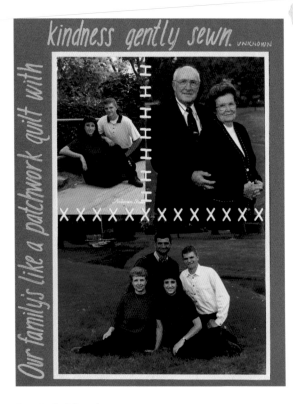

Punch Stitching Use a film strip border punch around a photo's outer edges, then weave raffia or ribbon through the holes and tie the ends in a bow. Photo Joyce Feil

Punch Quilting Create a photo quilt by using upper case "H" and "X" letter punches (Family Treasures) down the sides, at evenly spaced intervals, of adjoining photos. Other letter punches to try are "I," "V" and "Z." Photos provided by Alois Elrod (Broomfield, CO)

Punch Positive and Negative Effect Use a small snowflake punch, or any punch shape that complements your photo subject, to punch halfway into photo's edges. Flip punched snowflake halves down on black mat to complete design. Idea and photo JoAnn Colledge (North Ogden, UT)

Use Jumbo Punch as a Template Jumbo punches (Family Treasures, Nankong) work well as a template when cropping photos. Simply turn punch upside down, insert photo, adjust for placement of shape on photo and punch! Photo of child Sally Scamfer (Bellevue, NE)

Punch Realistic Florals From Photo Scraps Experiment with punch combinations to make realistic floral designs from floral photo scraps. To make a chrysanthemum, layer large hearts, ¼" and ¹⁄₁₆" hand-punched circles. Hand-cut stem and add large punched birch leaves. Idea and Photos Kathleen Paneitz (Boulder, CO)

2

PHOTO CROPPING TAKES SHAPE

CROPPING YOUR PHOTOS INTO DIFFERENT shapes provides a myriad of unique uses for photos. Here you will learn how to:

● use templates for basic shape cropping
● explore cutting your own shapes freehand
● cut into a photo to define a shape ● combine cropped photos with paper to create new shapes ● crop photos into a wide array of letters and numbers ● create puzzle pieces from your own handmade template ● use the Coluzzle® and Puzzle Mates™ template systems ● and make beautiful mats and page borders from cropped photos.

By learning all of the great ways to use shape cropping to transform everyday photos into unique works of art, you will be inspired to experiment with more artistic forms of creative photo cropping.

Shapes

WHETHER FREEHAND CUT OR
cropped with the use of a template,
shape cropping adds simple style to scrapbook pages while complementing the
photo's subject. Shape templates are inexpensive and available in a wide variety of designs
and themes. Transparent templates allow you to see the
photo beneath for accurate placement. You can also
make your own templates from plastic coffee can lids,
or you can use cookie cutters for patterns. Draw cropping inspiration from your photos to help determine
appropriate cropping shapes. Or, perhaps,
explore cropping copies of the same photo
with a variety of shapes to discover the effect
that you like best. Finally, experiment with
piecing cropped photos together to
make new shapes.

Shape Crop Life's Celebrations
For simple style and quick results, Marilyn
Garner (San Diego, CA) allows her birthday
photos to direct the shapes used, namely
presents, party hats, balloons and a cake,
to crop her photos creatively. Turn the page
for instructions on how to use templates
and clear dies to crop photo shapes.

It's a Party!

Rachel's 4TH Birthday

Shape Cropping

Add instant style to scrapbook designs by cropping photos into shapes that reflect the theme of your page. Photo shapes can be cropped using a wide variety of templates, ranging from plastic shape templates to clear dies to your own unique designs crafted from cardstock, stencil film, or plastic coffee can lids. Be creative and experiment with some of the options shown below.

1 *One option is to crop photos with shape templates (C-Thru Ruler Co., Provo Craft). First, place the template over the photo and center the photo subject. Then use a photo-safe wax pencil to trace along the inside of the shape template (Figure 1).*

2 *Next, cut out the traced shapes with scissors, cutting just a little to the inside of the cropping lines so no markings are visible (Figure 2) and mat with patterned paper.*

3 *Another option is to use a clear die (Accu-Cut, Ellison) to crop a shape. When using a clear die shape, place the photo face down on foam side of die. Center the photo in the see-through area of the die (Figure 3). Place the clear die foam side up on the die tray and roll through the die cut machine. To remove the photo, simply put a finger through the hole and push the photo out. To mat photos, mount on colored or patterned paper and trim around outside of paper leaving a ⅛" border.*

Crop Shapes Without Using Templates

Cropping pictures and piecing them together into a new, large shape not only brings photos to life, but gives your page a thematic focus. If you don't have a template for the shape you want to create, turn to children's coloring books for simple images with bold outlines. Size the shape on a photocopier and then, as Nancy Campbell (Coppell, TX) suggests, use a light box to trace the shapes over photos. Crop and piece together your new photo art.

Use Negative Space to Define Shape

It's easy to use negative space to define a shape. Simply place a shape, like this tulip die cut (Accu-Cut), across photos laid in place on a scrapbook page. Use a photo-safe wax pencil to trace around the die cut. Then trim photos on the tracing lines, discarding the shape scraps you cut out. Wipe off any wax residue and mount photos on page. Idea Loy Stevens (Kennewick, WA), photos Erica Pierovich (Longmont, CO)

Make a Freehand Shape

Without a template at hand, Debbie Vellucci (Livonia, MI) drew her own flower pattern and cropped photos to fit. The shape variation of the flower's petals and leaves adds originality to the freehand shape.

Trace a Pre-cut Paper Shape

Die cuts, for example, make great patterns for cropping photos into shapes. Cami Beegle (Loveland, CO) featured the Seattle seaport by tracing die cut skyline shapes (Ellison) onto photos and then cropping out the shapes.

Accent Shape With Photo Scraps Karen Nagel's (Wheathampstead, Herts, United Kingdom) creative cropping helped land a cute, fat-lipped fish. Karen cropped fishing photos with an oval template and then cut freehand shapes out of photo scraps to give her fish its characteristics.

Add Splash With Freehand Cropped Shapes Add splash to your page by creating a frolicking freehand design. Janie Thomas (Blakely, GA) filled her page with freehand cut water drops, capturing family pool playtime with a great splash!

Combine Shapes and Silhouettes Creatively cropped beach photos were used to "build" Teresa Villanueva's (Aurora, CO) sandcastle. The addition of a partially silhouetted photo of her son at play in the sand is a clever way of placing the sandcastle in its proper proportion and context.

Shape a Person's Silhouette
Photocopy and enlarge (or reduce) a profiled photo of subject. Cut out a photocopy of profile and use it as a pattern, tracing the profile onto photo of choice (we used a floral photo) with a photo-safe wax pencil and cut it out.

Pierce Details into Shapes Collect a treasure of seaside memories in shapes inspired by the sea. Janet Thompson (Santa Clarita, CA) cropped a freehand sand dollar shape and then pierced the cropped photo around the edges to mimic the detail of a sand dollar.

Crop Shapes Inspired by Photos
Reproducing golf club shapes helped Dona Carroll (Larkspur, CO) put together a bag full of miniature golf memories. Dona cropped freehand golf club shapes and then layered the clubs to look as if they're placed in a golf bag.

Draw Shape Inspiration From Other Sources

Spiritual photos take flight when crafted together to create a serene symbol. Bobbi Clarke (Middleburg, FL) enlarged the dove outline from a greeting card and then cropped and layered photos to fit, matting each with paper.

Crop Definition and Detail Into Shapes

Add definition by using a detailed stencil (Delta), those normally used for painting and sponging, to crop photos as Judy Weston (Poplar Bluff, MO) has done with her story-time photos.

Penns

Design an Original Shape

Laurie Herlson (Butte, MT) combined a cropped photo with paper to create this original paint-can design. Paper was added to complete the lid, handle and base of the can. To make more than one image of the same shape, save time and make a template out of cardstock. Vary the size by cropping inside or outside of template lines.

Crop Photos to Fit in Hand-Drawn Shape

Kimberly Meade (Redmond, WA) cut photos in freehand pentagons to fit her hand-drawn soccer ball shape. More photos, snipped with scissors to resemble blades of grass, border the bottom of the page.

Shape a Photomontage

Piecing together a patchwork of cropped photos was easy for Angie Davis (Golden City, MO), because she created the hand-drawn hot air balloon image first, and then mounted the photos on top, trimming as needed to fit her outline.

Create a Shapely State Make a special place for vacation and hometown photos, as Stephanie Boeshore (Fletcher, NC) did of her and her husband's family photos. Photos were cropped to fit in the outline of the families' native state, Pennsylvania.

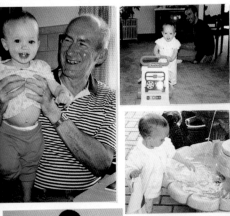

vania

Eric and I drove to Pennsylvania to visit for the week the last week in April. We stayed at Eric's parent's house. Samantha loved it because they didn't have a gate in front of their stairs going to the second floor. ...guess where she was everytime our backs were turned. We also enjoyed breakfast Thurs. at the Farmer's Wife with Eric's aunts and uncles.

One of the days my mom, Eric's mom, Samantha, and me went to Ashcomb's plant farm. We had a cart to put all of our plants on. Samantha started pushing the cart through the isles. It looked like the cart was moving on it's own because she's so small you couldn't see her above the plants (see pic. in top left corner.)

Another day Nicole took me to AC Moore Craft store, where they had tons of scrapbooking supplies! Afterwards we went to Heather's for lunch and so all the cousins could play together (Olivia was asleep the whole time.)

The last night in PA we had an early birthday party for Samantha so she could celebrate with her cousins and other relatives.

We had a great trip. Eric and I even went down to the Corvette after Samantha was asleep. We enjoyed the trip. Samantha's looking forward to playing with her cousins again too.

Combine Photos With Paper to Make a New Shape It's simple to crop photos to fit inside a shape when using a template (Puzzle Mates™). Just trace the shapes onto photos with photo-safe wax pencil, cut out images, mat on patterned paper (Keeping Memories Alive) and embellish with freehand drawn flowers. Photos Erikia Ghumm

Shape Photos to Fit Activity

Highlighting the many moves of a ballerina delighted Suzan Bellis (Albany, OR), so she framed photos of her granddaughter in freehand drawn and cut ballet slipper shapes. Showcase your own hobby and activity photos in subject-related paper shapes, allowing the shape to serve as a template for cropping your photo.

Every summer when the Monarch migrate, they stop off for a coup of weeks at our lake place in Hawic This is the first time that I've been successful in photographing them.

Piece Photos to Form Relevant Shape

Showcase photos by cropping and piecing them together to form a shape that is relevant to the photos' subject matter, such as Angela Pechin's (Gilroy, CA) fanned-out photos of a tranquil Japanese garden. Use this technique with your own travel photos, making new shapes that reflect your photos' subject matter.

Create a Beacon of Photos Vacation photos take form when cropped into striking shapes. The stature of a lone lighthouse came to life when Pat Feldhake (Cedarville, MI) created the lighthouse shape and then layered strips of paper and cropped photos to fit.

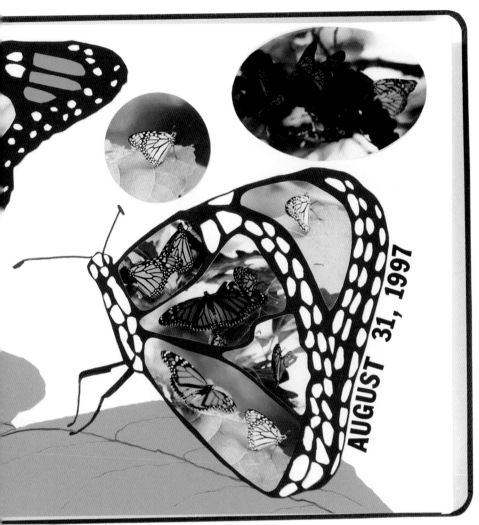

Duplicate an Intricate Pattern

Duplicating the intricate wing pattern of a freehand cut monarch butterfly was a delicate process for Terri Robichon (Plymouth, MN). Two photos were photocopied and enlarged, then traced over the cardstock butterfly image. The photos were then cropped into shapes to fit the wing design and white holes were cut into wing edges to complete the design.

Build a Scrumptious Photo

Sundae Creating a sundae out of photos cropped into circles sweetened the memories of Yona Mae Harvey's (Horsehead, NY) daughter's first birthday. The ice-cream "scoops" were topped with pre-printed paper (Current®, Inc.) and layered in a colorful dish. Try this with any celebration or food-related photos.

Cut Photos to Fill a Shape Cropping photos to fill an oversized shape helped Marsha Peacock (Jacksonville, FL) showcase her daughter's first attempt at photography. Marsha created a giant filmstrip and filled it with freehand shaped photos cropped in perspective to fit the filmstrip.

Layer Cropped Photo Collage Create a romantic and historical collage that spans the years by cropping photos into simple shapes and silhouetted images. Andrea Douglas (Escondido, CA) layered 58 photos to chronicle the six years she and her husband dated, and to show how times may change but true love remains.

Build a Boatload of Photos Bring an ocean adventure to life by building a boat full of photos. Kathleen Taylor (Kearneysville, WV) constructed the USS Stingray by hand, and then cropped photos to fit the hull, documenting her actual stingray experience. Letter stickers (Creative Imaginations) complete the design.

Crop a "Tree-mendous" Photomontage
Cropping photos into shapes and reassembling to form a shaped photomontage can add fun and focus to your page theme. Jenny Hoarty (Fairmont, NE) cropped images of her "tree-mendous" little sister into leaves and then layered them to form a tree montage.

Letters & Numbers

ANOTHER USEFUL VARIATION of shape cropping is cutting your photos into letters and numbers. Draw upon the photo's theme to cut appropriate letters and numbers to help commemorate a special occasion in an appealing way. Many letter and number templates are available and we've provided inspirational design ideas as well.

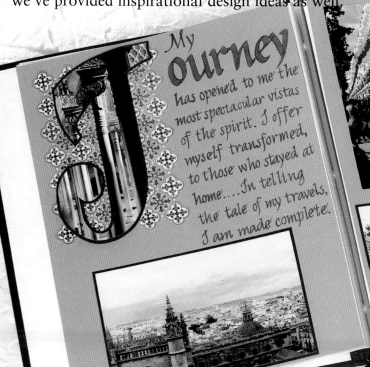

Make an Illuminated Photo Letter Illuminated letters, reminiscent of old European manuscripts, can be cropped from photos to embellish the simplest of pages. Using a template or computer font (fancy or script-style work best), print or photocopy the letter in desired size. Cut out letter and use as a template or pattern for photo shape. Use foam spacers to mount letter on "tile" designs, cropped from photo scraps or actual photos of tiling. Photos Deborah Mock (Denver, CO)

Use a pre-cut photo die cut letter

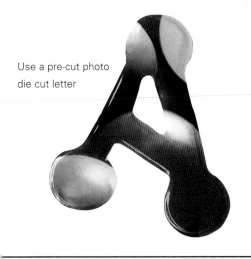

Crop photos to fit large template letter

Punch a letter

Piece a letter with photo scraps

Use die cut as a template on single photo

Mat a letter

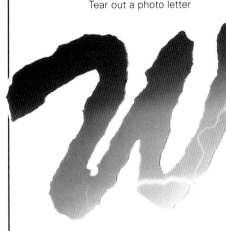

Piece a photomontage of tiny portraits

Trace around letter with pen-stroke stitching

Tear out a photo letter

Cut out negative space to form number

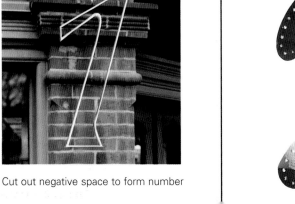

Embellish a heritage photo number with piercing

Place photo behind a negative die cut

...ce a freehand
...ter photomontage

Crimp a letter

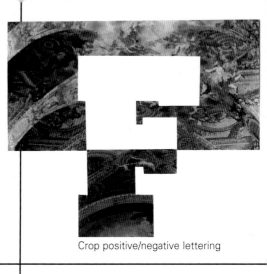

Crop positive/negative lettering

Use photo subject
to mimic a letter
shape

Place photo behind
hand-drawn letter
or open-faced font

Use photo scraps for lettering

...etch a freestyle outline

Pose people to
form a letter

Make a double
drop shadow with
die cut letters

Cut out a number
with decorative
scissors

Add a hand
drawn outline

Slice a number

See page 254 for sources.

Trim a Lettered Pop-Up Give lettering a third dimension by using a brass template (POP-UPS by Plane Class™) and a craft knife to carve the letters out on a photo. Add cropped photo to cardstock and fold. Photo Ken Trujillo

Crop Photo Subject Into Letters A photo subject came into shape when Terry Larkin (Jenison, MI) cropped photos of freshly baked Christmas cookies into letters that spell "cookies," for a page you can almost taste. Try this with any food-related photos.

Ho, Ho, Homemade Photo Letters
Cropping single photos into letters gives an instant photographic title to your page. Handmade letters, like Terri Robichon's (Plymouth, MN) "Ho, Ho, Ho," are wide enough to capture a large photo image. When creating your own letters, sketch them out on cardstock first to create a pattern. Place over photo, trace with a photo-safe wax pencil and cut out.

Crop a Photo to Form a Letter When using letter forms (*Letter Forms: 110 Complete Alphabets* by Frederick Lambert, Dover Publications) for a pattern to crop letters, "fill in the blank" creatively by cropping a photo subject that resembles a letter's shape. In this case, fish are used to help spell the word "fishing." Idea Tina Hall (Arlington, TX)

Crop a Letter Pop-Up Cropping photos into letters or numbers helps emphasize the focus of your page, just as Becky Carter (Oskaloosa, IA) has done with photos of her sleeping grandson. Using a freehand cut letter, Becky focuses on a la-Z-y theme by making a double pop-up of matted and layered photo letters.

Puzzles

CREATING PUZZLES FROM

cropped photos is quite popular. Whether you make your
own puzzle pieces or use puzzle templates, it's a convenient way to join many
photos on one page.

Piece Together a Puzzle Photomontage

Piecing together a page of over forty photos was easy for Tracey Bullock (Sparks,
NV), who created a puzzle photomontage
spanning ten years of her life. The steps
below show how you can piece together
a puzzle photomontage of memories.

1 *Make a grid of squares, adjusting
grid size to accommodate number
of photos and your page size.*

2 *Make a "notch" template by
punching a small circle into a
piece of cardstock. Use the
template to draw half circles
randomly on grid lines.
Erase lines through half circles to
form individual puzzle pieces (Figure 1).*

3 *Number each grid piece and photocopy for reference.
Cut out grid pieces with small scissors or a craft knife, then trace
pieces onto photos for use in the photomontage (Figure 2).*

4 *Write puzzle piece number on back of cropped photo and refer
to grid photocopy when assembling puzzle photomontage.*

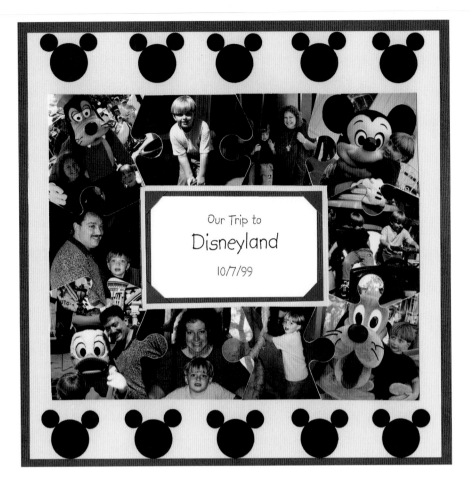

Collect photos and place under template, one at a time, to determine which photo to use for each puzzle piece. Slide one photo under the determined puzzle piece and hold securely. Place the tip of a swivel knife within each cutting channel and cut along the edge of the puzzle piece. Remove the template and trim edges still connected. Repeat for each puzzle piece. Assemble and arrange on your scrapbook page.

Using a Coluzzle® Puzzle Template Piecing together a single day's fun was a ride in the park when Michelle Rank (Cerritos, CA) used an 8 x 10" Coluzzle puzzle template (Provo Craft) to highlight her Disneyland adventure. Follow the tips to the right to see how easy your puzzle page can come together.

Fix a Puzzling Dilemma Assembling pieces of a photo puzzle became a challenge for Sabina Dougherty-Wiebkin (Lebanon, NH) when she realized that two of her cropped photo pieces didn't fit together like they should. The mistake was remedied by mounting the two mis-cut pieces askew, leaving openings large enough for journaling.

Use a Puzzle Template Using a template provided an easy solution to Claudia Hill's (Whittier, CA) desire to fit as many photos as possible onto one page. By cropping related photos using a puzzle template (C-Thru Ruler Co.), she was able to feature nine fun-in-the-sun photos on one scrapbook page.

Link Photos With Design Element Adding a simple design element to your puzzle can help tie photo images together. Debbie Meyer (Elida, OH) cropped her romantic sunset photos with an oval template (Puzzle Mates), then added the sailboat design in the center to accent her page theme.

Try Minimal Cropping for Maximum Image
Vertical photos don't need a lot of cropping or embellishing to make an extraordinary page. Turning an oval template (Puzzle Mates) sideways allowed Crista Quinn (N. Canton, OH) to minimally crop her vertical photos to create an expansive layout that resonates an uncrowded day at the beach.

Use Decorative Scissors to Crop Puzzle Page Achieve a puzzle page look by placing seven related photos on a page and cropping the four corners of the center photo diagonally with decorative scissors, as shown. Allowing ¼" space between all photos, crop six remaining photos to fit on page and to accommodate corner cuts of center photo. Idea Tina Hall, photos Pennie Stutzman

Crop a Puzzle Mates™ Photo Puzzle Photo puzzle templates not only provide simple, defined spaces for photos, but also make a perfect place for photojournaling. To use a Puzzle Mates puzzle template, place it on top of your photos, one at a time, and trace each shape using a photo-safe wax pencil, as shown. Crop photos with scissors, cutting just a little to the inside of the cropping lines so that no marks are visible. Photos Pennie Stutzman

They start you early in the morning
while the air is cool and
the winds are calm,
the sun had just started to lift
off of the horizon!
Finally, the balloon was full and up we rose;
how beautiful the world looks
when you're
peeking around a cloud!
We sailed so effortlessly,
and then before we knew it
we were back on the ground
packing it in.
What a perfect way
to spend a summer morning!

Mats

IF YOU LOVE TO TAKE POSED STILL-LIFE AND nature photos, but never know what to do with them, consider turning them into photo mats. This cropping technique accents the photo layered beneath the mat and makes great use of photos that might otherwise go unused. You might even be inspired to photograph things you may have never considered before.

NAVAJO RESERVATION • CHINLE, AZ • ERICA & ERIC YUTH

Crop a Landscape Mat

Scenic photo enlargements make great photo mats when paired with subject-related photos. The art on the previous page and below shows a photo of children, in traditional Navajo garb, placed behind a scenic photo mat. Note how the two photos complement one another.

The Shaping Memories Oval Cropper™ was used to create the hole in this mat. Below, you will find other mat cropping tools that you can use to create photo mats. Follow these steps to create your own scenic landscape photo mat.

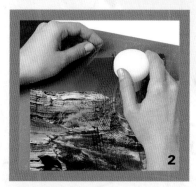

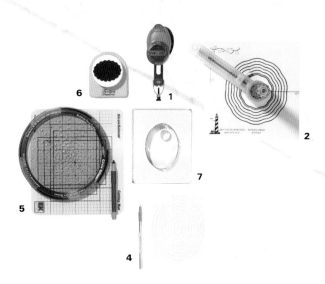

Alternative Mat Cropping Tools Making a photo mat can be difficult if you are trying to use a craft knife or scissors to make the hole in your photo. It can be done, but you will get smoother, cleaner results using one of the many cropping tools available for this purpose. Just a few of the cropping alternatives available are (clockwise, starting at the top): **1** Fiskars® Oval Cutter **2** Lighthouse Memories Ovals & More Cutter **3** Provo Craft graduated oval template **4** Provo Craft Coluzzle® Nested™ Oval Template and patented swivel blade knife **5** EK Success' Orbis™ Circle Scissor™, cutting mat, and patented cutting knife **6** Family Treasures jumbo scallop punch **7** Accu-Cut® Oval Acrylic clear die.

1 *Determine which numbered cropping line you will use to cut the mat's opening by positioning the clear cutting guide atop the photo to be framed by the photo mat (Figure 1).*

2 *First, lay the clear template on mat photo to find placement, then adjust cropper and place on clear template (Figure 2). Remove template and make the cut.*

3 *To complete the art, position and center your featured photo behind the mat and mount in place using a photo-safe adhesive (Figure 3).*

Photos Connie Mieden Cox (Westminster, CO), published with permission from Millie Roanhorse

Crop a Memorabilia Mat Create a showcase for your special photos and portraits with a still-life photo of subject-related memorabilia or souvenirs, as shown to the left. Photos MaryJo Regier

For another variation, crop a panoramic or enlarged photo of an event to mat a subject-related portrait, as shown below. Photos Dawn Mabe

Crop a Vacation Mat Cropping a mat of your vacation photos to frame a portrait of your family on vacation is a simple way to document the experience. Photos Dawn Mabe

Crop a Photocopied Mat Design This striking mat effect is easy to accomplish by using copyright-free, reproducible clip-art frames (*Creative Photocopying* by Stewart & Sally Walton, Watson-Guptill Publications) and scissors or a craft knife. For another example of the results of this type of technique, see the bookplate in the front of this book. Photo of children Orealy Hernandez (Holly Springs, NC), floral photo Deborah Knapp

Trim a Partially Silhouetted Mat Floral photo mats create a visual charm when caressing the portraits of children. Simply crop a shape in the center of any floral photo, partially silhouetting a portion of the flower or petals as you crop the center, or partially silhouetting the top of the photo mat. Mount a favorite photo behind mat. Infant and floral photos Linda Grudle (Broomfield, CO), photo of children Sally Scamfer

Grandeau of the Seas

Mat a Photo With Itself You can also create a photo mat by cropping an enlarged photo into a mat, as Cathie Allan (Edmonton, Alberta, Canada) has done. Begin by partial silhouetting and cropping out the center of a photo and set aside. The photo's outer edge then becomes a mat. Layer the inner edge of the mat with two different colors of paper, trimmed to create a matted, shadow box effect. Mount the photo's center portion behind the mat to complete the design.

Borders

PHOTO PAGE BORDERS PUT ALL OF THOSE left-over photo trimmings and snippets to good use. Experiment using photo scraps to create edge, corner and mosaic borders. Or, use "leftover" people shots, mini studio portraits and even index prints to create interesting photo page borders.

Extra Photos Make Eye-Catching Borders Cropping extra photos into 1¼" squares can create an eye-catching and colorful border, similar to the one Crista Quinn (N. Canton, OH) has created with a desert scene.

Kingwood
Gardens
flowers
+
animals

Use Photo Slices to Create Simple Borders

You can also create theme-related borders with slices from extra photos to frame your page with flair. Crista Quinn (N. Canton, OH) framed her garden snapshots above with a simple border of floral photo slices.

Similarly, cropping photos of beautiful surroundings into 1" slices made a natural border for the pages of Joy Carey's (Visalia, CA) lush outdoor photos shown at right.

Crop Triangle Page Corners Leanne Scott (Houston, TX) cropped 4 x 6" blueberry bush photos diagonally, from corner to corner, to make this corner border treatment. Try this technique with extra photos related to your special activities.

Crop a Mosaic Border

Put more photo scraps to use by using a small square punch to create a tumbling mosaic border. Simply use photo scraps that are complementary to your photos or your scrapbook page theme.

For another variation, crop ½" mosaic squares from photo scraps and assemble to frame a page. Idea Eileen Ruscetta (Westminster, CO)

Make an Index Print Border Those nifty little index prints that come with developed rolls of film also make interesting page borders when cut apart and mounted. Idea Lori Soloman (Old Bridge, NJ)

Crop a Decorative Ruler Border Use a photo-safe wax pencil to trace one of many available decorative ruler designs and crop a creative photo border. Debbie Kelly (Carl Junction, MO) uses a cloud-shaped decorative ruler (Creative Memories) to crop and piece together her sea and sky border.

Layer a Silhouetted People Border Silhouette and layer people photos for an interesting ancestral border, as Jeanine Faw Kamdar (Germantown, MD) has done. It's a great way to use many heritage or contemporary "family and friends" photos on one scrapbook page.

Use Photo Scraps to Make a Border Photo scraps, when cut into 1" squares and halved diagonally, make an interesting mosaic-type border. Use photo scraps of colors that are complementary to photos featured on your scrapbook page.

Punch a Border From Tiny Portraits Put those "itsy bitsy" portraits you get in portrait packages to good use as a page border by simply punching out the portraits with a large or jumbo shape punch.

3
ARTISTIC CROPPING TECHNIQUES

ARTISTICALLY CROPPED PHOTOS reduce the need for elaborate page decorations because the photo art truly speaks for itself. In this section, the many distinctive photo cropping techniques featured include:
• mosaics • quilts • building a scene • stained glass • kaleidoscopes • and illusions.

Few photo cropping techniques rival the gorgeous results of these. They are much easier than you might think. By experimenting with the various forms of artistic photo cropping, you will successfully transform your basic photo cropping "know-how" into photo cropping "wow!"

Mosaics

THE ART OF MOSAIC HAS FASCINATED
artists for centuries. Mosaic, defined as "a
surface decoration made by inlaying small pieces of
varyingly colored material to form a pattern or picture," is easily adaptable to scrapbook pages. Pieced
photo mosaics are a captivating way to display photos, whether you are cropping and reassembling a single photo or combining several photos. In addition,
photo mosaics are as diverse as the photos you
use, each lending its own fresh originality to
the finished design.

Creating a Photo Mosaic Many scrapbookers
also enjoy cooking, other crafts, and gardening
as well. If you love your garden, creating a photo
mosaic like Denise Steusse's (Sammamish, WA)
allows you to enjoy your flowers all year long.
Turn the page for illustrated steps on how to
create a basic photo mosaic.

I love my flowers! The blooms bring me joy and peace. All of these flowers are in my garden.

Creating a Photo Mosaic

1 Select photos and lay them out on a scrapbook page or background paper in a general format (Figure 1).

2 Using a photo-safe wax pencil and a ruler, create a grid of 1" squares on the back of each photo (Figure 2).

3 Number each square on back of photos by row (Figure 3), numbering backward to maintain proper order when photos are flipped over.

The concept of photo mosaics is basic—cut your pictures into square "tiles" and arrange them as you like. The easiest cutting technique involves slicing your photos vertically and horizontally using a metal straightedge ruler and craft knife or a small paper cutter. The arrangement of your photo tiles can range from simple to complex, depending upon how much time you want to spend on it and the look you want to achieve. The illustrated steps depicted here are for building a basic mosaic. You can apply these steps to create several variations of photo mosaics.

4 Cut photos into 1" squares and put individual photos in an envelope or plastic sandwich bag to keep them separated (Figure 4).

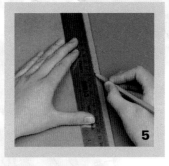

5 Lightly draw outer assembly guides on scrapbook page or background paper (Figure 5).

6 Arrange squares as desired, using the most interesting pieces of each photo, and mount in place (Figure 6).

Mosaic an Edge Border Simple cropping
of large squares make up Terri Robichon's
(Plymouth, MN) feline photo border. The
continuous solid-colored background gives
the illusion of three photos being one. Lettering
(Close To My Heart™) completes the design.

Frame a Mosaic Window Effect Looking at daily
life through a window can give a new view to
everyday family photos. Creating a windowpane
effect can be done in two ways; one is by slicing
photos into 1" squares and reassembling with
white space in between. Or, as Tamara Ruby
(McKinney, TX) has done here, by slicing thin
strips of white paper and placing the strips vertically and horizontally atop photos. Both techniques achieve the same mosaic window effect.

Vary the Mosaic Photo Tile Sizes

Different photos that are cropped into different sized photo tile pieces come together in a varied mosaic-like fashion in Kolleen Jenne's (Jordan, MN) collection of colorful flowers and foliage. Photos are cropped into both squares and rectangles, giving focus to each specimen's beauty while providing a refreshing mosaic variation.

Build a Multi-Photo Mosaic Scene

Making a mosaic can take different paths; either by cutting one photo into squares and reassembling, or, like Veronique Grasset's (Ruy, France) multi-photo mosaic, cropping numerous photos and reassembling them into a single image.

Using a Grid Template to Create Mosaics

Create mosaics easily by using a grid template to mark cropping lines. These mosaics were made using a 1" grid that was photocopied onto clear acetate (transparency film). A transparent grid template allows you to view your photo for quick placement and easy marking of cropping lines. The steps below illustrate how to use a transparent grid template to create a photo mosaic.

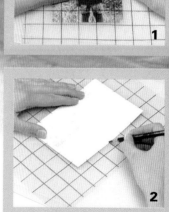

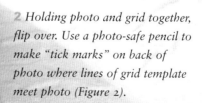

1 Move grid template over photo to find proper placement (Figure 1). On people photos, position grid over faces for minimal cropping on facial features.

2 Holding photo and grid together, flip over. Use a photo-safe pencil to make "tick marks" on back of photo where lines of grid template meet photo (Figure 2).

3 Use a ruler to connect tick marks, thus creating cropping lines on photo back (Figure 3). Then follow steps 3-6 on page 206 to complete the mosaic, reassembling either in original pattern or at random, as shown above.

Make Your Own Mosaic Grid Template

Transparent grid template—Hand draw or use a computer to make a grid. Photocopy onto clear acetate or transparency film. Opaque grid template—Hand draw or use a computer to make a grid on white copy paper. To view your photo for proper placement through an opaque grid template, place your grid and photo on a light box or against a sunny window. Then follow steps 2 and 3 to mark cropping lines.

COLOGNE CATHEDRAL

Köln

Piece Together a Panoramic Mosaic When Kristina Kuhl (Poreese, IL) tried to piece together a mosaic with three panoramic photos of the Cologne Cathedral, she found that they did not line up evenly. Her solution was to cut the photos into ¾" squares and reassemble into one magnificent mosaic. As you can see, mosaic pieces can be cut into all sizes.

Crop a Mosaic Frame One mosaic framing option is to use a center photo that documents where the photos were taken. In the case above, Heather Spurlock (Salt Lake City, UT) cropped three different botanical photos into 1" squares and reassembled them to frame a central photo that showcases the name of the garden from which the photos were taken. This is a great photojournaling technique that works well with sightseeing and vacation photos.

Similarly, framing a portrait with floral photo tiles helped Caroline Lebel (Toronto, Ontario, Canada) document the natural beauty surrounding her on her wedding day, as shown above right. The tile sizes were varied, as needed, to frame her treasured portrait.

In yet another framing variation, Celeste Knudsen (Auburn, WA) found herself hesitantly cropping lush landscape photos into squares, but was delighted at the outcome of her mosaic framing effect, shown at the right.

Punch a Mosaic Background Make a punched mosaic background from photo scraps to offset simple cropped photos. Ann Perry (Allen, TX) used a small square punch to create mosaic pieces of the sand, sea and sky for this decorative spread of her vacation at scenic Hilton Head Island. When working with such tiny mosaic pieces, your assembly work will go much quicker if you send photos through a Xyron® adhesive application machine prior to punching into mosaic pieces.

Crop a Mosaic Background A mosaic background brings foreground photos to life, while utilizing cropped photo leftovers. Making similar-sized mosaic tiles, Karen Holder (Jacksonville, NC) relied on scraps of water photos to produce a monochromatic background that doesn't take any attention away from her action photos.

Amsterdam, the 97 facets city ...

Amsterdam, la ville aux 97 facettes ...

Design a Mosaic Original Amsterdam, known as "the city with 97 facets," is showcased in a 97-piece original mosaic created by Veronique Grasset (Ruy, France). A small square punch was used to punch photo scrap pieces for the interior of the mosaic.

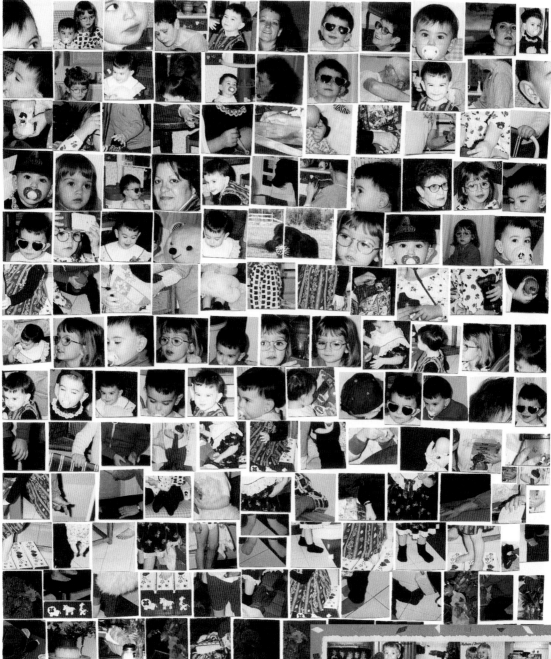

Crop a Mini Photo Mosaic Collage If every photo tells a story, then building a mosaic collage out of small photo pieces must compose a novel! Instead of filing extra photos away, Marah Rocco (Howard Beach, NY) cropped photos into various-sized pieces and reassembled them into a free-form mosaic collage that speaks volumes about a busy holiday season.

In a similar manner, Charla Campbell (Springfield, MO) cropped a year's worth of memories from 54 different photos to create a retrospective of the year 1999.

Place Silhouettes Into a Mosaic Incorporate silhouetted photos into a photo mosaic to create a spectacular work of art. This detailed page was made by first silhouetting selected images and then cutting photos into 1³⁄₁₆" squares. The use of three cropping techniques—silhouetting, partial silhouetting and mosaic tiles—gives this page its innovative look. Photos Erica Pierovich

Simple Shape, Unique Mosaic Crop photos into a diamond shape to create a fence-like mosaic. Barbara Christmann (Rohnert Park, CA) cropped photos with a Déjà Views template (C-Thru Ruler Co.) to create a patchwork trellis of nature's beauty.

Crop a Tri-Tone Mosaic For an interesting mosaic variation, crop a tri-tone mosaic using three 8 x 10" enlargements of the same photo—one in color, one in sepia, and one in black-and-white. These photos were reproduced on a digital photo machine, which had all three print options. Crop photos into a mosaic. Reassemble using black-and-white photo tiles for outer frame, then sepia, then color photo tiles for the center. Piece together your unused photo tiles for two more variations of the tri-tone theme. Photo MaryJo Regier

Piece an Abstract Mosaic Frame With Photo Scraps Another way to crop photos that might otherwise go unused is to crop them into tiny, geometric-shaped "shards" and assemble together in an abstract mosaic. Veronique Grasset (Ruy, France) pieced together this frame with photo scraps of grass, leaves and murky water to accentuate the green hues in her family's casual waterside portrait.

Augignac 08/98

Quilts

QUILTING AND SCRAPBOOKING HAVE SO MUCH
in common; using the same techniques as quilters, you
simply crop photos and mount, rather than cut fabric
and sew. Quilting patterns and templates are easily
adaptable to individual photos, which makes it a perfect cropping technique for special occasion, holiday,
scenic and people photos. The wide array of patterned
papers available will easily
complement your photos'
themes and colors.

Star Light, Star Bright Some variation of
the diamond or square shape forms the
base of most star quilt patterns. The star
design far outnumbers all other quilt patterns and is easy to work with because of
its straight lines. Experiment with any quilt
pattern, however, to see how you might
adapt it to make a photo quilt.

Crop a Dresden Plate Piecing together
many images of a single theme can
resemble a "quilted" look on your page.
Utilizing a quilter's Dresden plate stencil
(Wrights EZ Quilting), Liz Niemtschik
(Littleton, CO) cropped images of New
Mexico into a 20-piece photographic fan,
making use of many extra photos that
might have otherwise gone unused.

Make a Photo Quilt

Perhaps one of the easiest ways to create a photo quilt is by using nothing more than photos and a transparent shape template. Transparent templates allow you to move the template around on a photo to isolate a portion of the photo that you wish to use when creating a photo quilt.

Colors   of a

Pennsylvania   October

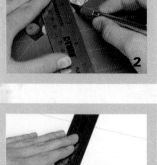

1 *Position template over photo. Use a photo-safe wax pencil to trace shape onto photo (Figure 1).*
Repeat with all photos selected until you have 30 photo diamonds. If you do not have a diamond template, simply photocopy the pattern below onto cardstock, cut out, and trace around it on photos.

2 *Use a metal straightedge ruler and craft knife to cut out all photo diamonds, cutting slightly to the inside of each cropping line so no marks are visible (Figure 2).*

3 *Use a pencil to lightly draw one vertical line down and one horizontal line across the center of a 12 x 12" scrapbook page (Figure 3) to serve as a grid for photo diamond placement.*

4 *Begin assembly in the center of the page, forming six diamonds to make a star. The remaining photo diamonds are then placed between the star's points to form the final design (Figure 4).*

Melinda Staley (Colorado Springs, CO) used a homemade diamond template to create her quilted homage to Pennsylvania's autumn landscape. She used 30 photo "diamonds," cropped from eight different photos.
To make your own diamond-shaped quilt, follow the steps above. In the pages that follow, you will see many ways to create photo quilts. To learn even more about quilted scrapbook pages, see *Memory Makers Quilted Scrapbooks.*

Quilt a Photo Pinwheel A triangle template, cropped from a 4" square of cardstock that was cut diagonally, creates a colorful pinwheel out of Twyla Slater's (Bozeman, MT) family photos.

Simplify Quilts With a Single Shape Cropping many photos into the same shape simplifies a quilted "honeycomb" look for Carolyn Perfetti's (Franklin, OH) vacation photos. Carolyn cropped her photos with a hexagon template (Creative Memories) and completed the design by using partial hexagons at the top, sides and bottom of the page.

Quilt a Centerpiece Barbara Christmann (Rohnert Park, CA) created a
corner fan design—quartered out of a circle, and then divided into thirds—
that successfully draws the eyes inward to the center photo of her quilt.
A punched border (Family Treasures) and square corner
photo tiles complete the design.

Quilt an Ohio Star Variation One of the most versatile motifs for quilting a page is the Ohio star pattern. Liz Niemtschik (Littleton, CO) simplified a more intricate star motif quilt pattern below (originally designed by Maureen Martins) by using large diamonds and squares, pieced together with small colored triangles. For a more intricate pattern, use four small squares to form one large square and two small triangles to form one diamond. The possibilities of pattern and color are endless!

Frame Photos With Small Star Quilt Scraps

Photo scraps can make the most beautiful frames for your photos, especially when cropped into geometric quilt-like shapes. Shelly Larson (Burnsville, MN) cropped triangles out of lush Florida foliage and assembled these stunning star frames. She also cleverly pieced together doubles of one photo to create a palm tree frond frame for the enlarged picture in the center.

Crop Photos to Create Quilt "Fabric"

Using photos as "fabric" for a quilt page creates a unique photographic effect. Elsie Duncan (Unity, Saskatchewan, Canada) cut triangles from 1½" squares of aquatic landscape photos and placed them point-to-point around the central photo.

Quilt Nature's Beauty

Displaying the simplistic beauty of wildlife in its natural setting was key to Pam Bailey's (Thornton, CO) layout. To do so, she cropped photos with an octagon template, and embellished the center photos with triangles snipped from octagon photo scraps.

Make Up Your Own Quilt Design Nancy Danielson's (Huntington Beach, CA) unique quilt page is a compilation of different templates. An enlarged hexagon template was used to make the center, while a leaf template (Family Treasures) was used to extend photo strips. Circle cropped photos complete this quilt of scenic Hawaiian memories.

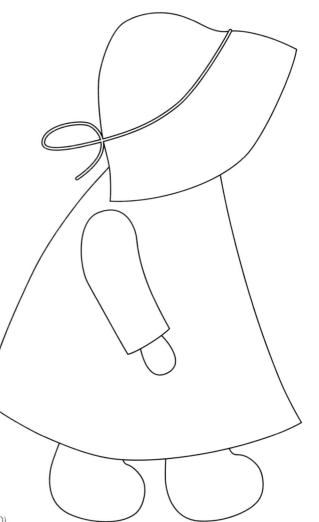

Quilt a 1930s Favorite Based on the popular 1930s "Sunbonnet Sue" quilt pattern and inspired by Elsie Duncan's (Unity, Saskatchewan, Canada) art featured in *Memory Makers Quilted Scrapbooks*, we re-created this art by enlarging the pattern shown and piecing together cropped photos to fit the pattern. Photos Stephanie Klish (Gunnison, CO)

Stack Horizontal Photos Vertically
Snorkeling memories are creatively preserved by Sherri Mendenhall (Carpintera, CA), who "stacked" underwater photos vertically with an above-water shot for great vertical depth and dimension.

Building a Scene

CUTTING AND LAYERING PHOTOS TO BUILD A SCENE is a captivating cropping alternative. This works well with travel and people photos, whether vertical, horizontal or panoramic. Try building a scene through creative photo cropping that incorporates what you have already learned about silhouetting and mosaics for a truly dazzling photo effect.

Combine Photos to Construct a Panorama

So simple is the idea, yet so splendid are the results of combining photos to form a panorama. Emily Neal (Bolingbrook, IL) matted and layered three progressive photos of the same Utah rock arch to build this panoramic view. Foam spacers were placed beneath the center photo to add dimension and height.

July 13, 1998

COTTONWOOD PASS
SAN ISABEL   GUNNISON
NATIONAL FOREST   NATIONAL FOREST
ELEVATION 12,126 FEET
CONTINENTAL DIVIDE
ATLANTIC   PACIFIC

Rebecca, Ruth, Reni
The panorama was taken from the top of this rise.

LOOKING WEST

O Lord, my God! When I in awesome wonder
Consider all the worlds thy hands have made,
I see the stars, I hear the rolling thunder
Thy power thro'out the universe displayed;
Then sings my soul, my Savior God to thee;
How great thou art, how great thou art!
Then sings my soul, my Savior God to thee;
How great thou art, how great thou art!

When thro' the woods and forest glades I wander,
And hear the birds sing sweetly in the trees;
When I look down from lofty mountain grandeur,
And hear the brook and feel the gentle breeze;
Then sings my soul, my Savior God to thee;
How great thou art, how great thou art!
Then sings my soul, my Savior God to thee;
How great thou art, how great thou art!

Layer Vertically to Show Progression
Cropped photos layered vertically help
Debbie Schubert (Phoenix, AZ) tell the
story of her family's individual rides
down an alpine mountain slide. In this
case, the vertical layering of four photos
gives the illusion that her family members came down the
slide simultaneously.

Layer Vertical Panoramas Instead of taking panoramic photos horizontally, behold a new vista by holding the camera vertically—a technique that
works great for building a scene. To achieve this effect, snap a series of
photos starting at the left of your scene. Move the camera a little to the
right and snap another photo. Continue with a couple more shots, overlapping a tiny bit of the previous shot through the viewfinder. Assemble
developed prints, overlapping as necessary to rebuild the scene; crop
outer edges as desired. Keep in mind that a panorama lens will pick up a
lot more sky than what you actually see in the viewfinder (as in the art
shown here), so aim your camera down a bit to capture more of the foreground. Photos Pam Klassen

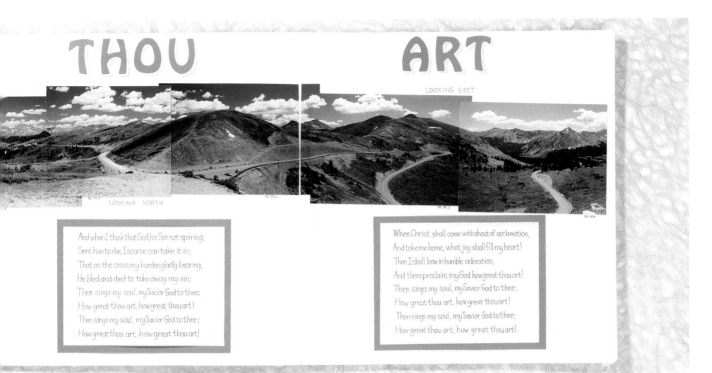

THOU ART

LOOKING EAST

LOOKING NORTH

And when I think that God, his Son not sparing,
Sent him to die, I scarce can take it in;
That on the cross, my burden gladly bearing,
He bled and died to take away my sin;
Then sings my soul, my Savior God to thee;
How great thou art, how great thou art!
Then sings my soul, my Savior God to thee;
How great thou art, how great thou art!

When Christ shall come with shout of acclamation,
And take me home, what joy shall fill my heart!
Then I shall bow in humble adoration,
And there proclaim, my God how great thou art!
Then sings my soul, my Savior God to thee;
How great thou art, how great thou art!
Then sings my soul, my Savior God to thee;
How great thou art, how great thou art!

Layer to Build an Expansive Panorama Snap a series of overlapping photos, pivoting from the same spot left to right, to capture a sweeping vista that's too large and breathtaking for one frame alone. Ruth Penick's (Dayton, OH) seven-photo series covers 270° of Colorado's Cottonwood Pass. After taping two additional scrapbook pages to this spread to create foldouts, the 4 x 6" photos were lined up in order and overlapped so that photo details matched. Then one-half of the overlap on top photos was trimmed off so that the photo underneath would still show. Photos were mounted and die cut letters (Accu-Cut) and matted journaling were added to complete design.

Layer Unrelated Photos to Build New Scene
Silhouette crop the top edges of scenic panoramic photos and layer with foam spacers to create a three-dimensional effect. This technique is a great way to showcase panorama photos. You can also enlarge photos to 8 x 10" and crop to panoramic size for layering. Just for fun, place a favorite silhouette-cropped person or pet photo in the foreground of your new scene. Cloud photo Loralee Dischner, mountain photos John Budden and MaryJo Regier, floral photos Linda Dennis and MaryJo Regier, photo of child Chrissie Tepe

Crop and Layer Tiny Subjects Vacation photos, particularly beach scenes, often result in numerous photos with tiny subjects. Annette Robison (Billings, MT) was disappointed that her family members were so tiny in these beach scenes, even after she had 5 x 7" enlargements made. Her solution was to crop 19 photos and layer on top of each other, lining up each photo to rebuild the beach, the waves and the horizon into a whole new scene. This technique is a great way to showcase many photos that might otherwise go unused.

Same Subject, Different Times of Day An interesting variation to building a scene is to use several photos of the same subject, shot at different times of the day. In this case, five photos of the Denver skyline were shot at various time intervals. The 4 x 6" prints were then cropped into mosaic pieces and reassembled randomly. Just enough variation was used to keep the art interesting, but not too much variation so as to distort the perspective of the original skyline photos. Try this with photos of your house, a favorite park or a city skyline. Photos MaryJo Regier

DENVER SKYLINE AT SUNRISE · NOVEMBER 2000

Stained Glass

IF YOU'VE EVER VISITED A CATHEDRAL, you understand the appeal of stained glass. Its beauty seems to transcend the ordinary hues of our lives. Like many artistic techniques, this art can be readily adapted to the scrapbook page. Whether you crop a photo into basic parts and mount on black paper, or trace a pattern onto your photos, crop and reassemble, you will love the newfound radiance this cropping technique brings to your photos. And while more intricate designs can be time-consuming, the results are stunning and rewarding.

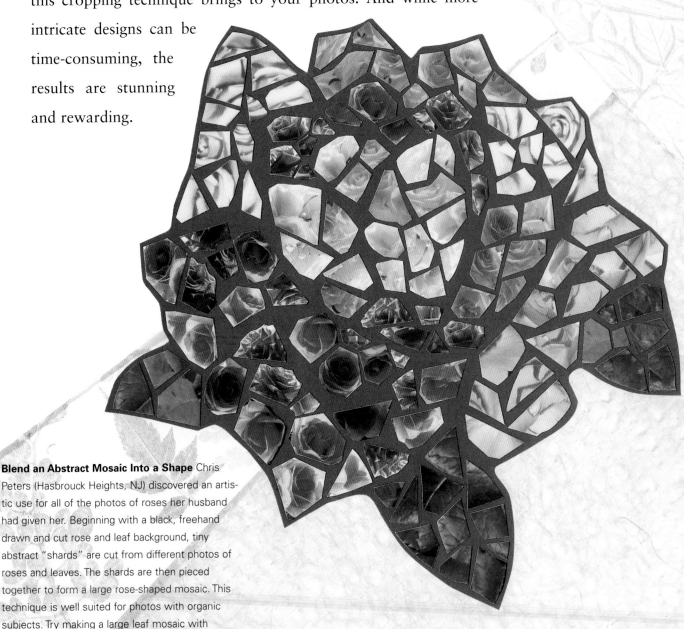

Blend an Abstract Mosaic Into a Shape Chris Peters (Hasbrouck Heights, NJ) discovered an artistic use for all of the photos of roses her husband had given her. Beginning with a black, freehand drawn and cut rose and leaf background, tiny abstract "shards" are cut from different photos of roses and leaves. The shards are then pieced together to form a large rose-shaped mosaic. This technique is well suited for photos with organic subjects. Try making a large leaf mosaic with abstract shards from several leaf photos or a large daisy mosaic with abstract shards from several different colored daisy photos.

Sweet little Angel
Caryn   1990

6 mo.

Crop a Stained-Glass Photo Design

Stained-glass photo designs are the perfect way to showcase a special portrait. This perfectly symmetrical octagon design incorporates both a photo and complementary-colored papers to form a striking arrangement. Follow the steps below to make your own illuminated masterpiece.

1 *To begin, use a photocopier to enlarge or reduce the pattern below to fit your photo. Then, use carbon paper or a light table to trace the pattern pieces onto the back of your photo, making sure that the center octagon is positioned over the center of your image. If your photo is smaller than the pattern, or if you want to add complementary-colored paper, trace the shapes and number the remaining pieces in the same manner as the photo. Use a metal ruler and a photo-safe pencil to retrace the pattern on the back of the photo, ensuring that all lines are straight (Figure 1).*

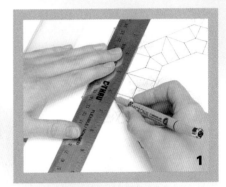

2 *Assign a number to each pattern piece on the back of your photo, numbering backward. Begin numbering at the center and work your way outward (Figure 2). This way, when the photo pieces are cut apart and turned over, they will be in the proper order for reassembly.*

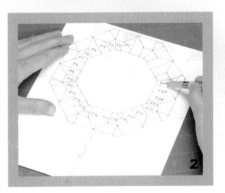

3 *With sharp scissors or a metal ruler and craft knife, cut around the inside edges of each piece (Figure 3), trimming away the traced line to create space for the background paper to show through.*

4 *Working out from the center octagon photo, mount each piece onto dark background paper using the pattern and numbered pieces as an assembly guide (Figure 4).*

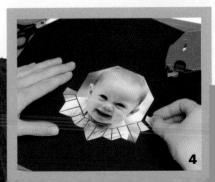

Photo Joyce Feil

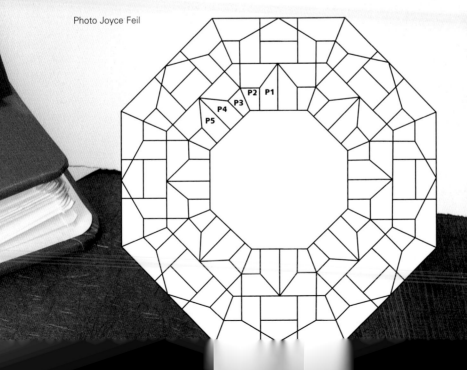

Shape a Geometric Design

Cropping inspiration can come from the most unlikely places, just as it did for Cathy Trapp (Mulvane, KS). After photographing fall foliage, Cathy was inspired to create this stained-glass design from a quilted hot pad she saw in a magazine. Geometric photo shapes were duplicated four times and then placed around the center photo, leaving space between each shape.

Simplify a Stained-Glass Window

Maintaining the focus of her scenic mountain photos is achieved by Loydene Brock's (Kansas City, MO) simple framing effect. Minimal cropping of the photos and placement of colored paper strips and shapes, backed in black, resembles the simplistic beauty of a stained-glass window.

Repeat a Cropped Geometric Pattern Create small stained-glass windows by cropping photos into mosaic-sized (1½" or smaller) pieces. Pam Friis (Castle Rock, CO) repeated the same stenciled design of geometric shapes multiple times, giving her photos the illusion of tiny, intricate stained-glass windows.

Mudflats where 1964 earthquake occurred~ Turnagain Arm

Kenai Peninsula~ an extension of Cook Inlet

A potlatch at the art museum in Anchorage

Carved bear at a Portage Glacier gift shop. (7 mo. PG

Crop Single Photo for Stained-Glass Look To create a stained-glass image, silhouette crop a photo into parts and mount on black paper, leaving about ⅛" space between cropped pieces. Karen Preston (Portland, OR) created her own stained-glass images of Alaskan landscape and artifacts by cropping her photos along natural cutting lines and reassembling on black cardstock.

Stained-Glass Scene Building Layering partially silhouetted landscape photos gave Julie Sawyer's (San Antonio, TX) Arabian pictures an interesting stained-glass effect. Julie matted each photo with black paper to create the "leaded" lines.

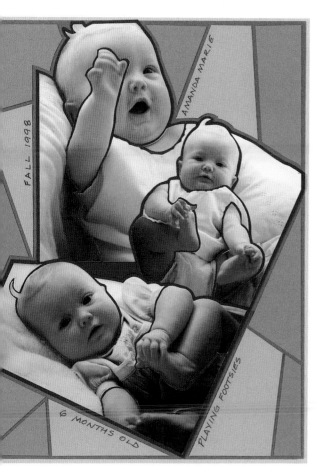

FALL 1998

AMANDA MARIE

6 MONTHS OLD

PLAYING FOOTSIES

Crop a Stained-Glass Design Without a Pattern It's easy to achieve a stained-glass scrapbook design without a pattern. All you need is a simple photo without a lot of detail in it. Follow the steps below to learn how.

1 To begin, silhouette crop the outer edge of the photo subject. Then, cut out each major "part" of the subject, as shown (Figure 1), cutting a little extra space between pieces to allow for space needed when reassembling.

2 To reassemble, begin with the central parts of the image and work outward. Mount each part onto black background paper, leaving a small gap between each piece to form "leaded" lines (Figure 2).

Photo Joyce Feil

Piece Together a Poinsettia Stained-glass images take on a new shape when pieced together into a floral design. Paper piecing this poinsettia page began as Sandra de St. Croix (St. Albert, Alberta, Canada) traced the flower image on a vellum-type paper and then placed it over her photos to see each petal image. The petal shape was then drawn onto the photograph and cut slightly smaller than the lines prescribed so it could be mounted on the red flower background. "Leaded" lines were hand drawn with a wide black pen. Try this technique with any floral pattern to create your own stained-glass scene.

Shape Stained-Glass Tulips Shape photos into a colorful bunch of stained-glass tulips by photo-copying the pattern below and enlarging to fit scrapbook page. Trace each flower piece onto the appropriate photo or piece of paper and cut just inside traced line. Mount each piece onto dark background paper. Trim paper to a ⅛" border and assemble. Idea Sandra de St. Croix (St. Albert, Alberta, Canada), photos Lora Mason

Kaleidoscopes

TRADITIONAL KALEIDOSCOPES HAVE BEEN designed, built and cherished for over 180 years. "Kaleidoscope" in Greek means "beautiful form to look at." Photo kaleidoscopes are a fun blend of photographs and angles. Nearly any photo can be used, but the most dramatic kaleidoscope effects are produced with photos that have repetitive patterns, intersecting lines, vivid colors, good light quality and lots of activity. In the pages that follow, you will see a number of different ways to make photo kaleidoscopes. If you would like to learn more about making photo kaleidoscopes for scrapbook pages, see *Memory Makers Photo Kaleidoscopes*™.

Creating a Basic Photo Kaleidoscope

Photo kaleidoscopes may seem complicated, but they are simple to make by using an equal number of original and reverse-image photos. Once you select a photo to use, follow the instructions below to create a basic, eight-piece photo kaleidoscope.

Original image   **Reverse image**

Supplies
- 4 original and 4 reverse-image 4 x 6" reprints
- 45° clear triangle
- Craft knife
- Metal straightedge ruler
- Cutting mat
- Ballpoint pen
- Removable tape
- Photo-safe adhesive

1 Determine Cutting Lines *Place a 45° triangle over the part of the photo that you want to use, lining up the triangle's 90° square corner with one of the corners of the photo (Figure 1). Hold a folding mirror against the side of the triangle to preview the kaleidoscope, if desired.*

2 Order Reprints *Have the photo lab make "exact match" original and reverse-image reprints from your negative (Figure 2).*

3 Cut Photos *Place the triangle over the part of the photo that you want to use, as determined in Step 1, and make the same single cut on each original and reverse-image photo (Figure 3).*

4 Assemble Cut Pieces *Place one cut original photo beside one cut reverse-image photo, lining up photos to form a pair (See Figure 2 on page 236 for example). Tape the pair together on the back with removable tape (Figure 4). Repeat with remaining photo pairs.*

5 Add Finishing Touches *Trim outer edges of the photo kaleidoscope in a pleasing pattern, if desired. On the back of the kaleidoscope, apply double-sided adhesive at center star and edges prior to mounting on a page (Figure 5).*

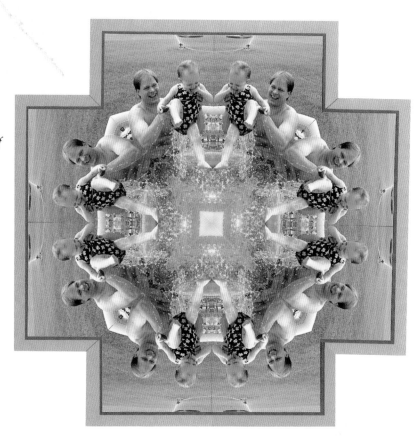

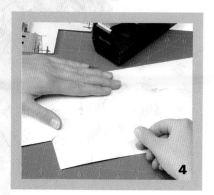

Original image

Kaleidoscope Edges In Tammy Stevenson's (Florrisant, MO) basic, eight-piece photo kaleidoscope, the edge of the photo was left intact to create this cross shape. Allow your photos to dictate the manner in which the outer edge is trimmed on the finished kaleidoscope. Some photos work best leaving the edge intact, while others are good candidates for cropping with scalloped edges or in points, silhouette cropping, or cropping with decorative scissors.

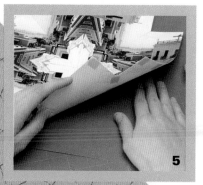

Cropping Kaleidoscope Mats

Photo kaleidoscope mats provide the perfect venue for showcasing cherished photos. These mats are simply a photo kaleidoscope with an opening in the center. The photo kaleidoscope to the left was made into a mat using the same photos shown on page 234. Follow the instructions below to make a 12 x 12" photo kaleidoscope mat.

Original image   Reverse image

You will need the same supplies listed on page 234, including four original and four reverse-image 4 x 6" photo reprints. You will make just one cut on each photo.

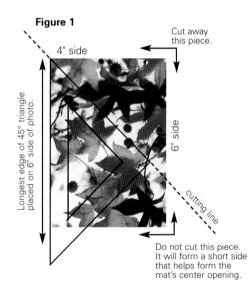

Figure 1

4" side

Cut away this piece.

Longest edge of 45° triangle placed on 6" side of photo.

6" side

cutting line

Do not cut this piece. It will form a short side that helps form the mat's center opening.

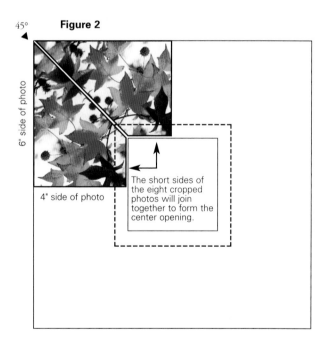

45°   **Figure 2**

6" side of photo

4" side of photo

The short sides of the eight cropped photos will join together to form the center opening.

1 Determine Cutting Lines *Place the longest edge of a 45° triangle along the 6" side of an original reprint, with the triangle point meeting a photo corner. Mark the cutting line (Figure 1) and make the cut. Repeat with the remaining three original photos.*

2 Cut Reverse Images *Layer one cut original photo on top of one uncut reverse photo and tape together at matching corners to cre-*

ate a mirror image. Place ruler over photo; cut on reverse photo. Now you have one pair (Figure 2). Repeat with remaining photos.

3 Assemble and Finish *Tape pairs together on back of photos to create kaleidoscope. In doing so, the short side of the cut photos will join together to form the center opening. Add center photo behind mat to finish.*

Photos Rita Brei (Mission Viejo, CA)

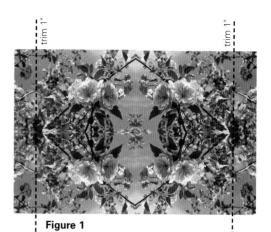

Figure 1

This kaleidoscope mat variation is easy to make, using just two original and two reverse-image photos. Follow the steps below to create an 8 x 10" photo kaleidoscope mat.

Original image

Figure 2

1 *Tape photos together into a foursome. Crop 1" from each side to make a 10" width (Figure 1).*

2 *Use a square template or ruler and craft knife to crop center opening (Figure 2). Add photo behind mat.*

Photos Sandra Yanisko (Barto, PA)

Craft a Wood Frame Mirage Florence Davis (Winter Haven, FL) captured her grandson's wet footprints as he watered flowers on her deck for an ingenious use of a photo in a photo kaleidoscope mat. Her eight-piece, 45° angle kaleidoscope creates the illusion that the center photo is in a wooden frame.

Original image (cropped)

Crop a Classic Photo Kaleidoscope

It's fun to experiment with a number of different triangle sizes to achieve different kaleidoscopic effects. When making a photo kaleidoscope, imagine that the part of the photo you have chosen to use is one slice of pie. The angle you use will determine the number of photo "slices" needed to make a 360° kaleidoscope "pie." The chart at the right illustrates this concept. Follow the steps on the next page to create a classic twelve-piece photo kaleidoscope with an open center.

Eight 45° pieces = one 360° photo kaleidoscope

Six 60° pieces = one 360° photo kaleidoscope

Twelve 30° pieces = one 360° photo kaleidoscope

Standard Triangle Sizes*

Triangle Chart

degree required	kaleidoscope pieces	# of original & reversed images
20º	18 =	9 each
* 30º	12 =	6 each
36º	10 =	5 each
* 45º	8 =	4 each
* 60º	6 =	3 each
* 90º	4 =	2 each

Use this chart to help you determine the number of reprints needed when experimenting with different sized triangles.

Original image

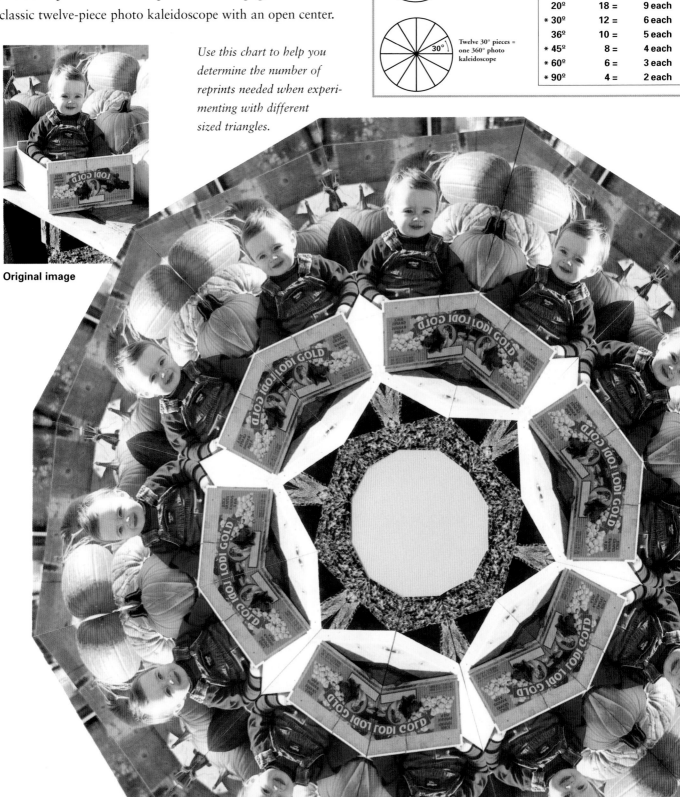

1 Determine Cutting Lines *To begin, place a 30° triangle over the part of the photo that you want to use, extending the triangle's tip beyond the edge of the photo to create the center opening (Figure 1). Conversely, when the triangle's tip stays on the photo, the result is a photo kaleidoscope whose points meet in the center, like those shown below.*

2 Cut Photos *Now find three or four reference points that fall along the edges of the triangle, points that include the part of the photo you want to use (Figure 2). Cut through these exact same three or four reference points on each original and reverse-image photo.*

3 Assemble and Finish *Follow steps 4 and 5 on page 235 to assemble and finish the photo kaleidoscope. See the following photo kaleidoscopes for ideas on how to fill the center opening.*

Photo Kaleidoscope Rachel Smith

Original image (cropped)

Fill Center With Mini Kaleidoscope
Donna Pittard (Kingwood, TX) uses photo scraps left over from cropping original and reverse-images, to create a mini kaleidoscope for her photo kaleidoscope's center opening.

Make a Classic Kaleidoscope While her family vacation photo is great all by itself, Karen Jakubowski (Massapequa, NY) recognized that the outstretched wings on the totem pole would join together perfectly to form a circle in this classic, eight-piece kaleidoscope made with 4 x 6" photos and a 45° triangle. Cropping the photo in this manner effectively removes the empty foreground to focus attention on the family.

Original image

Layer Photos Onto Kaleidoscope Layer cropped photos onto a finished kaleidoscope for an interesting embellishment, as Elaine Trinkle (Elizabethton, TN) has done. Note how the outer circle photos draw the eye inward to the center of the kaleidoscope.

Original image

Make a Graduated Frame Center A combination of journaling and photo frames cropped with a graduated template makes an interesting and informative center for Pam Kean's (Pierre, SD) kaleidoscope art. It successfully documents the birth of twin cecropia moths from one cocoon. You can also fill a kaleidoscope's center with a mini kaleidoscope made from the kaleidoscope's photo scraps, a matted photograph, a design element (such as a sticker or die cut) or journaling.

Original image

Original image

Silhouette Kaleidoscope Edges Another interesting variation for trimming a photo kaleidoscope's edges is to silhouette crop the edges. This works especially well with photos of people, as in the case of Sheryl Abbott's (Kingwood, TX) daughter holding a cherished bunny.

Illusions

PEOPLE HAVE BEEN FASCINATED WITH OPTICAL ILLUSIONS for centuries. And few scrapbookers can resist the allure of creating photo illusions through creative cropping, which extends the imagery of a conventional photograph. It's quite simple to use photo enlargements to exaggerate size or pair unlikely photo subjects for interesting, often comical effects. Equally intriguing are the dimension and depth that result when cropping photos for blocks and hexagon illusions. The following examples are sure to give you plenty of inspiration for cropping your own photo trickery.

Enhance the Illusory Effect
As you can see, just about any photo subject can be used when cropping photo illusions. Once your photo illusion is assembled, take a picture of it. By re-photographing, the cropped and layered edges become softened, giving the appearance of just one photo instead of a composite of cropped photos, thus enhancing the illusory effect.

Create a Prehistoric Pursuit Using an enlargement of the family's pet lizards and silhouette-cropped photos of her children, Christine Lees (Hallam, Victoria, Australia) crafted this Jurassic illusion. Flintstone-style garb was crafted from paper to clothe these primitive hunters, while letter stickers and freehand cut dog bones complete the design.

Silhouette a Fantasy Wildlife Park
Zoo photos make a capricious background when enlarged and layered with silhouette cropped photos of family and friends. We'll let you guess which is the real "wildlife" in this imaginary menagerie! Zoo photo Mark Duncan (Denver, CO), photos of children Judy Sorenson (Broomfield, CO)

Plant a Fantasy Flower Garden

Plant a fantasy garden of flowers and fairies by layering silhouettes of various sizes. Suzi Leverington (Narre Warren, Victoria, Australia) inspired scrapbook magic by taking photos of her "fairies" in various positions, combined with enlarged tulip photos. This is a great illusory technique to try with photos of any activity, particularly athletics and hobbies. To achieve this effect, use your own landscape, garden or outdoor photo enlargement for a background. Add silhouetted people photos to complete the illusion. To re-create this fantasy flower garden, follow the steps below.

Rebecca & Katie Sept 1999

1 *Take photographs of flowers and children posed in costume using a low-speed film, such as ISO 100, which allows for high quality enlargements. Pay attention to lighting and avoid harsh shadows with fill flash. Try to keep the same distance from your subjects for each photo so that the subjects are the same relative size in each photo. Pose the children in different positions. For example, have them sit sideways on a table, pretend to peer off in the distance or peek over the edge of a chair (Figure 1).*

2 *Take close-up photos of flowers. Check your camera's focus range so that you don't get too close and end up with blurry pictures.*

3 *Enlarge the children and flower photos to the appropriate relative sizes (Figure 2). Select one or two flower enlargements for use as the background.*

4 *Silhouette enlarged photos of both flowers and children. Layer photos and flower background (Figure 3), arranging into a pleasing scene prior to mounting permanently in place.*

1

2

3

Create an Off-Scale Scene Creative cropping takes on a grand scale when silhouetted enlargements are placed on regular-sized photo backgrounds to create a humorous, off-scale scene. Debra Helm (Tewksbury, MA) made a giant out of her son, giving the illusion that he is towering over a beautiful Antigua ocean, by silhouetting his enlarged image and placing him on the water's horizon line.

Duplicate the Action Create the illusion of full-court action by layering different sizes of photo silhouettes. Norma Bauman (Coon Rapids, MN) printed her son's slam-dunk
four times in sizes 4 x 6", 5 x 7", 8 x 10" and 11 x 14". She left the largest photo intact, but silhouetted the smaller three and then layered the image, from largest to smallest. Try this technique with any sports action shot.

Bounce Photo Subjects on Page
Raquel Pineira's (Tustin, CA) visit to Taco Bell's Discovery Space Center resulted in photos of her children perched on outdoor sculptures. By silhouetting the children and adding simple pen strokes, the children appear to be bouncing around on the page.

Piece a Metamorphosis Hobby photos are great candidates for cropping a metamorphosis because of their "start to finish" nature. Terri Robichon (Plymouth, MN) cropped a series of photos of her husband's plane-building project, aptly named "The Evolution of Flight," in this M.C. Escher-style metamorphosis—from left to right, the transition from squares to fish and birds.

Crop and Merge Different Photos Into One
Cheri O'Donnell (Orange, CA) created this Picasso-esque portrait by lining up three separate portraits (one of her, one of each of her daughters) to match features, such as eyes, noses and mouths. She then cropped and trimmed photos as necessary to create a new portrait. Add lettering (Current®, Inc.), zigzag border (Westrim Crafts) and journaling to complete design. Try merging portraits of you and your loved ones. You may just be surprised how much you really do look alike!

Create a Dual Image Take a double look. Is this one girl or two? The same person, or twins? Create a multiple illusion by using silhouetted images of different sizes, layered, to create dimension and illusion. LouAnn McKinney (Akron, OH) shows her daughter holding a lifelike doll, which is actually a small silhouetted photo of her daughter in the same outfit. Don't let your eyes fool you!

Pull a Cropped Giant Combining a silhouette-cropped enlargement with a silhouette-cropped panoramic photo of tug of war participants creates this fun illusion. Try it with an enlargement of your house, car, a favorite toy or other favorite object to create your own gargantuan effort. Tug of war photo Pennie Stutzman

Crop Some Anthropomorphics The optical trickery of anthropomorphics (placing animal heads on human bodies) has appeared and reappeared throughout the history of painting. It's an amusing concept to bring to the scrapbook page, especially when pairing favorite household pets with family portraits. Photos of wild animals are fair game for creating anthropomorphics as well. You can even make a reverse anthropomorphic by placing a human head on an animal body. Photos clockwise from top: tigers Lora Mason; surprised man Sally Scamfer; lions Jeff Neal (Huntington Beach, CA); dancers Dawn Mabe; boy in Hawaiian shirt, moose and walrus Pennie Stutzman; giraffe, tuxedo pair and German shepherd family MaryJo Regier

Layer an Imaginary Rush Hour What will parents ever do with all of those photos of toddlers in play cars? Just for fun, try silhouette cropping your "toddler at the wheel" photo and layer on top of an enlarged traffic photo. Then steer clear of the action! Photo of child Cheri O'Donnell, traffic photo Nikki Widner

Crop Some Tom Thumb Trickery
Re-create the tomfoolery of Tom Thumb, the diminutive hero of English folklore. Crop your own fantasy world by enlarging a still-life, close-up photo for the background and silhouetting a smaller-sized photo subject. Mount the silhouette on the background, keeping in mind that you want to make the scene look as "real" as possible. Toadstool photo Pam Klassen, photo of child Diane Perry (Broomfield, CO)

Silhouette a Lilliputian Scene Welcome to Lilliput, one of the lands of *Gulliver's Travels*, where miniature people dwell in the midst of a giant! To create this fun illusion, nestle reduced, silhouetted images of people among enlarged, partially silhouetted photos of feet, hands, or head and shoulders. Photos Dawn Mabe

Crop Diamonds to Form Blocks Cropping photos into the shape of diamonds creates a wonderfully simple block illusion, depending on how they are pieced together. Using a diamond template, Shelley Potter (Fairbanks, AK) combines three diamonds to create a cubed illusion of her stepson's favorite hobby.

Tumble a Block Variation Try something new with the block illusion by varying the amount of cuts made on one side. Inspired by a newspaper ad, RaeAnn Struikmans (Temecula, CA) detailed her photo cubes by cropping four small diamonds and placing them on one side of each cube. We've tumbled them down the page to show you what blocks can look like as a border.

Stack a Block Tower Stack a tower of blocks by cropping photos with a diamond-shaped template. Jennifer Thomas (Potter, NE) cut out three diamond shapes to make one block, and suggests working from the bottom up to create the building-block illusion.

Sea World

The first day we used our new park passes a large group of our friends went together.

My sister Michelle with

Blake, Garre...

March

2000

We had to take turns on the rides but the Killer Whale show we could all enjoy together

Orlando, FL

Design a Dimensional Hexagon Illusion

Designing a dimensional illusion with photos and paper adds depth and creativity to layouts. The Sea World hexagon illusion shown on the left takes the concept of illusional blocks a few steps further. For a cropped photo hexagon illusion, use light, medium and dark colored papers on the box sides, or try using similar-shaded photo scraps for an all-photo work of art. Follow the steps below to create your own hexagon illusion.

1 *After enlarging the pattern to fit your page, cut one of the blocks into pieces for a pattern using a craft knife and ruler (Figure 1). Keep a second copy of the pattern, uncut with each piece numbered, to use as a guide when reassembling.*

2 *Trace each piece of the block onto the appropriate colored or printed paper, using light, medium and dark shades to show dimension and perspective (Figure 2). Assemble the block.*

3 *Using a light box or sunny window, trace the pattern over the photo(s) and trim to fit the block (Figure 3). Accurate cutting will ensure properly fitting pieces. Repeat steps 1-3 for each block until all are complete. Crop and add center photo to complete design.*

Idea Hallie Schram (Bellgrade, MI), photos Lora Mason

Triad Optical Illusions *by Harry Turner; used with permission of Dover Publications, Inc.*

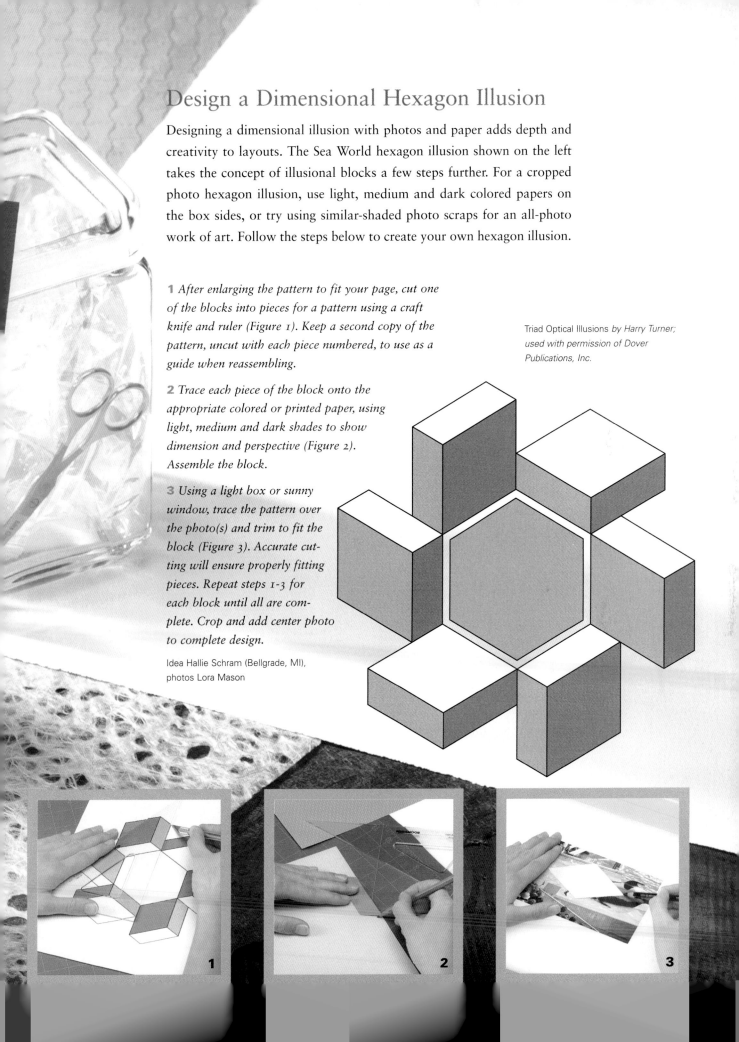

Gallery

WE ARE CONFIDENT THAT WE HAVE INSPIRED YOU to experiment with creative photo cropping on your own photos. As you can see in our gallery, many scrapbookers have already discovered the excitement it brings to scrapbook pages as they design cropped photo composites, each unique unto its own. Enjoy. Be inspired. Experiment. And please don't forget to send us a copy of your masterpiece!

1

2

3

1 Disney Anniversary Photomontage, Terri Sharp (Hillsborough, NY) **2** Framing With Slices, Pam Friis (Castle Rock, CO) **3** Angled & Cropped Collage, Dayna Silva (Katy, TX) **4** Photo Kaleidoscope & Silhouette Collage, Nancy Kazlauckas (Sauk Centre, MN) **5** Shaped Photo Mosaic, Tracy Beck (Salinas, CA) **6** Title as Photo Art, MaryJo Keith (Wildwood, MO) **7** Photo Kaleidoscope Variation, Idea Nancy Kazlauckas (Sauk Centre, MN)

Point Pinos Lighthouse

In September 1999, We went for
A trip over to the lighthouse in
Pacific Grove, CA

8

9

10

11

12

8 Illusional Photo Art, Terry Ann Benedict (Belt, MT) **9** Building an Illusional Scene, Julie Mix (Southlake, TX) **10** Honeycomb Photo Quilt, Veronique Grasset (Ruy, France) **11** Silhouetted Pop-Up Corral, Tracey Carpenter (Baldwin, NY) **12** Portrait Quilt, Lori Nelson (Gardners, PA) **13** Silhouetted & Layered Collage Scene, Sally Richards (Huntington Beach, CA)

13

Additional Page Instructions, Photo and Source Credits

Page 136

Photo Weaving

Weaving two of the same photos together is a fun cropping and reassembly technique that works great with any photo subject and any photo size. We used two 12 x 12" photo enlargements—one in color, the other in black-and-white. To create a two-tone woven photo, follow these steps.

1 Using a metal straightedge ruler and a photo-safe wax pencil, press lightly to draw vertical lines ½" apart across the color photo (Figure 1). Repeat this step on the black-and-white photo, drawing horizontal lines ½" apart down the photo. 2 Use your metal ruler and a craft knife to slice color photo strips apart. Number each strip on back in consecutive order to make reassembly easier (Figure 2). Repeat this step on the black-and-white photo as well. Then, trim black-and-white strips down to ⁷⁄₁₆" in width. By allowing ⁷⁄₁₆" less on black-and-white strips, weaving will be easier. 3 Weaving begins in the center, starting with the four center vertical color strips and the four center horizontal black-and-white strips (Figure 3). Our 12 x 12" photos, when cut into strips, resulted in 24 vertical and 24 horizontal strips. Our four center strips, both vertically and horizontally, were strips numbered 11, 12,

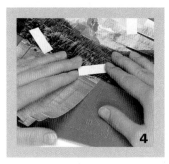

13 and 14. Weave strips together, matching photo features. Add a new strip each time you complete one weave, keeping a good balance going between the addition of color and black-and-white strips. 4 As the woven photo art grows larger, you might find it necessary to use removable artist's tape to hold the work-in-progress together (Figure 4). When all strips are woven together to complete the reassembly of the two photos, use permanent, photo-safe tape or a sheet of photo-safe adhesive on the back of the photos. Trim if needed and mount as desired. Remove artist's tape from the front of photos and wipe all fingerprints with an optical cleaning cloth or lint-free gloves. Photo John Budden, Owner of Shutter Priority, 303.460.9919

Pages 138-139

Photos Debra Fee (Broomfield, CO), Lora Mason, MaryJo Regier, Pennie Stutzman, Ken Trujillo

Page 140

Photos of children Lora Mason, Heritage photo Debbie Clark (Littleton, CO), Kodak Picture Maker photo courtesy of Eastman Kodak Co.

Page 172

Punch Quilting photo Anderson Studio 402.466.2951

Pages 186-187

A–photo die cut (Alphapics); B–letter template (Puzzle Mates), Idea & photos Melissa Weisner (Vienna, VA); C–letter punch (Family Treasures); D– Idea & photos Chris Peters (Hasbrouck, NJ); E–Fat Cat template (Frances Meyer); F–AlphaBetterLetter template (The Crafter's Workshop), Photo Deborah Mock; G–Wacky Letters template (Frances Meyer); H–die cut (Accu-Cut); I–Lettering Genie template (EK Success), Photos Erikia Ghumm; J–Classic Caps template (Frances Meyer), Photo Kelli Noto; S–Photo Denise Stuesse; T–die cut (Accu-Cut); U–Idea & design Connie Vogt (Frankfort, IL), Photos My Little Loves, Inc., 708.429.7570; V–Chubby Letters template (C-Thru Ruler Co.), Photo Kelli Noto; W– letter template (C-Thru Ruler Co.);

X–Lettering Genie template (EK Success), Photo Shelley Littlefield; Y–Photo Dona Carroll; Z–template (Frances Meyer), Photo Deborah Knapp; 1–AlphaBetterLetter template (The Crafter's Workshop); Photo Deborah Mock; 2–Classic Caps template (Frances Meyer); 3–Classic Caps template (Frances Meyer), Photo Kelli Noto; 4–6 AlphaBetterLetter templates (The Crafter's Workshop).

Page 224-225

How Great Thou Art © Copyright 1953 S.K. Hine. Assigned to Manna Music, Inc., 503.965.6112. Renewed 1981. All Rights Reserved. Used by Permission. (ASCAP)

Page 240

Silhouette Kaleidoscope Edges photo Portraits by Clare, 281.358.8965

Page 158 Conceal a Photo

Page 169 Photo Doll Chain Pattern

Sources

The following companies manufacture products used to create art or are featured in this book. Please check your local retailers to find these products. In addition, we have made every attempt to properly credit the trademarks and brand names of the items mentioned in this book. We apologize to any companies that have been listed incorrectly, and we would appreciate hearing from you.

Accu-Cut®
800.288.1670

AlphaPics™
508.822.7799

Close To My Heart™
888.655.6552

The Crafter's Workshop
877.CRAFTER

Creative Imaginations
800.942.6487

Creative Memories®
800.468.9335

The C-Thru® Ruler Company
800.243.8419

Current®, Inc.
800.848.2848

Darcie's Country Folk
800.453.1527

Delta Technical Coatings, Inc.
800.423.4135

Design Originals
800.877.7820

DMD Industries
800.805.9890

EK Success™
800.524.1349

Ellison® Craft & Design
800.253.2238

Family Treasures, Inc.
800.413.2645

Fiskars, Inc.
800.950.0203

Frances Meyer, Inc.®
800.372.6237

Graphix
800.447.2349

Keeping Memories Alive™
800.419.4949

Lighthouse Memories
909.879.0218

McGill, Inc.
800.982.9884

Nankong Enterprises, Inc.
302.731.2995
(wholesale only)

Plane Class™
319.378.8124

Provo Craft®
800.937.7686

Puzzle Mates™
888.595.2887

Shaping Memories
636.390.8529

Westrim Crafts/
Memories Forever®
800.727.2727

Wrights
800.660.0415

Xyron®
800.793.3523
(wholesale only)

Bibliography

Hoppen, Stephanie. *Decorating With Pictures*. New York: Clarkson N. Potter, Inc., 1991.

Lambert, Frederick. *Letter Forms: 110 Complete Alphabets*. New York: Dover Publications, Inc., 1972.

Turner, Harry. *Triad Optical Illusions*. New York: Dover Publications, Inc., 1978.

Walton, Stewart & Sally. *Creative Photocopying*. New York: Watson-Guptill Publications, 1997.

www. Polaroid.com

Illustrated Glossary of Cropping Techniques

3-D Photos

Using foam spacers between layers of photos to add depth and dimension can create 3-D photo art. See pages 162, 164, 166, 223, 225.

Borders

Photo borders put all of those leftover photo trimmings and snippets to use. Or, make great use of extra people shots and mini studio portraits by creating interesting photo page borders. See pages 198-202.

Building a Scene

Cutting and layering photos to build a scene is another fun cropping alternative. This works well with travel and people photos, whether vertical, horizontal or panoramic. See pages 223-226.

Collage

Collage is a collection of different photographs pasted together on a page. The elements may or may not overlap. See pages 163, 184, 214, 250, 251, 253.

Cropping

Traditionally, cropping means cutting or trimming a photo to keep only the most important parts of the image. This book gives creative cropping a whole new meaning, however, with a multitude of ideas, tips and techniques for using every bit of a cropped photo. See pages 139, 144-253.

Frames

Cropping frames into photos is an easy way to add class to your photos without taking attention away from the photo's subject, and the framing variations are many. See pages 148-154.

Illusions

Creating photo illusions through creative photo cropping extends the imagery of a conventional photograph. The trickery of photo illusions can exaggerate size and scale, pair unlikely photo subjects for interesting, comical effects or play upon dimension and light. See pages 241-249, 252.

Letters & Numbers

Another fun variation of shape cropping is cutting your photos into letters and numbers. Many templates are available for this use. We've provided examples of freehand cut designs to inspire you, as well. See pages 185-188, 251.

Mats

This cropping technique accents the photo layered beneath the mat and makes great use of photos that might otherwise go unused. See pages 193-197.

Mosaics

Pieced photo mosaics are a captivating way to display photos, whether you are cropping and reassembling a single photo or combining several photos. Photo mosaics are as diverse as the photos you use, each lending its own fresh originality to the finished design. See pages 204-216, 251.

Photo Kaleidoscopes

Making photo kaleidoscopes is "hands-on" cropping at its finest. They are intriguing and may seem complicated, but are really quick and simple to make using an equal number of regular and reversed photos. See pages 233-240, 251.

Photomontage

Montage is similar to collage, but the pictures or parts of pictures are superimposed, or overlapped, so that they form a blended whole. See pages 181, 184, 189, 250.

Pop-Up

Pop-up is the art of cutting, folding and mounting photos so that when you open a two-page spread, a design will "pop up" from the pages. See pages 168, 188, 253.

Punches

Discover the versatility and ease of using punches to crop photos. With so many different punches on the market today, photo cropping possibilities are as limitless as your imagination. See pages 143, 170-172.

Puzzles

Creating puzzles from cropped photos has grown tremendously in popularity. Whether you make your own actual puzzle photo pieces or use puzzle-like templates, it's a great way to join numerous, related photos on one page. See pages 189-192.

Quilts

Using the same techniques as quilters, you simply crop photos and mount, rather than cut fabric and sew. Quilting patterns and templates are easily adaptable to your individual photos, which makes it a perfect cropping technique for special occasion, holiday, scenic and people photos. See pages 217-222, 252, 253.

Shapes

Whether freehand cut or cropped with the use of a template, shape cropping adds simple style to scrapbook theme pages while narrowing the focus of the photo's subject. See pages 174-184.

Silhouettes

One of the most popular cropping techniques, silhouette cropping requires you to trim around the contours of the figures in your photos. For added interest, experiment with partial silhouetting to add a whole new dimension to page design. See pages 160-169.

Slices & Segments

Cropping a photo into random, angled, vertical or horizontal slices adds fresh perspective to page design. After cropping, you can reassemble the photos in countless ways for added impact. See pages 155-159, 250.

Stained Glass

Like many artistic techniques, this art can be readily adapted to the scrapbook page. The technique of cropping a photo or photos into "shards" and reassembling them will bring newfound radiance to your photos. See pages 227-232.

Weaving

Cropping and weaving two copies of the same photo together, one in color and one in black-and-white, is a unique and highly visual technique that works great with any photo subject and any photo size. See pages 136, 254.

SweetDreams

John
Michael
3 weeks
old

November
29
1997

MEMORY
MAKERS

Baby
Scrapbooks

IDEAS, TIPS AND TECHNIQUES
FOR BABY SCRAPBOOKS

**MEMORY
MAKERS
BOOKS**

DENVER, COLORADO

BABY

FACE

you've got the little baby face

face you've got

little baby

got the cutest little baby face you've go

Contents

p.350

p.308

DANIEL
4 MONTHS OLD

BEFORE YOU WERE BORN, I KNEW YOU. JEREMIAH 1:5

sasha, 6 mos.

anna, 6 mos.

Introduction

Of all the scrapbooks we are most likely to create, baby scrapbooks are among the most popular. When newborns enter our life, whether we're a parent, a grandparent or an aunt, they capture our hearts with deep emotion and unconditional love. Creating their baby scrapbook documents a piece of their life that they won't remember. It shows them they were loved and cared for, and points out personality traits that they've carried since birth.

Through my own three children, I have witnessed how swiftly their first year passes. And through the countless baby scrapbook pages graciously sent in by our readers, I've been able to share in the joyous celebrations of new life and all that babies bring to our lives and families. I hope you enjoy this same heartwarming experience as you look through the pages of this book.

We have featured many distinctive ideas. In addition, we tell the stories behind the pages. Included are page ideas for pregnancy, showers, name selection, birth, family and more. We also included adoption, ceremony and cultural pages, as well as treatments for portraits and heritage pages. And since a baby's daily activities are the equivalent of a parents' workday, we've paid extra attention to those all-important sleepytime, bathtime, mealtime, illnesses and boo-boos, playtime and growth pages. Lastly, we have included historical and informative baby-related sidebars and tips.

Baby's first year bustles with rapid growth and wondrous change. Few parents can resist capturing their wide-eyed innocence, toothless grins and miraculous "firsts" in photos. And with an estimated 4 million babies born each year, we're talking about a lot of photos.

Whether you're new to scrapbooking or a seasoned veteran, a grandparent or a parent-to-be, there is inspiration here for everyone.

DANIEL
(SEE PAGE 382)

michele and sasha, 1994

Michele

FOUNDER OF MEMORY MAKERS® MAGAZINE

Checklists

Like most parents, you will take a lot of photos and you will save everything!
Use these lists as the basic framework for organizing your photos and memorabilia.

BABY PHOTOS

- [ ] Positive pregnancy test
- [ ] Stages of pregnancy
- [ ] Mom receiving ultrasound
- [ ] Nursery preparation
- [ ] Baby shower guests, gifts, refreshments
- [ ] Hospital and hospital nursery
- [ ] Actual birth or adoption
- [ ] Doctor's and nurses' care
- [ ] Baby with doctor or midwife
- [ ] First time Mom and Dad hold baby
- [ ] Baby meets siblings and family
- [ ] Baby's tiny fingers and toes
- [ ] Leaving hospital and homecoming
- [ ] Baptism, christening, ceremonies
- [ ] Baby in baby equipment
- [ ] Sleeping and favorite blanket
- [ ] Nursing and mealtime
- [ ] Bathtime
- [ ] Playtime and favorite toys
- [ ] Monthly growth
- [ ] Baby with favorite stuffed animal each month
- [ ] Monthly weigh-ins and shots
- [ ] Milestones and firsts (see page 353)
- [ ] Funny faces
- [ ] Holidays
- [ ] Illnesses and boo-boos
- [ ] Baby with family pets
- [ ] Travel and outings
- [ ] Professional portraits

JOURNALING

Try to keep a daily journal that chronicles pregnancy, birth, the adoption process and life with baby. If there's no time for journaling, jot tiny notes on a calendar to add to the scrapbook later. Other things you might wish to record:

- [ ] *Reactions to news of pregnancy*
- [ ] *Pre-birth letter to Baby*
- [ ] *Name selection process*
- [ ] *Family tree with personal histories*
- [ ] *Trip to hospital*
- [ ] *Story of labor*
- [ ] *Timed contractions*
- [ ] *Names and comments of doctor and nurses*
- [ ] *Post-birth letters to Baby*
- [ ] *Beloved lullabies, poems, quotes and games*
- [ ] *Relationships with special people*
- [ ] *Milestones and firsts (see page 353)*
- [ ] *Baby's unique habits*

MEMORABILIA

- [ ] Baby's ultrasound photos
- [ ] Color-copied nursery wallpaper/fabric swatches
- [ ] Shower invitations and cards
- [ ] Squares cut from shower wrapping papers
- [ ] Gift list and registry
- [ ] Hospital bracelets, bassinet name tag
- [ ] Umbilical cord and circumcision rings
- [ ] Hospital and doctor bills
- [ ] Copy of doctor's notes
- [ ] Copy of birth certificate
- [ ] Foot and hand prints
- [ ] Birth announcement
- [ ] Newspaper clippings (see page 314, de-acidifying)
- [ ] Church bulletin announcements
- [ ] Congratulatory cards
- [ ] E-mail announcement and replies
- [ ] Letters to Baby from family and friends
- [ ] Ceremony mementos
- [ ] Baby photos of Mom and Dad
- [ ] Heritage baby photos of relatives
- [ ] Time capsule souvenirs
- [ ] Formula, food and diaper labels
- [ ] Growth and development records
- [ ] First lock of hair

Scrapbook Supplies

Use these lists of basic tools and supplies and unique design additions to help you get started on your baby scrapbook album.

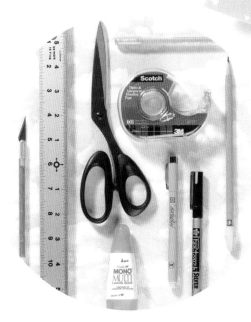

BASIC TOOLS & SUPPLIES

Albums & Scrapbook Pages
Colored and Printed Papers
Page Protectors
Pens and Markers
Permanent and Removable Adhesives
Ruler
Scissors

UNIQUE DESIGN ADDITIONS

Die Cuts
Fancy Rulers
Fancy Scissors
Journaling and Design Templates
Memorabilia Pockets
Paper Frames
Paper Trimmers/Cutters
Photo Corners
Punches
Stamps
Stickers

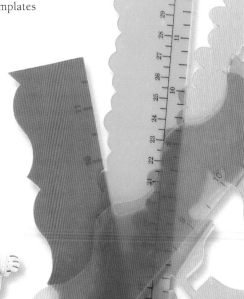

For preservation purposes, we strongly recommend the use of acid- and lignin-free albums and paper products, photo-safe adhesives, PVC-free plastics and pigment inks.

Children are the heart of the famil

Mommy
Daddy
and
Sawyer
1998

Getting Started

Infancy is fast-paced and filled with tender and meaningful moments. Moments that few parents, friends and relatives can resist capturing in photographs. While the thought of creating a baby scrapbook album may seem overwhelming, a little pre-planning, organization and inspiration will make the labor of love manageable and rewarding.

1 ORGANIZE PHOTOS AND MEMORABILIA

Use checklists on page 264 as a guide for organizing your photos and memorabilia. Jot down memories that your photos inspire which may have been neglected through journaling. Sort according to events or chronological order, determining if you will add pre-birth photos and memorabilia into the album. You may want to enlarge some photos. Assembling sorted photos and memorabilia to be included in the album will help determine the album's size, number of pages and page protectors needed.

2 ALBUM SELECTION

Albums come in three-ring binder, spiral, post bound or strap-style. The most popular, readily available sizes are 12 x 12" and 8½ x 11". Sturdy albums will withstand the test of time. Albums should provide an acid- and lignin-free and photo-safe environment for photos and memorabilia. Expandable albums are best for making baby's album an ongoing project.

3 VISUAL THEME SELECTION

Your baby album's visual theme will depend on your photos and memorabilia, as well as what fits your style and budget. The repeated use of a design element, color or unique border can give the album continuity. Shop with a list of page layouts and some photos to avoid any unnecessary spending.

4 CREATING LAYOUTS

Composition

Beautiful scrapbook pages and albums rely on balanced, eye-pleasing composition. For example, the page to the right is simple yet balanced. Consider using two-page spreads that are clean and basic as opposed to making each page a unique work of art. Save elaborate designs and fancy techniques for title pages and important photographs. Some basic concepts to help your page composition follow. And remember, layout an entire page or spread before mounting anything.

Focal Point

A scrapbook page may contain several photos, but one should be important enough to be a focal point. Use the rest of the page and photos to complement the focal point.

Creative Photo Cropping

Creative cropping breaks the monotony of a square or rectangular page while emphasizing the subject or removing busy backgrounds. You will find many successful examples of photo cropping throughout the pages of this book.

rhys, 9 mos.

Matting and Framing

You can focus attention on special photos with decorative mats and frames, which can be purchased or handmade with colored or printed papers, fancy scissors and templates. Selected colors should complement photos without stealing away any attention.

Adding Embellishments

Once your photos and memorabilia are in place, complete the layout by adding design embellishments such as stickers, die cuts, punched shapes and more.

5 JOURNALING

No page is complete without your own words to tell the story. Handwritten words add a personal touch. There are also computer fonts, lettering books and journaling templates available. We have also included lettering patterns and page title ideas (see pages 378-379) to help you. Try to tell your baby's story without relying solely on photos. Our journaling checklist (see page 264) will help bring your photographic story to life.

Morgan, Jackson, Aidan & Brendan
The Kelly Quadruplets
7 months old

Three Page Designs

We invited three artists to take a scrapbook challenge. In addition to a packet of the same scrapbook supplies (shown right), we also gave the three scrapbookers a set of photos of these cute quadruplets, provided by their mother, Tricia Kelly of Thousand Oaks, California. We then challenged the artists to unleash their personalities and imaginations on a baby scrapbook page.

While the three page designs are quite different, they all possess unique personality and imagination. And that's what scrapbooking is all about!

See page 382 for the materials included in the packets sent to the three artists.

Hug Please

TRY A SIMPLE BORDER PAGE

Michele's quick, basic design covers a 12 x 12" scrapbook page. She chose to use four individual portraits in an effort to capture the quadruplets as individuals. Note how Michele colored the stamped babies' outfits blue and pink, just as the real babies are dressed in the photos. Her easy, four-corner border, simple journaling and simple photo treatments also help keep the focus of attention on the photos themselves.

Michele Rank, Cerritos, California

Hug Me 1st, 2nd, 3rd and 4th!

TIE IT ALL TOGETHER WITH RIBBON

Linda's intermediate design incorporates silk ribbon, torn paper and miniature silk ribbon rosettes to help mimic the softness of the photos on this 12 x 15" scrapbook page. She has put her stamped babies with tiny strips of ribbon inside 3-D Keepers™ for the future addition of locks of hair from each baby.

Linda Strauss, Provo, Utah

Special Request, Please Open...

MAKE AN INTERACTIVE DRESSER

Efrat's advanced design showcases a whimsical, three-dimensional motif across a two-page, 8½ x 11" spread. The pop-ups and pull-outs emphasize the whirl of activity that there certainly must be with four babies in one house. Silhouette cut photos, stickers and the addition of magazine cutouts add to the unique personality of Efrat's design.

Efrat Dalton, Fort Collins, Colorado

Oh happy day!

On March 9, 1999, after 2 home pregnancy tests came out positive, (Tammy wasn't convinced the first time.) we learned we were expecting a baby! we caught the exciting moment with the self-timer on our camera. A visit to the doctor the following day confirmed the results of the tests.

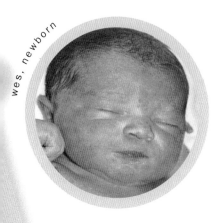

wes, newborn

jack, newborn

Getting Ready

A NEW BABY IS LIKE THE

BEGINNING OF ALL THINGS —

WONDER, HOPE, A

DREAM OF POSSIBILITIES

— *EDA J. LE SHAN*

We learn in an instant that a child is coming, but we believe it only in baby steps. The first flush of morning sickness. The little "swish-swish" of Baby's heart on the sonogram. When we search our souls for the name we've always known. Preparing for a baby means making room in your home and in your heart. But it will pass in the blink of an eye, so record it now. Save those ultrasound and pregnancy photos, shower cards and nursery fabric swatches. Record your emotions and life dreams, for they are about to come true.

emily, newborn

OH HAPPY DAY!
TAMARA SHIROMA
KAPOLEI, HAWAII
(SEE PAGE 382)

Lauren's Nursery

MATCH NURSERY DECOR

Sticker borders and stamped letters highlight photos of Cheri's garden-theme nursery. Start by layering photos on pale green parchment. For the title, stamp the beginning letters (Stampin' Up!) with green ink on gold paper; cut out and border with green dots. Stamp remaining letters directly on the background. Adhere fence, flower, leaf, butterfly and green line stickers (Frances Meyer). Stamp red ladybugs (Stampin' Up!).

Cheri O'Donnell, Orange, California

Marie's Story

While awaiting the arrival of their first child, David and Shawnee settled on a jungle theme for baby Alexis' nursery. David asked his mom, amateur artist Marie, to design a wall mural featuring jungle animals. Years earlier, Marie had painted David's childhood room with his beloved Fantastic Four® comic book characters.

After sketching the design in pencil on the bedroom wall, Marie put everyone in the family to work. "At first they were all scared to death that they would ruin the painting," says Marie. "But with a little encouragement, the mural slowly came to life."

The family painted lions, zebras, giraffes, elephants, monkeys, parrots and hippos, which Marie later re-created for a pop-up page in her scrapbook. Shawnee's favorite animals are rabbits, which you don't usually find in the tropics. "Of course there aren't any rabbits in the jungle," laughs Marie. "But our mural indeed has rabbits sitting on top of a giraffe."

By the end of the day all of the novice painters commented on how well they did. Their self-affirmation didn't surprise Marie one bit. "I believe we all have artistic ability," she says. "That ability just needs cultivating."

Marie Valentino, Happy Scrappin'
Shelton, Washington

See page 328 for instructions on how to make a bathtime pop-up.

Showered With Gifts

When Juanita adopted her daughter, she was showered with generosity. First, print title letters on blue paper. Cut each letter into a water droplet shape and mount along top borders. Print colored umbrellas (Sierra On-Line); mount along bottom borders. Silhouette cut and layer photos of baby gifts.

Juanita Yager, Gurnee, Illinois

UNIQUE BABY SHOWER GAMES

BINGO *Bingo with baby words instead of numbers.*

CREATE-A-CAPTION *Guests write captions for funny expressions of baby photos torn from magazines.*

DECORATE ONESIES *Guests decorate gift onesies with paints.*

DRESS BABY *Teams dress baby dolls fast and accurately.*

FILL BABY'S PIGGYBANK *Guests add pocket change to piggybank when "off limit" words or actions are exposed.*

GIFT BINGO *Bingo played during gift opening with gift words.*

GUESS THE BABY *Match each guest to his or her baby photo.*

IT'S IN THE BASKET *Display basket filled with baby items for 20 seconds; hide. Guests try to remember basket's contents.*

NAME GAME *Forming words with letters in Baby's name.*

OFF LIMITS *Certain action or word "off limits" during shower.*

RICE BOWL *Find safety pins in bowl of rice while blindfolded.*

ROUND-THE-TUMMY *Guests estimate size of Mommy's tummy with lengths of string or toilet paper.*

SCRAPBOOK *Guests make baby pages for Mommy to add photos to; guests write notes to Mommy and Baby.*

SHOWER-IN-A-BOX *Out-of-town relatives and friends participate in gift-giving by mail; opening of gifts is videotaped or photographed and sent to "guests" with thank-you notes.*

STORY-GO-ROUND *Start baby story with "Once Upon a Time..." Each guest adds to story; see what develops by "The End."*

TIME CAPSULE *Guests bring contemporary items to encapsulate for Baby to open some day.*

WHISPER CHAIN *One guest whispers baby advice to another guest. See how good the advice is once it has come "full circle."*

Baby Shower

Basic punches add quick decorations to Kim's festive umbrella. Use umbrella stencil (Puzzle Mates) to create umbrella from printed paper. Trim photos to fit umbrella. Cut rectangles for gift boxes. Trim strips for ribbons and freehand cut polka dot bow. For gingham bow, punch two medium hearts and a small circle. For polka dot flowers, punch medium flowers and $1/4$" circles. For edge of umbrella, punch medium flowers, small circles and mini swirls. Freehand cut lavender and silver handle.

Kim Heffington, Avondale, Arizona

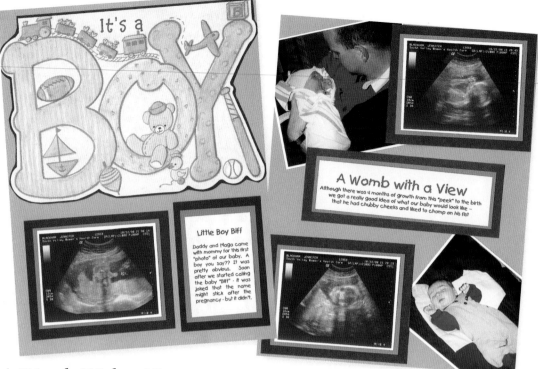

A Womb with a View

Although there was 9 months of growth from this "peek" to the birth we got a really good idea of what our baby would look like – that he had chubby cheeks and liked to chomp on his fist

Little Boy Biff

Daddy and Maga came with mommy for this first "photo" of our baby. A boy you say?? It was pretty obvious. Soon after we started calling the baby "Biff" - it was joked that the name might stick after the pregnancy - but it didn't.

A Womb With a View

MATCH BEFORE/AFTER PHOTOS

The ultrasound of Jennifer's son not only showed that he was a boy but also that he had chubby cheeks and liked to suck on his fist. After he was born, she took pictures of him in similar positions. To create this fun layout, use a blue or pink background. Double mat printed journaling (DJ Inkers) and ultrasound photos. Single mat photos and greeting card.

Jennifer Blackham, West Jordan, Utah

BABY DOLLS
Hand cut babies from printed paper; assemble. Add ¼" punched circles for cheeks and punched mini heart on dress; draw details.

Michelle Lizz King, Ceres, California

BABY'S DEVELOPMENT

From conception to delivery, Baby's miraculous growth is fun to follow.

1ST MONTH *Baby is a tiny, tadpole-like embryo, smaller than a grain of rice.*

2ND MONTH *Baby looks more human as facial features, fingers, toes, eyes and ears begin to develop.*

3RD MONTH *Baby is now 2½ to 4" long and weighs about ½ ounce. Organs are developing, including reproductive organs. Gender is still hard to detect.*

4TH MONTH *At 4 to 6" in length, baby nourishes from the placenta and is developing reflexes. Tooth buds, nails, hair, eyebrows, eyelids and eyelashes are forming.*

5TH MONTH *Mommy begins to feel movements of her 8 to 10" baby. Lanugo and vernix cover its body, hair begins to grow on its head and brows and white eyelashes appear.*

6TH MONTH *Baby weighs about 1¾ pounds and is about 13" long. All essential organs are formed.*

7TH MONTH *Three-pound Baby can now suck its thumb, hiccup and even cry. It can taste sweet or sour and responds to pain, light and sound.*

8TH MONTH *At 18" long and 5 pounds in weight, active Baby can now see and hear. Brain growth is tremendous but lungs are still immature.*

9TH MONTH *Weighing about 7 pounds and about 20" in length, Baby becomes less active in its confines as it prepares for birth.*

joshua, 2 mos.

LET'S GO TO THE VIDEOTAPE

"When Stephen was born, we didn't have a good camera or any good shots of him as a newborn," says Anne Heyen of Glendale, New York. "So we photographed shots from his video on the television screen with a new point-and-shoot camera from 4-5 feet away."

The Incredible Expanding Woman

SHOW PREGNANCY'S PROGRESSION

During four months of bed rest, the only time Cheri got "made up" was for these monthly photos. After collecting a pregnancy photo series, use a balloon template (Extra Special Products) to trim photos into balloon shapes. Silhouette a head photo and mount above pregnant body die cut (Accu-Cut). Journal and draw details with colored pens. Adhere heart and angel stickers (source unknown) on die cut.

Cheri O'Donnell, Orange, California

Life on the Inside

PROFILE A PRECIOUS PRISONER

The ID number for Melissa's "prisoner" was her daughter's actual birth date printed in the Brittanic Bold font (Sierra On-Line). To make the striped background, cut ½" white strips and space ½" apart on black paper. Write the birth story using a humorous "prison record" style. Print the title and story. Mat all elements with black paper.

Melissa Jordan, Cassville, New York

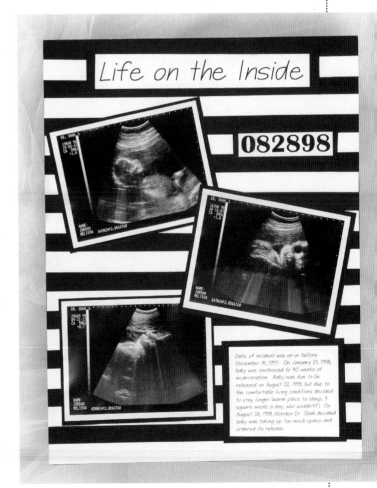

Expectation...

We found out that we would be blessed with a second child on Thanksgiving day! Well that's definitely something to be thankful for...

A new chapter in our lives is about to begin. We are both a little afraid... both excited... both wondering about the changes a new life will bring to our family...

Bethany is thrilled to find out there will be a little brother or sister joining her... She's telling everyone she is going to have a baby. She says there is a baby in her tummy too!

Nine months suddenly seems like such a short time to prepare... There is so much that needs to be done, and yet nine months seems almost an eternity to wait... What does this new baby look like? What kind of child will it be? The heart is already beating inside me, I am in awe of the precious gift that is growing inside my body...

Wonderment, Joy...

Expectation

REFLECT ON FUTURE BIRTH

Using a greeting card illustration, Dale wrote simply and beautifully about the joy and wonderment of expecting her second child. For the titles and first letters of each paragraph, use a thick blue calligraphy pen. Journal and draw embellishments using thin blue, green and pink pens.

Dale Caliaro, Oviedo, Florida

NAMING BABY

Naming Baby is a thoughtful and enlightened process. With heritage, cultural and religious considerations to ponder, as well as distinction, style and character attributes, the evolution of the naming process will continue to change over time.

TEN MOST POPULAR BABY NAMES...THEN AND NOW*

	1899			1999	
MALE	**FEMALE**		**MALE**	**FEMALE**	
1. John	Mary		1. Michael	Emily	
2. William	Anna		2. Jacob	Samantha	
3. George	Margaret		3. Matthew	Madison	
4. James	Helen		4. Christopher	Ashley	
5. Joseph	Marie		5. Joshua	Sarah	
6. Charles	Elizabeth		6. Austin	Hannah	
7. Frank	Florence		7. Nicholas	Jessica	
8. Robert	Ruth		8. Tyler	Alyssa	
9. Henry	Ethel		9. Joseph	Alexis	
10. Edward	Alice		10. Andrew	Kayla	

From the Social Security Administration's Office of the Chief Actuary

annelise, newborn

YOUR NAME

You got it from your father,
It was all he had to give.
So it's yours to use and cherish
For as long as you may live.

If you lose the watch he gave you,
It can always be replaced.
But a black mark on your name, son,
Can never be erased.

It was clean the day you took it,
And a worthy name to bear.
When he got it from his father,
There was no dishonor there.

So make sure you guard it wisely,
After all is said and done.
You'll be glad the name is spotless
When you give it to your son.

-Author Unknown

Sasha Kiev

TELL THE NAMING STORY

This page not only recalls the process of choosing Sasha's name but also lists Mom's and Dad's favorite names. First print the "What's in a name?" story directly on cream paper. Trace printed titles onto lavender paper using a purple pen. Mat story, photos and titles. Arrange elements on page and write favorite names. Freehand cut pink roses and lavender ribbons; punch small and mini swirls for centers. Use the swirl border punch #2 (Family Treasures) for the leaves.

Michele Gerbrandt, Memory Makers

INTRODUCING......

May flowers fill your heart with a fresh perspective and new life!

Our family has grown... and we have a new sprout!

JACK CONNOR WEGE BAYLESS

SPROUTED
MAY 5, 1999
9:55 AM
HT. 23 1/2 INCHES
WT. 10LBS. 3 OZS.

PROUD PARENTS

SCOTT AND KATY BAYLESS

BAYLESS FARMS
organically grown

FIVE MAGIC BEANS
NET WT 10 g

Magic Beans   (HYBRED)

Children are like seeds, in each there is a promise of the future. Nurture them with love.

type	inches	grows best	days to germinate
annual	23 1/2"	full sun	280

PLANTING INSTRUCTIONS

Sow in fertile soil giving lots of love and affection. Water and feed often. After becoming well established, harvest after 18-21 years. Comes from good stock.

tori, newborn

kendall drue, 3 days

Birth

WHEN OUR BABY STIRS AND STRUGGLES TO BE BORN, IT COMPELS HUMILITY: WHAT WE BEGAN IS NOW ITS OWN.

— ANNE RIDLER

As Baby makes his or her debut, thinking gives way to doing as new life springs forth. And trusted people are there to help. Your spouse, partner, doctor or midwife. Maybe older children. Try to dictate labor milestones for your partner to record. Maybe allow photos from discreet angles. Bask in the moment your child's eyes first meet yours. Then gather up everything: hospital bracelets, APGAR scores, headlines from the day's newspaper and announcements to help make these fleeing moments last on a scrapbook page.

marco, newborn

INTRODUCING JACK BAYLESS
KATY BAYLESS
ALHAMBRA, CALIFORNIA
(SEE PAGE 382)

THE RED ROSEBUD ON THE CHANCEL TABLE TODAY announces the birth of Ellis Levi Ackerman on February 11. Ellis was born to Chris and Sara Ackerman and very proud grandparents are Steve and Debra Rodney.

Ellis Levi Ackerman stepped into our lives on February 11th, 1999 at 5:14 in the morning

IT'S A BOY!

It's a Boy!

CREATE A PHOTO MOSAIC

As a neonatal nurse practitioner, Debra witnessed her grandchild's birth and performed his first physical exam. Her photo mosaic is the perfect way to document a fast-paced day. Titled by stickers (Mrs. Grossman's) and printed journaling, Debra's photo mosaic blends ten separate photos. Begin by using a ruler and pencil to lightly mark the horizontal and vertical cutting lines (to create 1" squares) on the back of the photo. Number the back of each square photo piece in chronological order to make reassembly easier. Slice photos vertically and horizontally on cutting lines using a small paper cutter. Piece together mosaic.

Debra Rodney, Tucson, Arizona

Special Delivery

POSTMARK THE NEW ARRIVAL

An old envelope provided the template for Arlene's pocket. Print the postmark onto solid blue paper using PrintShop Deluxe software (Broderbund). Mat with blue gingham. Unseal an envelope and trace the edges onto gingham paper; cut out, fold and seal. Arrange photo, printed journaling and stamped footprint encased in memorabilia pocket (3L Corp.) in envelope. Adhere "It's a Boy!" sticker (Frances Meyer).

Arlene Santos, Mililani, Hawaii

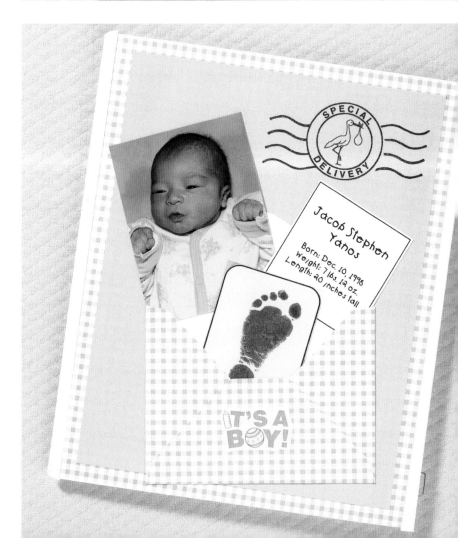

SPECIAL DELIVERY

Jacob Stephen Yanos
Born: Dec. 10, 1996
Weight: 7 lbs. 12 oz.
Length: 20 inches tall

IT'S A BOY!

jackson, 6 mos.

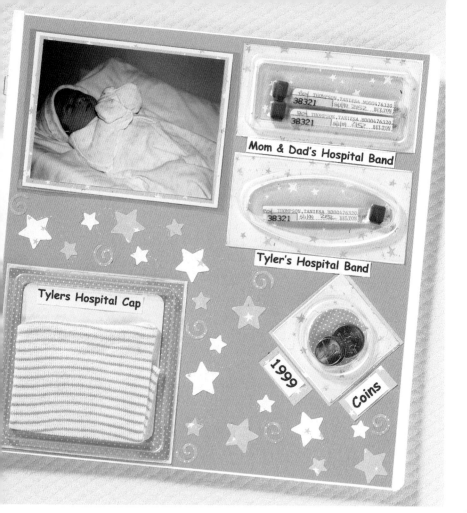

Mom & Dad's Hospital Band

Tyler's Hospital Band

Tylers Hospital Cap

1999

Coins

Tyler's Birth

DISPLAY 3-D MEMORABILIA

To protect the items related to her son's birth, Taniesa used 3-D Keepers™ (C-Thru Ruler Co.). These ¼" thick clear plastic boxes provide a sturdy home for just about any semi-flat object. Mount decorative paper beneath the boxes to help memorabilia stand out. To copy the star design, punch swirls and medium and small stars from printed paper. Draw details with silver pen. Print and mat titles. Double mat photo. Arrange elements on a dusty blue background.

Taniesa Thompson, Gilroy, California

Worth the Wait

SHOW DELIVERY BY THE CLOCK

Billie waited nine months and spent two days in labor to see her newborn son, a feat she documents in timely fashion. To make a similar page, cut a 7" black circle and a 6¼" white circle for clock face. Mount with freehand cut stem and hands; set time to your delivery time. Add cropped and silhouetted photos. Adhere number, letter and nursery stickers (Creative Memories). Finish with journaling.

Billie Martin, Seffner, Florida

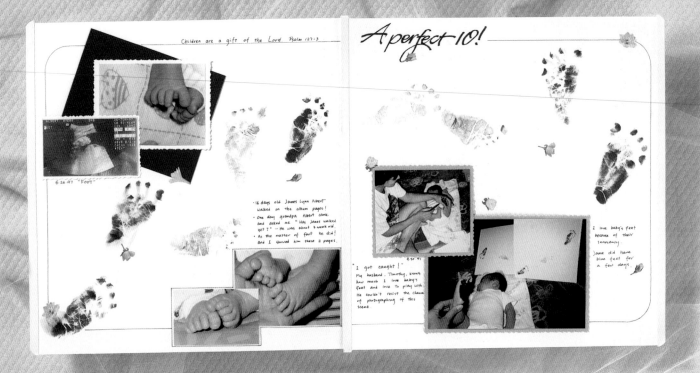

A Perfect 10!

STAMP PRECIOUS FOOTPRINTS

Hyeran's son had blue feet for a few days after "walking" on her page. She suggests that an easy way to stamp baby footprints is to first tape the paper to sturdy cardboard. Then, holding the ankle firmly, tap an ink pad onto baby's foot. Carefully stamp the footprint by pressing the paper against the foot. For the layout, first crop and mat photos. Draw title with a thick black pen. Draw thin black border lines, drawing corner curves using a small round object. Adhere rose stickers (Mrs. Grossman's). Journal with black pen.

Hyeran Albert, Martinez, California

Splashing Good News!

TUCK CARDS IN A PEEK-A-BOO POCKET

A duck shape is perfect for Tracy's country-style pocket page. First adhere a strip of gingham paper along the top of the background page. Draw a curved wavy line along the top of a separate page and cut away the top portion to create top of pocket. Punch ¼" holes along the wavy edge. Weave two lengths of yellow ribbon through the holes, starting from the outside edges, and tie a bow. Trace an enlarged duck die cut (Ellison) onto the pocket and cut out, creating the "peek-a-boo" opening. Adhere the pocket to the background page along the left, bottom and right sides. Using a wavy ruler, mount a wavy gingham strip along the bottom edge of the pocket. Punch small yellow ducks.

Tracy Haynes, Boynton Beach, Florida

Dear Justin,
You are one day old in this picture. You were loved from the very deepest parts of my soul from the day you were born. I was unprepared for what a special person you would become. My dreams for you are fulfilled every day as the story of your life unfolds. As I want to experience it with your unparalleled enthusiasm, may you always exceptional compassion. More than anything, and of our lives together. You to know, that I have loved every I want of the moment miracle of being your mom.
April 1999

Love Letter

PIECE A STAINED-GLASS FRAME

Karen's stained-glass technique provides a lovely frame for her one-day-old son. Start by cutting a vellum crescent for the moon. Trace a bear design onto vellum using a black pen. Color the backs of these elements with chalk. Outline the moon with black pen. To create the stained-glass window frame, cut vellum and black strips. Color one side of the vellum strips with colored chalks. Layer the vellum strips beneath black strips. Double mat photo and trim corners. Write a love letter to the newborn; adhere.

Karen Wilson-Bonner, Tapestry in Time, Livermore, California

TIPS FOR BETTER BABY PHOTOS

Babies are popular photographic subjects. For the best baby photos follow these simple tips:

- *Keep camera loaded and handy.*
- *Use the right film speed (400 inside, 200 outside).*
- *Hold camera steady.*
- *Experiment with soft, available lighting and no flash.*
- *Use flash in low light and to fill shadows.*
- *Back-lighting can silhouette baby or highlight hair.*
- *Side-lighting illuminates baby's profile.*
- *Get in close to eliminate busy backgrounds.*
- *Take both horizontal and vertical photos.*
- *Frame baby off-center.*
- *Get down to baby's level to capture perspective.*
- *Try black and white film; it's forgiving of skin blemishes.*
- *Thumb through magazines for photo inspiration.*

BRIDE'S HANKY BABY BONNET

"My son, Ethan, wore a 'Bride's Hanky' bonnet home from the hospital," says Donna Hasker, of Temple Hills, Maryland. "One day his bride can remove the stitches and use it on her wedding day."

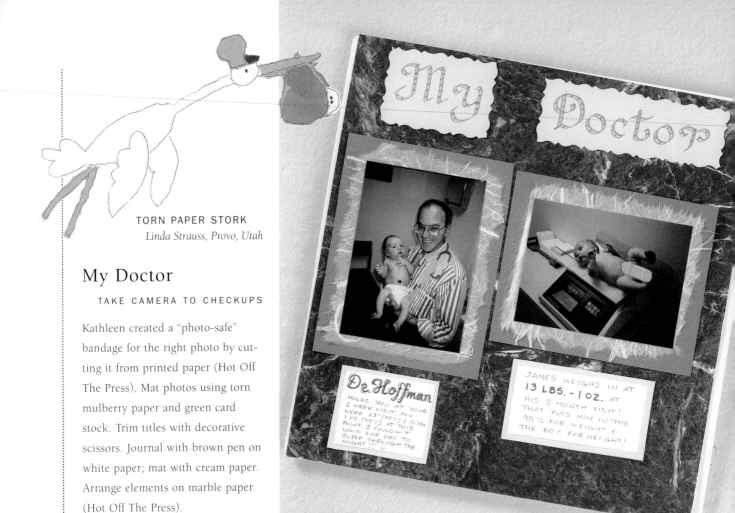

TORN PAPER STORK
Linda Strauss, Provo, Utah

My Doctor

TAKE CAMERA TO CHECKUPS

Kathleen created a "photo-safe" bandage for the right photo by cutting it from printed paper (Hot Off The Press). Mat photos using torn mulberry paper and green card stock. Trim titles with decorative scissors. Journal with brown pen on white paper; mat with cream paper. Arrange elements on marble paper (Hot Off The Press).

Kathleen Fritz, St. Charles, Missouri

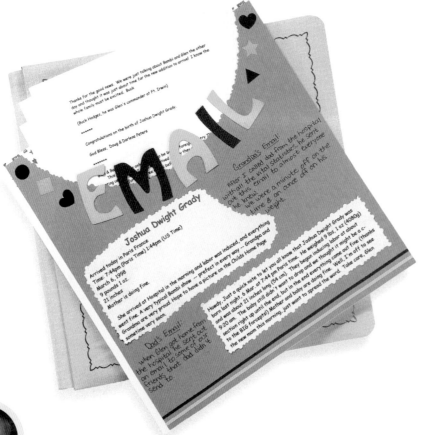

E-mail

SAVE COMPUTER GREETINGS

Congratulatory e-mails from friends and family fill Bamber's bright pocket. First mount printed paper (NRN Designs) on background page. Using a dinner plate, mark a cutting line on the top edge of the pocket; trim with decorative scissors. Adhere pocket to background page. Mount letter die cuts (Creative Memories). Adhere heart, square, circle and line stickers (Mrs. Grossman's). Trim printed e-mails with decorative scissors. Journal with red pen.

Bamber Grady, Fort Hood, Texas

mitch, 4 mos.

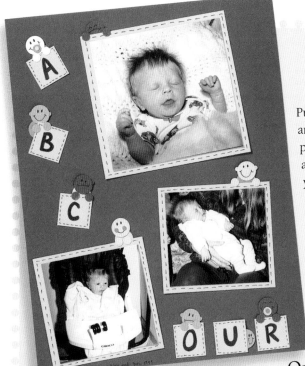

PUNCH ART

Punch art is easy. All you need are a few punches and some paper to create captivating art from simple, punched paper shapes. Punch art adds charm and whimsy to scrapbook pages. It can also extend your scrapbooking budget by making good use of paper scraps that might otherwise be thrown away. Punch art truly offers versatility and endless possibilities. There are two more cute examples of baby punch art on page 318. And for more baby-related punch art, see *Memory Makers Punch Your Art Out Volumes 1 & 2*. (See page 383 for ordering information.)

Our Baby

MAKE PUNCH ART ALPHABET BABY BLOCKS

Anissa's punch art alphabet baby blocks accent a simple page spread of unrelated baby photos. To make this spread, mount mint green matted photos on a forest green background. Punch 1" squares (Family Treasures) for blocks from mint green paper. For babies, punch ⅝" or small circles for heads and shoulders, ¼" round hand punch for hands and pacifiers and ⅛" round hand punch for ears, cheeks and pacifier grips and ¼" swirls (Family Treasures) for hair; assemble and adhere to blocks (see below). Finish with punched letters (Family Treasures), pen stroke stitching on blocks and photo mats and face details.

Anissa Stringer, Port Ludlow, Washington

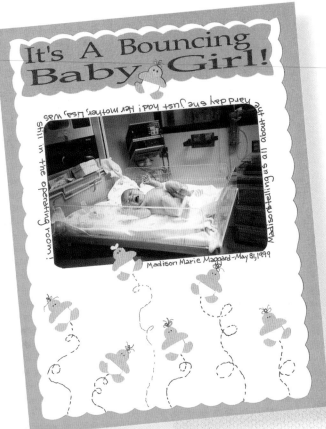

It's a Bouncing Baby Girl!

PUNCH TINY DIAPERED NEWBORNS

Julie's first granddaughter inspired these whimsical babies made with a teddy bear punch. For the background, trim white paper with large scallop scissors and layer on blue or pink. Print title and trim with scallop scissors. Round photo corners. Punch bears from flesh-colored paper, trimming off the ears. Punch an equal number of white bears, trimming into diaper shapes. Arrange babies with diapers. Draw dashed curly black lines and pink bows if desired.

Julie Bahr, Blue Springs, Missouri

News on the Day Gigi Arrived

EDIT PERSONALIZED FRONT PAGE

Joyce cut and pasted articles summarizing current events on the day her daughter was born. To make her own front page, Joyce started with a headline cut from a local paper. Cut out and arrange different articles, including the birth announcement if available. Photocopy and reduce onto white paper. For the page background, trim right edge of mauve paper using a scallop ruler to draw the cutting line. Punch small hearts. Joyce then color copied and enlarged the Diaperene® logo baby; cut out and layer with newspaper.

Joyce Schweitzer, Greensboro, North Carolina

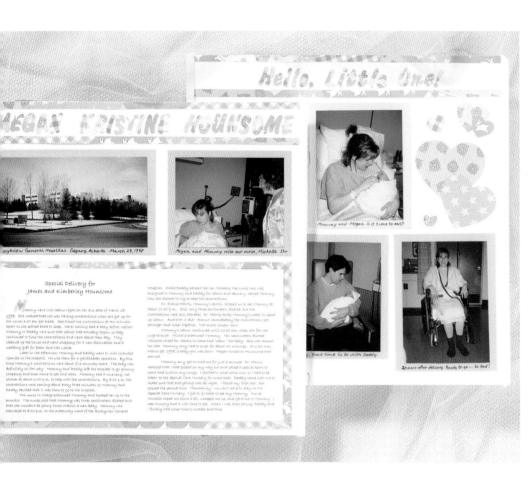

Megan Kristine Hounsome

JOURNAL ABOUT BIRTH

To make the title, Kimberley printed the letters on white paper using the Challenge Extra Bold font (Microsoft). Then she traced the letters onto the wrong side of printed paper (Frances Meyer) and cut them out with cuticle scissors. To complete the layout, cut matching strips of printed paper to border the title letters. Mat photos and the printed birth story. Write photo captions.

Kimberley Hounsome
Calgary, Alberta, Canada

Krista's Story

A mother-to-be's worst fears came true for Krista when her water broke prematurely during her 19th week of pregnancy. During several uneasy weeks of waiting, hoping and praying, the baby maintained stability. But when Krista began having contractions, the doctors sadly informed her that their fourth child was no longer showing a heartbeat and would be stillborn. The family was devastated.

Krista found that making a scrapbook page about Elizabeth helped her in her journey of grief. "I wanted a page to honor her brief time with our family and that the kids could look at when they feel like seeing her or talking about her," says Krista. Some of Elizabeth's mementos, however, were too painful to include in the album.

Krista finds the pages are a good way to talk with others about Elizabeth. She especially appreciates the times when neighbors or family see Elizabeth's tribute. "It makes me feel better that someone is interested in her," says Krista.

Krista Lee Feairheller, Kettering, Ohio

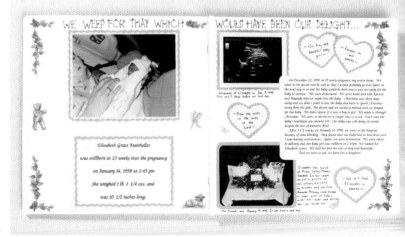

Punch Art Album

Amy Talarico, Northglenn, Colorado

Punch art offers a world of endless possibilities for baby scrapbook albums. The album that Amy created for her daughter is a gorgeous testament to the dimensional simplicity of baby punch art.

Amy had a Lucy Rigg™ baby book, which she adored. However, she wanted to create a scrapbook album that would last forever, complete with page protectors. Her solution was to combine elements from the Lucy Rigg book with her own scrapbook and punch art talents to create a truly unique baby scrapbook album.

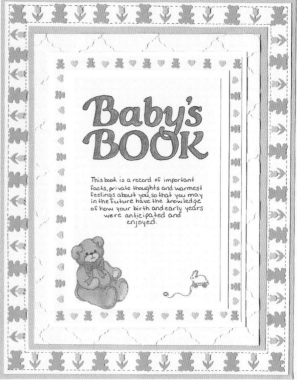

Coming Home

The day and date ___Monday December 29, 1986___
Who came to take you home ___Grandma Haliw & Aunt Diane Haliw___
Where your family lived at the time ___we lived with Grandma___
___Haliw at 2305 W 92nd Ave #111 in a trailer.___
Who was waiting to greet you ___Aunt Kristy Haliw, Cousin Tabi___
___Haliw and Uncle Bob Haliws girlfriend Natalie Kaylor.___
How your room was decorated ___you shared a room with___
___mom. It was small but it was ours.___

Amy's consistent use of a few simple punches and decorative scissors, combined with soft pastel papers and extensive journaling, give the album its classic appeal.

Amy spent untold hours creating the punch art and placing it carefully on the pages. Her album is a record of important facts, private thoughts and warmest feelings about her daughter. The result is a scrapbook album that gives her daughter the knowledge of how her birth and early years were truly anticipated and enjoyed.

Adoption

Adoptive families make memories that are unique to their experience: fragments of the search for their child, word of the baby's birth, details about the child's native country or biological family. All are vital to record, for adopted children will ask questions one day that your baby scrapbook album may help answer.

WE'RE HOME!

Frank & Maureen Robertazzi's 22-hour flight from China to New Jersey with their newly adopted baby landed at night, resulting in dark, unappealing photos. To enhance the photo of Aubri looking out the plane window, Frank removed the dark background by adding a digital photo of New York City at sunset. "It's the greatest city in the world," says Frank.

Maureen Robertazzi, East Hanover, New Jersey

Sharon's Story

Sharon stood in the middle of the Haitian orphanage surveying over 80 children. She felt overwhelmed by the inquiries posed. "Will you be my mama?" and "Can I go live with you in Canada?" With a husband and three boys waiting anxiously for her at home, Sharon wondered how she could possibly choose the right children to adopt.

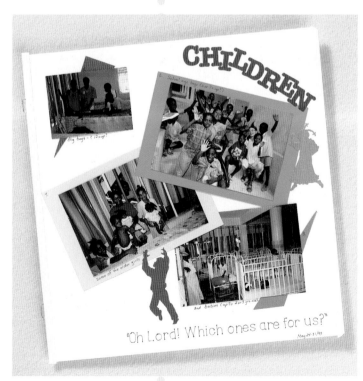

"I wanted to take them all," says Sharon. "But I knew I couldn't." She eventually narrowed her picks down to a two-year-old girl and a pudgy baby boy. All too soon after the selection came a tearful goodbye, with promises to the two children that they could come live with their new family soon.

Daniel and Amanda finally arrived to a joyous welcome from their new family following 17 months of seemingly endless waiting. After watching her older boys treat the newcomers like guests for months, Sharon was actually relieved the first time she heard all of the kids squabbling. "Any mother gets tired of her children fighting," says Sharon. "But this time I thought, 'Oh! We're finally a family.'"

Sharon Fehr, Fort St. John, British Columbia, Canada

Babies Are Heaven Sent

PRESERVE ADOPTION ANNOUNCEMENT

Chris begins baby Joey's adoption story with a simple page showcasing his announcement card. Mount yellow triangles on page. Adhere announcement and cropped photo. Embellish with stickers (Mrs. Grossman's, Sandylion).

Chris Peters, Hasbrouck Heights, New Jersey

Adoption

WRITE A THOUGHTFUL ACRONYM

This layout honors Michele's best friend, Becky Homan, who adopted twin girls born prematurely. Start by mounting the adoption announcement across the center of the layout. Mat photos and printed journaling using soft colors and decorative scissors. Adhere baby booties die cut (Making Memories) and small punched bears. Color in printed letter outlines for the word "adoption" with colored pencils.

Michele Lea, Oxford, Ohio

Adoption Album

Melanie Penry Mitchell, Overland Park, Kansas

Scrapbooks have proven to be an important tool for teaching adopted children about their past and their path, as they became part of a new family. Melanie's special album tells the story of the journey to adopt Mary, a Chinese baby girl, from start to finish: the ocean of paperwork, the months of waiting, packing for the trip to Beijing, sightseeing in China before getting Mary and meeting friends and family back in the United States.

Another fun and unique aspect of Melanie's album is her rebus journaling on the clothing page. It successfully documents the layers and layers of clothing Mary was wrapped in on the day of her adoption–a good idea since the adoption director asked for all of the clothes back except for the quilted suit seen in the center photo.

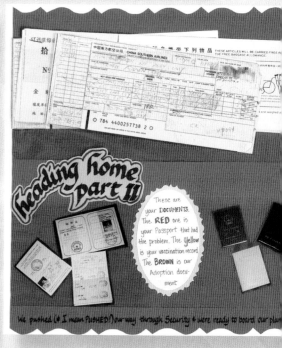

It's Official!!

They called us back & looked over our paperwork. We expected an "interview" but all they asked was if we had moved since we applied. A little small talk & then "Ta Da"- You were OurS Forever! YIPPEE!!

This is one of my FAVORITE pictures! You look so cute/happy!

Melanie employs hand-lettered journaling, great photos and lots of memorabilia throughout the album for a truly personal touch. And Mary, now 3, loves to look at her memory book. "You can never fill in all the blanks for adopted children, but it's important for her to know what a great experience it was to become a family," says Melanie. "We wouldn't have traded it for anything."

We wished, hoped, prayed & dreamed but never realized what a wonderful child you would be & how much we would fall in love with you!

When You Wish Upon a Star - Your Dreams Come True!

... journaling to you many years ago— We didn't know then that we had to wait for you to be born — But you were worth the wait!

a happy, exhausted family

We travelled around the world on an extraordinary trip we'll never forget...

to bring you home and make us a family forever and ever

A baby's body is a joy and delight in his parents arms

Aaron

Jan 1997

kirstie and nathan, newborn

akemi and alexis, 1 mo.

Family

A BABY IS GOD'S

OPINION THAT LIFE

SHOULD GO ON.

— CARL SANDBURG

A baby's urgent cries and blissful smiles enliven our spirits and renew our family bonds. What was once a collection of individuals with singular needs now becomes a unified circle of caregivers. This warmth and unity of purpose changes families forever. Mark it with photographs of those first feedings with Grandma, sibling inter-actions and precious snuggles with Daddy. A handwritten sample of your baby's sleep schedule and a list of first-time visi-tors will also make great additions to Baby's scrapbook album.

bryan, jessica and nile, 3 mos.

A BABY'S BODY...
DEANNA HAMMER
KELOWNA, BRITISH
COLUMBIA, CANADA
(SEE PAGE 382)

Sarah and Grandma

CHRONICLE A NEW RELATIONSHIP

The dusty colors of Liza's layout create a gentle setting. Start with pale yellow for the page background. For top border, trim edges of blue strips using the Teardrop Corner Lace Edge punch (Family Treasures) with the guides removed. For title, adhere outlines of letter stickers (Creative Memories) to floral photos; cut out each letter leaving a ¹⁄₁₆" border. Crop and mat photos using the Teardrop Corner Lace Edge and corner rounder punches. Mat oval for journaling. Cut and layer pieces for baby in high chair. Journal with black pen.

Liza Wasinger, Fairfax, Virginia

Cathryn's Story

Cathryn was returning to work following the birth of daughter Natalie and required child care for her baby and older son, Win. Luckily, Cathryn's niece Alice desired to attend the junior college near her home. Alice found a home, and Cathryn a trusted caregiver for her children.

The house was soon filled with Natalie's squeals as she played with Alice. "I could see them forging a very sweet bond," remembers Cathryn. Alice's fiance, Aaron, and twin brother, Jake, joined her in doting on Natalie.

Cathryn's scrapbooking supplies frequently engulfed the living room table, so it wasn't long before Alice was hooked on the hobby.

Alice also provided Cathryn with welcome diversions. "We painted our toenails purple and bought toe rings, danced to Janet Jackson and watched 'Road Rules' on MTV," says Cathryn. "For me it was a yearlong slumber party."

Alice now attends San Francisco State and doesn't get to see the family as much. When she does get to visit, Natalie joyfully runs to the door calling for her cousin 'La La'.

Cathryn Vance, Santa Rosa, California

alexis, 13 mos.

katelyn, 4 mos.

PHOTO TRADITION

"My dad has pictures of all seven of his grandchildren in his cowboy hat," says Amy Talarico of Northglenn, Colorado. "It's a family tradition now!"

Austen and Mommy

COMBINE COLOR WITH BLACK-AND-WHITE

Cindy's color photos and classic black-and-whites capture the timelessness of a mother's love. For the background, adhere border stickers (Mrs. Grossman's) on light khaki card stock. Cut a sheet of soft plum paper in half diagonally to form triangles. Crop and mat photos using decorative scissors and templates. Double mat title using deckle scissors and corner rounder punch. Accent title with small flower sticker (Mrs. Grossman's).

Cindy Mandernach, Fraser, Michigan

I Love My Aunts

Kelley took the time to photograph her baby with five doting aunts for this special scrapbook page. To copy the look, start with floral background (Frances Meyer). Crop photos and trim corners using Nostalgia corner scissors (Fiskars). Mat photos with striped paper (Hallmark) and trim mat corners. Mount light green triangles beneath each mat corner. For title words, adhere letter stickers to white paper and trim edges with decorative scissors. Mat with light green paper.

Kelley Blondin, Grand Blanc, Michigan

Snuggle Your Daddy

SHOWCASE A TENDER MOMENT

Amy's page features a favorite father-son snapshot. Create the border by trimming red strips with decorative scissors; mount along top and left edges of background paper (MPR Assoc.–paper discontinued). Mount ⅜" strip of striped paper (Provo Craft) along top edge. Mat photo with red paper; mat again with striped paper. Cut and mat hearts using red and striped paper. Draw black line accents. Adhere gold letters (Making Memories) to red paper and cut out. Write remaining title letters with red pen.

Amy Giacomelli, Monrovia, California

mackenzie, 6 mos.

A Father — holds his son's hand for a little while, but his heart forever.

October 3, 1998

War Eagle Mill, Arkansas

PHOTO KALEIDOSCOPES

Photo kaleidoscopes are made by using multiples of both the original and the reversed (or mirrored) image of a photo. Cutting these photos on an angle and piecing them together again will give you a dramatic kaleidoscopic design.

For best results, select a photo that has vivid colors, good light quality, lots of activity, repetitive patterns or intersecting lines. For more on creating photo kaleidoscopes, see *Memory Makers Photo Kaleidoscopes™*. (See page 383 for more information.)

A Father

MAKE A PHOTO KALEIDOSCOPE

Donna's photo of her husband and son captures a touching moment that creates an endearing photo kaleidoscope. To make your own photo kaleidoscope, first mount background paper of choice. Then follow the directions at right; trim to frame photo and mount. Mat a favorite poem (as Donna did), photo or other artwork; mount in center.

Donna Pittard, Kingwood, Texas

1 *For a 12 x 12" page, start with four regular and four reversed-image (made by photo lab, printed from flipped negative) photos. Place a clear, 45° triangle on one photo to determine cutting lines. Move it around until the part of the picture you wish to use is visible beneath the triangle (Figure 1). Find three distinct reference points on the photo, which fall along the edges of the triangle. You will cut through these exact points on each original and on each reversed-image photo.*

2 *Line up your triangle to match the three preselected reference points on each photo. With a craft knife, cut the photo using your triangle as the straight edge. Repeat exact cut on the seven remaining photos (Figure 2).*

3 *Using one cut piece from a regular photo and one from a reversed-image photo, place cut sides together, matching them into mirror-imaged pairs along your predetermined reference points. Secure with removable tape. Repeat with all pairs of photos; assemble into page border matching all reference points. Trim center opening to frame poem, photo or other artwork; mount (Figure 3).*

Note: For an interesting variation, see page 369 for how to make photo kaleidoscope mats.

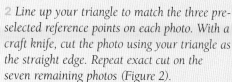

Daddy's Little Princess

CRAFT A ROYAL PAGE

Paper piecing and punch art helped Christiane savor this father-daughter moment. Print title and mat with pink. Punch large flowers and small circles. Layer on photo mats; adhere photos. Freehand cut crowns from gold glittery paper (Sandylion), blonde hair and dresses from floral paper (source unknown). Punch large and small flesh hearts for body. Punch large and small circles for faces. Draw faces with black pen; smudge cheeks with pink chalk.

Christiane Wilson-Grove, Kirkland, Washington

1-2-3 Kids

WATCH A FAMILY GROW

Charlotte's thought bubbles humorously illustrate her sister's growing family. To re-create this funny page, mat photos using colored rectangles and triangles. For the numbers corresponding to each child, adhere number stickers (Creative Memories) to small ovals. For the thought bubbles, freehand cut cloud shapes and punch ¼" circles. Write thoughts and outline clouds and circles. Adhere footprint stickers (Creative Memories, Frances Meyer).

Charlotte Wilhite, Fort Worth, Texas

Big Brother, Little Sister

CAPTURE SIBLING BONDING

The birth of little sister Rachel made such an impact on big brother Ryan that Jill wanted to honor their special relationship. Start with a selection of sibling photographs; silhouette all but one. Freehand cut the title letters from blue and pink gingham paper. Layer photos with letters. Journal with blue and pink pens.

Jill Andersen, Marietta, Georgia

Little Sister Store

LAUGH AT SIBLING RIVALRY

A funny "sibling rivalry" poem aptly fit the result of Kelley's attempt to photograph her two daughters. To create the "store," mat photo with blue paper. Trim bottom edge of dark pink rectangle for roof. Layer stickers (Mrs. Grossman's) along bottom edge of photo. Print the poem on cloud paper (Hallmark) and cut into a cloud shape. Cut an additional cloud shape. Mat clouds with blue paper. Adhere sun die cut (source unknown). Journal and draw blue dots.

Kelley Blondin, Grand Blanc, Michigan

Our Family Has Grown By Two Feet

STAMP SOME TINY FOOTPRINTS

A catchy title and matching footprints highlight Laura's new-baby layout. For the border, cut ¾" strips from yellow printed paper (Keeping Memories Alive). Stamp blue title letters (Close to My Heart™/D.O.T.S.).

Round corners of stamped footprints. Mat photos and footprints with red printed paper (Keeping Memories Alive). Cut two additional circle photos. Journal with blue pen.

Laura Thompson, Spanish Fork, Utah

my daddy does silly things with me

my daddy can touch his finger to the moon

He comforts me when I'm sick

My Daddy and Me Theme Album

FOCUS ON BABY'S ULTIMATE HERO

Ruth gave each of her twin daughters a storybook of her special bond with Daddy for a one-of-a-kind Christmas gift. The books' easy-to-read captions and the fun-loving use of stamps and humor make these storybook albums a perennial favorite of Ruth's family. Note how the photos selected successfully fit the limited scope of the book–My Daddy and Me. "The girls love their stories about what they did and how they acted as babies," says Ruth.

Ruth Freitas, North Dartmouth, Massachusetts

For more baby specialty album ideas, see pages 290, 294, 306, 329, 349, 359 and 375.

Sewing Album

Madeline Gordon, Orlando, Florida

Madeline made her tribute theme album, Nannie's Dream Stitches, as a Mother's Day gift in 1998. Madeline's mother, an accomplished seamstress, makes heirloom-style dresses for granddaughter, Ellie Claire.

Nannie's Dream Stitches

Fabric: Sea Island Cotton
1½ yds. at $26.⁰⁰ per yd.

Pattern: Party Ribbons smocking
Cherry Williams Bishop

Size: 1 (18 mos)

Notes: Nannie made a similar dress for Sarah when she was one. I loved it so she made it when I was pregnant with Grant. He never wore it.

Ellie Claire   July 1997

"I had 'sew' much fun working with my mother on the dresses and putting together an album to document these priceless heirlooms," says Madeline. "When she received the gift album, she was nearly in tears and said it was the most thoughtful thing anyone had ever done for her."

As Ellie Claire's collection began to grow, so too did Madeline's desire to document her mother's handiwork by photographing Ellie Claire in her dresses and putting them in a special album.

Madeline uses fabric swatches from the dress as background "paper." Most of the dresses are hand-smocked with great detail and the extensive journaling about each dress makes this album a one-of-a-kind historical keepsake.

Ceremonies & Culture

All cultures have private and public celebrations to welcome babies into the family and the community. For your baby scrapbook album, save ceremony invitations and letters to Baby from loved ones to mark this special time when all commit to the care and protection of your child and all children.

Certificate of Baptism

DISPLAY JOYOUS MOMENT IN ELEGANCE

Donna chose elegant, laser-cut frames to showcase these precious photos of her twins' baptismal celebration. To make a similar spread, frame cream card stock background with ⅛" strips of taupe card stock. Mat baptism certificates on taupe card stock; adhere. Double frame photos with laser-cut frames (SDL Corp.); adhere. Add stickers (Mrs. Grossman's); journal with gold ink.

Donna Pittard, Kingwood, Texas

Alissa Rose

REPRODUCE A CHERISHED GOWN

(RIGHT) Teresa's paper-piercing mimics the smocking of her baby's gown. Add ½" strip of trimmed polka dot paper to black background. Crop photos; mat and adhere. Freehand cut dress, bonnet and name. Pierce dress and bonnet with a pin to add detail; layer around photos. Add journaling.

Teresa Quick, Cabot, Arkansas

alexis, 6 mos.

CJ's Dedication

PRESERVE A PRAYERFUL MOMENT IN TIME

Julie used photos of CJ's church dedication and journaled a special blessing as a reminder of God's love for him. Double mat ceremonial photo on blue and angel paper (Design Originals); trim with deckle scissors and adhere. Mat family photos on blue paper; trim with deckle scissors and adhere. Trim a 1" strip of angel paper with deckle scissors; place at bottom of page. Journal with blue ink.

Julie Staub, Loveland, Ohio

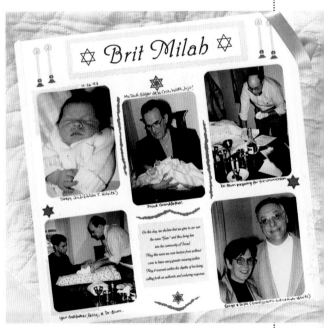

Brit Milah

CONFIRM FOREFATHERS' COVENANT

Annette's page commemorates son Julian's introduction to the Jewish community. Trim photo corners; adhere. Print title on white paper; trim with deckle scissors. Mat title on cream paper; trim with deckle scissors and adhere. Print blessing on cream paper; trim with deckle scissors and adhere. Finish with tiny strips of blue paper trimmed with deckle scissors and Judaic stickers (Creative Memories).

Annette Hilvitz, Overland Park, Kansas

The Blessing

CAPTURE ANCESTRAL CULTURE

Margie used a purple background, the color of royalty, for her page celebrating nephew Alec's traditional Japanese baptism at the landmark Meiji Shrine in Tokyo. Using purple lilac paper (Hot Off The Press) for a background, adhere double-matted photos. Finish with rattle and star die cuts (Hallmark) and journaling.

Margie Higuchi, West New York, New Jersey

Naming Ceremony

PRESERVE RITE OF PASSAGE

Kimathi Onome's first rite of passage was an ancestral naming ceremony performed by a priest trained in the Akan (Ghana, West Africa). The symbols on Sekile's page are taken from a symbolic language called Adinkra and from her own inspiration. To begin, crop and trim photos; adhere to page. Trim two 1" strips of tan card stock with deckle scissors; mount on outer edge of pages and add gold photo corners (Frances Meyer). Journal on tan card stock; trim with deckle scissors and adhere. Freehand draw symbols in gold ink. Finish with pen stroke stitching around photos.

*Sekile Nzinga-Johnson,
Lanham, Maryland*

kira, 8 mos.

Dutch Nursery Rhymes

RECORD FAVORITE LULLABIES IN NATIVE TONGUE

Dutch native Nicole and her husband sing Dutch songs to baby Destinee in an effort to raise her in a bilingual household. The scrapbook pages will help her remember these cultural melodies when she is older. To make a similar layout, mount red and white trimmed paper on a royal blue background. Draw ribbon border in black ink. Freehand cut flag and flagpole; adhere. Layer trimmed and matted photos. Layer double-matted, hand-lettered nursery rhymes and matted title. Adhere windmill cut from printed paper (Northern Spy) embellished with punched tulips. Add pen stroke stitching on windmill and flag to finish.

Nicole Ramsaroop, Orlando, Florida

Boys' Day

SHOWCASE CULTURAL SYMBOLISM

Every year, Jolene creates a page illustrating the symbolic significance of Boys' Day, a traditional Japanese holiday. In this manner, baby Brandon will grow up with an understanding of those who came before him. Start with a red background. Use Crayola® mini stamp marker to stamp yin/yang symbol on background paper. Photocopy "happi coat" kimono for border strips. Trim and crop photos. Double mat oval photo with red paper and kimono paper; trim edges with decorative scissors. Silhouette crop full-body photo; adhere with foam spacer. Finish page with journaling, arrow and target from kimono paper and origami koi fish.

Jolene Wong, Walnut Creek, California

Heritage

To know who they are, children must know where they came from. Babies' connections to their ancestors are biological, but their bonds to family are everlasting. Showcasing family resemblances and displaying your family tree and history will help your child find his or her place in the world.

Family Resemblance?

YOU BE THE JUDGE

Tracy color copied her and her husband's baby pictures to create this side-by-side comparison. Start by writing the page title with thick black pen on a tan background. Mat and layer photos. Journal with black pen.

Tracy Yonker, Alto, Michigan

Ancestors

PASS DOWN FAMILY HERITAGE

Along with a detailed genealogy, Linda included quotes from famous African-Americans about the value of family heritage. Print family tree (Family Tree Maker, Broderbund Software) or draw by hand. Print photo caption and quotations; mat with yellow paper. Mat baby photo with star die cut (Hallmark). Layer elements with star printed paper (Frances Meyer).

Linda Keene, Golden Valley, Minnesota

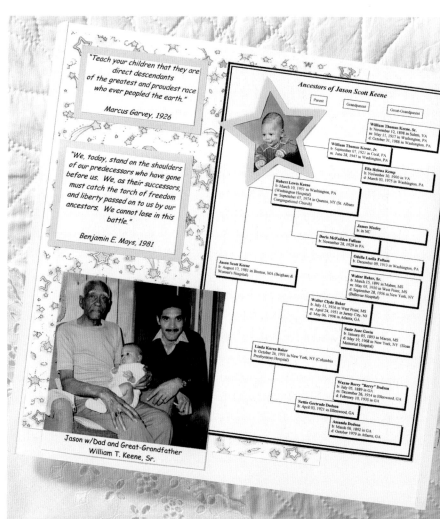

My Family Tree

DECORATE YOUR FAMILY TIES

Heather's drawings beautifully embellish the mats and bows tying together four generations. First crop and double mat the oval baby photo. Crop remaining photos into circles using a large circle punch. Double mat each circle photo with colored circles, ovals and rectangles. Cut bows from colored and gingham paper. Punch small hearts. Embellish mats, bows and hearts using opaque colored pens (Pentel Milky Gel Rollers). Title page and label photos with a thin black pen.

Heather Schram, Belgrade, Montana

Father and Son

COMPARE BABY PICTURES

Mary's son not only looks like his father but is also wearing the same blue velvet outfit. First mount a brown triangle on a white background, dividing the page in half diagonally. Cut photo mats using decorative scissors. Layer cream paper on upper left portions of two blue heart die cuts (Accu-Cut). Outline and draw stitches on all die-cut edges. Adhere die cuts and stickers (NRN Designs, Frances Meyer). Write titles and captions.

Mary Lisenby, Wichita, Kansas

For an archival-quality album environment:
- *Assume all memorabilia is acidic; never let photos and memorabilia touch.*
- *To preserve old newspaper clippings and announcements, spray with de-acidification spray (such as Archival Mist™ by Preservation Technologies) or photocopy the clippings onto oatmeal-colored paper (to preserve antique look) prior to mounting.*
- *Use only acid- and lignin-free paper, photo-safe adhesives and pigment inks.*
- *Handle photos with care; avoid direct light.*
- *Use nonpermanent mounting techniques (photo corners, sleeves, etc.) for easy removal for copying or restoration.*
- *Keep cropping to a minimum; background objects tell their own stories of place and time.*
- *Don't trim or hand-tint old photos. Have reprints made first.*

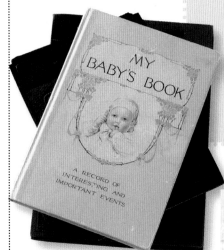

When We Were One

COMPARE FAMILIAR FACES

Digging up old family photos helped Julie settle a family "feud" about which side of the family her son most resembled. For each photo, cut a tan and brown mat. Print and trace the Playbill font (Sierra On-Line) for the title words; double mat each word. Journal and write photo labels with black pen; mat with tan or brown.

Julie Gustine, Murrieta, California

austin, 7 mos.

I think that
I shall never see...

Grandpa 'Boppa' Don Regier, 3 months, 1933

Dylan, 3 months, 1989

Jacob, 3 months, 1992

Colt, 3 months, 1986

Hunter, 3 months, 1999

·whose ancestors came to America from Southern Russia in 1879·

Four grandsons who look more like me!

I Think That I Shall Never See...

OLD ART LINKS PRESENT, PAST

An old illustration of a ship helps link contemporary photos of MaryJo's sailor-suited sons to their ancestors' voyage to America. Begin with a navy background (Canson); add ¼" strips of gold paper at top and bottom. Photocopy clip art on cream paper; mount. Add navy-colored oval trimmed with deckle scissors above ship. Journal on vellum; trim with deckle scissors and adhere. Oval crop photos; adhere. Adhere matted title at top and bottom of page. Finish with embellishments (Creative Beginnings).

MaryJo Regier, Littleton, Colorado

Precious Legacy

1928
Harold Eugene Cain

1955
Harold Joe Cain

1981
John Harold Cain

Three Generations

Three Generations

FRAME A PHOTO LEGACY

Efrat's hand-tinted photos and museum-like framing of three generations of the Cain family is reminiscent of yesteryear. Use striped paper (The Family Archives) for background "wallpaper." Triple mat photos with gold, cream and burgundy papers. Layer gold frame (Sonburn) over photos. Finish with matted journaling and gold ribbon.

Efrat Dalton, Fort Collins, Colorado

SweetDreams

John
Michael

3 weeks
old

November
29
1997

meagan, 9 mos.

...len, 11 mos.

Activities

QUIET DOWN COBWEBS,

DUST GO TO SLEEP,

I'M ROCKING MY BABY AND

BABIES DON'T KEEP.

–ANONYMOUS

While your baby's arrival may have seemed to move in slow motion, now that he or she is here, nothing will ever be slow again. You and your busy, busy baby will have many golden moments together: tender lullabies, fitful naps, splashy baths and eager feedings. Treasure every one of these moments, as well as the not-so-sunny moments of unforeseen illness and injuries. They, too, shall pass. Quicker than you could ever imagine.

sarah, 12 mos.

SWEET DREAMS
MELISA THORNTON
MUNFORD, TENNESSEE
(SEE PAGE 382)

Sleepytime

Nothing's as sweet as a slumbering baby. Capture these moments on film and record how you achieved them. Was it the blankie's satin edge that did the trick? A soothing lullaby? The security of falling off to sleep is a memory you will cherish and your baby will carry in his heart forever.

CLASSIC GOOD-NIGHT RHYMES AND LULLABIES

Lullabies help parents and Baby wind down at the end of the day and nothing sounds sweeter to Baby's ears than Mommy's and Daddy's loving voices in song. Some old-time favorites:

Golden Slumbers kiss your eyes...
Hey Diddle Diddle, the cat and the fiddle...
Hush, Little Baby, don't say a word...
I See the Moon, and the moon sees me...
Kumbaya, my Lord, Kumbaya...
Rock-A-Bye, Baby, on the treetop...
Sleep, Baby, Sleep, thy father guards the sheep...
Star Light, Star Bright, first star I see tonight...
Twinkle, Twinkle, Little Star...
Wee Willie Winkie runs through the town...

**SWINGING ON A STAR &
BABY BUGGY PUNCH ART**
Tonya Jeppson, Boise, Idaho
(instructions on page 382)

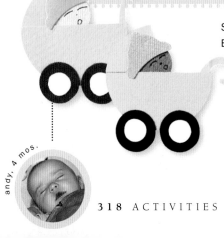
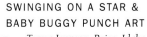

andy, 4 mos.

Twinkle, Twinkle Little Star

ROCK ON A CRESCENT MOON

(UPPER RIGHT) The stamps provided Cathy's design idea. To make the border, stamp and emboss blue dots and dashes, blue crescent moons and yellow stars (Stampin' Up!). Color stars and moons yellow and baby clothes blue. Cut large crescent moon and baby blanket from printed paper (The Paper Patch); layer with silhouetted photo. Add dimension to moon and blanket edges with Liquid Appliqué (Marvy Uchida). Adhere ribbon bows. Write titles in yellow.

Cathy Lay, Lake Zurich, Illinois

Sleeping Baby Quilt

SNUGGLE UP IN A QUILT PAGE

(UPPER FAR RIGHT) Jessica's photos lend the perfect focus to a baby quilt. Start by mounting photos in desired positions. Fill white spaces with colored and printed paper (Provo Craft) strips. Cut heart, star, flower and duck shapes. Punch ¼" circle for flower center. Finish with pen stroke stitching.

Jessica Fisher, California

The Story of Pooh and Twin

PHOTOGRAPH TREASURED TOYS

(LOWER RIGHT) When Cindy bought her son a "spare" Pooh as a backup, he soon needed both to sleep. For the page background, use yellow printed paper (Keeping Memories Alive). Double mat photos with soft blue solid and printed paper (Keeping Memories Alive). Cut soft blue mat for journaling. Punch Pooh bears (All Night Media) along the bottom of the mat. Write title, using the punched shapes for the "O" letters in "Pooh." Adhere Pooh stickers (Michel & Co.).

Cindy Mandernach, Fraser, Michigan

A Little Bird Told Me...

BUILD A COZY NEST

(LOWER FAR RIGHT) Barbara crafted this Geddes-style page for her granddaughter's birthday. Print the lettering and clip art bird directly on lavender background paper. Color bird. Freehand cut nest shape, trimming top edges with large oak leaf punch. Crumple thin brown strips. Layer photo and nest pieces with punched oak leaves and vine die cut (Ellison). Journal and draw details with black pen.

Barbara Parks, Auburn, Washington

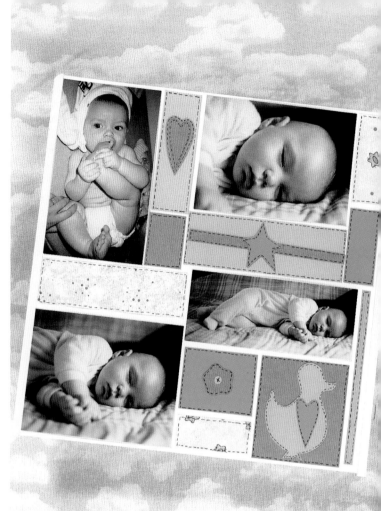

Austen got his Pooh bear from Nana at his baby shower. He had become so attached to Pooh that we had to buy a spare. No store had them anymore so I logged on to the Internet to see if the company could direct me to a store that carried it. They did and we bought TWIN. Now Austen is attached to BOTH bears and needs both to sleep. He loves his Pooh's.

a little bird told me
there's someone new in
the nest......

... Jessica Lynn ...

June 15, 1991

Slumber Softly Little One

EMBOSS A POCKET-PAGE SPREAD

Heat-embossed celestial designs richly enhance Genevieve's pocket pages. Use 8½ x 11" tan card stock for background; layer with trimmed sky papers (Carolee's Creations). Silhouette cut clouds from angel/cloud paper (The Paper Company); adhere to pages at sides and lower edges, leaving top edge open for pocket. Circle crop photos; mat with gold paper and adhere. Silhouette cut angels from angel/cloud paper; mat with bronze paper; layer over photos. Stamp and heat emboss stars (Stampabilities), sun and moon (Rubber Stamps of America) and birds (Personal Stamp Exchange). Cut out; adhere. Journal with gold ink (Sakura).

Genevieve Glassy, Tenino, Washington

HEAT-EMBOSSED STAMPING

Heat-embossed stamping is an appealing way to add detailed illustrations to your scrapbook layouts.

To heat emboss a design, you must use a pigment stamping ink, which will dry slowly, allowing you to stamp several images before you sprinkle all of them with embossing powder. Embossing powders are available in a variety of colors and styles. Opaque embossing powders completely cover the ink with the color of the powder, so you can use any ink color. In contrast, clear embossing powders let the ink color show through.

To heat emboss a stamped image, follow the steps below. Be sure to keep your photos away from the heat gun or other heat source.

1 Stamp the image with clear pigment ink. Liberally cover the designs with gold embossing powder (Figure 1).

2 Tap off the excess, using folded paper to return extra powder to the container. Gently sweep away any tiny bits of powder using a soft brush.

3 Apply heat with a heat gun until the ink "rises and shines" (Figure 2).

UP ALL NIGHT

Most of all the other beautiful things in life come by twos and threes, by dozens and hundreds. Plenty of roses, stars, sunsets, rainbows, brothers and sisters, aunts and cousins, but only one mother in the whole world.
Kate Douglas Wiggin

Mommy and Justin
June 1999

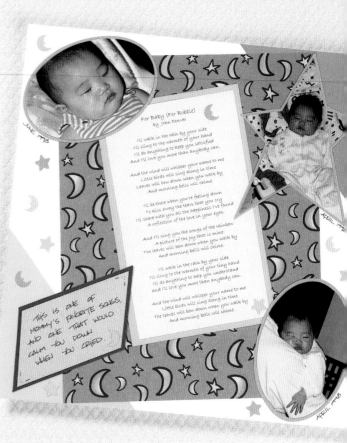

For Baby (For Bobbie)
by John Denver

I'll walk in the rain by your side
I'll cling to the warmth of your hand
I'll do anything to keep you satisfied
And I'll love you more than anybody can.

And the wind will whisper your name to me
Little birds will sing along in time
Leaves will bow down when you walk by
And morning bells will chime.

I'll be there when you're feeling down
To kiss away the tears that you cry
I'll share with you all the happiness I've found
A reflection of the love in your eyes.

And I'll sing you the songs of the rainbow
A picture of the joy that is mine
The leaves will bow down when you walk by
And morning bells will chime.

I'll walk in the rain by your side
I'll cling to the warmth of your tiny hand
I'll do anything to help you understand
And I'll love you more than anybody can.

And the wind will whisper your name to me
Little birds will sing along in time
The leaves will bow down when you walk by
And morning bells will chime.

JUNE 1993

APRIL 1993

APRIL 1993

THIS IS ONE OF MOMMY'S FAVORITE SONGS, AND ONE THAT WOULD CALM YOU DOWN WHEN YOU CRIED.

Babies Smile in their Sleep because they are listening to the Whispering of Angels

Special Delivery

Hannah June Ivens
Delivered - December 18, 1997
Weighing - 7lbs 12ozs
Length - 19 1/2 inches

Up All Night

REMEMBER THE WEE HOURS

(UPPER FAR LEFT) Susan recorded that unforgettable part of new motherhood–sleep deprivation. The pictures tell the story, so keep them the focal point with simple shapes and mats. For the window, freehand cut moon, curtain rod and curtains; layer with white strips on star paper (Creative Memories). Adhere letter stickers (Creative Memories) for title; accent with black dots. Journal with thick black pen.

Susan Gilmore, Orlando, Florida

Mommy's Favorite Lullaby

CHRONICLE A SOOTHING SONG

(UPPER LEFT) Sleeping baby pictures illustrate John Denver's "For Baby," a song that often calmed Stacey's daughter. For the background, mount gold and purple triangles in lower left and upper right corners. Print song lyrics and double mat with orange and star/moon printed paper (Colors By DESIGN). Crop and mat diamond shape for journaling and star and oval photos. Punch small stars and moons.

Stacey Shigaya, Denver, Colorado

Special Delivery

FRAME A NEWBORN BABE

(LOWER LEFT) Matching borders tie Kathi's theme page to her portrait page. For the page borders, draw scalloped lines using a thick purple pen. For the portrait, trim photo corners using a corner lace punch (McGill) and mount on printed clip art frame. Layer strips of printed quilt clip art around edges. Trim photo in envelope using corner heart punch (McGill). For stamps, cut and mat small photos, printed title, and printed clip art; trim mats with stamp scissors (Fiskar). For mailbox, print clip art and layer with silhouetted photo. Adhere small punched heart and floral clip art. Journal with black pen. (All clip art from Microsoft's® *Greetings Workshop* CD.)

Kathi Ivens, Truckee, California

Mason Garret Collins

PHOTOCOPY A TREASURED HEIRLOOM

To customize a baby gift page made for Mason's mother, Donna photocopied Mason's great-great-great-grandmother's quilt for background. Note that baby is sleeping on quilt in photo, too. To make the photo frame, quadruple mat with red, white and mulberry paper. Print title and trim with deckle scissors; mat with red paper. Adhere red ribbon bow.

Donna Leicht, Appleton, Wisconsin

COUNTING SHEEP

Freehand cut pieces; assemble.
Cathy Blackstone, Columbus, Ohio

Bathtime

Most babies have a love-hate relationship with bathtime, but it can be the most interactive and intimate part of Baby's and your day. When you can, bathe with your baby for extra bonding. And be ready to capture the giggles and tears.

Isaac

CREATE A PHOTO STAINED GLASS

Bobbie's page is part of a gift album she and her siblings compiled for their mother. For detailed instructions on photo stained glass, refer to *Memory Makers* Issue 5, page 55. To make the stained glass, cut the photo into an octagon shape. Cut the edges into a symmetrical pattern. Mount photo and "glass" pieces on black paper, leaving small gaps in between each piece. Extend the stained glass design using pieces of printed paper (Amscan, Hot Off The Press). Trim completed design into an octagon shape and mat with pink and black paper; center on blue background. Mount black triangles in corners. Label photo with black pen.

Bobbie Jacobson, Shaker Heights, Ohio

Our Little Stinker

TEAR A SWEET SKUNK

Torn paper adds a furry look to Linda's expressive animal. First mat photos with white paper and arrange on an aqua background. Layer black and white torn paper to create skunk. Trim thin white strips for whiskers. Draw eye and nose details with white pen. For title, punch white squares, mat with black paper, and write letters. Draw black and white line borders. Journal with black pen. Accent with yellow duck punches.

Linda Strauss, Provo, Utah

raelyn, 7 mos.

Nice hair do . . . you too!

Andrew at age 3 and Emily at age 1   August 22, 1988

annelise, 8 mos.

QUILLING

Quilling, an ancient art originally known as paper filigree, involves rolling thin strips of paper into various shapes and arranging those shapes into a design. Perhaps you made quilled art as a child. Quilling supplies are quite inexpensive and as you can see, quilling adds a fun and playful touch to baby scrapbook pages. The standard width of quilling paper is ⅛", but wider and narrower sizes are available. Besides quilling paper (Lake City Craft Quilling Supplies), you'll need glue and a slotted or needle tool. Rolling paper around the tool makes various shapes, while the number of coils made determines the thickness of the shape.

HOW TO ROLL QUILL SHAPES WITH A NEEDLE TOOL

1 *Cut off a strip of paper to the desired length.*

2 *Slide paper strip into slot of tool and press the end of the paper around the tool with your thumb.*

3 *Roll the paper while holding the tool steady, keeping the strip's edges as even as possible (Figure 1).*

4 *Pinch ends, as needed (Figure 2).*

5 *Glue shapes together (Figure 3); adhere to page.*

HOW TO ROLL VARIOUS SHAPES

LOOSE SCROLLS: *Roll one end, leaving the other end loose.*
LOOSE CIRCLES: *Roll, remove from tool and let the coil loosen. Glue the loose end.*
TEARDROPS: *Roll and glue a loose circle. Pinch one side of the circle to a point.*
MARQUISE: *Roll and glue a loose circle. Pinch on both ends.*
TIGHT CIRCLES: *Roll, slip the tool from the roll's center and hold it to keep it from unwinding. Glue the loose end of the paper to the side of the roll.*

Bathtime Buddies

QUILL A SPLASHY DESIGN

Gail enjoys trying fun new techniques to enhance her scrapbook pages. Her quilled duck and fish designs can be a whimsical addition to any baby's bathtime page. To make this page, mount double-matted photos onto double-matted background. Use the quilling techniques described at the left to roll loose blue scrolls for waves; loose yellow circles for duck heads; yellow teardrops for duck bodies; large orange marquise shapes for fish bodies; small orange marquise shapes for fish tails and fins; and tight blue circles for fish eyes and bubbles. Glue rolled designs together to form ducks and fish. Adhere designs to page using tiny drops of glue. Finish with dot letter die cuts (Accu-Cut) and journaling.

Gail Birkhead, Tyngsboro, Massachusetts

*No baby album is complete
without an adorable "blackmail" page!
Concept/Poem by Gina Emerson,
Salisbury, North Carolina
Photo by Deleise Klaassen
Edmond, Oklahoma*

I'm
bringing home
my girlfriend
to meet my Mom and Dad.
We'll laugh and have a good
time, but then it will turn
bad, when Mom gets out the
Scrapbook when I was "oh

The Girlfriend Page

so cute" and that
first page that
she will show
is me in my
Birthday
Suit!

BY MOMMY

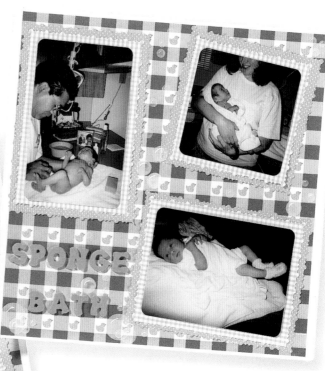

Olivia's First Sponge Bath

BLOW BUBBLES AROUND FOAM LETTERS

Craft foam matched the sponge-bath theme of Tracy's
fun layout. Start with duck printed paper (The Paper
Patch) for page background. Round corners of photos;
double mat using decorative scissors and gingham and
polka dot paper. Trace title letters (Pebbles In My
Pocket) onto craft foam and cut out. Mat yellow gingham duck die cut (Creative Memories); cut foam beak,
black eye and wing detail. For bubbles, punch and
layer different sizes of vellum circles, highlighting with
white and blue markers.

Tracy Cabello, Granger, Indiana

brad, 12 mos.

Bath Time

DECORATE OLD-FASHIONED BATHROOM

Nancy cut checkerboard paper into square tiles to mimic her parents' 1940s bathroom. Start with a green background. Cut and mat circle photos and "bubble" for title. Cut white strips for chair railing and windowpane. Arrange squares of checkerboard paper for tile pattern. Cut pieces for bathtub, tub feet and window. Layer photo and stickers (Stickopotamus) beneath tub. Adhere additional stickers.

Nancy Chearno-Stershic, Bel Air, Maryland

Bathtime

SPLASH AMONG THE BUBBLES

The gray grout lines give Jacqueline's page a bathtub backdrop. After drawing the gray lines, cut faucet handles, spout and water droplet. Write title with thick and thin blue pens. Circle cut and silhouette photos. Layer photos with bubble stickers (Frances Meyer), duck die cuts (Creative Memories) and blue and white circles. Color ducks' beaks orange. Draw details with blue and black pens.

Jacqueline O'Beirne, Lake Barrington, Illinois

BATHTIME POP-UP

Pop-up pages are full of surprises, magic and fun. And best of all, making pop-ups is easier than you might think!

1 *Use a white 12 x 12" scrapbook page for background. Silhouette cut large bubble paper (Hot Off The Press); adhere to lower left corner of page.*

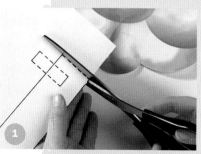

2 *Sandwich together one 8½ x 11" sheet of large bubble paper and one 8½ x 11" sheet of small bubble paper (Hot Off The Press) with right sides out; glue. Repeat with a second set of large and small bubble paper. Silhouette cut each bubble paper "sandwich." Layer together and adhere top of bubble papers to top ⅓ of background page. Fold up bottom ⅔ of bubble paper to form lift-up flap.*

3 *Transfer pattern on page 381 and center it on an 8½ by 11" sheet of white card stock. Fold card on fold line; cut on dotted lines (Figure 1).*

4 *Open card and carefully push out on the strips created to form the pop-ups (Figure 2).*

5 *Cover top half of pop-up with striped paper (NRN Designs) for "wallpaper" and bottom half with quilted paper (The Paper Patch) for "linoleum," trimming where needed to accommodate pop-up flaps (Figure 3). Lift up bubble paper flap and mount pop-up card to page.*

6 *Freehand cut bathtub and sink. Silhouette crop photos for bathtub; adhere to bathtub and add bubble stickers. Mount on pop-up strips (Figure 4). Add toiletry stickers (Mrs. Grossman's, Stickopotamus), placing foam spacers under bathroom scale, soap and some bubbles for added dimension. Trim a piece of old washcloth with fancy scissors for floor mat; adhere. If desired, make "puddles" on floor by using two coats of thick, clear embossing enamel.*

7 *Silhouette cut photos for front of pop-up card. Adhere to front of pop-up card, tucking under silhouetted bubbles where needed. Journal front of pop-up to complete.*

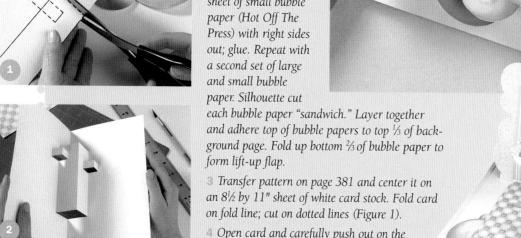

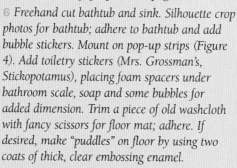

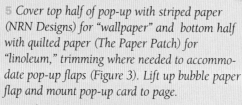

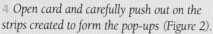

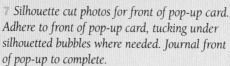

Rub-a-Dub-Dub

CRAFT A BUBBLY POP-UP

Pat's delightful bathtime pop-up page is complete with wallpaper, linoleum, toiletries and tiny "puddles" of thick, clear embossing enamel. Silhouette-cropped bubble paper and photos add to the excitement—even the family dog has a spot in the action! To make your own bathtime pop-up page, follow the instructions at left.

Pat Murray, Edmonton, Alberta, Canada

katie, 11 mos.

Grandma's Brag Book

CELEBRATE FIRST GRANDCHILD IN EXPANDABLE THEME ALBUM

Becky's mother lives 12 hours away, so when her first grandchild was born, Becky shared the moments in a "Grandma's Brag Book" theme album. The expandable album (Creative Memories) allows Becky to send her mother pages to "keep Grandma updated" on Baby's growth and activities. And even though the color theme varies from page to page, simple page treatments give the book its consistent look.

Becky Scott, Wenatchee, Washington

Mealtime

It is the best of times and the worst of times. The skin-to-skin intimacy of nursing gives way to the wonder of strained carrots suspended in midair. Labels from formula and favorite foods make great memorabilia. Photos of when mealtime is overtaken by sleepytime, as Baby nods off in the high chair, do as well.

Cheerios® Boy

POUR A BOWL OF FUN

Tracy's son stars in the cover photo for this cereal-box page. For the background, use bright gold paper. Double mat photo with gold and black paper. Freehand cut bowl, spoon and splashing milk. Cut ¾" tan circles for Cheerios; punch ¼" holes in centers. Freehand cut black title letters or trace from cereal box.

Tracy Yonker, Alto, Michigan

Cookies

BAKE PUNCH-ART GOODIES

Her daughter's love for cookies prompted Kathryn's mealtime photo shoot. To bake your own batch, punch and layer 1¼" jumbo colored circles. Punch ¹⁄₁₆" holes from Oreo cookie top. Punch ¼" brown circles for chocolate chips. Take a "bite" using scallop scissors. For pink cookie, trim tan icing with deckle scissors; punch small circle from center. Add layered die cut letters for title. Crop and mat photos and layer with cookies. Journal along border with thin black pen.

Kathryn Neff, Bel Air, Maryland

sara, 6 mos.

SWEET PEA

"I considered these photos 'throwaway shots' until I cropped them to remove a busy background," says Emily Tucker of Matthews, North Carolina. "I added them onto a hand-cut pea pod and now it's one of my favorite album pages."

Spaghetti and Meatballs

MAKE SQUIGGLY NOODLES

Alex's love of spaghetti was the inspiration behind mom Joanna's pasta page. Use wavy ruler to cut spaghetti strips; adhere. Crop photos with circle template. Mat with colored paper; trim with decorative scissors and adhere. Add fork die cut (Ellison) and extra "noodles" to complete.

Joanna Barr, Belmont, Michigan

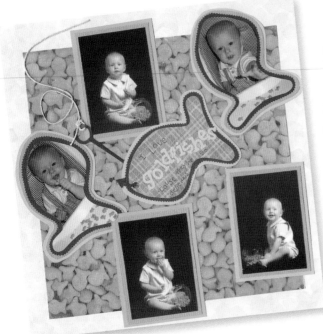

I Love Goldfishes

MAKE YOUR OWN PRINTED PAPER

To match the theme of the portraits, Michelle color copied crackers in a plastic bag. Start by layering photocopied paper on a blue printed background (Provo Craft). Double mat portraits. Crop snapshots and orange paper into fish shapes; double or triple mat, trimming the black mats with decorative scissors. Write title and adhere letters stickers (Frances Meyer). Freehand cut hook and put through punched hole. Tie twine around the fishhook eye.

Michelle Gowan, Macon, Georgia

Too Pooped to Eat

CAPTURE A CLASSIC MEALTIME MOMENT

Rather than wake a sleeping baby, Michelle's husband made a pillow for their sleeping son. Use striped paper (Keeping Memories Alive) for background. Mat photos with white, checkerboard and printed paper (Keeping Memories Alive); trim yellow mats with fancy scissors. Cut title letters with template (Frances Meyer). Punch large white flowers and small yellow circles for centers. Freehand cut white flower and large yellow circle; journal and draw details.

Michelle Gowan, Macon, Georgia

jakob, 8 mos.

Logan's First Cereal

FEATURE YOUR GERBER® BABY

Mena replaced the Gerber logo baby with photos of her son. Start with a bright orange background. Crop and mat circle and oval photos. Next, Mena cut out and color photocopied cereal box parts and layered with smaller photos. Print and mat journaling.

Mena Spodobalski, Sparks, Nevada

BYGONE DAYS OF INFANT FEEDING

Long before Cheerios and Gerber foods were part of Baby's daily staples, infant feeding experienced a touching and often tragic past. While breastfeeding has always been essential for the survival of the human race, artificial or hand feeding has long been used when the breast would not or could not perform. Some interesting historical highlights include:

• Sheep, goat and calve horns are some of the oldest feeding vessels, readily available to hunters, gatherers and livestock farmers.
• Jug- and boat-shaped vessels of pottery and earthenware have survived from the Neolithic, Late Bronze and Early Iron Ages onward. Such vessels evolved into the feeding can, or Bubby Pot (16th century England) and still survive today as the spouted "sippy cup" used by toddlers.
• Late Medieval wooden, glass and other upright feeding vessels with screw tops and artificial nipples evolved over 500 years into the precursors of today's modern bottles.
• Pap-boats, used to feed pap or panada (gruel made from bread or grains and boiled water or milk), were used from the 17th to the 19th centuries.
• Sucking bags, the forerunner of today's modern teethers, are of ancient origin. Made of gauze or other thin cloth, these were soaked in pap or panada, squeezed of excess liquid and given to babies to suck.
• Nineteenth-century America saw the dawn of pediatric medicine, the scientific analysis of human vs. cow's milk, the campaign for sanitary milk supplies and widespread production of glass nursing bottles.
• The 20th century witnessed a decline in breastfeeding with the manufacturing of infant formulas and canned baby food.
• By the end of WWII, the U.S. Patent Office had issued over 230 patents for glass nursing bottles.

Twins feed from glass "turtle" nursers, introduced from England in 1864. They were commonly used for years until it was learned that countless infant deaths could be attributed to bacterial buildup in the bottles' feeding tubes.

Baby's first year is generally healthy and happy, interrupted only by common illnesses and minor injuries. But Baby heals quickly with tender loving care from Dr. Mom and Dr. Dad, and these photos and mementos will help shape your child's sense of compassion for life.

Chicken Pox

ILLUSTRATE THE MISERY

A coloring book helped Bonita design this poor sick character. Start by rounding corners of photos and mats; layer on navy background. Draw and mat "fever" style title using thermometers in some of the letters. Cut and layer pieces for sick giraffe using printed paper (Paper Parade) for body. Draw details with colored pens.

Bonita Warren, Tillamook, Oregon

Emergency

PRESERVE MEMORY EVEN WITH NO PHOTOS

Cathy tucked get-well cards from her daughter's 1971 bout with croup into this medical-theme pocket page. For the top border, adhere line, letter and hospital-theme stickers (Creative Memories, Frances Meyer). For the pocket, cut a rectangle about half the size of the page and adhere along left, bottom and right sides. To decorate the pocket, mount polka dot paper along with a strip of white paper trimmed with decorative scissors. Outline with border stickers. Accent page with additional stickers and black dots.

Cathy Murphy, Downingtown, Pennsylvania

MEMORY WHEEL

Memory wheels are easily adaptable to scrapbook pages and are great space savers, using five photos at a time.

1 *Cut two 10½" circle "wheels." Glue together for strength. Trim outer edge with zigzag scissors for firm grip when turning wheel. Insert brad fastener through center of wheel and attach to center of background page (Figure 1). Spin wheel to ensure that it spins freely on page.*

2 *Cut five horizontal photos using photo pattern on page 381, positioning narrow part of pattern at bottom of photo subject. Mount photos securely on wheel with narrow bottoms surrounding center of wheel (Figure 2).*

3 *Use window pattern on page 381 to cut window opening 1½" down at center of cover paper that will cover the entire wheel. Place window opening over wheel, centering one photo in the window.*

4 *Lay window cover over mounted background and wheel; line up all edges. Use slot pattern on page 381 to mark slot for wheel on window cover paper over edge of wheel underneath and 1" from page edge (Figure 3). Slot should point to left if wheel will turn on left side of page, right if wheel turns on right side of page. Remove window cover; cut open slot.*

5 *Place cover on background; slide edge of wheel through curved slot (Figure 4). Adhere cover to background at corners and edges, without capturing any of the wheel. Journal about the wheel's photos; decorate as desired.*

The Big Accident

TAKE A "SPIN AND PEEK"

Chris uniquely turned a horrible double accident into a soothing memory wheel scrapbook page. She used two sheets of 12 x 12" red paper to encase the wheel and matted journaling, lettering (Provo Craft) and stickers (Frances Meyer) to finish the page. To make your own memory wheel, follow the steps at left.

Chris Peters, Hasbrouck Heights, New Jersey

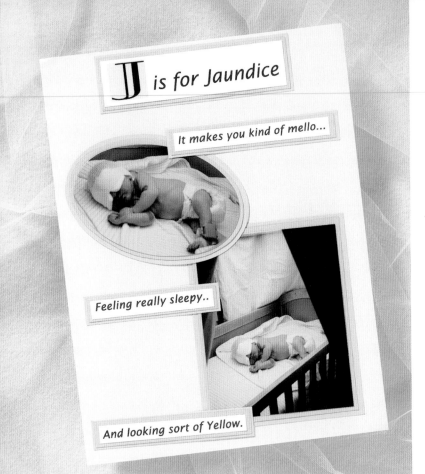

J Is for Jaundice

PRESERVE A SINGSONG VERSE

Nancy's husband sang these words to Hunter when he was hospitalized for low blood sugar and developed jaundice. Print the letter "J" using the New Yorker Engraved font (Print Shop Deluxe). Print remaining words using Lucida Sans font (Broderbund). Double mat titles and photos with soft yellow and blue. Layer elements on yellow background.

Nancy Kurokawa, Chula Vista, California

First Cold

SING THE SNIFFLE BLUES

Yuko's cute blue characters aptly express a head-cold mood. Start with blue checkerboard paper for the page background. Cut five doctor bags and layer using padded adhesive. Adhere letter and plus sign stickers (Creative Memories). Print and mat journaling. Circle cut and mat center photo. Cut two hot water bottles as mats for other photos. Cut and layer pieces for blue characters; punch eyes with ¼" round hand punch. Draw details with blue pen.

Yuko Neal, Huntington Beach, California

My Twelve-Month Check

SAVE THOSE BOO-BOO BANDAGES

Colorful bandages from her son's immunizations provided the idea for Cindy's Kermit® page. To make the frog pattern, Cindy photocopied and enlarged the bandage design. Cut and layer paper to build Kermit, outlining each piece with black pen. Mat journaling, bandages and photos. Adhere "ouch," bandage, stethoscope, syringe and doctor bag stickers (Frances Meyer).

Cindy Mandernach, Fraser, Michigan

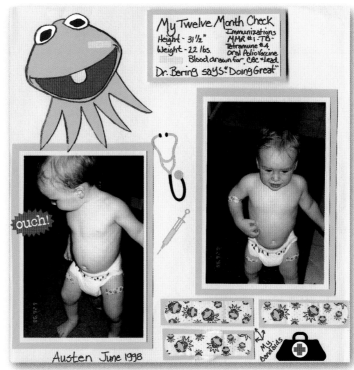

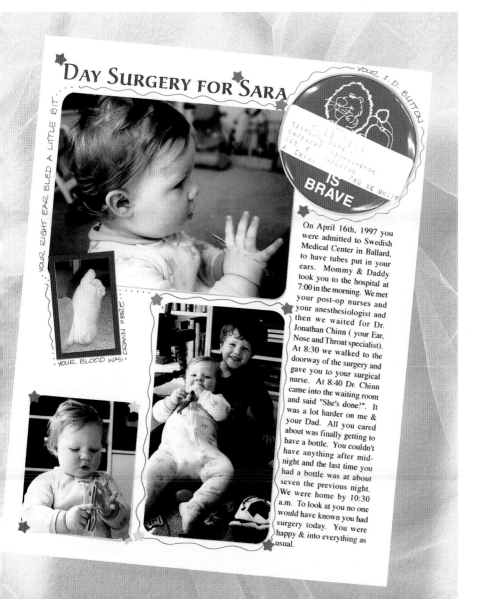

Day Surgery for Sara

DOCUMENT MEDICAL HISTORY

Kim saved the hospital ID button from her daughter's ear-tube surgery and color copied it for this page. Print the title and journaling directly on the page background. Crop and mat photos as desired. Label photos and draw details with blue pen. Adhere star stickers (Mrs. Grossman's).

Kim Owens, Lynnwood, Washington

torin, 3 mos.

savanna, 7½ mos.

Playtime

PAT-A-CAKE, PAT-A-CAKE,

BAKER'S MAN

BAKE ME A CAKE AS FAST

AS YOU CAN...

Playtime may be fun for you, but your baby is on a mission. Behind those bright eyes and joyful giggles, little wheels are turning. Baby is learning about object permanence (peek-a-boo), word and action combinations (itsy-bitsy spider) and language skills (one, two, buckle my shoe). But more than that, baby is rapidly becoming a social butterfly. Preserve these playful photos, favorite games and baby nicknames while they are still fresh in your mind.

ariel, 7 mos.

BABY FACE
CHAR BEHUNIN
RUPERT, IDAHO
(SEE PAGE 382)

Our Little Olympian

PHOTOGRAPH A LITTLE GOLD MEDALIST

Inspired by the winter Olympics, Lesli posed these
cute photos for different events. Cut two blue wavy
strips and a 1¾" gold circle for medal. Mat photos and
printed journaling; adhere. Add journaling and
pen stroke stitching to medallion.

Lesli Erickson, Slayton, Minnesota

bobsled

weight lifting

sumo wrestling

our little olympian

rings

Chitchi's Story

New parents often marvel at the accomplishments of their offspring. Each "first" is greeted with thoughts of the genius we have produced. The same is true for Chitchi and Louis and their son David. But one activity worried them a bit at first.

"David would crawl away to amuse himself, and we would find him with a line of objects stretching across the floor," says Chitchi. "We asked ourselves, 'What is he doing that for?'" Other parents whose children exhibited similar talents later reassured them. "We've come to realize that it's normal, especially for boys," says Chitchi.

Some of David's favorite items to line up are CDs, books, magnetic letters, placemats, shoes and cars. David will often call his line of books his "train."

"He really takes after his dad's organizational skills," says Chitchi. "David has always put his toys away without being asked."

David has recently graduated to a higher level of organization. Previously he would line up all of mom's punches, regardless of size or shape. Now he sorts punches into distinct lines, separating the border, mini and jumbo tools into their own paths.

David doesn't line up things as often anymore, which makes Chitchi glad she documented his efforts on a special scrapbook page.

Chitchi Tabora, San Francisco, California

Get in line! And see how our son David would line things up like a pro! Ever since David was about 15 months, we would often walk into a room and find all the books laid out on the floor, lined up from one wall to the other! We can't explain why he does this but it's sure fun to watch him do it. And don't you dare take any of the objects out of formation, David is pretty serious about this job of his!!!

hunter, 6 mos.

Brad vs. Crusher

FEATURE A FRIENDLY FEUD

Patti's humorous page captures the times her older son tried to show little brother who was boss. For the wrestling ring, cut navy mat and tan poles. Draw lines to enclose the ring. Cut free form white pieces for the words "slam" and "pow" and outline with thick black pen. Silhouette photo. Adhere small (Current) and large letter stickers (Creative Memories) for titles.

Patti Barnes, West Bend, Wisconsin

Next?

ENLARGE A MISCHIEVOUS SNAPSHOT

Liz scanned her son's pajamas to re-create the fabric's giraffe design. For the giraffe's spots, punch ⅛" and ¼" red circles; adhere. For title squares, stamp "Wasn't there, didn't do it" design (Rubber Monger), heat emboss and cut out. Mount giraffe and stamped squares. Punch ¹⁄₁₆" dots and mount around giraffe. Stamp title letters (Stampendous) in each square.
Mat portrait with red paper and trim with jumbo deckle scissors (Family Treasures).

Liz Kajiwara, Palmdale, California

The Baby Patch

Cathie's embossed stamping highlights this berry-licious page. Use black paper for background; add ⅛" white paper border. Layer trimmed heart and matted checkered papers (The Paper Patch). Mat cropped photos; adhere. Stamp coneflowers (Mostly Animals), angels and fairies (Stamposaurus), sign (DJ Inkers), bunnies (Artistic Stamp Exchange) and berries (Son-Light). Emboss stamped designs; cut out and adhere. Journal sign and page edges.

Cathie Allan,
Western Educational Activities Ltd.
St. Albert, Alberta, Canada

So Many Names

PRESERVE BABY'S NICKNAMES

Kris and her family had so many nicknames for her son that someone once commented that Samuel might never learn his name. The words are printed directly on the background paper. To do so, use a computer to print the title and different names using a variety of fonts. (The page shown uses two horizontally overlapping 8½ x 11" pages.) Position the names so that they fit around a silhouetted photo.

Kris Morrison, Hastings, Minnesota

quinton, 7 mos.

PEEK-A-BOO PIE

Scrapbook artists are continually searching for creative ways to use more and more photos on one scrapbook page. The peek-a-boo pie technique is a fun and easy solution. For another variation, try the Memory Wheel on page 335.

1 Mount berry paper (Frances Meyer) for background.

2 Cut one 11" circle (top crust) and one 10" circle (bottom crust) from tan card stock. Trim top crust using cloud scissors (Fiskars) to form pie's "scalloped" edge (Figure 1).

3 Transfer pie pattern on page 380 to top crust. Use a craft knife to carefully cut on all dotted lines (Figure 2). Scoring with a stylus will help create nice, crisp folds on flaps.

4 Adhere top crust to bottom crust; mount on background leaving enough room for page title.

5 Silhouette cut six favorite photos and mount beneath flaps onto bottom pie crust (Figure 3). Journal about each photo on inside of pie flaps. Add title lettering.

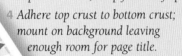

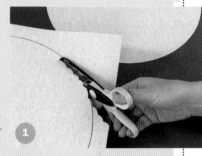

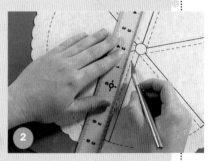

Cutie Pie

SHOWCASE PEEK-A-BOO PHOTOS OF YOUR "CUTIE PIE"

Kathleen's check on her napping baby girl brought the inspiration for creating her 12 x 15" "cutie pie" page. Each lift of a pie slice reveals a precious photo underneath. Kathleen's use of berry paper (Frances Meyer), cloud scissors (Fiskars) and red die cut lettering helps carry out the berry-licious theme. To make your own peek-a-boo pie, follow the steps above.

Kathleen Dodd, Dublin, Ohio

Couch Potato

An abundance of photos of her daughter propped up on the couch resulted in Amy's humorous theme page. To cut symmetrical couch halves, hold two 8½ x 10½" yellow rectangles together and trim three sides as shown. Mount pieces in a mirror image across the center of the layout. Draw couch details. Cut blue pillows and layer beneath silhouetted photos and white thought bubble. Circle cut two photos and mat with pillow shapes. Cut additional pillows for journaling. Outline title letters and color in.

Amy Paltelky-Flynn, North Muskegon, Michigan

100 Aker Wood Playground

PAINT A WHIMSICAL BACKGROUND

Hand-painted illustrations provide a storybook backdrop to Efrat's playground snapshots. First sketch tree and other elements around placed photos, outlining with thin black pen. Paint with watercolors. Adhere photos.

Efrat Dalton, Fort Collins, Colorado

Big Girls Do Cry

SHOW THE SUNSHINE AND RAIN

A photo shoot gone sour gave Carla the idea for this happy/sad page. For the background, cut yellow lightning bolt and sky blue and brown triangles. Crop and mat photos as desired. Use Print Master Gold software (Broderbund) to print large lightning bolt and small clouds with lightning. Freehand cut sunshine and additional clouds. Adhere umbrella die cut (Punkydoodles) and water droplet stickers (Mrs. Grossman's). Journal and draw details.

Carla Daniel, Bowling Green, Kentucky

Playtime

SPOTLIGHT ON FUN

Renee's page was one of her
first experiments with hand lettering. To start, freehand draw title
letters on green paper; cut out and outline with dark green pen.
Silhouette cut and mat photos. Layer photos and letters on printed
background (Close to My Heart™/D.O.T.S.).

Renee Sherman, Fort Collins, Colorado

Mommy's Work Is Never Done

MAKE A MESS WITH STICKERS

Cindy's border humorously illustrates the reality of life with baby.
Adhere border stickers to page edges. Add red wavy lines with a
wavy ruler. Layer furniture and object stickers (Mrs. Grossman's) to
create your own chaos. Crop and layer photos. Adhere letter stickers (Frances Meyer).

Cindy Mandernach, Fraser, Michigan

The Many Hats of Annie

LAYER A FUNNY FACES MONTAGE

When photographing her daughter in various hats, Molly often drapes the background with a sheet to keep the focus on the subject. After silhouetting each photo, layer on bright pink paper. Trim around entire photomontage, leaving a small border. Mount photomontage on a purple background. Journal with colored pens.

Molly Sheedlo, Blaine, Minnesota

Baby's Fantasy

PUT WORDS IN THEIR MOUTHS

An imaginative and funny page was Stephanie's answer for what to do with all those extra baby pictures. For the background, lightly sponge clouds, mountains, trees and grass using template (All Night Media) and stamping ink. Layer silhouetted photos with stickers (Mrs. Grossman's, Creative Memories, Sandylion, Paper House Productions, Michel & Co.) and other cut-out elements. Draw and cut out thought bubbles.

Stephanie Dueck, Whitehall, Montana

The Dreaded Dust Bunny
One fun filled morning the dreaded dust bunny came for a visit. Zachary and Maxwell were playing quite well together in their bedroom. Mom was monitoring their activities from the front room when she grew quite concerned. Their laughter was a bit disturbing, so she decided to take a look. Much to her surprise the dreaded dust bunny had arrived. Zachary had gotten a hold of the baby powder and layered a nice layer of power all over the room and on his younger brother Maxwell. All mommy could see of her youngest was these two baby blue eyes peeping out of a pile of dust. Needless to say mom was not amused at the time, but decided it was a "Kodak moment". Lucky Mom got to clean up the boys and bedroom. We hope the dust bunny does not come back for a visit any time soon.

The Dreaded Dust Bunny

IMMORTALIZE A MISCHIEVOUS MOMENT

When her little ones had too much fun with the baby powder, Michele decided it was a Kodak moment. Start by cutting $\frac{3}{4}$" gray strips and four $2\frac{1}{2}$" gray squares. Cut squares in half diagonally. Stamp and emboss winter daisy border (Close To My Heart™/D.O.T.S.) on strips and triangles. Mount triangles in corners of parchment background. Layer strips around each photo. Print story; trim story edges with decorative scissors and mat with gray paper. Stamp, emboss and cut out bunnies. Color pink bunny ears and cheeks.

Michele Rank, Cerritos, California

Even
ANGELS
Have Bad Days
As a rememberance of your first birthday on Valentine's Day, mommy wanted to have a special "cupid" picture taken of you. Since you were just getting over an ear infection and fell asleep on the way to the studio, these pictures represent the sequence of events... your wings wouldn't stay on, your nose ran most of the time, and even fishy crackers couldn't make you happy! We scheduled another appointment right away which went much better (these pictures are in your professional portrait album)

Even Angels Have Bad Days

USE UP THOSE "BAD" PROOFS

When Renee's normally angelic son decided he didn't want to be Cupid for his first Valentine's Day birthday, she made the best of it as well as this adorable page. Cut the title using letter die cuts as templates. Mat main oval photo with white paper; trim with decorative scissors. Arrange with other oval photos on colored background; trim edges with decorative scissors. Write title and journaling. Adhere angel stickers (Creative Memories).

Renee Belina, Apple Valley, Minnesota

daniel, 9 mos.

Pop-Up, Pull-Out Storybook Album

MAKE A POP-UP, PULL-OUT STORYBOOK FOR YOUR CHILD

Susan turned her granddaughter Bailey's love of books into a storybook for Bailey. The album is full of little pop-up, pull-out, slide, peek-a-boo and wheel pages, always an entertaining favorite of young children. The album's high-energy colors work well with photos of busy Bailey. Also included are photos of grandparents and other relatives. "I wanted her to be able to see us when we can't be around," says Susan.

Susan Combs, The Chocolate Scrapbook, Louisville, Kentucky

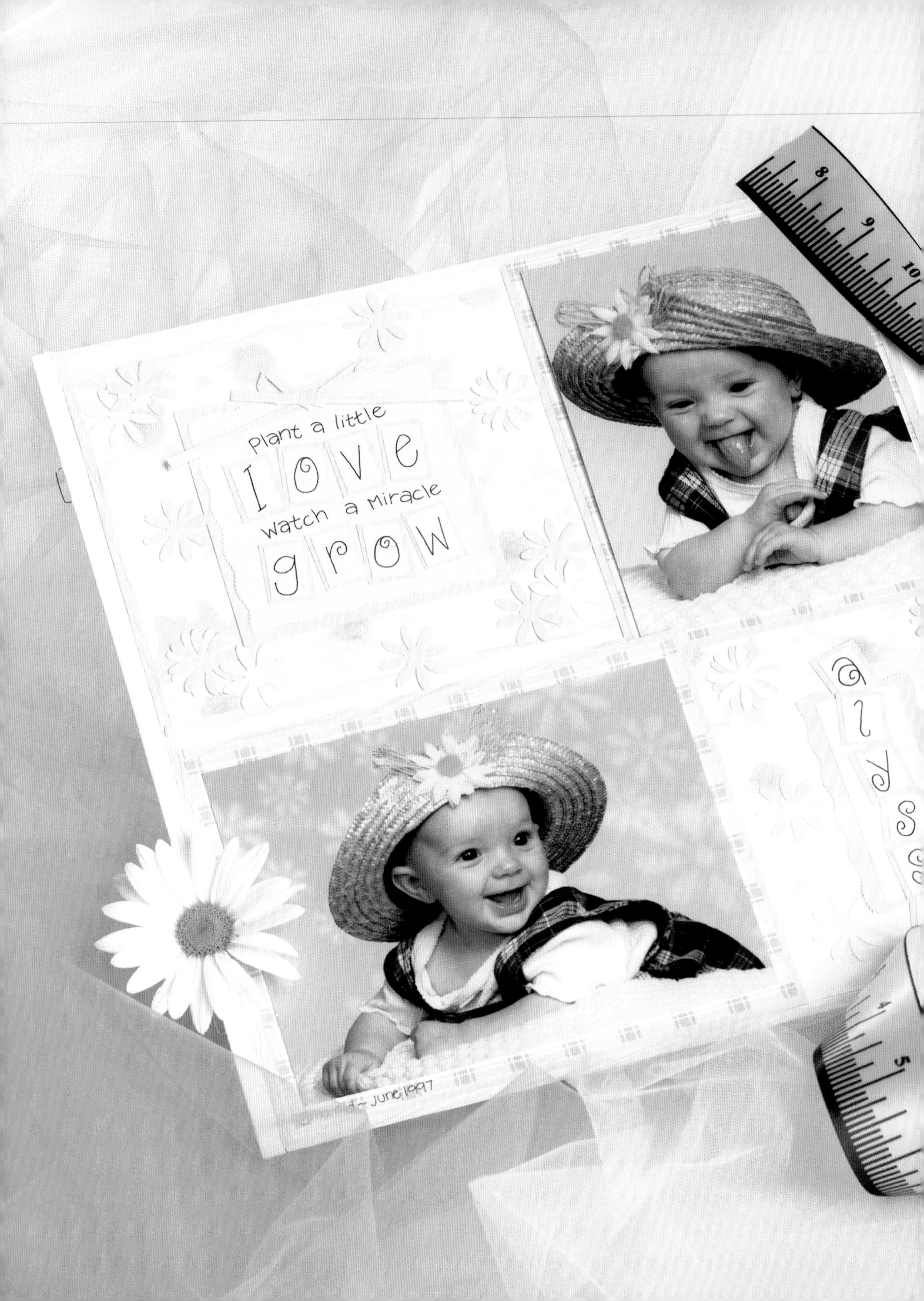

Plant a little
love
watch a Miracle
grow
June 1997

kalen, 12 mos.

colby, 9 mos.

Recording Growth

GROWING INCH BY INCH

AND SMILE BY SMILE, BABY

STAYS LITTLE JUST

A SHORT WHILE...

Babies come into the world fragile and defenseless and emerge from infancy a year later as a strong and independent toddler. In her first year, your baby will likely triple her birth weight, learn to convey her likes and dislikes and acquire the roots of language. She will also learn to turn over, sit up, crawl and perhaps walk. And she realizes she is separate from you. Your child may never change and grow so much in a single year again. Keep a pad and pencil handy and take lots of photos to capture all of these once-in-a-lifetime events.

zachary, 12 mos.

PLANT A LITTLE LOVE
CYNTHIA CASTELLUCCIO
CARROLLTON, VIRGINIA
(SEE PAGE 382)

Aidan's 1st Shoes

CUT OUT PHOTO FOOTPRINTS

Ellen cleverly traced around her son's shoes to help record his first steps. To make the path, diagonally piece 5½" light gray strips on a green background. Adhere grass stickers (Mrs. Grossman's) along edge of path. Freehand cut dark gray pebbles to fit on the path. Make a template from a baby shoe to crop the photos. Deckle trim brown photo mats. Tear and crumple brown paper for journaling to look like a piece of trash for the ants to carry away. Adhere ant stickers (Provo Craft).

Ellen Underhill, Seattle, Washington

My First Haircut

BUILD BARBER POLE BORDERS

After five homemade haircuts, Kim took her son to the barbershop. To make the barber's pole borders, use a wavy ruler to draw parallel wavy lines about ½" apart on red and blue paper. Cut two blue and two red wavy strips. Intertwine a red and blue strip for each border. Cut gray rectangles for the tops and bottoms and connect with black lines. Crop and mat circle, oval and octagonal photos using decorative scissors. Place hair in memorabilia pocket (3L Corp.). Adhere haircut-theme stickers (Frances Meyer).

Kim Penrod, Overland Park, Kansas

BABY'S MILESTONE MEMORIES

Your baby's infancy will be packed with important "firsts." While it may sound like a lot of work to photograph and record these incidents, you will never regret it. Be on the lookout for the following milestones to enhance your baby's scrapbook album:

- Clapping
- Crawling
- Drinks from cup
- First bath
- First birthday
- First haircut
- First holidays
- First illness
- First laugh
- First outing
- First smile

- First solid food
- First steps
- First tooth
- First words
- Lifts head
- Pulling self up
- Reaches for objects
- Rolling over
- Sitting up
- Standing
- Waving

ANGEL BABY

To turn your baby into an angel, silhouette photo; add hand-cut halo and wings.
Pam Joutras, Lincoln, Nebraska

Monopoly

COVER THE FIRST YEAR HIGHLIGHTS

The spaces on Kathleen's Monopoly® board summarize her son's growth milestones and family events during his first year. Start by drawing the game board outlines with thick black pen. Label and decorate spaces for first year's events using stickers (Mrs. Grossman's, Colorbök), cut-out shapes, punches and colored pens. Crop and mat photos, matching the mat colors to the board spaces. Adhere letter stickers (Creative Memories) for title.

Kathleen Fritz, St. Charles, Missouri

Meghan's Milestones

RECORD PHYSICAL PROGRESS

Ellen's "road to success" highlights her daughter's milestones
from crawling to walking. White dots add even more dimension. To complete the background, cut a yellow sun, green
grass and black road, layering as shown. Draw road and sun
details with a yellow opaque marker. Cut gray stones and
layer with silhouetted photos. Adhere flower (Mrs.
Grossman's) and insect (Michel & Co.) stickers. Add title
stickers (Making Memories); outline with white opaque pen.
Journal and draw details.

Ellen Miller, Syracuse, New York

The Baby Boy Who Could

RIDE A GROWING-UP TRAIN

(BOTTOM RIGHT) Jennifer built the photo mountain by piecing photos together and cutting the
top edge. For the train track, layer small brown
rectangles on a thick black line. Silhouette
photos and layer with the train die cuts (Ellison)
along with black and colored circles and strips.
Cut various sizes of light blue clouds. Adhere
letters stickers (Frances Meyer) for the title and
journal with black pen.

Jennifer Brookover, San Antonio, Texas

camille, 8 mos.

First Airplane Ride

CONTAIN EVENT WITH EASY BORDER

Bamber's page commemorates not only moving from Paris to the United States, but also surviving an international plane ride with an infant. Start by mounting photos and airplane die cut (Creative Memories). Print title letters in an open faced font. Cut out title letters, mat with blue, and color in yellow. Adhere airplane stickers (Mrs. Grossman's).

Bamber Grady, Fort Hood, Texas

5 Days Old
1 Month Old
3 Months Old
7 Months Old
8 Months Old
2 Months Old
9 Months Old
10 Months Old
11 Months Old
1 Year Old

Age	Vital Statistics	
	Weight	Height
Birth		
2 weeks	7 lbs 9 oz	
2 months	7 lbs 13 oz	20"
3 months	10 lbs 13 oz	20"
4 months	12 lbs 6 oz	23 ¼"
5 months	13 lbs 10 oz	25 ¼"
6 months	14 lbs 6 oz	25 ¼"
7 months	16 lbs 4 oz	26"
10 months	16 lbs 3 oz	27"
1 Year	18 lbs	28"
	19 lbs 7 oz	29 ¼"
		30 ¼"

Growth Spurt

SHOW A YEAR OF SMILES

Circle photos and just two paper colors keeps Linda's layout simple to document progress. To make the title, adhere letter (Creative Memories) and toy (Hallmark) stickers to white paper strip; mat with light green paper. Crop and mat photos. Print, cut out and mat growth chart and photo labels. Arrange elements on page with rattle die cut (Creative Memories). Accent with additional toy stickers.

Linda Keene, Golden Valley, Minnesota

Watch Me Grow

SEE THE TRANSFORMATION

Mary labeled her pictures by putting a sign in each monthly photo. Use bear and swirl printed paper (Design Originals) for background. Round corners of photos; mat and adhere. Print title using the Market font (Microsoft). Adhere die cuts (Colorbök).

Mary Hortin, Albion, Illinois

Watch Me Grow!

I'M 1 MONTH OLD TODAY! 9-21-96
I'M 2 MONTHS OLD TODAY! 10-21-96
I'm 3 months old today! 11-21-96
I'M 4 Months old today! 12-21-96
I'm 5 Months old today! 1-21-97
I'm 6 months old today! 2-21-97

Aidan's Teeth

DESIGN A DENTAL BORDER

Ellen scanned the tooth chart from a baby book and changed the colors to match her page. To complete the chart, deckle cut black and white mats and cut a pink oval for the center. For the border, cut pink gums with a scallop ruler and round corners of white rectangles for teeth. Circle cut photos. Double mat the larger photos with white and pink, trimming the white mats with notch scissors (Fiskars). Draw and mat title and adhere toothbrush and toothpaste stickers (Mrs. Grossman's). Journal on the dental chart and write photo captions. Layer page elements on a black background.

Ellen Underhill, Seattle, Washington

Hannah's First Birthday

CREATE A BALLOON BORDER

Marilyn created a classic birthday page using simple shapes and muted colors. For the balloon border, cut 10 mauve ovals using template (Delta). Trim crescents from three balloons and layer as shown. Crop and mat photos using oval template, corner rounder and decorative scissors. Cut pieces for cupcake. Punch small hearts. Emboss cake (Plaid) on lavender rectangle. Adhere candle and flower stickers (Mrs. Grossman's). Write title and draw details.

Marilyn Garner, San Diego, California

Happy Birthday

COLOR A CLASSIC MILESTONE

Cher colored her black-and-white birthday photos using SpotPen™ hand-coloring pens. To try out this technique, follow the package instructions to pre-moisten the photograph and apply the colors. Round corners of photos and mats and arrange on printed paper background (The Paper Patch). Apply rub-on cupcake, candles, letters, number, balloons, stars and presents (all Provo Craft). Print and mat journaling.

Cher Fudge, Wilmington, Ohio

My First Words

DOCUMENT BABY'S FIRST WORDS

Her daughter's growing vocabulary compelled Holly to create this vivid layout. Use patterned paper (Close to My Heart™/D.O.T.S.) for background. (LEFT PAGE) Mount large oval of patterned paper; layer with assorted paper scraps; adhere trimmed photo. (RIGHT PAGE) Double mat photos with patterned paper; trim with decorative scissors and adhere. Stamp words in red and black using Brush Stroke Caps (Close to My Heart™/D.O.T.S.); adhere.

Holly Johnson, La Quinta, California

Some just love to
play outdoors
Beneath the cool
rain showers!

They start to grow the day they're born—!
And some can get quite tall!

Little Blessings
♡♡
A story about
Meghan Alison McCallister
from birth to 5 mos.

3½ mos.

4 mos.

As little blessings grow and learn

They need a helping hand.

Little Blessings Storybook Album

RECORD BABY'S RAPID GROWTH IN A STORYBOOK ALBUM

In three days, Melissa made four of these charming "Little Blessings" books for relatives as Christmas gifts. The book's theme, based on a Precious Moments™ book titled *Little Blessings*, helps share baby's good times with someone dear. The album's photos convey the story of Meghan's first five months for grandparents and great-grandparents who might have otherwise missed out on her joyful, daily growth. Note how the simple page treatments and captioning help draw attention to the baby's photos. "The storybooks were a big hit on Christmas day!" says Melissa.

Melissa McCallister, Gainesville, Florida

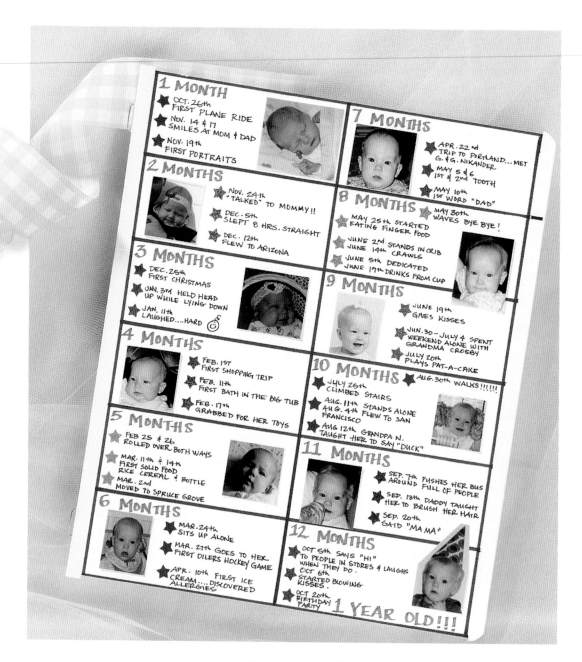

One to Twelve Months

SUMMARIZE WITH BULLET JOURNALING

Linda's journaling style is a quick way to cover a year's progress. Start by dividing the page into twelve equal boxes using a ruler and thick black pen. Crop and mount photos. Write month titles. Adhere star stickers (Mrs. Grossman's) and journal about each month's milestones.

Linda Crosby, Phoenix, Arizona

mason, 6 mos.

My First Year

GROW A CIRCLE OF LIFE

A softly penciled tree trunk provides the background for Kathy's vine of baby faces. First lightly outline trunk and branches. Shade with brown pencil. Use colored pens to write blue title and draw thick green vine. Cut out faces and mount in chronological order along vine. Adhere flower, butterfly and ivy stickers (Mrs. Grossman's).

Kathy Maggard, Edmond, Oklahoma

My First Home

REMEMBER HOME SWEET HOME

A square punch made it easy for Kathleen to build a brick house. Start by trimming 1" and ½" brown strips with deckle scissors, arranging as shown. Punch and trim cream and tan squares for bricks. Deckle trim black triangle for roof and brown rectangle for journaling. Crop and mat photos, drawing accents with thick brown pen. Mat cream triangles for photo corners. Write title and journal with white opaque pen.

Kathleen Fritz, St. Charles, Missouri

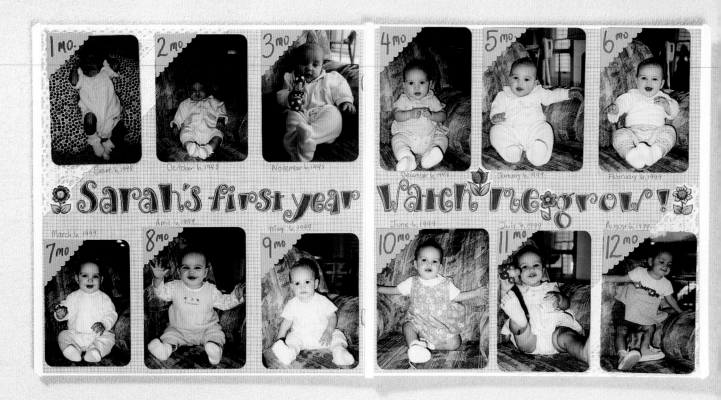

Sarah's First Year

After completing this layout, Liza was amazed to see how her daughter had changed from a tiny baby. Start with green printed paper (Keeping Memories Alive) for the background. Cut square lace doily (Close To My Heart™/D.O.T.S.) into two triangles for upper left and lower right corners. For the upper left corner of each photo, trim the long edge of a lavender triangle. Round remaining three corners on each photo. Write title letters using purple, magenta and white pens. Journal with pink pens. Adhere flower stickers (Provo Craft).

Liza Wasinger, Fairfax, Virginia

GROWING LIKE A WEED PUNCH ART

FLOWERS—Small snowflakes layered, ¼" round hand punch.
LEAVES—Medium foot, small oval.
ROCKS—Small oval, small egg trimmed.
Punch all shapes and assemble. Finish with bug stickers (Mrs. Grossman's) and hand-drawn stems and outlines.

Marcella Casebolt, Freemont, California

 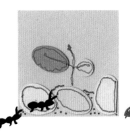   

BUTTERFLY BABY

To turn your baby into a butterfly, silhouette photo; add hand cut wings and antennae.

Suzi Leverington, Narre Warren, Victoria, Australia

Calendar Girl

PIECE A TWELVE-MONTH QUILT

These pages are part of a four-page layout Kathryn displays using panoramic page protectors. For the title, adhere letter stickers (Making Memories) on gray background. Layer quilt design using square photos and colored and printed strips and shapes. For bunny (Design Originals *Punchin'*), punch medium and small gray hearts. Cut hearts in half for ears, feet and hands. Punch mini red hearts for tongue and nose. Accent each bunny with a monthly or seasonal theme using additional punches or cut-shapes. Journal and draw details and outlines with black pen.

Kathryn Neff, Bel Air, Maryland

kara, 9 mos.

lauren, 8 mos.

Portraits

A BABY'S PORTRAIT CAPTURES

THE ESSENCE OF SPRINGTIME

– ALL OF THAT WHICH

IS FILLED WITH HOPE

AND PROMISE.

GRIN AND BEAR IT
LINDA STRAUSS
PROVO, UTAH
(SEE PAGE 382)

A baby is truly a study in contrasts. Most times, he is covered with sand and strained peas, his hair in playful disarray. But for that brief shining moment in the studio, he is a beautiful vision in his birthday suit or Sunday best, his flawless skin scrubbed and every ringlet combed into place. Perhaps that's why we go to the trouble and expense to stage formal portraits of our babies, to capture on film the instant in which they really look in our hearts: healthy, happy, perfect. These special portraits command special treatment in your baby scrapbook album.

katelyn, 11 mos.

HUNTER
10 mos.

teddy bear... teddy bear... that will do!... teddy bear

1997

teddy bear...go upstairs...teddy bear teddy bear

Hunter

PIECE A TEDDY BEAR FRAME

Tucking the photo corners beneath the hands makes Angie's bear appear to hold the portrait. Freehand cut the bear parts or photocopy and enlarge this page to make a pattern. Cut head, hands and feet from brown paper and clothing from gingham and star papers. Cut small pink half circles for the ears. Mat photo and layer with bear. Journal with black pen.

Angie Pitre, Kentville, Nova Scotia, Canada

Two Months Old

CRAFT A BABY BEAR

To add interest to simple portrait pages, Linda often re-creates photo elements such as this bear from her son's vest. Start by matting the photo with gingham paper. Cut navy triangles for the mat corners. Write and double mat title. Cut and layer pieces for bear. Draw details with black pen.

Linda Crosby, Phoenix, Arizona

TWO MONTHS OLD

AUSTIN RICK CROSBY NOV. 96

PRESIDENTIAL
GREETINGS FOR BABY

"A congratulations card for your new baby from the president and first lady makes a wonderful scrapbook album souvenir," says Marsha Hudson of Seattle, Washington.

You can send baby's name, address and birth date to White House Greetings Office, Room 39, Washington, DC 20500. Sorry, no e-mail or phone requests accepted.

Zachary's First Portrait

FRAME THE SMILES WITH STYLE

Stacy's color choices are perfect for these classic little boy portraits. Start with a navy background. Print the titles on cream paper using the Party font (Microsoft Publisher); double mat with hunter and cream. Mount photos on cream mats using clear photo corners. Cut hunter green strips and layer around portrait as shown. Punch brown and green swirls.

Stacy Hutchinson, Whitehouse, Ohio

Eric

ACCENT WITH STRIPES AND PLAIDS

A monochromatic color scheme adds a classic appeal to Christina's portrait page. First border a solid blue background with 1" strips of striped paper (Keeping Memories Alive). For corners, mat four ⅞" navy squares with white. Cut oval frame from printed paper; mat with white and dark navy. Write names on oval frame background and in two corners using a white pen. Cut and draw "My First Year" banner. Layer banner and silhouetted photo with oval frame. Freehand cut first letter of name; mat with white paper; trim with deckle scissors. Cut 2" navy squares and printed mats for remaining letters of name. Write letters and draw dots with white pen.

Christina Storms, Scotch Plains, New Jersey

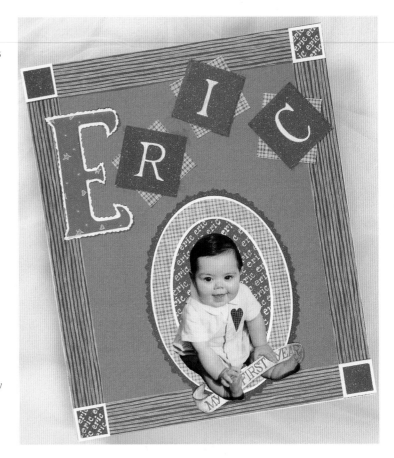

Seth

TAKE TIMELESS BLACK-AND-WHITES

When her son was seven months old, Tracy took photos of her favorite baby parts. For the portrait frame, cut a wide black mat. Write silver words and outline leaves and flowers; color in with colored pencils. Cut a slit around the design in the upper left and lower right corners. Tuck photo beneath slits. Mat remaining photos. Arrange elements on a gray background. Write saying (from *Naked Babies*, a book by Nick Kelsh & Anna Quindlen) with black pen.

Tracy Yonker, Alto, Michigan

caitlin, 6 mos.

Avalon

MAKE A FLORAL PHOTO KALEIDOSCOPE MAT

Carey enjoys making photo kaleidoscopes and found that a picture of her garden made a perfect frame for her adorable niece, Avalon. The striking garden photos successfully draw attention inward to the center photo of the baby. To create your own 12 x 12" photo kaleidoscope mat, follow directions at right; trim to frame photo and mount.

Carey VanDruff, Santa Ana, California

PHOTO KALEIDOSCOPE MATS

Photo kaleidoscope mats allow you to showcase cherished baby photos or create highly personalized gifts. For a polished look, the photo kaleidoscope mat should be created using a photo with colors that complement the center photo.

Making a photo kaleidoscope mat is easier than you might think, as you will see in the steps below. To learn more on creating photo kaleidoscopes, see *Memory Makers Photo Kaleidoscopes*™. (See page 383 for more information.)

1 *Select the photo you will use to create the photo kaleidoscope mat; have four original 4 x 6" duplicate photos and four reverse 4 x 6" photos made (Figure 1).*

2 *Using one original print, place the longest edge of a 45° triangle along the 6" side of the photo with the triangle point meeting a corner of the photo; mark the cutting line (Figure 2). Repeat with the remaining three original photos.*

3 *Layer one original cut photo on top of one reverse uncut photo and tape together at matching corners to create a mirror image. Place ruler over photo; cut on reverse photo. Now you have one pair (Figure 3). Repeat with remaining uncut three reverse photos to make three more pairs.*

4 *When finished cutting, mount all pairs onto page. Place another selected photo or artwork in the center and then frame as desired.*

Note: To make an 8 x 10" photo kaleidoscope mat, follow the instructions above using two original and two reversed-image 4 x 6" photos.

FIGURE 1

FIGURE 2

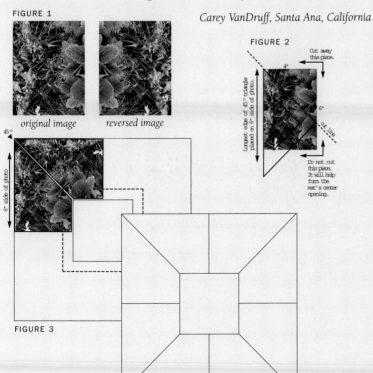

FIGURE 3

original image *reversed image*

45°

6" side of photo

Cut away this piece.

4"

6"

Longest edge of 45° triangle placed on 6" side of photo.

Cut line

Do not cut this piece. It will help form the mat's center opening.

Baby Girl

—down through a field of
stars & moonbeams, you were born
into this world and the happiness
and blessed joy you bring to us is
more radiant than the sun and
older than the moon. The world
belongs to you, Baby Kitty, along
with all our love.

Kathryn
Elizabeth
Pittard

8 Months Old   June 8 1991

Baby Jussie Bear, our boy
born on the wings of hope and
dreams, you are overflowing with the
purity of innocence and all our
promises of tomorrow. The world
belongs to you and as you begin your
journey, always remember how
very much we love you.

Triston
Michael
Pittard

It's a Boy

8 Months Old   June 8, 1997

It's a Boy & Baby Girl

Stickers with a clear background (me & my BIG ideas) make Donna's pages look like custom printed paper. First mount each portrait on a colored background. Journal with silver and highlight with white. Outline page titles with silver and fill in with white. Trim and adhere stickers around portrait, borders and titles.

Donna Pittard, Kingwood, Texas

Cameron and Kyle

Leatha's monthly portrait sessions successfully document her twins' growth, while the large portraits provide an easy focal point for her cheerful page designs. For the "January 1997" page (LEFT), adhere line stickers (Mrs. Grossman's) about ½" from bottom edge. Draw red and blue vertical lines about ¾" apart using thick pens. Layer bear stickers (Michel & Co., Paper House Productions, Suzy's Zoo) over line stickers. Crop and mat photos, title and journaling. Trim mats with deckle scissors.

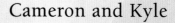

January 1997
~ 8 Months ~

Cameron and Kyle love to go to Aunt Lucinda's room and visit with her bears. They climb up in the chair with the bears then dump them on the floor and drag them around.

For the "6 Months Old" page (RIGHT), start with striped background (Frances Meyer). Triple-mat large photo with gingham, polka-dot (Frances Meyer) and red papers; adhere. Double-mat smaller photos and add red triangles at two corners. Trim title with decorative scissors; mat and adhere.

Leatha Ogden, Athens, Alabama

6 Months Old

Wearing My New Outfit

PUNCH A "BEARY" CUTE PAGE

The blanket in the photos provided the inspiration for Kristi's punch-art bears. To build the background, randomly punch ⅛" holes from ½" colored strips. Arrange strips as shown. For bears, punch large circles for faces and small circles for ears. Punch ¼" circles for inner ears. Freehand cut bows. Draw faces and other details with black pen. Mount photos and journal with pink pen.

Kristi Loudon, St. Charles, Missouri

Becca

PIECE A PUZZLE PAGE

The Sunbonnet Sue design ties in the baby quilt made especially for this portrait of Robyn's daughter. First cut a small oval photo for the page center. Print journaling, adjusting the margins as necessary. Mat the journaling and a similar size white rectangle. Use an oval template (Puzzle Mates) to cut the center oval mat and trim the surrounding elements. Cut pieces for Sunbonnet Sue using printed (Provo Craft) and cranberry paper. To decorate the bonnet, punch small yellow circles and mini cranberry swirls. Draw details with black pen.

Robyn Dunkleberger, Ponca City, Oklahoma

Hey Diddle Diddle

CRAFT A DIMENSIONAL NURSERY RHYME

Large, whimsical design elements and a large silhouetted photo of Katelyn work in unison to bring a favored nursery rhyme to life. To make a similar 8½ x 11" page, start with purple cloud paper (Current) for background. Journal nursery rhyme down right side of page in purple pencil. Locate the patterns on pages 380-381 and then follow the steps below to make the design elements. To assemble, layer moon, cow, saucer, teacup, spoon and stars onto background, using foam spacers to lift the cup and stars for added dimension.

MAKING THE DESIGN ELEMENTS

MOON—*Transfer moon pattern to yellow card stock; cut out. Sponge dark yellow ink on outer edges to shade.*

COW—*Transfer cow pattern to white card stock. Using a thick dark purple pen, trace over all lines and color in spots and hooves. Color nose pink.*

CUP AND SAUCER—*Transfer teacup and saucer patterns to white card stock; cut out. If desired, trace cats along top of cup using stencil (Delta). Use a tiny sponge eyeshadow applicator to apply green, orange, pink and yellow inks as shown. Journal name on cup. Slit teacup with craft knife along front lip; insert silhouette-cut photo of baby.*

SPOON—*Transfer spoon pattern to blue card stock; cut out. Sponge sky blue ink on outer edges to shade (see below).*

STARS—*Trace stars using stencil (Provo Craft); sponge with blue and purple ink and cut out. (All inks used were from Paintbox2® by Clearsnap.)*

Hey! Diddle, Diddle!

The cat and the fiddle,

The cow jumped over the moon;

The little dog laughed

To see such sport

And the dish ran away with the spoon.

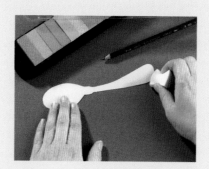

The photos in the album contain the following captions:
- Once my knee made me sad
- Or I can be elegant and dressy
- My name is Katherine Mei Dawe
- This is my family

Portrait Storybook Album

COMBINE PORTRAITS AND CANDID PHOTOS IN A STORYBOOK

Julie combined professional portraits and candid photos of her daughter Katie into a storybook. Punch art and stickers, along with the simple captioning and photo matting, give her little album its clean, crisp appearance.

"Katie loves to read her album because the story and pictures are all about her," says Julie.

Julie Dawe, Fort Collins, Colorado

PAPER FOLDING

Paper folding is a fun and unique way to embellish your scrapbook pages. With a few folds here, a few tucks there and some creative assembly, you can frame your photos with paper art that is reminiscent of ancient origami. And it's easy to do.

There are many different folds you can use. Here we feature the pointed petal corner fold. It's a great fold to use for experimenting with paper positioning. By assembling folded pieces in a ring, you can create a round frame.

Altering the number of folded pieces and the assembly method can yield square frames or smaller wreaths, with no openings, to use as embellishments.

For the wreath shown here, you'll need twenty-five 2½" squares (twenty-one for the frame and four for the corners) of lightweight denim paper (Hot Off The Press). One 8½ x 11" paper will yield twelve squares. Fold each piece following the steps below. Try folding a practice piece first.

POINTED PETAL CORNER FOLD

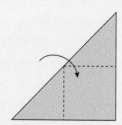

1 With pattern side facing up, fold C and D to A and B and crease.

2 Open flat, fold A and C to B and D and crease.

3 Open flat and turn paper over with pattern side down.

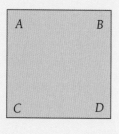

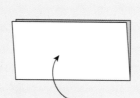

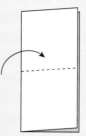

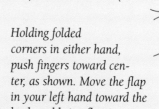

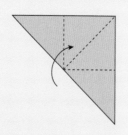

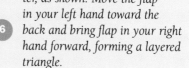

4 Bring A to D, forming a triangle and crease.

5 Open flat, fold C to B, forming a triangle and crease.

6 *Holding folded corners in either hand, push fingers toward center, as shown. Move the flap in your left hand toward the back and bring flap in your right hand forward, forming a layered triangle.*

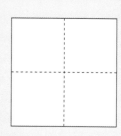

Paper folding technique by Kris Mason of Folded Memories and Laura Lees of L Paper Designs. Photo Cher Fudge, Wilmington, Ohio

Brandon

FOLD A DENIM WREATH MEMORY

The denim overalls on this adorable little guy inspired this denim folded paper wreath page. Begin with navy background (Canson). Cut twenty-five 2½" squares from denim paper (Hot Off The Press). Fold pieces following illustrations below. On separate sheet of white paper, use circle cutter to cut a ring that is 4½" on the inside and 5¼" on the outside. Use the ring and follow assembly instructions below. Place a 5 x 7" photo behind frame; trim if needed and adhere. Mount remaining four folded pieces at corners; finish with journaling.

ASSEMBLY

- *Line up twenty-one pieces on circle's edge with even spacing and using the same reference points on each folded paper as shown below.*
- *Holding two pieces with closed points facing same direction, place flap of one piece into space between flap and diamond of the other.*
- *Snug up pieces so that the long open end of inserted piece is flush with edge of diamond of other piece.*
- *Secure with adhesive.*
- *Repeat remaining pieces, sliding first piece into last to finish.*

7 *Bring top right flap to left side.*

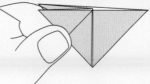
8 *Fold top left flap down along centerline and crease.*

9 *Slide finger between remaining left flaps.*

10 *Bring top left flaps to right side.*

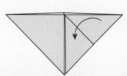
11 *Fold top right flap down along centerline and crease.*

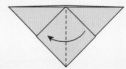
12 *Bring top right flap to left side.*

For more on paper folding, see Memory Makers® Memory Folding™. *(Ordering information is on page 383.)*

Lettering Patterns & Page Title Ideas

If you wish, use these convenient lettering patterns to add an elegant finishing touch to your baby scrapbook pages. Simply photocopy the lettering pattern, scaled to the size you need, and trace onto your page in pencil using a light table. Retrace and color in pen color of your choice. Or make your own patterns from the page title ideas listed by theme.

PRE-BIRTH
A womb with a view
Life on the inside
Showered with love
Twinkle, twinkle little star...how I wonder what you are
Under construction

Sugar and Spice *and everything nice*

Our Little Angel

a Star is born

LABOR & DELIVERY
A labor of love
A star is born
Baby's coming!
On the day you were born
Special delivery
Welcome little one
Your shining hour

BABY ANNOUNCEMENTS
B is for baby
Heard the news?
It's a boy!
It's a girl!
Meet our new arrival
News from the cradle
Oh what joy, a baby boy!
Sugar and spice and everything nice
Welcome home baby

FAMILY
Brotherly love
Cuddles for Mommy
Daddy's girl
Daddy's little slugger
Daddy's pride and joy
Family ties
Grandpa's little princess
It's all relative
Like father, like son
Like mother, like daughter
Love my Grandma
Mommy's little stinker
Mommy's little angel
My heart belongs to Daddy
Our new grandchild
Proud grandparents
Sisters forever
That's our boy

cute as a Button

Grandpa's Little PRINCESS

TWINS
Diaper daze
Double delight
Double trouble
Seeing double
Twice blessed
Two by two

Special Delivery (LOVE YOU SO MUCH!)

DIAPER DAZE

born to be wild

SLEEPYTIME

Angel baby
Good night, moon
Hush-a-bye baby
Now I lay me down to sleep
Off to dreamland
Rock-a-bye-baby
Sleep, baby, sleep
Sleep tight, little one
Sleeping beauty
Snug as a bug
Sweet dreams, baby
Sweet slumber

BATHTIME

Bath time makes life bearable
Bathing beauty
Best-dressed baby
My bath runneth over
Rub-a-dub-dub

ACTIVITIES

Born to be wild
Busy hands
Feed me, burp me, change me, cuddle me
Fun in the sun
Hug me, squeeze me, love me
I'm on a roll!
Let's go bye-bye!
Look at me, I'm crawling!
Look, Ma, no hands!
Make a joyful noise
My first steps
Pat-a-cake, pat-a-cake
Peek-a-boo
Shake, rattle and roll
So much to do, so little time

FINGERS & TOES

A perfect 10!
Our family has grown by two feet
Priceless parts
Tiny fingers, tiny toes

SENTIMENTS

A baby is love
A blessing from above
A wee bit of heaven
Babies are a gift from above
Babies are a miracle of love
Babies are heaven sent
God's little lamb
Heart of my heart
Jesus loves me
Little one, you hold my heart
You are my sunshine
You are loved

GROWTH

Born to bloom
Growing by leaps and bounds
Growing inch by inch
How does our baby grow?
Inch by inch, growing is a cinch
SOOO BIG!
Watch me grow!

MILESTONES

My 1st adventure
My 1st bath
My 1st Christmas
My 1st Easter
My 1st food
My 1st haircut
My 1st home
My 1st smile
My 1st steps
My 1st tooth
My 1st words
My 1st year

PORTRAITS

Cute as a button
Lookin' good
Our little angel
Our little superstar
Sitting pretty
You oughta' be in pictures
You're so doggone cute!
You've got the cutest little baby face
Unbearably cute

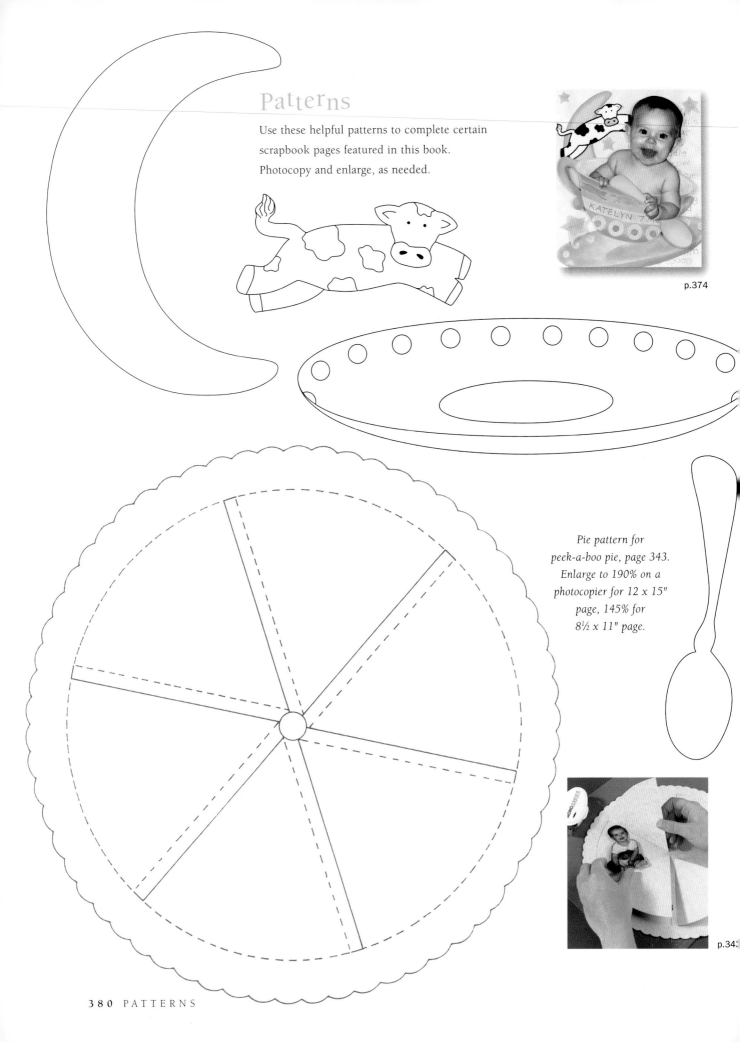

Patterns

Use these helpful patterns to complete certain
scrapbook pages featured in this book.
Photocopy and enlarge, as needed.

p.374

*Pie pattern for
peek-a-boo pie, page 343.
Enlarge to 190% on a
photocopier for 12 x 15"
page, 145% for
8½ x 11" page.*

p.343

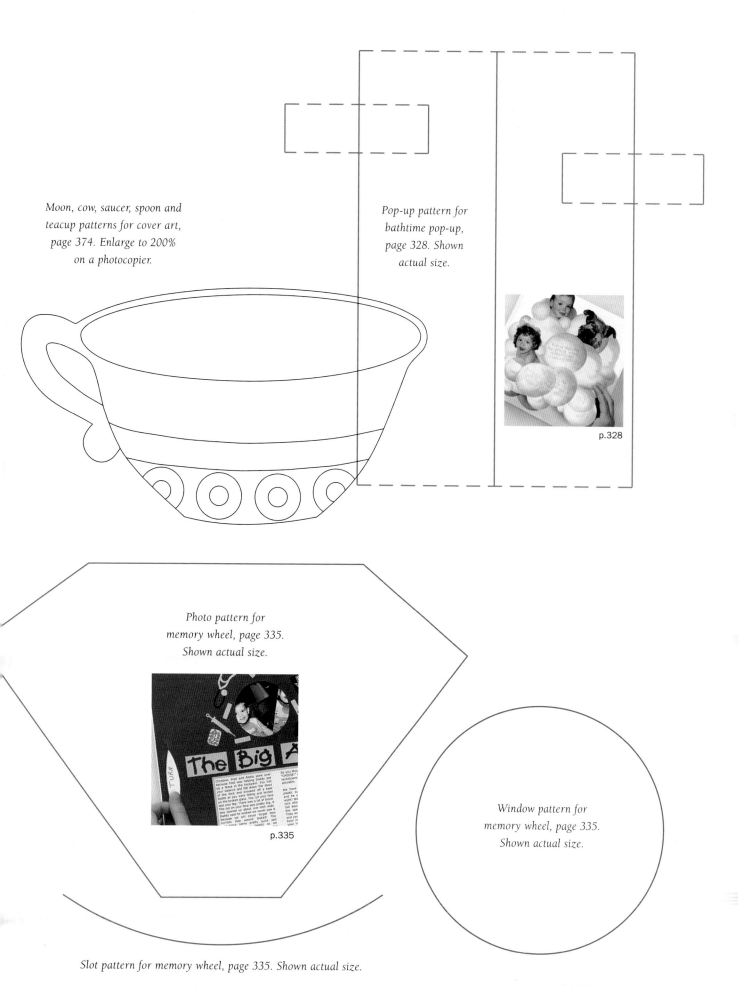

Moon, cow, saucer, spoon and
teacup patterns for cover art,
page 374. Enlarge to 200%
on a photocopier.

Pop-up pattern for
bathtime pop-up,
page 328. Shown
actual size.

p.328

Photo pattern for
memory wheel, page 335.
Shown actual size.

p.335

Window pattern for
memory wheel, page 335.
Shown actual size.

Slot pattern for memory wheel, page 335. Shown actual size.

cover photo
Katelyn Stephanie Barnard,
Laguna Nigel, CA

title page
Cameron, 9 mos. Christina Husted,
Kokomo, IN

page 262
Daniel
Use cream paper for background.
Punch pastel papers (Canson) with
large circle punch; adhere randomly. Mount photo. Freehand cut matted frame; adhere with foam spacers. Finish with matted journaling
and ¼" hand punched pastel dots.

pages 266-267
Children Are...
Alex's button-adorned quilt spread
is the perfect homespun layout for
showcasing sixteen unrelated photos. Begin with teal background.
Trim sixteen photos to 2¼" squares;
mat with 2½" yellow patterned
squares (The Crafter's Workshop)
and set aside. Cut sixteen more
2½" squares from patterned papers
(The Robin's Nest, Hot Off The
Press). Randomly decorate fourteen
squares with freehand cut and
punched mats and buttons, using
foam spacers under buttons.
Journal last two squares. Assemble
quilt, evenly spacing all squares ½"
apart and ¼" from edges of pages.

page 268
Rhys Michelle Fletcher, Phoenix, AZ

page 270
Andrew Anne Detter, Dover, PA
Three Page Designs Artists were
supplied with products from the
following companies to create their
pages: PAPERS–The Crafter's Workshop,
K & Company, Keeping Memories Alive,
MiniGraphics, Paper Adventures and
Royal Stationery. STICKERS–Frances
Meyer, Mary Engelbreit, me & my BIG
ideas and PrintWorks. STAMP–Uptown
Rubber Stamps. 3-D KEEPERS™–
C-Thru® Ruler Co.

page 271
Kalen Jamia Bankhead,
Lancaster, CA

page 272
Oh Happy Day!
Tamara's photo exudes her expectant
joy over her positive pregnancy test,
a great piece of memorabilia. Start
with a sheet of textured paper. Cut
another sheet of lavender paper into
a starburst pattern; mount every
other strip on the background.
Double mat photo and punch large
flowers and small circles for corner
embellishments. Print and mat journaling. Cut out handmade title letters; mat and cut out each word.
Print and mat journaling. Mount
pregnancy test.

page 273
Wes Michele Rank, Cerritos, CA;
Jack Mark Lewis, Denver, CO;
Emily Heather Schram,
Belgrade, MT

page 274
Paige Janelle Harris, San Rafael, CA

page 276
Joshua Jewelene Holverson,
Pocatello, ID

page 277
Carlos Lara Janeen Lezcano,
Pembroke Pines, FL

page 278
Annelise Renee Sherman,
Fort Collins, CO

page 279
Derek Claudia Smith, Denver, CO

page 280
Introducing Jack Bayless
Katy's birth announcement was
inspired by the story of Jack and
the Beanstalk. For your own organic page, use decorative scissors to
trim photo and background yellow
square. Mount blue gingham paper.
Mat photo and announcement with
black and gold paper. Stamp green
vines (Hero Arts) and sun (DJ
Inkers). Adhere letter stickers
(Frances Meyer), white fence and
ivy stickers (Mrs. Grossman's) and
bee stickers (Provo Craft).

page 281
Tori Wendy McKeehan, Sugar
Grove, IL; Kendall Drue Lisa
Elfstrum, Susan City, CA; Marco
Kathy Medina, Carrollton, TX

page 282
Jackson Tricia Kelly,
Thousand Oaks, CA

page 283
Taylor Claudia Smith, Denver, CO

page 284
Brenna Laurie Herlson, Butte, MT

page 285
Logan Shelley Price, Lakeland, FL

page 286
Mitch Joy Carey, Visalia, CA

page 287
Bethany Cindy Kitchin,
Lemoore, CA

page 288
Mercedes Julie Trujillo,
Thornton, CO

page 289
Jourden Barbara Wegener,
Huntington Beach, CA

page 292
Tucker Alison Beachem,
San Diego, CA

page 293
Katie Beth Ortstadt, Wichita, KS

page 296
A Baby's Body...
Deanna's love of classic black-and-
white photos in natural light and
simple embellishments give this
page its timeless appeal. Adhere
large photos to page. Crop and mat
smaller photos on yellow paper.
Freehand cut large and small
daisies and leaves; adhere. Finish
with pen stroke stitching and journaling.

page 297
Nathan Gerrie Kerby, Joplin, MO;
Alexis Jill Aiello, Chatsworth, CA;
Nile Jamie Getskow, CA

page 298
Alexis Lisa Garnett, Littleton, CO

page 299
Katelyn Stephanie Barnard,
Laguna Nigel, CA

page 300
Mackenzie Tina Hall, Arlington, TX

page 301
Cameron Shawna Sanner,
Des Arc, AR

page 302
Holly Kelley Blondin,
Grand Blanc, MI

page 304
Hannah Karen Humayun,
Timonium, MD

page 308
Alexis Tracey Carpenter,
Baldwin, NY

page 309
Samantha Victoria Sherman,
Apopka, FL

page 310
Kira Beth Smith, Auburn, WA

page 312
Doug Jeanne Ciolli,
Dove Canyon, CA

page 313
Jason Linda Keene,
Golden Valley, MN

page 314
Austin Jadelyn Alvarez, Folsom, CA

page 315
Amanda Nicole Donatucci,
Ottawa, Ontario, Canada
Three Generations
Photos provided by Karen Cain,
Denver, CO

page 316
Grandma's Heart chenille pillow and
lamp Provided by Highlander
Marketing, (800) 836-3810,
wholesale only
Sweet Dreams
Melisa's page conveys her sleeping
newborn's peacefulness with soft
nighttime colors. Start by cutting
clouds and stars from white, denim
(Close to My Heart™ /D.O.T.S.) and
yellow (Keeping Memories Alive)
paper using template (PrintWorks).
Freehand cut yellow moon. Mat
stars and moon with white paper.
Double mat photo. Layer elements
on dark blue patterned background
(Keeping Memories Alive). Use
template (Pebbles In My Pocket) to
cut yellow title letters; mat with
denim paper. Journal and draw
details with gold and navy pens.
Tie bow with gold embroidery
floss.

page 317
Darien Arlene Cano, Burbank, CA;
Meagan Lisa Coultas, Lebanon, OH;
Sarah Liz Dubenetzky,
Carlsbad, CA

page 318
Andy Jenny Palamar, Kennesaw, GA
Swinging on a Star punch art
MOON & STARS–Lg. circle cut into
crescent, sm. and mini stars. HEAD
& TORSO–Sm. circle. ARM &
FEET–Sm. oval. Freehand draw
details.
Buggy Baby punch art
BUGGY–Lg. circle cut. HEADS &
WHEELS–Sm. circle. WHEEL
CENTER–3/16" round hand punch.
HANDLES–Sm. spiral, negative piece
from scroll border punch. HAT–Lg.
bell cut. Freehand draw details.
(For more baby-related punch art,
see Memory Makers® Punch Your Art
Out Volumes 1 & 2. Information,
page 127.)

page 323
Katherine Julie Dawe,
Fort Collins, CO

page 324
Raelyn Ellen O'Dell, Campbell, CA

page 325
Annelise Renee Sherman,
Fort Collins, CO

page 326
Brad Denise Dawn, San Jose, CA

page 327
Hannah Karen Humayun,
Timonium, MD

page 328
Katie Beth Ortstadt, Wichita, KS

page 330
Sara Kim Owens, Lynnwood, WA

page 331
Jessica Barbara Parks, Auburn, WA

page 332
Jakob Rebecca Goodrich,
Missoula, MT

page 333
Alison Susan Brochu, East Berlin,
CT; Antique infant feeder and photo
Provided by Allen Morawiec,
Littleton, CO, private collector and
member of The American
Collectors of Infant Feeders.

page 334
Emily Jennifer Wilkinson,
Lynwood, CA

page 335
Maxwell Michele Rank, Cerritos, CA

page 336
Samuel Rebecca Goodrich,
Missoula, MT

page 337
Jakob Rebecca Goodrich,
Missoula, MT

page 338
Baby Face
Bright colors and a simple design
highlight black-and-white photos of
Char's daughter. For the border, write
the "Baby Face" song lyrics separated
by black lines. Crop and mat photos
using bright colors and deckle scissors.
Piece photos into a square design.
Write title words on white strips.

page 339
Torin Michelle Fletcher, Phoenix,
AZ; Savanna Pat Asher, Camarillo,
CA; Ariel Lori Creamer,
Belle Harbor, NY

page 340
Hunter MaryJo Regier, Littleton, CO

page 341
Andy Jenny Palamar, Kennesaw, GA

page 342
Quinton Cara Currier,
McMinnville, OR

page 343
Amber Pennie Stutzman,
Broomfield, CO

page 345
Jared Beatriz Boggs,
Delray Beach, FL

page 346
Tucker Amy McGrew,
Miamisburg, OH

page 347
Lindsey Denise Alford-Ray,
Crofton, MD

page 348
Daniel Angie Ojeda-Kreiman,
Fairport, NY

page 350
Plant a Little Love
When the photographer wanted to
throw out the photo of her daughter sticking out her tongue, Cynthia
told her, "No way!" Create a similar
sunny page by double matting portraits using patterned (The Paper
Patch) and yellow paper. Arrange
portraits with rectangles of daisy
paper (Geographics). Use black
pen, decorative scissors and cream
and yellow paper to create titles.
Punch large cream and yellow flowers. Adhere raffia strips and bow.

page 351
Colby Cindy Browning, Chatham,
NJ; Kalen Jamia Bankhead,
Lancaster, CA; Zachary Michelle
Peters, North Aurora, IL

page 352
Amanda Pam Klassen,
Westminster, CO

page 353
Brad Denise Dawn, San Jose, CA

page 354
Camille Sylvie Abecassis,
Denver, CO

page 355
Morgan Jennifer McInnes,
Coarsegold, CA

page 358
Ashley Amy Talarico,
Northglenn, CO

page 360
Mason Wendi Hitchings,
Isaquah, WA

page 361
Ellie Wendi Hitchings, Isaquah, WA

page 363
Kyle Kim Skattum, Broomfield, CO

page 364
Fiesta Plush polar bears Provided
by Summit Connection,
(800) 777-1292, wholesale only
Grin and Bear It
Linda's freshly bathed baby and
bunches of bears made for a perfect
spur-of-the-moment portrait. First
mat and mount the portrait; then
draw a black line border around
the page edges. Freehand cut
thought bubbles for journaling.
Punch white and gray bears and
draw faces. Layer bears around
portrait, using foam spacers for
dimension.

page 365
Lauren Cheri O'Donnell, Orange,
CA; Kara Pam Kopka, New Galilee,
PA; Katelyn Stephanie Barnard,
Laguna Nigel, CA

page 367
Morgan Cathy Shepherd,
Santee, CA

page 368
Caitlin Dawn Mabe, Broomfield, CO

page 369
Dylan Holly Gressett,
Springdale, UT

page 373
Trinton Lydia Rueger, Denver, CO

page 374
Rebecca Becky Burgeron,
Egg Harbor Township, NJ

page 376
Jessica Barbara Parks, Auburn, WA

SOURCES

The following companies manufacture products featured in this book. Please check your local retailers to find these materials. In addition, we have made every attempt to properly credit the trademarks and brand names of the items mentioned in this book. We apologize to any companies that have been listed incorrectly, and we would appreciate hearing from you.

3L Corp. (847) 808-1140

Accu-Cut Systems® (800) 288-1670

All Night Media®, Inc. (800) 782-6733 (wholesale only)

American Tombow, Inc. (800) 835-3232

Amscan, Inc. (914) 345-2020

Artistic Stamp Exchange (800) 232-5399

Broderbund (800) 395-0277

Canson, Inc. (800) 628-9283

Carolee's Creations (435) 563-9336

Clearsnap, Inc. (800) 448-4862

Close to My Heart™/D.O.T.S. (888) 655-6552

Colorbök (800) 366-4660

Colors by DESIGN (818) 376-1226

The Crafter's Workshop (877) CRA-FTER

Creative Beginnings (800) 367-1739

Creative Memories® (800) 468-9335

The C-Thru® Ruler Company (800) 243-8419

Current®, Inc. (800) 848-2848

Delta Technical Coatings, Inc. (800) 423-4135

Design Originals (800) 877-7820

DJ Inkers™ (800) 944-4680

Ellison® Craft & Design (800) 253-2238

Extra Special Products Corp. (937) 548-9388

The Family Archives™ (888) 662-6556

Family Treasures, Inc. (800) 413-2645

Fiskars®, Inc. (800) 950-0203

Folded Memories (425) 673-7422

Frances Meyer, Inc.® (800) 372-6237

Geographics, Inc. (800) 426-5923

Hallmark Cards, Inc. (800) HALLMARK

Handmade Scraps (877) 915-1695

Hero Arts Rubber Stamps, Inc. (800) 822-HERO

Hot Off The Press®, Inc. (800) 227-9595

K & Company (888) 244-2083

Keeping Memories Alive™ (800) 419-4949

L Paper Designs (425) 775-9636

Lake City Craft Quilling Supplies (417) 725-8444

Making Memories (800) 286-5263

Marvy Uchida (800) 541-5877

Mary Engelbreit® Studios (800) 443-MARY

McGill, Inc. (800) 982-9884

me & my BIG ideas (949) 589-4607

Memory Makers® *Memory Folding™, Photo Kaleidoscopes™* and *Punch Your Art Out Volumes 1 & 2* (800) 366-6465

Microsoft Corp. microsoft.com

Michel® & Company (800) 533-7263

MiniGraphics (800) 442-7035

Mostly Animals Rubber Art Stamps (800) 832-8886

MPR Associates®, Inc. (800) 454-3331

Mrs. Grossman's Paper Co.™ (800) 457-4570

Northern Spy (530) 620-7430

NRN Designs (800) 421-6958 (wholesale only)

Paper Adventures® (800) 727-0699

The Paper Company (800) 426-8989

Paper House Productions (800) 255-7316

Paper Parade (717) 898-1212

The Paper Patch® (801) 253-3018 (wholesale only)

Pebbles In My Pocket® www.pebblesinmypocket.com

Pentel of America, Ltd. (800) 421-1419

Personal Stamp Exchange (800) 782 6748

Plaid Enterprises, Inc. (800) 842-4197

Preservation Technologies (800) 416-2665

PrintWorks (800) 854-6558

Provo Craft (800) 937-7686

Punkydoodles (800) 428-8688

Puzzle Mates (888) 595-2887

The Robin's Nest (435) 789-5387

Royal Stationery™ (800) 328-3856

Rubber Monger (888) 732-0086

Rubber Stamps of America (800) 553-5031

Sakura of America (800) 776-6257

Sandylion Sticker Designs (800) 387-4215

SDL Corp. (509) 476-4580

Sierra On-Line, Inc.® (800) 757-7707

Sonburn, Inc. (800) 527-7505

SonLight Press International (888) SON-LITE

SpotPen™ Hand Coloring Pens (505) 523-8820

Stampabilities (800) 888-0321

Stampendous!® (800) 869-0474

Stampin' Up! (800) 782-6787

Stamping Station, Inc. (801) 444-3828

Stickopotamus® (888) 270-4443

Suzy's Zoo® (800) 777-4846

Uptown Rubber Stamps™ (800) 888-3212

Westrim® Crafts (800) 727-2727

PROFESSIONAL PHOTOGRAPHERS

page 262
Daniel
Joyce Feil
Denver, CO

page 276
Joshua
Kapture Kids Portrait Studio
(800) 238-1195

page 282
Special Delivery
First Foto
(800) 443-0855

page 312
Family Resemblance
CPI Corp.–Sears
Grand Rapids, MI 49512

page 313
Father and Son
Heitz Photography
8008 W. 19th North
Wichita, KS 67212

page 320
Slumber Softly Little One
Diane Perry
5140 W. 120th Ave.
Westminster, CO 80020

page 332
I Love Goldfishes
Sears Portrait Studio
Macon, GA 31206

page 346
Tucker
Expressly Portraits
Beavercreek, OH 45431

page 348
Even Angels Have Bad Days
David T. Brown Photography
13800 Chestnut Dr., #215
Eden Prairie, MN 55344

page 350
Plant a Little Love
Lifetouch Portrait Studios
J.C. Penney
Hampton, VA 23666

page 353
Monopoly
First Foto
(800) 443-0855

page 365
Lauren
Ruth Clark Photography
20793 Valley Blvd., #D
Walnut, CA 91789

Kara
Sears Portrait Studio
Menaca, PA 15061

Katelyn
Lifetouch Portrait Studios
Laguna Hills, CA 92653

page 367
Morgan
Expressly Portraits
Foster City, CA 94404

Zachary's First Portrait
Moto Photo 533
Toledo, OH 43614

pages 370-371
It's a Boy & Baby Girl
Expressly Portraits
Foster City, CA 94404

page 372
Cameron & Kyle
Rogers Portraits
115 W. Washington St.
Athens, AL 35611

page 373
Becca
Cope Photography
202 E. Grand
Tonkawa, OK 74653

page 375
Storybook Album
Senger Portraits LLC
2190 W. Drake Rd.
Fort Collins, CO 80526

BIBLIOGRAPHY

Cone, Thomas E., Jr., M.D. *200 Years of Feeding Infants in America.* Columbus, OH: Ross Laboratories, 1976.

Eisenberg, Murkoff, Hathaway. *What to Expect When You're Expecting.* New York: Workman Publishing, 1984, 1988, 1991, 1996.

Emerson, Sally. *The Nursery Treasury.* New York: Bantam Doubleday Dell Publishing Group, Inc., 1988.

Fildes, Valerie. *Breasts, Bottles and Babies.* Edinburgh: Edinburgh University Press, 1986.

Hague, Michael. *Sleep, Baby, Sleep–Lullabies and Night Poems.* New York: Morrow Junior Books, 1994.

McKellar, Shona. *A Child's Book of Lullabies.* New York: DK Publishing, Inc., 1997.

Pfister, Marcus. *I See the Moon–Good Night Poems and Lullabies.* Switzerland: North-South Books, 1991.

WEB SITES

www.acif.org (The American Collectors of Infant Feeders)

www.ssa.gov/OACT/NOTES/note139/note139.html (Social Security Administration's Office of the Chief Actuary)

Casey was adorable in the dress that I made for her first day of school at Turtleback Elementary. She was so excited to start school. Special memories of this year were: her best friend Joy, her wonderful teacher Mrs. Brown, Pajama Day, Farmer Day and art time. 1995

MEMORY
MAKERS

SCHOOL DAYS
Scrapbooks

Ideas, Tips & Techniques for
Scrapbooking the Grade School Years

**MEMORY
MAKERS
BOOKS**

DENVER, COLORADO

SAMANTHA, KINDERGARTEN

► Contents

OUR LITTLE ARTISTS

Sasha - Kindergarten

Daniel - 1st grade

Anna - 2nd grade

Each of our children loves to create their own masterpieces. Painting and drawing are an important part of our lives.

Introduction

Each year, as summer winds down and my children and I head out for the "back-to-school" shopping experience, it is easy to get caught up in the excitement and anticipation that a new school year brings and the memories of school days gone by. My earliest grade school memory goes back to kindergarten. I vividly remember walking to school and clanging my metal lunch box against my knees while waiting with a group of kids for the crossing guard to allow us to cross the street. I couldn't wait to get to class and be with my teacher.

Children have a natural love of learning, and as much as school life has changed since I was in school, some things remain constant. Who can forget the pride of owning your very own, shiny backpack and sharpened pencils for the first time? And remember wondering who would sit next to you and the aroma of food wafting down the hallway from the cafeteria, making your stomach grumble?

Some things you just never forget as your senses rush over you and the mental images replay. However, the details of such important events can fade over time. When you preserve your or your children's school memories and activities, it is easy to reminisce by simply flipping through the pages of a unique scrapbook album.

In this book, we provide countless page ideas to help you document all of the hard work, the triumphs and the tribulations, the opportunities and the special details that capture the essence of grade school. We've included ideas for everything—from back-to-school experiences, daily school life, activities and special events to home schooling, documenting the difficult times and unique treatments for school portraits. In addition, we feature fun techniques, original paper piecing patterns, reproducible page patterns and more to help you get started. You'll also get to hear from kids who are creating their own scrapbooks. Maybe their stories will inspire your own grade-schooler to start scrapping.

One thing is certain. At no other time in a child's education will more school papers, photographs, and memorabilia come home than in grade school—each item with its own unique story to tell. I hope this book will inspire you with new pages to create and photographs to take. With these great ideas, your school days pages are guaranteed to make the grade!

Michele

MICHELE GERBRANDT
FOUNDER OF *MEMORY MAKERS* MAGAZINE

OUR LITTLE ARTISTS
(SEE PAGE 507)

1 Getting Started

The years spent in school are very busy, packed with many memorable moments, events, friendships and accomplishments you don't want to forget. Ideally, you could do your school scrapbooking as it happens and as your child grows. Unfortunately, that is not the case for most of us. Therefore, some organization and planning are essential. Here are some easy steps to help you get started.

1 Set Up a Work Area

Your work area should have a level work surface, good lighting and good access to your scrapbooking supplies, photos and other memorabilia. Preferably this is an area you can leave and come back to without much time spent on setup or cleanup. You may also want to make sure you are near an electrical outlet, especially if you use a light box, embossing gun, extra lighting or computer.

2 Decide on a Format

Decide how much information you want to include for each grade. Remember that the amount of information you choose to use will have a direct result on the size and the amount of time you spend on the scrapbook. If you're a scrapbooker who likes to scrap everything, you may want to consider dividing your school scrapbook into two or three separate scrapbooks (primary and secondary or elementary, middle and high school).

3 Create Categories

Write categories for your photos and memorabilia on sticky notes. Categories can be in chronological order, by theme or even modeled after the chapters in this book. See the photos and memorabilia checklists on page 395 for ideas. You can add or remove categories as you go.

4 Organize Photos & Memorabilia

Good organization is key to being successful in your scrapbooking. Try to store and save all school photos and memorabilia in the same area of your home. This eliminates wasting time trying to remember which shelf, box or closet holds which photos. It is important to try to label or make notes about photos as soon as possible. Jot details on sticky notes or on the backs of photos with a photo-safe wax pencil. This will help prevent forgetting special moments and will assist you when it's time to journal.

5 Store Photos & Negatives

Any time you put this much time and effort into something as special as your child's scrapbook, it deserves the added effort of making sure it will last. Store extra photos and negatives in archival quality binders, boxes and sleeves to help secure your memories for future generations.

SCISSORS & PAPER TRIMMER

Keep a pair of sharp, straight-edge scissors and a paper trimmer at hand. Also, use decorative scissors for creative edges on photos and mats. Turn decorative scissors over to achieve a varied cutting pattern.

2 Basic Tools & Supplies

Once you've chosen a format and organized your photos and memorabilia, you're almost ready to create your first page. But first, gather the following tools:

ADHESIVES

Use scrapbooking adhesives, such as glues, tapes and mounting corners, that are labeled "acid-free" and "photo-safe." Rubber cement, white school glue and cellophane tape contain chemicals that can harm photos over time.

PAPERS

Acid- and lignin-free decorative papers are available in countless colors and patterns. Use these versatile papers for a background, an accent, or to mat or frame photos.

ALBUMS

Albums come in strap-style, three-ring binder or post-bound, allowing you to remove, add, or rearrange pages as needed. Spiral-bound albums make great theme albums for children or gift albums. The quantity and physical size of your photos and memorabilia will help determine the size of album you need.

DESIGN ADDITIONS

Unique design additions can give a page theme continuity. These can include stickers, die cuts, memorabilia pockets, photo corners and more. Shop with a list of needed supplies and some photos to match colors and avoid any unnecessary spending.

RULERS & TEMPLATES

Use rulers and templates to crop photos or trace shapes onto paper, to cut decorative photo mats or to create your own die cuts.

PENCILS, PENS & MARKERS

Journaling adds the voice and pertinent facts to your scrapbook. A rainbow of journaling pens and markers, with a variety of pen tips, make penmanship a snap. Pigment ink pens are best because of their permanence.

3 Create a Layout

FOCAL POINT

Choose an enlarged, matted, unique or exceptional photo for a focal point on the page to help determine an eye-pleasing layout. This is where the eye will look first. Other photos on the page should support this image.

BALANCE

Place your photos on a one- or two-page spread. Large, bright or busy photos can feel "heavier" than others, so move the photos around until the page no longer feels weighted or lopsided. Remember to leave enough space for journaling.

COLOR

Choose background and photo mat papers and design additions that complement the photos, making them stand out rather than compete for attention. Sometimes less is more. Too much color can be distracting.

4 Crop-n-Assemble

CROPPING

Photo cropping (Figure 1) can add style, emphasize a subject or remove a busy background. See *Memory Makers Creative Photo Cropping for Scrapbooks* for hundreds of cropping ideas.

MATTING

Single or layered paper photo mats focus attention and add balance to a page. Use a paper trimmer (Figure 2), decorative scissors, a template or freehand cut a mat, leaving a border around the photo.

MOUNTING

Mount photos on your page with double-sided tape (Figure 3) or liquid adhesives for a permanent bond. Paper or plastic photo corner triangles allow for easy removal of photos, if needed.

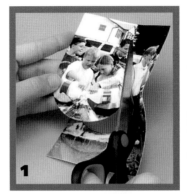

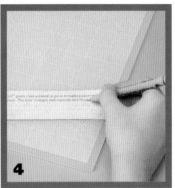

5 Journaling

The stories behind the photos are details that can be lost forever if they're not included on your page. Start with one, or a combination, of these simple journaling styles:

JOURNALING TIPS

- Write freehand in light pencil first, then trace with ink.
- Journal on a separate piece of paper (Figure 4), cut it out and mount it on the page.
- Use a pencil to trace a lettering or journaling template on the page, then trace with ink.
- Print journaling on your computer. Crop, mat and mount journaling or trace the journaling onto your page using a light box.
- Journal onto die cuts or mats, write around your photos in curved lines or turn paragraphs into shapes.
- Photocopy and color the lettering patterns on pages 500-501 for quick page titles.
- Use the journaling checklist on page 395 to help bring your photographic story to life.

STORYTELLING

Give details about those in the photo at the time the photo was taken. Include everything from clothing, background items, mood, and conversation—perhaps even the weather!

QUOTES, POEMS & SAYINGS

Search for your subject on quote-related Web sites, in poetry books, in the Bible, even on T-shirts! Or write your own.

BULLETS

List the basics of who, what, when and where in bullet form.

CAPTIONS

Expand on bulleted information with complete sentences, allowing for more creative expression.

- Leah, age 11
- 6th Grade
- Science: studying volcanoes
- Community Christian School
- 2001

Volcano! Leah made an erupting papier-mâché volcano for 6th grade science.
Community Christian School
Age 11
2001

There once was a girl named Leah
Who just couldn't wait to be a
Science class whiz
Her volcano did fizz
And everyone yelled, "Mama Mia!"

Community Christian School
2001
6th Grade
age 11

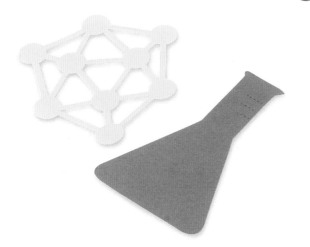

Leah's 6th grade class worked in pairs to make papier-mâché volcanoes. The kids' vinegar, baking soda and food-coloring concoctions made for great eruptions! The kids learned that teamwork leads to success. The whole school loved this project! Community Christian School, 2001   Age 11

Teams: (left to right) Traci and Leah Jason and Alexia, Brittany and Ian with Sara watching, Brandon and Chris with Levi watching.

6 The Complete Page

It's easy to get caught up in the avalanche of scrapbooking products available, but it's important to stay focused on the purpose of scrapbooking when completing a page—to preserve your memories. With that in mind, make sure your page has the five basic elements of a great scrapbook page: photos, journaling, complementary color, effective design and long-lasting construction.

Photos Dawn Brough, Broomfield, Colorado
Design Pam Klassen, Broomfield, Colorado

Checklists

Throughout your child's school years, you'll gather lots of photos and memorabilia that you'll want to preserve. Use these lists to help collect and organize memorabilia for your school days scrapbook.

PHOTOS

- [ ] Individual portraits
- [ ] Class portraits
- [ ] Favorite teachers
- [ ] Best friends
- [ ] Growth
- [ ] Favorite things
- [ ] What I learned
- [ ] First day of school
- [ ] Last day of school
- [ ] Field trips
- [ ] Doing homework
- [ ] Special school clothes
- [ ] School building
- [ ] Daily routine:
  - waking up
  - getting ready
  - catching the bus
  - class
  - lunch
  - recess
  - after-school activities
- [ ] Sports
- [ ] Scouting
- [ ] Performances
- [ ] Awards
- [ ] Science/Social Studies/History/Math fair
- [ ] Field day
- [ ] Reading
- [ ] Studying
- [ ] Honors
- [ ] Class pets
- [ ] Fundraisers
- [ ] Recess
- [ ] School lunches
- [ ] Field trips or travels
- [ ] School carnivals or festivals
- [ ] Art, 4-H or other exhibitions
- [ ] Celebrations or holidays
- [ ] Snow days
- [ ] Pep rallies
- [ ] Community service
- [ ] Student council
- [ ] Talent show
- [ ] What I did over spring break
- [ ] What I did over summer break
- [ ] Teacher or student appreciation
- [ ] E-mail or pen pals
- [ ] Summer school
- [ ] What I want to be when I grow up
- [ ] Remembering a classmate (In memory of)
- [ ] Graduations
- [ ] Your child with:
  - friends
  - teachers or principal
  - coaches
  - exchange students
  - family and siblings

JOURNALING

You can't go to school with your child, so make sure you ask them lots of questions or get them to journal themselves. Some things you might wish to record:

- [ ] Favorite things at a given age
- [ ] What your child learned in a given year
- [ ] How your child felt about teachers, classmates and classes
- [ ] First day of school mishaps
- [ ] Educational milestones and successes
- [ ] Your child's strengths and weaknesses
- [ ] What happened during the year? (world events)
- [ ] Information off school Web site
- [ ] School or club song, pledge, cheer or motto
- [ ] School rules or dress code
- [ ] Your child's growth
- [ ] Autographs from classmates
- [ ] Some of your child's opinions
- [ ] Some of your child's quotes
- [ ] History of school or school mascot
- [ ] The funniest thing that happened in school
- [ ] Most embarrassing moment in school
- [ ] Best moment in school
- [ ] What is unique about your child?
- [ ] Personality and character traits of your child
- [ ] Why you are proud of your child
- [ ] Moving from elementary to middle school

MEMORABILIA

Keep the memorabilia that's important to your child and your child's elementary school experience. Consider photographing an overabundance of memorabilia for your album if necessary.

- [ ] Artwork
- [ ] Handwriting samples from each grade
- [ ] Copies of homework
- [ ] Certificates, ribbons and awards from organized activities
- [ ] Notes from classmates and teachers
- [ ] Pieces of projects
- [ ] Class schedule
- [ ] School supplies
- [ ] Copies of textbook covers
- [ ] Report Cards
- [ ] Special test scores
- [ ] Newspaper clippings
- [ ] School bumper stickers or pennants
- [ ] Programs or fliers from special events
- [ ] Meaningful doodles
- [ ] Handprints
- [ ] Receipts
- [ ] Ticket stubs
- [ ] Photocopy of school images, logos, pledges, etc.

Jake's Backpack

receipt
for all of Jake's backpack stuff

	16.99	T
	3.09	T
	2.99	T
GLUE STICK	1.59	T
PENCILS	3.09	T
FILLER PAPER A	.59	T
KODAK FILM	4.99	T
STEP-IN	19.99	T
	87.87	
VISA/VS		
CHANGE	.00	

Jake starts school with his very own shiny new supplies! It takes a big boy to handle such a heavy backpack!
August 15,1996

Back to School

Some of our most powerful childhood memories are of those magical days when the lazy sweetness of summer gave way to the fresh-scrubbed structure of school. After all, getting ready is a happy shock to the senses: the fresh, woody smell of newly sharpened pencils; the crisp, orderly feel of folders and notebook paper; the sweaty adrenaline rush of shopping for the "cool" apparel; the tugs of combing through summer's tangles and the panic of searching for socks, much less socks that actually match. It's all worth it, though, when hand and heart come together for The Pledge of Allegiance and the first lessons of the school year. These are the times when both kids and parents will find endless possibilities—and endless memories to treasure and share.

"SCHOOLS DAYS, SCHOOL DAYS;

DEAR OLD GOLDEN RULE DAYS.

READIN' AND WRITIN' AND

'RITHMETIC; TAUGHT TO THE TUNE

OF A HICK'RY STICK."

—Will D. Cobb (1876-1930)

JAKE'S BACKPACK
(SEE PAGE 507)

LEROY DRIVE ELEMENTARY, 1ST GRADE

Back-to-School Shopping Madness

OUTFIT AN ARMOIRE WITH SCHOOL CLOTHES

Kathleen took photos of her daughter's back-to-school shopping spree "finds" to create a two-page "room" spread complete with a stocked armoire of her own design—an idea that works equally well for both girls and boys. Like Kathleen, you may want to feature a combination of actual clothes and paper-pieced clothes in the armoire. First, follow the tips on page 399 for *Photographing for Proper Perspective* to take pictures of your child in different outfits. Then "wallpaper" the page backgrounds with floral and striped patterned papers (Colorbök); add floral sticker strips (Mary Engelbreit).

For the left page, triple mat computer-printed journaling and title block (Broderbund) and adhere. Decorate "room" with furniture punch-outs (Mary Engelbreit). Silhouette-crop and mat photo of child in classic modeling pose. For the right page, follow the steps on page 399 to create and assemble the armoire and the clothing to hang in it. Accent page with more punch-outs to complete the spread.

Kathleen Lindner, La Palma, California

Photographing for Proper Perspective

Begin by photographing your child in a classic "modeling" pose, like the one Allison struck on the page at left. Use tape to mark the spot on the floor where your child stands for the first picture. Also mark where you are standing to take the pictures, thus ensuring that the same distance is between the two of you for all photos to gain equal perspective in all photos. Also, be sure that your child is posed the same in each photo. If her left arm is extended outward, as Allison is doing, be sure that her same arm is extended in all photos in the same manner.

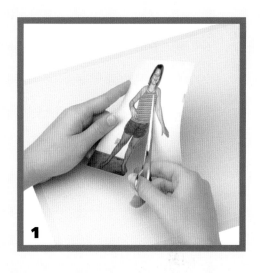

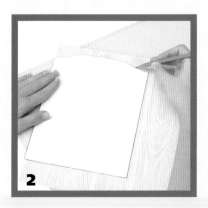

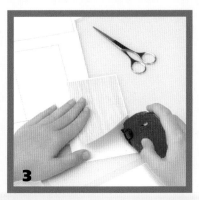

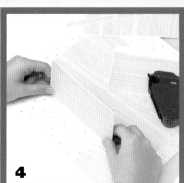

1 *Use small, sharp scissors to silhouette-crop photos of child (Figure 1), staying true to the outline of the child and being careful not to lop off fingers, toes, hair and ears. Repeat with photos of child in different outfits, keeping just the outfits this time.*

2 *Copy and enlarge the armoire pattern on page 502, sizing to fit page and perspective of your child's photos; cut out pattern pieces. Trace around pattern pieces (Figure 2) onto wood-grain patterned paper (Provo Craft). Cut out wood grain pieces, cutting a tiny bit to the inside of the traced lines.*

3 *Adhere armoire doors (Figure 3) and lower drawer to white cardstock. Fold doors along dotted lines to form "hinge" on which you will mount doors onto dresser.*

4 *Using the photos on the opposite page as a guide, adhere the doors to armoire (Figure 4), then assemble remaining dresser components.*

5 *Grab an actual wire hanger from your closet to use as a guide; twist craft wire in the same fashion to create wire hangers (Figure 5) on which to hang "clothes."*

Summer's end brings back the back-to-school shopping experience. It's an annual tradition that parents, and their wallets, have come to expect. But in 1993, that tradition came with a twist for Sabina's family. A family friend, who owned a children's clothing store, asked Sabina's permission for her children to pose in a newspaper ad and television commercial for the store. The event turned into a scrapbook page.

"I see this as an opportunity to remind my children of some of the neat things they got to do when they were young," she says. "Not every child gets to be in a TV or newspaper ad." After posing in the August heat for many shots and lots of videotape footage, the ads were completed and Sabina's kids were allowed to keep the new clothing.

"To me it's special because these are my children, but for future generations it will say a lot about our time, the style of dress for children and how items were promoted for sale," says Sabina.

Beyond the historical significance, she hopes her albums will have personal meaning for her descendants as well. "I love seeing photos of my ancestors when they were children," she says. "It gives me a glimpse of them that I might not otherwise have. I expect my albums to do the same for future generations."

Sabina Dougherty-Wiebkin, Lebanon, New Hampshire

Wake Up

PHOTOJOURNAL A "GETTING READY" PAGE

Joyce kept school mornings running smoothly by designing a "get ready for school" page and hanging it on her daughter's door during the school year. Begin by stamping (Stampendous) a colorful background design. Crop and mat photos into circles with decorative scissors (Creative Memories). Layer and overlap title letters (Creative Memories) and photos on page. Add clock clip art (source unknown) to complete.

Joyce Schweitzer, Greensboro, North Carolina

Back to School

CHRONICLE A MORNING ROUTINE

Kimberly remembers her kids' first day of school with photos documenting the morning's activities. Begin by mounting two 5" paper strips along left and right sides of page. Adhere sticker letters (Creative Memories). Crop photos using oval template (Creative Memories) and decorative scissors. Circle cut clock faces; mat with solid paper and detail with pens.

Kimberly Trachtman
Sharpsville, Pennsylvania

The Bus

PAPER-PIECE SCHOOL BUS FRAMES

Donna brings her twins' favorite song to life with a cleverly crafted school bus frame. Cut brown patterned paper (MPR Assoc.) into road shape; mount on plaid background paper (Provo Craft). Paper-piece freehand-cut bus shapes by cutting yellow arches, silver bumpers, black wheels and stripes, and red lights. Adhere sticker letters (Provo Craft) to red paper; trim around letters. Complete page with journaling and words to the song.

Donna Pittard, Kingwood, Texas

School Time

PEN CHALKBOARD PHOTO CORNERS

Heather shows her four boys traveling on the
road to school with a collection of photos from
their first day. Create background by layering
2½" strip of black cardstock trimmed along the
top with decorative scissors (Fiskars); layer over
patterned paper (NRN Designs). Punch large
white rectangles (Family Treasures) for road
lines; slice horizontally in half and mount on
black road. Adhere crosswalk sticker (Frances
Meyer); draw white post. Freehand draw and
cut out school bus. Silhouette photos and
layer; mount with self-adhesive foam spacers.
Crop remaining photos; mat circle-cut photo
on black cardstock square. Cut black photo
corners; detail with white pen.

Heather Spurlock, Salt Lake City, Utah

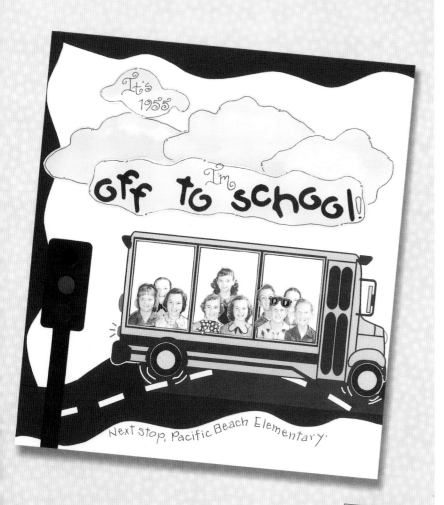

Off to School
TRANSPORT FRIENDS IN STYLE

Nadine created a clever school bus full of kids from vintage photos of her fifth-grade class. Begin by creating road and borders with decorative ruler (EK Success). Punch and halve white rectangles (Family Treasures) for road lines. Silhouette-crop school bus from patterned paper (Hot Off the Press); layer over road. Silhouette-crop "students" from copy of class photo; layer behind bus windows and add stickers (Mary Englebreit, Mrs. Grossman's). Mount red, gold and green metallic paper (Making Memories) scraps behind traffic signal die cut (Ellison) prior to mounting on page. Freehand cut clouds from patterned paper (source unknown). Adhere title sticker letters (Provo Craft) and complete journaling and cloud details with black pen.

Nadine Babbitt, San Diego, California

1st Day of Kindergarten
PHOTOGRAPH THE SCHOOL BUILDING

Rachel captured the excitement of her daughter's first day of school with classic first-day photos. Begin by cropping a large triangle with decorative scissors; mount on page. Craft school bus and chalkboard using a template (Provo Craft). Handcraft paper dolls; detail with pen and chalk. Mount dolls behind bus windows and adhere to page. Crop photos; round corners and mat. Adhere first day photo with black photo corners. Complete page with pen details and journaling.

Rachel Vezeau, Cary, Illinois

Stamping

Stamping lends a versatile and artistic touch to scrapbook pages, whether you stamp simple border designs or an entire background. The wide array of available stamp designs and ink colors makes it easy to create the perfect accent for school days pages, regardless of their theme.

I Pledge Allegiance

ACCENT A PATRIOTIC MOMENT

Stamping a red, white and blue background proved to be the perfect backdrop for photos of Julie's children, learning "The Pledge of Allegiance" from their father before school starts. Follow the steps below to stamp this background. Then create photo and journaling mats with a three-star corner slot punch (All Night Media); mount on page. Add punched and layered jumbo and small stars (Emagination Crafts); detail with pen strokes. Finish with stamped title (Stampin' Up!); color, mat and adhere.

Julie Swanson, South Milwaukee, Wisconsin

1 *In red ink, stamp double line stitch (Stampin' Up!) diagonally across page at 1" intervals. Repeat in blue ink starting at a different corner to create the crisscross pattern (Figure 1).*

2 *Apply color to stars and stripes of heart-shaped flag stamp (Stampin' Up!) with blue and red stamping markers (Stampin' Up!) as shown (Figure 2).*

3 *Stamp background in the squares that are created by the crisscross pattern (Figure 3) of the line stamping.*

Your First Day of Kindergarten

PUNCH A TITLE BLOCK

Sally reflects on her daughter's first day of kindergarten with a wonderful story to remember, accented by a punched title block. Crop and mat photo using corner rounder. Adhere crayon stickers (Frances Meyer) for border; draw black lines. Punch small red apples (Marvy/Uchida); trim off stems and layer on page as shown. Draw letters, stems and leaves, highlights and rest of title with pens. Complete page with journaling.

Sally Scamfer, Bellevue, Nebraska

Phyllis' Story

"When I first started writing about the memory of my daughter's school bus ride on her first day of kindergarten, I couldn't get past the picture of that tiny little girl stretching up so far to reach the first step," says Phyllis. "A box of tissues was gone before I could finally continue with my work. There is definitely a therapeutic element to this hobby!"

Phyllis Dollman, Culpeper, Virginia

RELIEVING FIRST-DAY JITTERS FOR CHILDREN AND THEIR PARENTS

The first day of school is a long-anticipated occasion. But mixed in with the excitement is often a lot of anxiety—not only for children, but for parents as well. Avoid first-day jitters by doing a little "homework" before the first day of school.

• Take your child on a tour of the school and, if possible, introduce her to the teacher, principal and other key adults.

• If your child will be taking a school bus, find out if you and your child can take a trial run on the bus before the first day of school. If your child will walk, practice following the route to and from school.

• Organize a get-together with other families in the neighborhood whose children attend the school so your child can get to know future schoolmates.

• Plan a fun after-school activity to do with your child so she has something to look forward to even if she has a tough first day.

• Read a book or watch a video about school, and talk about the characters' experiences with your child.

• Set a good example by staying calm and appearing confident. Children look to adults as role models. If you act nervous and tearful, so will your child. If you have a positive outlook, your child will have one as well.

• Play school. Set up a desk and chalkboard, and take turns assuming the roles of teacher and student.

• "Early to bed and early to rise" really will help a child to succeed. At least one week before school starts, change your child's sleep schedule. Well-rested children tend to be less anxious.

• Go shopping. Let your child select a back-to-school outfit that he or she will look forward to wearing on the first day of class. (Be sure to check the school's dress code beforehand!)

• Tuck encouraging notes and goodies into your child's backpack and lunch bag to give her a confidence boost during the day.

Will Does Kindergarten

ADD A MINI JOURNALING ALBUM

The special feature of Susan's spread is a handmade mini spiral album that features lots of space for journaling. To begin, layer patterned (Provo Craft) and wood-grain stamped paper (Coop Stamps) with solid paper for background. Freehand cut, crimp, punch and assemble schoolhouse; add pen stroke details. Cut schoolhouse in half and adhere to center of spread. Cut grass border with decorative scissors (Provo Craft) and stamp (All Night Media); adhere in front of schoolhouse. Use a ⅛" round hand punch to punch holes around edges of pages; insert cording and tie off on back of pages. Crop, mat and layer photos across spread, accenting photo mats with stamped designs (All Night Media, Inkadinkado, Judikins, Posh Impressions, Rubber Stampede, Stamps "N" Memories, Toomuchfun Rubberstamps) on mats, corner triangles and squares. Freehand cut apple; stamp leaves (Stampin' Up!), crimp stem and add photo. Add school bus picture frame and stickers (Creative Imaginations). For title, mat letter stickers (Provo Craft), accent "kindergarten" die cut (Memories Forever) with white ink, lace with more cording and insert freehand cut and drawn pencils. To make flag, cut ¼" strips of red and white paper; adhere to paper rectangle with punched square (Family Treasures) and stars (McGill). Crimp whole flag; cut rectangle into blocks and adhere with blocks set slightly askew. Follow instructions to the right to make the mini spiral album. Journal in album and accent with cropped photos and stickers to complete.

Susan Badgett, North Hills, California

To make mini spiral album, crop cardstock "book" using one color for cover and another color for interior pages. Punch ⅛" circles every ¼" along the "binding" of cardstock book. Place a kabob skewer or an embossing stylus atop binding holes; wrap craft wire around skewer and weave through the punched holes to create spiral. Hide the wire ends behind the booklet before mounting on page.

Cody Wendt

Kindergarten

FEATURE STUDENT'S SCHOOLWORK

Gretchen loves to save samples of her stepson's schoolwork without having many papers to file, so she reduces them on a copy machine and creates a coordinating layout. For photo mat, layer patterned paper (The Paper Patch) over solid, leaving ¼" border for the background. Mat portrait on patterned paper; trim solid paper with decorative scissors (Fiskars). Adhere yellow sticker strips around photo. Add sticker letters (Provo Craft) to matted title blocks. Mount scissors die cut (Ellison). Double mat child's autograph; accent with pencil sticker (Mrs. Grossman's). Color photocopy and reduce school papers; mat on solid paper.

Gretchen Wendt, Once Upon a Time
St. John, Indiana

School Days

USE A READY-MADE POCKET

An old manila folder made a perfect pocket
for Joy's kindergarten memorabilia. Spray
folder and memorabilia with Archival Mist™
(Preservation Technologies); mount folder
with clear photo corners and insert memorabilia. Crop photo and mat on solid paper;
freehand cut apple. Design title art (Provo
Craft) with pen and watercolors. Write subtitle letters with template (Pebbles In My
Pocket) and white pen. Add journaling.

Joy Carey, Visalia, California

PRESERVING MEMORABILIA

School days scrapbooks would not be the same without ribbons,
certificates, programs, receipts and more to personalize the pages.
Follow the tips below to help preserve memorabilia.

- Assume that all memorabilia you wish to add to your scrapbook
  is acidic; don't let memorabilia and photos touch.

- De-acidify newspaper clippings and announcements with Archival
  Mist™ (Preservation Technologies).

- Use PVC-free memorabilia protectors to encapsulate memorabilia
  before mounting on page.

- Consider using a photograph of the memorabilia as an alternative
  to mounting actual memorabilia, thus reducing added bulk in
  your scrapbook album.

Kindergarten

CREATE A QUICK-AND-EASY POCKET PAGE

Janna created a simple pocket page to hold her daughter's kindergarten memorabilia. Begin the quick-and-easy pocket by adhering an "overall" (EK Success)
to yellow cardstock; trim top into wavy design as shown. Slice four ½" strips of
red cardstock; mount around edges of "pocket" and at bottom of overall where
it overlaps yellow cardstock. Turn page pocket over; apply adhesive to sides and
lower edge, leaving the top open to form pocket. Mount pocket on patterned
paper background (Me & My Big Ideas). Mat and mount photos and title (EK
Success). Adhere stickers (Mrs. Grossman's), silhouette-cropped crayons and face
(EK Success). Complete page with journaling and pen strokes on photo mats.

Janna Wilson, Rudy, Arkansas

First Day of School

STAMP A SCHOOL-THEME BORDER

Michele's selection of primary colors and school-theme stamps reflects the excitement of her kindergartner's first day of school. Stamp designs (Close To My Heart) on white paper; color with pens and chalk. Cut and mat 2¾" tall borders with decorative scissors; mount on printed background paper (Close To My Heart). Print title and text block; chalk edges. Double mat and trim with decorative scissors. Mat again; detail with pen strokes. Crop photos and mat, adding freehand cut paper corners to highlight largest photo.

Michele Rank
Cerritos, California

On 9/7/00 Zachary went to his first day of Kindergarten. His school is Benito Juarez Elementary School, and it is right around the corner from our house. His teacher is Mrs. Arbourn and he is in class number A-3. There are 20 classmates for Zach to get to know. School starts at 8:40 AM and he gets out at 1:25 PM. Lunchtime at school is at 11:45. To prepare for Kindergarten Zachary got to pick out a brand new Backpack & supplies, lunchbox and clothes. As a special treat for starting school Zachary got to a special gift, lunch at McDonald's lunch & a toy monster trucks. When I picked up Zach from his first day of school, he would not stop talking about his new friends and how much fun he had. We are sure Zach will thrive in his new school.

First Day of School

COORDINATE BORDER WITH PHOTO MATS

Kelly combined a variety of border stickers
(Me & My Big Ideas) to coordinate with
photos matted with patterned paper. Begin
by cropping photos; double and triple mat on
solid and patterned (The Paper Patch) papers.
Print text; double mat on solid and patterned
(Provo Craft) papers. Adhere title and school-
theme stickers (Me & My Big Ideas) on white
paper; silhouette and layer on page.

Kelly Angard, Highlands Ranch, Colorado

My First Day

ADD DETAIL WITH POETIC JOURNALING

A poem becomes the perfect title and caption
for Melissa's daughter's first-day photos. Print
poem and crop photos; mat on solid paper.
Mount die cut (My Mind's Eye) on solid paper;
trim to size. Adhere all pieces on patterned
paper (The Paper Patch).

Melissa Rhoads, Nibley, Utah

First Grade

SILHOUETTE CROP A STAMPED BORDER

Oksanna stamped and silhouette-cropped a bushel of apples to frame photos of her first-grader's special day on a crisp, two-page spread. Begin background design by trimming patterned (Frances Meyer) paper to 7¼ x 9¾" with decorative scissors (Fiskars); mount on pages atop patterned paper (Frances Meyer) as shown.

For upper page, use decorative corner punch (Fiskars) to create photo mat; insert double-matted photo trimmed with decorative scissors (Fiskars).

For lower page, cut journaling block; use corner rounder punch and add swirl border punch (All Night Media) after journaling with gold pen. Mat on patterned paper; adhere to page. Circle crop second photo; double mat on patterned and solid paper and adhere to page.

For both pages, mount stamped and silhouette-cropped apples around border. Complete pages with title letters cut from templates (Accu-Cut, C-Thru Ruler); mount as shown. Add swirl punch (All Night Media) details to letters and dragonfly punch (EK Success) for date at bottom of page.

Oksanna Pope
Los Gatos, California

2nd Grade

PAINT A COLORFUL SCHOOL-THEME BORDER

Joy found inspiration for her colorful, hand-painted border and books from a piece of stationery. Begin by drawing border lines and details with pen; paint with watercolors. Crop photos; mat on solid paper trimmed with decorative scissors (Memories Forever). Freehand cut apple shape; color with watercolors. Crop individual portrait to fit apple; round corners. Finish with journaling.

Joy Carey, Visalia, California

1st Grade

COLOR BLOCK A SIMPLE SPREAD

(LEFT) A treasured postcard from a new teacher set the tone for a wonderful school year for Angie's daughter, featured on this simple color-block spread. Create border by slicing ¼" strips of solid paper; mount down sides of paper. Adhere school-theme stickers (Provo Craft) to 1½" squares; mount at corners of page. Mount postcard with clear photo corners (3L Corp.). Adhere cropped triangles to corners of one photo; mount photos. Paper tear title block; mount to page with nested eyelets (Impress Rubber Stamps; technique on page 474). Adhere sticker letters (Provo Craft). Complete page with pen line details at border, around photo and on photo corners.

Angie McGoveran, Festus, Missouri

Back 2 School

HIGHLIGHT CERTIFICATES AND REPORT CARDS

(BELOW) Including report cards and special achievement certificates helps Jennifer remember why her "good old school days" were so good! Start with alphabet paper (Me & My Big Ideas) background to provide the borders. Mat class photo and reduced color copies of school memorabilia; layer on pages. Crop die cuts (The Beary Patch) and adhere school theme stickers (Frances Meyer, Me & My Big Ideas). Cut and color title design from pattern. Cut and mat text blocks; add journaling.

Jennifer Moll, Ponca City, Oklahoma

First Day of 3rd Grade

PRESERVE LIST OF CLASSMATES' NAMES

Kerri used apple die cuts and a computer-printed list of her daughter's classmates for this easy, back-to-school page spread. Begin with patterned paper (Creative Imaginations) background. Crop, corner round, double mat photos and mount. Print and double mat captions and class list. For title, layer apple die cuts (Accu-Cut) and adhere letter stickers (Provo Craft). Mount apple below class list. Freehand cut bus shape. Accent bus with chalk, black paper stripes, black and gray circles for wheels, and pen stroke details. Silhouette-crop faces (Cock-A-Doodle Design) and layer behind windows; mount bus on page. Adhere letter stickers on bus to finish.

Kerri Brookins, Burleson, Texas

4th Grade

HIGHLIGHT PHOTO WITH PAPER FRAME

Oksanna frames her son's first day of school photo with a large apple frame and graffiti-style writing for a boyish look. Insert classroom photo into mat made with a corner slot punch (McGill); double mat on corrugated (DMD Industries) and patterned (Northern Spy) paper. Adhere to denim background paper (Frances Meyer). Freehand cut and color leaves; add to apple photo frame (Cock-a-Doodle Design); mount on page. Create title with lettering template (source unknown) and sticker letters (C-Thru Ruler). Punch small leaf (McGill); adhere to numeral "4." Finish page with graffiti journaling in thick watercolor pencils and stamped swirls (All Night Media) at bottom of page.

Oksanna Pope, Los Gatos, California

MIDDLE SCHOOL RULES

FIRST DAY OF
MIDDLE SCHOOL
SIXTH GRADE
September 7, 1999

Johnie, George, Stephanie and Rachel have been going to school together since preschool – that's 9 years! They were very ready for middle school but the moms weren't. The girls are 11 yrs old and the boys are 12. (Oh, and by the way, they spent the entire first day of school going through all the rules in each class!)

Middle School Rules

DOCUMENT AN IMPORTANT TRANSITION

The long-awaited first day of middle school was a letdown for Karen's kids because they had to learn a whole list of their new teachers' rules and regulations. Mount patterned paper (The Paper Patch) triangles at opposite corners. Crop photos; double mat and mount. Cut title letters from template (Frances Meyer). Cut text block, double mat and add journaling. Cut rectangle for ruler; detail with black pen.

Karen Regep Glover
Grosse Pointe Woods, Michigan

the Science Fair

— or —

the tale of a 3rd grade smart guy

First he tried out his idea, and then Sean presented it to the judges. The next thing we knew he was on his way to the district show - Way to go Sean! Febr 2000

All in a Day's Work

The most important lesson we learn in school is how to love learning. The daily lessons on math and science and language are simply the yardsticks by which we measure our success. What important and memorable yardsticks they are! Volcano models that erupt on command, that first watercolor self-portrait, a poem that brings tears to a teacher's eyes—the work of school, punctuated by the finer points of lunchroom and social etiquette, forms the structure of learning and life for children and adults. Offering their own unique mix of structure and freedom are home schooling and summer school. Yet all schoolwork produces treasures beyond compare, reminders of lessons learned, worthy of preserving and sharing with future generations.

"THEY KNOW ENOUGH WHO KNOW HOW TO LEARN."

—Henry Adams,
author and historian
(1838-1918)

THE SCIENCE FAIR
(SEE PAGE 507)

MELISSA, KINDERGARTEN

Spiders

ENCOURAGE CHILD'S CREATIVITY

One of Amy's son's favorite kindergarten activities was making (and eating) edible spiders. Amy not only captured the fun in photos, but also by letting her son draw his own spider renderings on paper for the photo's background. Crop photos; round corners with decorative corner rounder punch (Marvy/Uchida). Mat on paper using decorative scissors (Frances Meyer) and add journaling to photo mats.

Amy Rognlie, Littleton, Colorado

Homework

DOCUMENT A FAVORITE ASSIGNMENT

Oksanna showed that some homework assignments can be fun and fuzzy ... like when her daughter had to take care of the "class bear." For left page, begin by layering plaid paper (Provo Craft) over solid background, leaving a ¼" border. Create photo mat using corner slot punch (All Night Media), insert photo and mat solid paper trimmed with corner rounder. Paper-piece bear (Windows of Time); detail with pen strokes. Print journal caption; trim with decorative scissors (Fiskars) and double mat. Add mini bear punches (All Night Media) on last mat. For the right page, layer plaid rectangle on background in upper right corner. Crop photo and mat; trim corners with decorative scissors. Mat two more times; trim one with corner rounder. Add punched border swirls (All Night Media) and pen strokes. Stamp bears (Duncan Enterprises); silhouette-crop and mount. Reduce and photo-copy homework page; mat and mount on page. Cut heart from template (C-Thru Ruler) and adhere; embellish with sticker letters (C-Thru Ruler), pen strokes and paw print design (All Night Media). Cut title letters using template (Provo Craft); fill in openings of letters with egg punch (EK Success); mount across bottom of both pages.

Oksanna Pope, Los Gatos, California

BEST-LOVED BOOKS ABOUT SCHOOL

Help your child fall in love with reading
AND school with these fun and popular
books about school!

KINDERGARTEN AND 1ST GRADE

- Arthur's Teacher Moves In *by Marc Brown*
- Froggy Goes to School *by Jonathan London*
- Hooway for Wodney Wat *by Helen Lester*
- I Spy School Days *by Jean Marzollo*
- Lilly's Purple Plastic Purse *by Kevin Henkes*
- Little Spider at Sunny Patch School *by David Kirk*
- Miss Bindergarten Gets Ready for Kindergarten *by Joseph Slate*
- Miss Nelson Is Missing *by Harry Allard*
- Officer Buckle and Gloria *by Peggy Rathman*
- Rotten Ralph Helps Out *by Jack Gantos*
- Timothy Goes to School *by Rosemary Wells*

1ST GRADE AND 2ND GRADE

- All About Stacy *by Patricia Reilly Giff*
- Amanda Pig, School Girl *by Jean Van Leeuwen*
- Junie B., First Grader (at Last) *by Barbara Park*
- Lionel at School *by Stephen Krensky*
- Marvin Redpost: Class President *by Louis Sachar*
- Meet the Barkers: Morgan and Moffat Go to School *by Tomie dePaola*
- Never Spit on Your Shoes *by Denys Cazet*
- Pinky and Rex and the School Play *by James Howe*
- Sparky and Eddie: The First Day of School *by Tony Johnston*
- The Bride of Frankenstein Doesn't Bake Cookies *by Debbie Dadey*
- Young Cam Jansen and the Lost Tooth *by David A. Adler*

3RD GRADE AND 4TH GRADE

- A Letter to Mrs. Roosevelt *by C. CoCo De Young*
- Amber Brown Goes Fourth *by Paula Danziger*
- Captain Underpants and the Perilous Plot of Professor Poopypants *by Dav Pilkney*
- Frindle *by Andrew Clements*
- Horrible Harry Goes to the Moon *by Suzy Kline*
- Judy Moody *by Megan McDonald*
- S.O.R. Losers *by Avi*
- The Best School Year Ever *by Barbara Robinson*
- The Magnificent Mummy Maker *by Elvira Woodruff*
- Thirteen Ways to Sink a Sub *by Jamie Gilson*
- Wayside School Is Falling Down *by Louis Sachar*

5TH GRADE AND 6TH GRADE

- Children of the Dust Bowl *by Jerry Stanley*
- Harry Potter series *by J.K. Rowling*
- I Was a Sixth Grade Alien *by Bruce Coville*
- Joey Pigza Swallowed the Key *by Jack Gantos*
- My Life as a Fifth Grade Comedian *by Elizabeth Levy*
- My Louisiana Sky *by Kimberly Willis Holt*
- No More Dead Dogs *by Gordon Korman*
- Outrageously Alice *by Phyllis Reynolds Naylor*
- Secret Letters from 0 to 10 *by Susie Morgenstern*
- Sixth Grade Can Really Kill You *by Barthe DeClements*
- The Austere Academy *by Lemony Snicket*
- The View From Saturday *by E.L. Konigsburg*

GRALAND COUNTY DAY SCHOOL, 2ND GRADE

List courtesy of Sharon S. Ball, Multitype Consultant, North Suburban Library System, Wheeling, Illinois

Winnie, 2nd Grade
STITCH STAMPED IMAGES

Ann chose symbols to reflect the subjects her son studied in summer school. Begin by layering patterned paper (source unknown) over white paper, leaving ⅛" border. Crop photo; mat and mount with photo corners (Therm-O-Web). Cut title and journal blocks, double mat and punch ⅛" circles at bottom of one text block and top of another. Tie together with thin jute twine. Mount gauze (Pulsar) strip down side of page. Stamp images (Plaid Enterprises) with colored ink (Clearsnap); emboss with clear embossing powder (Ranger Industries). Crop images into rectangles and squares; stitch borders with sewing machine or by hand. Complete page with journaling.

Ann McElfresh, Tempe, Arizona

Dinosaur Dig
MAKE YOUR OWN PAPER-PIECING PATTERN

Marilyn caught her budding paleontologist uncovering a hidden fossil during a class project. Crop photos; mat and trim with decorative scissors (Family Treasures). Add freehand cut photo corners to one photo. Create dinosaur skeleton from photocopied and enlarged clip art (source unknown) used for a pattern; piece together and mount on page. Adhere sticker letters (Creative Memories) for title. Complete with journaling.

Marilyn Garner, San Diego, California

my day in grade 2

Julia Sydney Shannon

Friends

Ms. Rockwood
My teacher showing us how to make bookmarks.

My work

Book nook

This is the lunch room. The lunch lady is making nachoes.

Me and Andrea Walking to scohll.

This is my ↑ desk. picder of me and Melissa scohll supplise. favorite book. Skeeter's puppys picture.

I am writing in my think shop with my favorite pencil.

I am on the swings with Alina. I am at Recess.

We thought it would be fun to send a young student and scrapbooker "on assignment" to document a typical day at school. We found a willing participant in Blair, an enthusiastic second-grader at a local elementary school. To prepare for her photojournalism assignment, she made a list of all of the important photos that she planned to take—photos about things that she "wanted to remember" when she was older.

Armed with her photo list (which she later lost); a camera borrowed from her mom, Cynthia; and her teacher's permission, Blair set out one December morning to show what life is really like at her school. She began with a photo of herself and a friend trudging through the snow to school, followed by a close-up of the contents of her desk—her school supplies, photos of friends and the family dog, and a favorite reading book.

Blair also captured on film her classroom's reading nook, herself—hard at work in "the think shop," and recess fun on the swings. Some people asked Blair what she was doing, and her friends were eager to pose for pictures—some a little too eager. "My friends were crazy, and they all wanted their pictures taken," she says. "But my best friend didn't want to be in the pictures. I don't get that!"

Photos of the school lunchroom and "the lunch lady making nachos" provide great mealtime insight; while a photo of her teacher, cropped into the shape of a heart, tells a story all its own. Speaking of story, Blair's journaling tells us what her pictures could not on scrapbook pages that she created when she got her photos back from the photo lab.

Blair learned some important lessons from her assignment. "It is hard work being a photographer, and without these scrapbook pages, I think I would only remember people's faces," she says. "What will make these pages special in the future is seeing the clothes and hairstyles on the people—also my teacher's look. In 100 years, she will be 124 years old!"

We are not sure that Ms. Rockwood would like that thought, but she would probably agree with us about the grade that we gave Blair for her incredible effort to document a day at school—an "A+"! Nice job!

Blair Kacynski, Superior, Colorado

Lunch

PAPER PIECE CAFETERIA FAVORITES

Capture one of the most fun parts of a school
day with paper-pieced foods! Copy and size
patterns on page 503. Transfer to papers of
choice, cut out and assemble.

Pamela Frye, Denver, Colorado

School Lunch

SERVE UP A TRAY FULL OF GOODIES

Sue relived the yummy days of lunch in the cafeteria at her grandson's school. Begin by silhouette-cropping meal tray from patterned paper (Hot Off The Press); layer on background paper. Slice out one section of the tray with a craft knife; mount photo behind cut-out area. Photocopy and size pattern for pretzels and other food items (see page 503); transfer to papers of choice and cut out. Detail with white pen. Adhere cookie stickers (Frances Meyer). Circle-cut photo and mat on patterned paper (The Paper Patch). Freehand-cut napkin from white paper, shade with pencil to create "folds." Adhere title stickers (Stickopotamus); trim and mat. Finish page with journaling.

Sue Shute, Beaver Dam, Wisconsin

Friends

ADD PLAYFULNESS TO PUNCHED SHAPES

Bold primary colors and simple use of eyelet embellishments reflect Helen's good eye for design and balance on a fun playground page. Begin by slicing ⅛" and ¼" strips of primary-colored paper. Mount ¼" strips on three sides of background paper. Crop photo and double mat. Print title and journaling; mount ⅛" strips of colored paper slightly askew around edges of text block. Add eyelets (Impress Rubber Stamps; see page 474 for technique) at paper strip intersections. Punch large flowers (Family Treasures); mount on 1¾" squares. Adhere to page and then add eyelets to center of flowers.

Helen Naylor, San Diego, California

Mad Science
CREATE THEMATIC FUN WITH FONTS

Oksanna captured the unpredictable outcome of a science experiment with a comical, paper-pieced "mad scientist" and type fonts to match. Triple mat photo using corner slot punch (McGill) for navy mat; layer on printed background paper (Provo Craft). Print titles (downloaded from Internet; source unknown) and captions on denim (Provo Craft) and colored paper; double mat caption. Cut out title letters; mat with scraps of green mulberry paper. Write small title word with black pen. Cut paper doll pieces and science "blob" monster from patterns (Scrapable Scribbles). Punch eyes with small oval and ¼" circle punches and eyebrows with moon punch (Fiskars). Cut flask from vellum paper. Complete doll science blob monster with chalk and pen stroke details.

Oksanna Pope, Los Gatos, California

Nora Loves Homework...Not!
DOCUMENT DRUDGERY WITH HUMOR

Karen loves to capture day-to-day events, even when they show one of her daughter's least favorite things to do. Note Nora's priceless expression in the lower picture. Begin by layering solid paper over patterned paper (Keeping Memories Alive), leaving ⅛" border. Crop photos and mat. For title, adhere sticker letters (C-Thru Ruler) and cut letters from template (Frances Meyer). Adhere school supplies (Stickopotamus) and student (Provo Craft) stickers to complete design.

Karen Regep Glover
Grosse Pointe Woods, Michigan

Throughout his third-grade year, Johnny created beautiful, priceless projects for art class. But the paper and clay weren't going to last forever, and some of the objects were too big to save. How could he preserve his artwork for the future?

With the help of his mom, Johnny took pictures of himself with his artwork and created a scrapbook spread that would keep the memories of his artwork fresh for years to come. Not only will Johnny remember his artwork, he'll remember how he looked when he made it as well. And his scrapbook page isn't just for him.

"My children and grandchildren will be able to see the things I made when I was in school," he says.

Now Johnny always takes pictures of his artwork so he can remember his projects. And with his use of stickers and paper tearing, his scrapbook pages have become their own works of art to remember and cherish.

Johnny Zieske, Priest River, Idaho

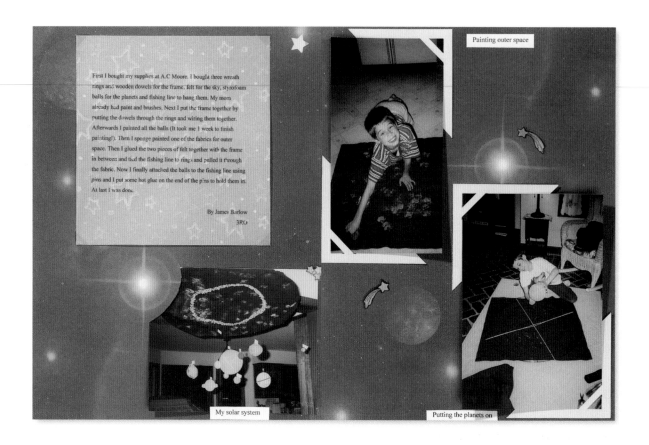

First I bought my supplies at A.C Moore. I bought three wreath rings and wooden dowels for the frame, felt for the sky, styrofoam balls for the planets and fishing line to hang them. My mom already had paint and brushes. Next I put the frame together by putting the dowels through the rings and wiring them together. Afterwards I painted all the balls (It took me 1 week to finish painting!). Then I sponge painted one of the fabrics for outer space. Then I glued the two pieces of felt together with the frame in between and tied the fishing line to rings and pulled it through the fabric. Now I finally attached the balls to the fishing line using pins and I put some hot glue on the end of the pins to hold them in. At last I was done.

By James Barlow
3RO

Painting outer space

My solar system

Putting the planets on

Putting the frame together

Painting the planets

James' Story, 3rd grade

In kindergarten, James tested into his school's "gifted program," but a little trouble with small motor skills affected his ability to write well enough to do the work required in the program. "James' mind often raced ahead of his hands, which was a real frustration for him," recalls his mom, Patty. "Scrapbooking encouraged James to journal as well as to do other small motor skill functions that helped to improve his abilities."

In third grade, James put his mastered skills to the test for an assignment in Mrs. Roche's class: He designed and built a solar system and documented his project in a scrapbook. His celestial success includes photos that show every step of the project. And his grade? "100% or an 'A'," says James.

"I liked making it but not doing the oral presentation," he says. "And everyone loved it! I was the only one who used a scrapbook or even used pictures." Years from now, James will likely remember that he got an awesome grade on the project, but without the scrapbook, "I don't think I'd remember how I made the solar system," he says.

James still scrapbooks about his dad, his mom, his activities and his cat. James' advice to other students about scrapbooking class projects? "Try it; it's cool. And you just might get a really good grade!"

James William Barlow III, Downingtown, Pennsylvania

In fifth grade, Gary had to visit a California mission and then build a replica, make a videotape or write a report about the mission and the trip. "My mom was scrapbooking, and I thought it might be more fun and easier than the other choices," says Gary.

"I liked visiting the San Juan Capistrano Mission and taking the photographs," he continues. "I liked matching the colors to the page and drawing the swallows. I like to draw and this gave me a chance to include my drawings in the project."

Gary had never worked on a scrapbook before, and he worked on the project at a scrapbook workshop he attended with his mom, Elisa. "My teacher really liked the album, and Mom shows the book to all her scrapping friends," Gary says.

In his opinion, "journaling helps keep track of what is going on at the time, where you are, and when it is. It helps you remember things later," says Gary. "I didn't think I'd like that part (the journaling), but I kept wanting to add things I had forgotten, so I'd just write them on the page."

Since his school project, Gary has created enough scrapbook pages to fill an album. His pages feature his cats, the zoo, bowling, his own lettering and his drawings. He attends a scrapbook workshop monthly. "Most of the time I am the youngest person there and almost always the only guy," he says with a smile.

"Without my album, I probably wouldn't remember much about the trip," says Gary. "Maybe the Mission won't be here 100 years from now and people will be able to see what it was like and learn about it from my album."

The final touch on Gary's album? A tiny photo of him cleverly tucked behind an old mission door on the very last page. It is the perfect ending.

Gary Purnell, Camarillo, California

Mission San Juan Capistrano

Mission San Juan Capistrano was founded twice. The first time was in 1775 by Father Lauseun and the second time was in 1776 by Father Serra. Father Serra dug up the bells that Father Lauseun had buried before and hung them from a tree.

The Mission today

by Gary S. Purnell
1999

Much of the memorabilia that finds its way home during the grade school years is a child's artwork. Like many parents, the art covers the refrigerator, or like Theresa's, it is featured on a "wall of fame" at home. One such piece of art is a playground drawing that her daughter, Audrey, created for a contest.

Audrey was a finalist in a "Draw Your Dream Playground" contest sponsored by the Elizabethtown Playground Committee. "I learned that I could let my imagination run free with ideas of things that I'd really like to have on my own dream playground," Audrey says. "Now I can remember the contest every time I look at the page Mom did!"

Construction on the playground began last spring. "It was a special moment in Audrey's life, and hopefully she can reflect on it with her children or grandchildren and they can go visit the real playground together!" says Theresa.

Theresa Smith, Elizabethtown, Kentucky

Brice's Winning Streak
RECORD SCHOLASTIC ACCOMPLISHMENTS

Donna was inspired by a timeline feature in a previous issue of *Memory Makers* magazine to create a layout of her daughter's academic triumphs. Begin by slicing ¼" strips of paper; mount vertically to create "columns" and show direction on patterned paper (Keeping Memories Alive) background. Crop photos; trim with corner rounder and mat on pat-terned paper (source unknown). Print journaling; crop to size and mat on solid paper. Adhere sticker letters (Creative Memories) for title and category headings on white paper; trim to size and mat. Adhere school-theme stickers (Creative Memories, Frances Meyer).

Donna Fenton, Williamstown, West Virginia

We Pick This Class!

PAPER PIECE SCHOOL-THEME SYMBOLS

Debbie records fond memories of teaching with timeless school symbols. Begin by slicing six ½" wide strips; mount over solid background paper at edges. Adhere small fasteners (HyGlo/American Pin) at outside page corners. Crop photos; single and double mat. Copy and size book and apple patterns (see page 502). Cut pattern pieces from solid and patterned papers (Doodlebug Design, Frances Meyer, Making Memories); piece together and layer on page as

shown. Adhere pencil sticker (Me & My Big Ideas) on white cardstock; silhouette and mat with self-adhesive foam spacers. Print script font title, journaling and alphabet; cut to size and mat before mounting on page.

Idea and Patterns Chris Peterson
Lakewood, Colorado

Photos and Layout Debby Schuh, The Memory Bee
Clarence, New York

Punch-n-Stitch

It is easy to create homespun appeal on a scrapbook page by using a variety of stitches, such as a simple running straight stitch, a cross stitch or an overcast stitch, shown on the page below. Experiment with stitches like the blanket stitch, chain stitch, or daisy stitch for completely different effects. You don't have to be a needlepoint enthusiast to skillfully add this look to your scrapbook pages. Your local library or the Internet (search words: needlepoint stitches) can provide great illustrations of basic to complex stitches.

School

STITCH A PUNCHED PAGE

Alison's simple stitching is a charming complement to her scrapbook page that features classroom photos. Although Alison's page is a 12 x 12" scrapbook page, you can easily use this technique on any size page. To create your own similar look, begin with a cardstock background in the color of your choice. Crop and mat photos; adhere to page. Cut white mats from cardstock for journaling block and for stitching. Then follow the steps below to create the page. Finish with journaling.

Alison Beachem, San Diego, California

1 *To begin, use a ruler and a pencil to draw "dots" that will serve as punch guidelines at ½" intervals around the page's edge and around pre-cut mats (Figure 1).*

2 *Use a ¹⁄₁₆" round hand punch to punch dots (Figure 2), creating the "holes" used for stitching.*

3 *Thread embroidery floss of choice into a sewing needle and stitch around the page's edges and the mat edges (Figure 3); tie off ends on back of page and mats.*

4 *To create lettering on mats, use a pencil to draw dots to form letters. Pierce the dots with a sewing needle to create holes for stitching. Stitch letters using a simple running stitch (Figure 4). If desired, stitch edges of apple die cuts, as shown; adhere to mat. Assemble all stitched mats and mount in place on page.*

Crafty Crayons

PUNCH AND PIECE A CRAYON BORDER

Alexandra's colorful punch art border is a perfect accent for scrapbook pages that display children's art and art class photos. Begin with a 2" strip of black paper for border background. Punch white 1¹¹⁄₁₆" deco squares (Family Treasures); adhere to background. Punch picket borders (Emagination Crafts) from primary-colored papers; cut pickets in half to form "crayons." Add freehand-cut rectangles of same-color shades of primary colors atop crayons to create "paper wrap." Assemble four crayons atop each white square with tips meeting in center as shown.

Alexandra Bleicher, Chilliwack, British Columbia, Canada

Notebooks

PUNCH SCHOOL SUBJECTS THEME BOOKS

Class curriculum scrapbook pages get off to a quick-and-easy start with Alexandra's simple punched border of "notebooks." Start with a 1⅞" strip of red paper matted with a 1½" strip of black paper for background. For each notebook, punch two ¾" squares (The Punch Bunch) from colored paper and one from white paper. Assemble notebook "pages" as shown; adhere to border strip. Accent pages with white halved ½" squares (The Punch Bunch); add subject title with pen.

Alexandra Bleicher, Chilliwack, British Columbia, Canada

Loving Hands

PUNCH A HANDPRINT BORDER

Alison's punched handprint border is a nice complement to scrapbook pages featuring a child's handprint or other artwork. First, create "mats" by layering punched 1⁹⁄₁₆" and 1¼" squares (Family Treasures); assemble and adhere on page in an offset manner as shown. Top squares with punched hands (EK Success) accented with mini hearts (Fiskars).

Alison Beachem, San Diego, California

Home Schooling

Basketball practice, math and English class, social studies and art. Just another busy day at school, except that in this school classes take place at the kitchen table, recess is in the backyard and the ballgames are all played at the local recreation center. With everything happening under their own roofs, home-schooling families certainly have no shortage of material for their scrapbooks. Read on for scrapbooking stories from home schoolers.

Johnna's Story

While students in traditional schools are slide shows of the Renaissance painters, Johnna Pierson and her children are visiting the museums of Paris. And while the kids back home are studying the history of Latin America, Johnna's family is standing at the base of pyramids in Mexico.

As a scrapbooking veteran Johnna knew there was no better way to document their traveling classroom than to bring scrapbooking into school. "It's a great way to remember where we've been and whom we have met," she says. Johnna has everyone carry his or her own camera, take pictures and make scrapbook pages of family field trips.

Not only does scrapbooking provide a format for preserving great memories, it has also helped with virtually every aspect of schoolwork, Johnna says. She sees improvements in handwriting and a better understanding of logic. "It has helped with learning to 'see' things that would make a good page," she says.

And with her husband's job taking the family someplace new every ten months, Johnna has been able to incorporate some amazing sights into her daily lesson plan. For Johnna, home schooling doesn't always mean school "at home." Between field trips to the pyramids of Mexico, the Eiffel Tower in Paris and all the monuments in Washington, D.C., it's obvious that Johnna doesn't take the "home" part of home schooling too literally.

Johnna Pierson, Greenville, South Carolina

Second Grade
at home

1995-1996

Chattahoochee
Pond Life Field Trip
Ranger Nancy introduced 33 homeschoolers to the wide variety of
life in a pond.   May 1999

Adrian's Story

Choosing to home school your children can provide your family with certain freedoms not available to families using traditional schools. Your children are able to learn at a pace best suited for them; your family can travel any time of the year. And you can ensure that your children are getting the attention they deserve and need. But there are some things home schoolers don't get that children in regular classrooms do—yearbooks, class pictures and other mementos. Adrian found a simple and creative solution to that problem. "I create a page for each grade for their own albums, documenting some of the special, and ordinary, activities they do in school," she says. Throughout the year she takes pictures of everything from the days spent studying at the kitchen table to the days spent out on field trips. "My children will never forget the autumn we went on a Caribbean cruise," she says. "They had home school on the pool deck a few mornings, in their bathing suits, with a view over the ocean."

When it comes to other forms of memorabilia, Adrian believes that the occasional "Student of the Week" or "Best Improved Handwriting" goes a long way. However, she prefers her scrapbooks to contain mainly photos and keeps the other memorabilia in personal journals. "It's the student's own work that holds meaning in years to come," she says.

Adrian Noren, Marietta, Georgia

Susan's Story

When Susan began home schooling 13 years ago, she knew she would be facing an uphill battle to convince others that she was doing the right thing. "I also wanted to prove to people that I don't sit around eating bonbons and watching soap operas while my kids read books," she says. Susan's need to prove herself inspired her to begin keeping what she calls a "school portfolio," or scrapbook, for each of her four children. In the scrapbooks, she includes samples of their schoolwork as well as photos from activities and field trips that show that her children really were having school. But Susan's style of "record-keeping" did more than just convince her friends of the legitimacy of home schooling. They liked the idea of keeping samples and memorabilia so much that some of them began creating their own scrapbooks.

Today, with the pressure to prove herself long gone, Susan is able to use scrapbooking as a way to make school more fun. Her children work on their own scrapbooks in art class—cutting, arranging and choosing their photos—which allows them to explore and express their creativity. And best of all, Susan is able to look at these books and recall how much fun they've had and how much her children have grown.

"I'm glad that I felt pressured to prove myself to others because now I have great school scrapbooks to look through," she says.

Susan Seydel, Bonita, California

Home Schoolers: Busy as Bees!

Our new Homeschool support group, Midcoast Christian Homeschoolers, just started this semester. Some of the kids who are also in AWANA needed to visit an historic place to complete one of the sections in their books. So, we decided to visit the Maine State Museum in Augusta. Four families met there and toured the whole place. We Mom's decided that we would like to take our own trip there, just so we could take the time to read all the info at our own pace!

Later in the semester we had a spelling Bee. Dawn got behind that and ran it wonderfully for us. She gathered up grade level spelling lists to study. On that day we lined the kids all up according to grade level and tested them from their own lists. All of the kids did very well. In the end, Katherine Nadeau, one of our second graders, proved herself most proficient at her list! She was awarded a ribbon donated to us by the shop that we bought the participation awards from. I think we will do this event again!

Diane's Story

Whenever anyone questions Diane's decision to home school her children, she has one perfect response: her scrapbook. "When it comes to convincing those who are unsure about the fact that we home school, a viewing of the scrapbook usually will open eyes and minds," Diane says.

The days of the isolated home schooler are long gone, and Diane is more than happy to help shatter that image. Her scrapbooks of spelling bees and field trips to museums and farms are proof enough that her children aren't lacking in any socialization or public recognition. "Home-school families take such pains to be sure that their children have outside interaction in the 'real world' that we need a place to stash those achievement certificates," she says. With awards earned through sports, scouting, church, reading and countless other activities, Diane's children have received as much as, or even more, recognition than many students in public school.

But Diane doesn't believe that all of her children's accomplishments need to be recognized with assemblies and award ceremonies. "The most valuable recognition comes when extended family and friends see their scrapbooked school memories and applaud them with hugs and words of encouragement!" Diane says. "At times like those, family members often launch into their own memories of school days." That's when her children learn more about their family heritage—something that they could never learn in a traditional classroom. "I wouldn't give that up for all the recognition assemblies in the world!" she says.

Diane Simmler, Bath, Maine

With scrapbooking, Amy is able to provide the home-school review board with more colorful records of her children's schoolwork than just a written list of what they've studied. "It's one thing to show our portfolio with the sentence 'We cooked an Egyptian meal for Grandma and Grandpa,' and quite another to take them through our unit study in pictures!" she says. And with many of their lessons being hands-on projects, Amy says she would rather not drag all of the models, costumes and meals they make to the review office. But the scrapbooks aren't just for the review board.

Amy uses them to bring her family closer together. "It's a nice way for the kids to sit down with aunts and uncles and grandparents and go over what they've done." The books also add fun to the classroom. "I tend to be very artistic, so we bring lots of little scrapbooking concepts into class. If I can hand them something that's creative to do, the learning will sink in," Amy says. But beyond helping to educate her children, Amy says there's another, even greater benefit to the time she and her kids spend scrapbooking. "I'm bonding with the most important people in my life," she says.

Amy Moxley, Mount Airy, Maryland

Activities & Special Events

"HOW DOTH THE LITTLE BUSY BEE
IMPROVE EACH SHINING HOUR,
AND GATHER HONEY ALL THE DAY
FROM EVERY OPENING FLOWER!"

—Isaac Watts, Author (1674-1748)

If schoolwork is the pencil sketch, then activities and special events are the colors that complete the masterpiece of education. In sports, children learn the value—and the challenges—of teamwork. On stage, they harness the butterflies within to soar aloft. During field trips, kids step through Alice's looking glass to touch new worlds. Celebrations set the hearts of children free. With awards and ceremonies, children learn to honor not just achievement but also the quest for achievement itself. The more a child does, the more photos and memorabilia there are to treasure and preserve in scrapbooks. Be sure to save sports ribbons, citizenship certificates and copies of recited poems. Each reveals a golden moment worth remembering.

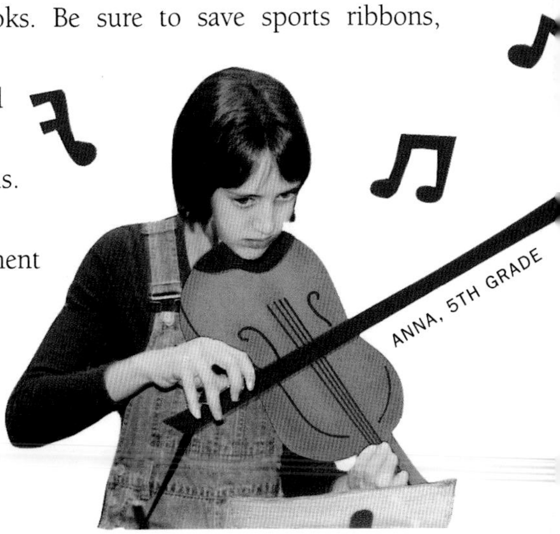

ANNA, 5TH GRADE

LADY STORM
(SEE PAGE 507)

Sports

Whether children participate in a team or an individual sport, playing sports teaches children valuable lessons in perseverance, discipline and integrity. Preserve these memories with photos of the special people involved and memorabilia that captures the excitement of a season. Win or lose, children's sports memories are an important part of the grade school experience.

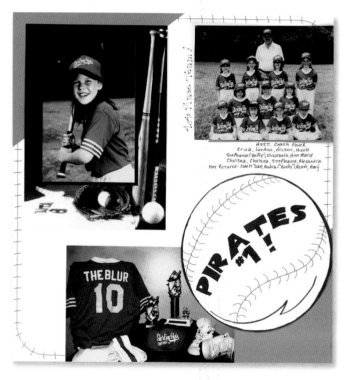

Pirates #1!

PHOTOGRAPH SPORTS MEMORABILIA

Tammy's daughter loves to play a variety of sports, so at the end of every season, Tammy makes sure she photographs the team uniform amongst season-winning memorabilia. Mount colored triangles in two colors. Crop photos; mount one on colored triangle. Circle-cut large baseball. Add red "stitching" to ball and around page with pen. Complete page with team name on ball and journaling under photo. See page 507 for tips on photographing memorabilia.

Tammy Meerschaert, Sterling Heights, Michigan

Bear Creek Bears

HIGHLIGHT STAR PLAYER ON THE FIELD

MaryJo's son enjoyed a winning season and superstar status on a page highlighting his achievements. Begin by slicing ⁷⁄₈" strips of patterned paper (Frances Meyer); mount at upper and lower edges of page. Add pen stroke details to football die cut (Creative Memories); tuck behind lower border as shown. Crop photos; double mat on solid and patterned papers (Frances Meyer). Crop an oval into one photo to highlight player; double mat and adhere over original photo with self-adhesive foam spacers. Mount photo player card; layer die-cut footballs (Creative Memories) with pen stroke details in white ink. Cut title letters using template (Scrap Pagerz) from solid and patterned papers. Mat and silhouette; add dimension with chalk around the edges. Complete with journaling and football stickers (Creative Memories).

Design Kelly Angard, Highlands Ranch, Colorado

Photos MaryJo Regier, Littleton, Colorado

2001

11-12 Year old
Little League
Health care
Resources
Team

Coaches: Dale Moran, Philip Shelton Bob Gray
Players: Ryan Holmes, Bruce Beddingfield, Matt Moran, Clint Snoddy, Casey Beddingfield, Chris Harris, Eric Berngruber, Rob Gray, Zerian Mastin, Chris Shelton, Chris Mitchell, Jeremiah Thomas

Sports Theme Album

PRESERVE THE SEASON'S HIGHLIGHTS

Long after the equipment is put away and the blood, sweat and tears have dried, the memories remain in Cathy's sports albums—all four of them!

Because she has so many games to record, Cathy separates the seasons by repeating the same design elements—in this case, stamped and silhouette-cropped stars, computer-printed journaling and the same paper colors—within each particular sports season.

Cathy's albums also include newspaper clippings, great action shots, still photos, even photos of the scoreboard. Lest a memory be forgotten, her extensive journaling includes names of coaches and players, inspirational sports-related sayings, season stats and highlights, trivia about the team, and quotes about the coaches and the season offered by individual players. One thing is certain: Win or lose, sports albums score!

Cathy Gray, Fayetteville, Tennessee

Did You know?
- Hot Dogs at the concession stand sell for $1.00
- Cokes for $1.00
- Nachos and cheese- $1.25
- An Easton Bat- 189.00
- A uniform- $50.00
- A glove $60.00- 100.00
- Cleats $60.00
2001

Little League- A Nervous Break Down one inning at a time.

How to identify a real fan?
- hears "Please return all foul balls to the concession stand" in his dreams
- sets up a chair but never sits in it because they're too nervous
- has a passion for the game
- plans summer vacations around baseball games
- goes to the ballpark early and stays late to watch the other teams play
- is know to say "just one more out boys" about 20 times a game
- Sunflower seeds are his favorite snack
- Can't sleep after a close game
- Over analyzes every game
- Starts 50% of his sentences with "If we just had _____ (fill in blank)

My favorite game- who can possibly forget this one? 1 to 1 in the seventh inning. Rob and Chris pitched fantastic. No errors in the field. Eric came in and pitched like a man. We lost, but I was so proud of the boys. They played their hearts out.

Indian Heights Basketball

SHOW CONTINUITY ON A TWO-PAGE LAYOUT

Heather searched for a way to display a full season of basketball photos while maintaining a cohesive two-page design. To create the nine-photo layout on the left, she used an octagon template and arranged photos in a circle. Center large photo; fill white spaces with small solid and patterned (Hot Off The Press) paper triangles. Crop and double mat photos on righthand page with same papers. Create border down side of page with triangles in same size and papers as opposite page; adhere to page leaving white space between triangles. Complete page with border lines on both pages and journaling with calligraphy pen.

Heather McWhorter, Kokomo, Indiana

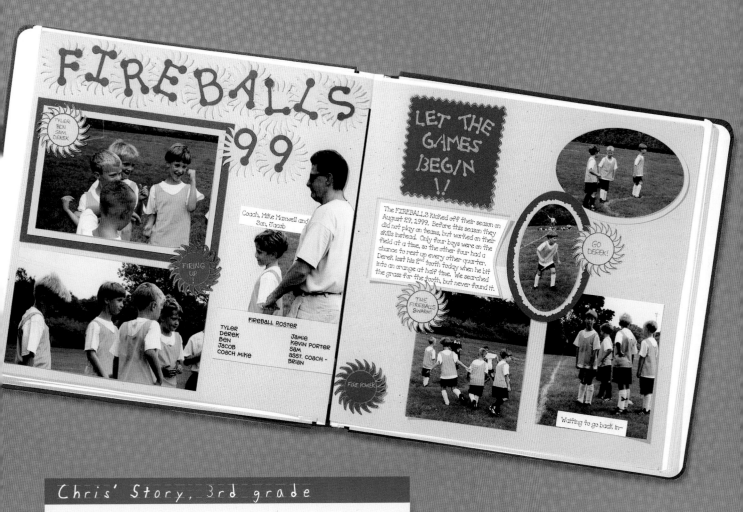

Chris' Story, 3rd grade

School activities pass so quickly; it can be hard to remember all the details. Chris recorded his memories of a charity event by scrapbooking about it.

"What I like most about scrapbooking is that you get to keep the memories more accurately than when you just have pictures," he says. Years later, he'll remember what happened and who was there.

"It will show me some of my childhood friends and the things I liked to do. And I'll be able to share it with other people," he says.

Scrapbooking has taught him a valuable lesson. "If you want to preserve memories well, think about it and do not just throw something together or not even do it at all," he says.

Chris Tardie, Berlin, Vermont

Fireballs 99

ADD PUNCH TO PAGE TITLE

Joellyn captures the enthusiasm of her son's first soccer team experience. Begin by cropping photos into ovals and squares. Single and double mat a few; trim one mat with decorative scissors. Punch jumbo suns (Family Treasures); layer across top of page. Mount die-cut title letters (Accu-Cut) over sunbursts. Stamp sun design (Stampabilities) on punched suns; layer on page for photo caption blocks. Crop printed journaling and mat and mount on page. Draw subtitle letters with template (source unknown); cut to size and trim with decorative scissors.

Joellyn Borke Johnston, Des Moines, Iowa

Lone Star Cyclones

CREATE A "FLIP-UP" MINI ALBUM

Heather found a way to display many photos by integrating a "flip-up" mini album on her pages. Begin by cropping photos for flip-up layers to 4 x 4½"; slip into clear photo sleeves (DMD Industries). Layer on background patterned paper (NRN Designs) as shown; adhere with wide sticker strips (Mrs. Grossman's) cut to size. Crop side photos; mat one and adhere stickers at corners (It Takes Two). Mount other photo behind decorative paper frame (My Mind's Eye). Cut 2" strip of patterned paper (Sandylion) for title block. Layer ¼" paper strip over patterned paper. Cut title letters using template (EK Success); mat and silhouette. Mount star fasteners (HyGlo/American Pin) on letters. Complete page by printing journaling; cut to size and mat.

Heather Shepherd, Sanger, California

Angelica

DESIGN A TEAM JERSEY

After attending a goal-making soccer game, Suzy knew her niece deserved to be highlighted in her scrapbook! Begin by mounting a solid, team-colored triangle in the corner. Copy and enlarge "jersey" pattern (see page 502); detail with hand-cut numbers and sticker letters (Making Memories). Crop photos and round photos' corners. Mount soccer ball die cut (Ellison); detail with pens and mat on cardstock. Cut out text block, mat and journal.

Suzy Quimbaya, Maumee, Ohio

Performances

In the center-stage spotlight, children learn how to channel their jitters into something wonderful—a sparkling performance that is a gift to the audience. Tuck away scripts and programs from plays and sheet music from recitals for display in your scrapbooks.

My Little Flapper
SAVE TIDBITS OF COSTUME

Cheryl sets the stage with feathers saved from a costume and a paper doll dressed to match. Begin with patterned paper background (Fiskars). Slice a 2" strip of solid brown paper; stamp wood print (Clearsnap) design to resemble stage floor. Crop photos and mat. Stamp doll parts (Joyful Hearts Stamps); silhouette, assemble, and add details to match photo. Punch mini swirls (All Night Media) for hair; mini oak leaf and mini flower (EK Success) for dress; and freehand cut bow for hair. Add pen and chalk details. Add feathers around photo. Journal on vellum; mount to page with colored eyelets (HyGlo/American Pin).

Cheryl Delavan, Cherry Valley, Illinois

Friends
SHOWCASE A SPECIAL PERFORMANCE

Lisa's daughter felt like the star of the show in a new dress at her kindergarten musical show. Begin by layering patterned paper (Design Originals) over solid, leaving ¼" border. Crop photos and reduced, photocopied musical program; single and double mat. Mount treble clef die cuts (Ellison).

Lisa Langhans, Lake Villa, Illinois

California Hoedown

FRAME PHOTOS WITH ROPE DESIGN

Jeanne's son got "roped" into square dancing at his school's
country hoedown. Begin by cropping photos into ovals;
mount on page. Freehand draw rope design to "lasso"
photos. Add "caller" clip art (source unknown); color with
pencils. Write title, journaling and dot details with pens.
Adhere musical note stickers (Mrs. Grossman's).

Jeanne Ciolli, Dove Canyon, California

School Program

PHOTOCOPY PROGRAMS OF PLAYS

Pat enjoyed creating her punch-art piggies to accent photocopies of her granddaughter's school play. Crop photos and
mat. Reduce and photocopy program; mat on solid paper.
Silhouette-crop and mat page topper (Cock-a-Doodle
Design) for title. Create punch-art piggies with 1¼" and
⅝" circle, small swirl, mini heart, small bow for feet, mini
diamond and dot for eyes and large maple leaf (all Family
Treasures), trimmed for ears. Freehand cut and slice colored
paper for sticks, straw and bricks. Circle-cut text block and
mat. Punch and assemble daisies (Family Treasures); adhere.
Freehand cut arrow and add journaling to finish the page.

Pat Asher, Camarillo, California

Musical Celebration

LAYER A MUSICAL MONTAGE

(ABOVE) Sarah documents a lovely afternoon picnic and end-of-the-year musical event put on by the children at her daughter's school. With her photo montage, she is able to fit a lot of photos onto each page. Begin by cropping photos, overlaying them as you go to fit within the frame of the patterned paper (Design Originals). When you are pleased with the arrangement of the photos, mount in place with adhesive.

Sarah McKenna, Gloucestershire, England

The Lion King

COORDINATE THEME WITH PATTERNED PAPERS

(BELOW) Patti shows her daughter is star of the show by combining wild animal prints and stickers with photos of an exciting stage production. Crop photos; mat photos on solid and animal print patterned papers (Frances Meyer, The Paper Patch). Crop and place photos behind large paw print die cut (Ellison). Adhere large animal stickers (Mrs. Grossman's), incorporating them to look as if they are holding photos. Adhere title sticker letters (Making Memories); outline with black pen.

Patti Holland, San Jose, California

Clubs & Activities

From merit badges and honor ribbons to service projects and after-school meetings—
as your children become joiners, their efforts build a pool of memories and mementos.
Clubs and activities provide a venue for individual and group achievement as
children learn that the power of "we" is far greater than the power of "me."

Oceanography Club

PAPER TEAR A "SEA-NIC" ADVENTURE

Maggie incorporated photos from a weekend field trip into a paper-torn
sea scene. Freehand tear paper pieces for sun, boat, whale and land. Crop
and silhouette photos; layer among paper torn scene. Adhere sea life
stickers (Mrs. Grossman's, Stickopotamus). Write title, journaling and
photo captions; accent with decorative pen strokes, swirls and details.

Maggie Bilash, Mesa, Arizona

4-H

PRESERVE A NEWSPAPER CLIPPING

Heather documented her daughter's showmanship experience at the
county fair by including a newspaper photo encased in an acid-free memorabilia envelope (Creative Memories). Create the colorful border by drawing the thick and thin straight lines first. Use decorative ruler (Creative
Memories) to draw the ribbon effect; shade with pen. Freehand draw four-
leaf clover in corner. Adhere colored paper triangles in opposite corners;
mount 4-H letters (Creative Memories). Crop photos and round corners.
Complete page with journaling and cat and rabbit punches (Nankong).

Heather McWhorter, Kokomo, Indiana

Troop 265
DRESS UP A BACKGROUND

As a Brownie Scout troop leader, Lorie values the importance of celebrating girls and their achievements. Freehand cut vest for background. Punch medium and small circles for "buttons" and "pins"; add flower and star stickers (Creative Memories, Stickopotamus). Cut triangles and mat to resemble patches and adhere stickers (Creative Memories, Mrs. Grossman's). Adhere black stickers (Provo Craft) for title. Adhere white sticker letters (Creative Memories) for troop identification; cut to size and mount. Crop photos; mount on page. Complete page with journaling.

Lorie Graham, Lexington, South Carolina

Chess
CRAFT OVERSIZED GAME PIECES

Oksanna's son takes on a new challenge by joining his school's chess club. Layer patterned paper (Provo Craft) over solid paper for the background. Freehand cut chess piece from solid paper. Crop photos; mat one and mount all on page. Cut title letters using template (C-Thru Ruler); add pen stroke details. Stamp ornamental design (All Night Media) and complete with pen stroke detail around photo.

Oksanna Pope, Los Gatos, California

Girl Scout Cookie Time
STACK A PILE OF COOKIE BOXES

When Angela's daughter sold almost 300 boxes of Girl Scout cookies, her living room turned into a cookie warehouse with stacks of boxes all around. Crop panoramic photo and mat. Freehand cut cookie boxes from colored cardstock; detail with pens. Write creative title letters with pens on vellum trimmed with decorative scissors; double mat. Punch 1" circles from brown paper for cookies; detail with pen. Complete page with matted journaling.

Angela Newton, Pewee Valley, Kentucky

Junior Girl Scout Rachel

PRESERVE UNIFORM WITH PAPER DOLL

Even without any photos, Karen found a way to capture her daughter's year in junior Girl Scouts with a paper doll and a photocopy of a vest. Begin by layering two colors of cardstock over background paper, leaving ⅛" border at each layer. Lightly pencil journaling border with a decorative ruler (Creative Memories). Journal with pen and erase pencil lines when ink is dry. Create paper doll (Stamping Station); add vest details with metallic stickers (Hambly Studios), punched mini circles and pen stroke details. Reduce and color photocopy front and back of vest to show patches earned; silhouette-crop photocopies and layer on page. Create "wood" frame for text block by slicing strips of patterned paper (Hot Off The Press) trimmed at the ends with decorative scissors. Mount thin twine tied into a bow and add journaling to complete.

Karen Regep Glover
Grosse Pointe Woods, Michigan

Crossing Over

TIE UP A SCOUTING ACHIEVEMENT

Gail's son "crossed over" to a new level in the Cub Scouts with countless hours of dedication and determination. Begin by cropping triangles; use fleur-de-lis corner punch (All Night Media) to accent corners before mounting at page corners. Crop photos and double mat on solid paper. Punch fleurs-de-lis at corners of second mat; mount on page. Photocopy and size pattern for neckerchief (see page 502). Cut from two colors of solid paper and assemble. Create lion cub pin from jumbo sunburst, 1" circle and small oval (Family Treasures) punches. Layer and detail with pens. Complete page with title sticker letters (Creative Memories) and add journaling.

Gail Birkhead, Tyngsboro, Massachusetts

Scouting

COMBINE PAPER SIZES

Kym found a way to integrate the perfect 8½ x 11" patterned paper for her son's scouting photos on a 12 x 12" page. Layer patterned paper (Bo-Bunny Press) over solid background paper. Crop photos; triple mat. Cut text block; triple mat. Cut 1⅝ x 10⅜" strip for title block; double mat. Freehand cut title letters; mount on title block.

Kym Gould, Greensboro, North Carolina

Bear Graduation

ADD A REALISTIC ELEMENT WITH COLOR COPIES

Jeanne added a realistic element to a Cub Scout graduation scene by nestling reduced copies of Boy Scout periodicals into the hands of paper dolls. Begin with patterned paper (Sonburn) background. Crop photos and round corners. Mat on cardstock trimmed with decorative corner and fleur-de-lis punches (Family Treasures). Mat again on cardstock; trim to size of first mat and add ¼" paper strips. Stamp title letters (Close To My Heart) on 1" squares; shade with colored pencils and mat. Stamp paper dolls (Joyful Heart Stamps); silhouette-crop and assemble. Add reduced, color-copied magazine covers; layer under boys' hands. Freehand draw flags; embellish with star and fleur-de-lis punches and pens. Slice ¼" strips and punch ⅛" circles from gold and silver metallic cardstock (Paper Cuts) for flagpoles. Complete page with paper caps (Ellison); cut front panel in complementary color and add Boy Scout stickers (Boy Scouts of America).

Jeanne Ciolli, Dove Canyon, California

St. Matthew's Catholic School

SHOW OFF CLUB EMBLEM

Donna created a clean and classic layout for her favorite Cub Scout portraits. Double layer tan speckled cardstock (Bazzill) over orange and blue cardstock, leaving ¼" border at each layer. Crop photos and double mat. Create large fleur-de-lis from pattern (Windows of Time) to mimic emblem ; mat on solid paper. For title block, mat rectangle and layer over matted square. Add title text and pen stroke stitching to finish.

Donna Commons, Jacksonville, Florida

Field Trips

On field trips kids get a chance to step outside of their normal routine and discover new worlds. The warm, yeasty smell of the bakery; the sounds of all the farm animals; the bustle of the factory all yield wonderful memories that can be captured with journaling and photos.

Frozen Field Trip

PAPER PIECE FAVORITE PART OF A FIELD TRIP

A little winter weather didn't spoil the fun of Lori's son's kindergarten field trip. Begin by layering patterned paper (Making Memories) over solid paper, leaving ¼" border. Paper piece school buses with pattern (Windows of Time); detail with pen. Add freehand paper-pieced bus driver and photo on back of bus. Crop photos; single and double mat.

Layer photos, buses and white paper-torn strips for "snow" on page. Print poem; trim and mat. Add small photo silhouette and freehand cut arrows to highlight child. Freehand draw title letters on 1⁵⁄₁₆" squares and large rectangle. Outline title; color with pencils and mat.

Lori Bowders, Waynesboro, Pennsylvania

Field Trip

ADD PIZAZZ WITH CORNER PUNCH DETAILS

There's no better school day for a student than one that includes a field trip, no matter where the destination. Oksanna documents her son's trip to a research center with bold colors and simple details. Start with patterned paper (The Robin's Nest Press) background. Crop photos into shapes. Single and double mat photos on solid paper; detail two mats with decorative corner slot punches (Fiskars). Create title letters with template (Provo Craft) in two colors and layer to create shadow effect; fill in holes in letters with swirl punch (All Night Media). Complete page with punched stars (Emagination Crafts) and journaling.

Oksanna Pope, Los Gatos, California

Field Trip to the Farm

ADD DIMENSION WITH CREATIVE LETTERING

Jacquie looked no further than her photos for inspiration when designing and selecting colors for her son's field trip page. Begin by cropping photos; round corners. Single and double mat. Layer over patterned paper (Sandylion). Craft farm scene at bottom of page with die cut barn (Ellison), fence (Stamping Station) and grass (Accu-Cut). Adhere farm animal stickers (Mrs. Grossman's). Slice thin strips of ivory cardstock; overlap and adhere together to form parts of letters. Complete letters with pen. Adhere sticker letters (Provo Craft) for title and date.

Jacquie Lomax, Long Beach, California

Our Field Trip to Chief Mountain

CRAFT SOME CLASSROOM BUDDIES

An adventure to the great outdoors is featured in Megan's photos accented by punched and pieced "classmates." Begin by cropping photos into rectangles and ovals; mount on background of patterned paper (Creative Imaginations). Cut title banner using wavy ruler; double mat, trimming the first mat with decorative scissors. Adhere sticker letters (Sandylion). Use a jumbo circle punch to form children's "heads." Freehand cut "hair" and trim with a variety of decorative scissors; layer atop heads. Complete page with pen stroke details on "faces," journaling and photo captions.

Photos Megan Bennett, Denver, Colorado

Design Stacey Shigaya, Denver, Colorado

Take Our Daughters to Work Day
DOCUMENT A VALUABLE EXPERIENCE

An enriching day for Cheri's daughter "at the office" was documented with pride. Crop and silhouette photos; mount on patterned paper (Masterpiece Studios) background. Mount certificate and event artwork. Crop text block; add border punch (Family Treasures) details and journaling.

Cheri O'Donnell, Orange, California

Lindsey's Story, 6th grade

As a sixth-grader, Lindsey visited the Florida Keys with her summer school class. She took many pictures of the memorable trip. Lindsey cleverly displays her landlubber photos above a sticker "sea level" and her underwater photos below.

"I wanted to include my photos on a page in a unique way, so I decided to make half of my page look like it was water," says Lindsey. "I cut out some of the underwater pictures like fish to make them look like they were swimming under water!"

Lindsey Sebring, Sebring, Florida

Celebrations

In celebrating moments large and small, children learn how to invite joy into their lives. As important as marking holidays and birthdays is the simple revelry in finding how sweet ice cream tastes dripping down your arm. Saved treasures from celebrations help us remember the past and build our hope for the future.

Jammie Day
ENHANCE THEME WITH PAPER DOLLS

Cindy created a bedtime thematic page for photos taken at her daughter's kindergarten pajama day. Begin by cropping photos; round corners. Mat on patterned (NRN Designs) and solid paper. Create bedtime scene with paper dolls, pillow, teddy bear and book (EK Success), layered with die-cut bed (Stamping Station). Detail die cuts with pen and chalk. Complete page with die-cut title letters (Accu-Cut) cut from patterned paper (NRN Designs). Mat letters and silhouette; mount on page. Add journaling in white ink to finish.

Cindy Roberts, Bel Aire, Kansas

Here's the Scoop!
CHRONICLE A DELICIOUS DAY

Cindy captured the fun and delight of building sundaes at an ice-cream social at her daughter's school. Begin by mounting triangles on opposite corners of the page. Crop photos; use template (Creative Memories) for special shape and round corners. Mat photo; mount all photos on page. Draw title words and artwork with pen. Complete page with pen details and journaling.

Cindy Kacynski, Superior, Colorado

My Funny Valentine

PACKAGE A POCKET FULL OF CARDS

Cheryl preserved the fun and good feelings associated with her daughter's Valentine's Day party, even without a photo from the event. Begin by mounting a clear memorabilia sleeve (Creative Memories) to solid paper; trim paper with decorative scissors. Punch mini hearts at each corner. Adhere sticker hearts (Mrs. Grossman's) around sleeve. Draw and color cherubs. Complete by writing title with pens and inserting valentine cards.

Cheryl Padia, Riverside, California

Valentine's Day

PUNCH A SWEET VALENTINE'S TREAT

Alison created a box of candy conversation hearts spilling around a sweet-faced valentine. Begin by trimming cardstock 1" from the bottom with decorative scissors (All Night Media). Punch mini heart and dot to resemble lacy design. Mount 1½" strip of white cardstock behind punched design. Crop photos into circles and heart with template (Family Treasures); double mat, trimming with decorative scissors (Frances Meyer). Freehand cut candy box from cardstock. Punch jumbo heart (Marvy/Uchida); adhere vellum behind punched shape to create window. Punch small hearts from a variety of pastel colors; layer behind box and across page. Punch jumbo hearts from vellum. Finish page with journaling and pen stroke details.

Alison Beachem, San Diego, California

St. Patrick's Day 2000 – Jordan's Class had a St. Patrick's Day Contest…Who could make the most interesting "Shamrock Poster"? Each child brought "green" items from home, and their teams decorated their "Shamrock Posters" and the class voted. Everyone wore green, and at the end of the day there was a great party to celebrate! There were green Jolly Ranchers, Green Jelly Beans, Green Sour Apple Candies (Mom's favorites!) and Shamrock Cookies. There were yummy cupcakes with green sprinkles, and Mrs. Brezden-Toney made her famous punch, which of course, was green!

Shamrock Shenanigans

PAPER PIECE A LUCKY LEPRECHAUN

Inspired by the luck of the Irish and a home-decorating magazine, Michele captured the fun of a St. Patrick's Day celebration at her son's school. Begin by chalking vertical lines 1½" apart to add dimension to solid background paper. Crop photos and round corners; mat on green paper. Paper piece an original leprechaun design and draw with chalk and pen strokes. Punch shamrock with jumbo heart punch (McGill); layer and mount on page. Punch jumbo squares (Family Treasures) for title block; adhere sticker letters (Frances Meyer). Complete page with computer-printed journaling.

Michele Weinberg
San Juan Capistrano, California

Party Theme Album

DOCUMENT HOLIDAY CELEBRATIONS

At no other time during a child's education are there more holiday parties than in grade school. Linda preserved her child's festivities in a school days album, which was part of a tribute to her child's beloved teacher, Mrs. Bochiechio.

The wide array of patterned papers and holiday-theme stickers, die cuts, stamps and punches available make it easy to create party pages. Note the patterned paper back grounds used on the "Spring Party" and "Trick or Treat" pages shown here. Linda takes advantage of the shapes in patterned papers by cropping the shapes out and placing her candid photos behind the paper—a great way to frame photos without adding extra bulk to a scrapbook album.

With a little creative cropping of your own, your classroom party pages will be something to celebrate!

Linda Foster, Williamsville, New York

"LE LION EST MORT CE SOIR"...

PETITS LIONS ET OURS

À LA FÊTE DE LA JUNIOR SCHOOL 1999

EMILIE ET SES COPAINS

LUDIVINE, AURELINE,

ALIX, FLORENCE, ALIZEE, C

Castille's Halloween Parade

INCORPORATE DESIGN INSPIRATIONS

Jeanne seeks inspiration for her pages wherever she can...even if it's from a design she sees on a piece of clothing! Crop photos, round corners. Mat on patterned papers (The Paper Patch). Adhere sticker letters (Frances Meyer). Layer die-cut stars (Ellison) on page; detail with pen strokes.

Jeanne Ciolli, Dove Canyon, California

Le Lion
CRAFT A COSTUME BACKGROUND

Natalie captures a fun day of dress-up with her wild, paper-crafted animal face. Begin by freehand cutting yellow and brown paper to resemble a wild and woolly mane; layer over solid background paper. Crop two photos into circles; mat on solid paper and layer over large white ovals for eyes. Slice panoramic photos into 1⅛" strips; mount over eyes. Freehand cut muzzle, nose and eyebrows. Slice ¼" paper strips, trimmed with decorative scissors for whiskers. Freehand craft mouth and teeth; layer photos behind teeth. Complete with journaling on whiskers with white pen.

Natalie Papin, Arnas, France

Thanksgiving Feast
PRESERVE PRECIOUS HAND PRINT

Wendy found a special way to preserve her daughter's handprint and thankful words from a school Thanksgiving feast. Begin by drawing pen stroke border with ruler for guide around pages. Stamp fall designs (Stampin' Up!); color and detail with watercolor pens. Crop artwork with decorative scissors (Family Treasures). Mat handprint and artwork on cardstock textured with paper crimper (Fiskars). Add raffia bow. Crop photos; mount on page. Complete page with title and journaling.

Wendy Rueter
Rancho Santa Margarita, California

The Big Feast

DOCUMENT A DAY'S EVENTS

Susan and her daughter's kindergarten class gathered together for a traditional Thanksgiving feast, complete with pilgrim and Native American costumes made by the students. Adhere border stickers (Me & My Big Ideas) at bottom of pages. Crop photos and mat. Write title and mat. Frame title block with harvest stickers (Me & My Big Ideas). Complete page with journaling and photo captions.

Susan Brochu, East Berlin, Connecticut

november 24, 1999

THE
BIG
FEAST

You model your homemade vest and headband.

Both morning kindergarten classes celebrated Thanksgiving together with a big feast in the cafeteria. Places were set with placemats you had decorated yourselves, and the menu included fruit cup, homemade corn, pumpkin and cranberry breads and milk. Each student chose whether to dress as a pilgrim or a Native American. Since I was one of the room parents for your class, I was able to help with the festivities (and I brought my camera, of course!).

Maggie, Lia, Julia, Ambyr, Melissa & Shane

Almost time to dig in!

We thank you, LORD, for all these blessings...for family and friends and turkey dressing.

Your placemat

one more picture & then you can eat!

"Smile and say 'We're stuffed!'"

Melissa, you, Daniel & Jordan

Gingerbread House Party

ASSEMBLE A YUMMY COLLECTION OF TREATS

Alison features the edible tools of the trade that her son used to make his first gingerbread house. Double mat patterned paper (Making Memories) for background. Crop photos; single and triple mat on solid paper. Cut title letters using template (Scrap Pagerz); detail with chalk. Print rest of title words and photo captions from computer; cut to size and mat. Crop rectangles from brown cardstock; detail with chalk and colored pencils to resemble graham crackers. Crop "gumdrops" from colored paper; sponge stamp with white ink (Tsukineko) for sugary effect and layer at top and bottom of pages. Mount red cording (Darice) to look like licorice by stitching an "X" at loops.

Alison Beachem, San Diego, California

Field Days

On your mark, get set, GO! What a great celebration of athletics field days are, blending the salty taste of sweat with the sweetness of fresh air, friendly competition and laughing so hard it hurts. Blue ribbons, winners' medals and photos of friends and rivals make great displays to mark these glorious, heart-pounding days.

Juarez Olympics

SHOW ACTION WITH PAPER DOLLS

Michele documented her son's unique "Olympic" activity at school, using muted background colors and paper dolls to highlight event activities. Begin by matting white cardstock over gray cardstock, leaving ½" border. Crop and mat photos; mount on page. Computer journal title and text block on vellum; layer over gingham paper (Close To My Heart) and mat. Using a circle cutter, cut circles, then overlap and interlock as shown to create Olympic rings. Create paper dolls with template (Close To My Heart) and design outfit to match photos; detail with pen and chalk. Complete pages with pen lines around edges.

Michele Rank, Cerritos, California

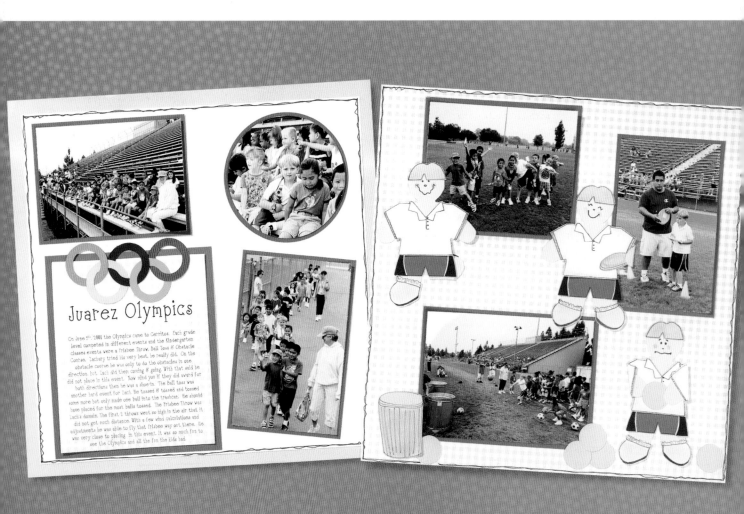

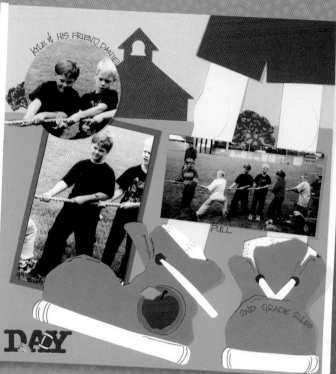

Franklin School Field Day

FEATURE AN INTERESTING POINT OF VIEW

Lorna shows the fun of field day from the ground's point of view, featuring knobby knees and laced-up sneakers. Layer solid green cardstock over a 3½" strip of blue cardstock for the background. Mount school die cut (Ellison) and school bus and tree stickers (Mrs. Grossman's) to complete the background. Copy and size the leg and sneaker patterns (see page 502) to fit page. Cut pieces and assemble. Add texture to white paper with crimper (Fiskars) for socks. Adhere apple stickers (Mrs. Grossman's) and detail shoes with pen stroke details. Crop photos; mat a few and layer on page. Adhere title sticker letters (Creative Memories); layer with school-theme stickers (Mrs. Grossman's). Complete page with journaling.

Lorna Dee Christensen, Corvallis, Oregon

Field Day

RE-CREATE PARTICIPANT AWARDS

An award-winning day of fun and friendly competition is reflected on Rosemary's page full of ribbons. Crop photos; round corners and mat a few. Freehand cut awards using decorative scissors (Fiskars) for ribbon ends. Adhere sticker letters (Frances Meyer) and star stickers (Mrs. Grossman's). Complete with photo titles written on banner stickers (Frances Meyer).

Rosemary Palawski, Davison, Michigan

Awards & Ceremonies

Ceremonies and awards serve to honor not just achievement itself but also the hunger and hope to try. Invitations, programs and certificates are naturals for preservation and display in scrapbooks; they remind children of when they reached for the stars and, for a grand moment, touched one.

SEAN, 3RD GRADE

Erin's Awarding Year
PHOTOCOPY SCHOOL CERTIFICATES

Tami shows her daughter's "awarding" year with a page full of reduced copies of certificates earned. Punch award die cut (Ellison) on background paper; mount yellow cardstock behind to show through. Reduce color copies of certificates; cut to size and mount. Mat school portrait; trim with decorative scissors. Punch stars; mount on page. Complete page with journaling on award.

Tami Comstock, Pocatello, Idaho

D.A.R.E. Graduation
PRESERVE A PROUD MOMENT

Mary features her daughter's completion of the D.A.R.E. program along with her fifth-grade class. Cut two sheets of colored paper in half diagonally with decorative scissors (Fiskars) to form large triangles; mount on page as shown. Adhere border stickers (Mrs. Grossman's) at upper and lower page edges. Crop photos; mat or outline with stickers. Add program, sticker and journaling to complete.

Mary Browder, Shreveport, Louisiana

Approved Workmen Are Not Ashamed
CREATE AN AWARD-WINNING LAYOUT

Jolene captures her daughter's award-winning smile and achievement by re-creating the red ribbon awards on her page. Begin by drawing three horizontal lines across the top of the page. Circle-cut photos to look like medallions, focusing on award winners. Mat and add gold pen stroke details. Cut red cardstock into long "V" shapes to look like ribbons; detail with gold pen. "Hang" ribbons with medallions at the bottom from third horizontal line. Silhouette-crop photo and add title with pen at top of page. Complete page with journaling.

Jolene Philo, Boone, Indiana

Kindergarten Awards
SHOW OFF SCHOOL ACHIEVEMENTS

Rhonda captured her son's proud smile after he earned two special kindergarten awards. Start by drawing title frame and border; layer over background paper (Keeping Memories Alive). Triple mat photo; mount over ribbons. Complete page with paper doll (EK Success) dressed in clothes to match the photo.

Rhonda Scott, Fairfield, California

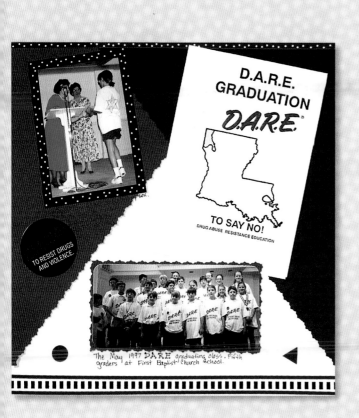

Graduation

All at once a child is not just a person and a classmate but a member of the "Class of..." Graduation ceremonies make this rite of passage real, complete with all the pomp and circumstance. Tassels, programs autographed by classmates and photos make great pages to remember this special time.

You're a Star!

PRESERVE A SPECIAL DOCUMENT

Debbie documents her son's rite of passage from elementary school to middle school with a star-studded layout. Begin by triple matting patterned paper (Stamping Station) for the background. Crop photos and double mat. Reduce and color copy diploma. Craft paper doll (DJ Inkers); detail with pens and chalk. Adhere shadowed sticker letters (Making Memories) to white paper strip. Mount to page with eyelets (Magic Scraps); detail title block with pens. Draw stars, silhouette; add details with pens. Mount to page with foam spacers (All Night Media).

Debby Schuh, The Memory Bee
Clarence, New York

Celebrate

PAY TRIBUTE TO GRADUATES

Narda captures the excitement of a spirited graduating class with bright colors and decorative pen work. Begin by cropping photos into rectangle and oval shapes; mat one photo. Freehand cut graduation caps; detail with pen. Triple-mat title block on solid and patterned paper (Provo Craft). Use decorative ruler as a guide for text written in a wavy fashion; pencil large letters around smaller words. Use two pen colors for lettering; add star and dot details on title block and around photos. Complete page with journaling.

Narda Poe, Midland, Texas

Little Huskies

SILHOUETTE PHOTOS OF FRIENDS

Carole gathered a number of graduation photos of her daughter's friends and silhouette-cropped them to fit on a one-page layout. Begin with a large, colored triangle layered with patterned paper (Hot Off The Press) for the background. Mount silhouette-cropped photos. Add die-cut heart (Creative Memories), title and journal quote.

Carole Parma, Albuquerque, New Mexico

Diploma

LAYER DIE-CUT ENHANCEMENTS

Jeanne assembled fun and colorful elements to reflect the joy of her son's sixth-grade graduation. Begin by silhouetting and cropping photos; triple mat on solid and patterned paper (The Paper Patch). Layer photos on page with computer-generated "diploma" and graduation cap die cuts (Ellison). Adhere graduation-theme stickers (Frances Meyer) on background and photos. Complete page with freehand-drawn lettering and pen stroke details.

Jeanne Ciolli, Dove Canyon, California

Graduation Day

FEATURE CLASSMATES' SIGNATURES

Tami documents her son's kindergarten graduating class with his classmates' signatures surrounding his handmade bear. Mount artwork at center of page. Crop individual signatures and mat; mount on page in random fashion. Adhere sticker letters (Creative Memories) and graduation cap stickers (Mrs. Grossman's). Finish page with journaling.

Tami Emricson, Woodstock, Illinois

Rachel's in the News!

FILL A POCKET WITH MEMORABILIA

Karen collected her daughter's fifth-grade awards, newspaper clippings and special keepsakes in a pocket page emblazoned with positive headlines. Create pocket page by cutting cardstock to one-half the height of page. Apply adhesive to three sides of cardstock, leaving the upper edge open to form pocket. Silhouette-crop "5th grade" title (Cock-a-Doodle Design) and images; mount on cardstock and mat. Circle-crop photo, adhere sticker letters (C-Thru Ruler) and insert memorabilia to complete page.

Karen Regep Glover
Grosse Pointe Woods, Michigan

Grad

FEATURE GRADS IN OVERSIZED CAP

Debi created a full-page smiling graduate to display photos of a grade school graduation. Begin by layering patterned paper (The Paper Patch) over white, leaving a ¼" border. Freehand cut large circle and hair; detail with pen and chalk. Cut an 8" square from black paper for back of graduation cap; layer behind head, overlapping corner behind page. Crop photo using semi-circle template (Puzzle Mates); mat on black paper and mount over hair to complete cap. Add freehand-drawn tassel and diploma. Crop second photo; triple mat. Punch stars (Family Treasures). Complete page with title letters cut from template (Puzzle Mates); mat on yellow paper and silhouette.

Debi Adams for Puzzle Mates, Anaheim, California

Kindergarten, Class of 2001

DRESS DOLLS TO DOCUMENT MILESTONE

Michele captures the pride and excitement her son experienced at his kindergarten graduation with a succession of celebratory paper dolls. Begin by layering patterned paper (Close To My Heart) trimmed with decorative cutter (Fiskars); layer over speckled background paper (Close To My Heart), leaving ⁵⁄₁₆" border. Add pen stroke lines around wavy border. Print title and journaling; trim and triple-mat. Crop photos and double- or triple-mat. Craft paper dolls and clothes with stencils (Close To My Heart). Stamp faces (Close To My Heart); add chalk and pen stroke details. For "diploma," roll paper scrap, flatten and glue together. Adhere small paper strip to look like diploma tie.

Michele Rank, Cerritos, California

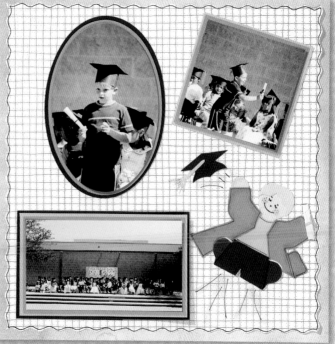

Casey

Casey was adorable
in the dress that I
made for her first
day of school at
Turtleback
Elementary.
She was so excited
to start school.
Special memories
of this year were:
her best friend Joy,
her wonderful
teacher Mrs. Brown,
Pajama Day,
Farmer Day
and art time.
1995

Portraits & Milestones

"EDUCATION IS FOR IMPROVING THE LIVES OF OTHERS AND FOR LEAVING YOUR COMMUNITY AND WORLD BETTER THAN YOU FOUND IT."

—Marian Wright Edelman, author (1939-)

There they are: the whole class and teacher together, every hair combed into place, just perfect. Captured on film are friends for a lifetime. Creating pages to display class and individual portraits helps to mark the passage of time. Eager yet timid preschoolers cross that threshold into kindergarten, then blossom with each passing year, laying the foundation for all learning that life will bring. Scrapbooking about a child's elementary years will help you remember, of course. But it also helps a child to build self-esteem. Kids see how our culture honors and remembers great leaders with formal portraits. How fitting, then, to display children's portraits in scrapbooks. For they too will soon take their place in history.

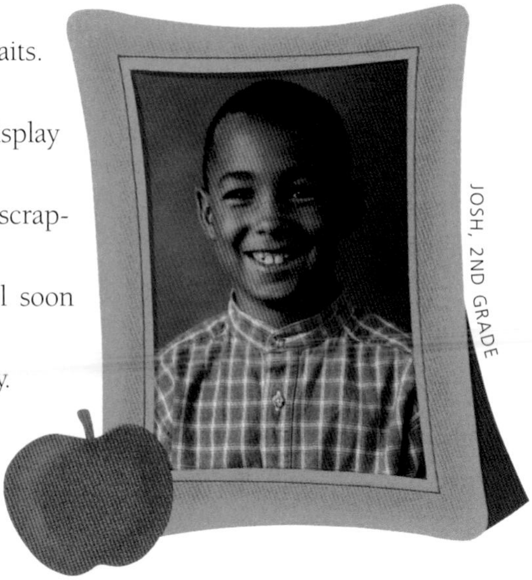

JOSH, 2ND GRADE

CASEY
(SEE PAGE 507)

BIG USES FOR SMALL PORTRAITS

Try these fun and creative uses for those tiny photos that come in professional portrait packages:

- Add to a growth "timeline" to document grade school years.

- Add to mini "filmstrip" made with paper and filmstrip border punch.

- Create a shaped photomontage, like the schoolhouse to the right.

- Crop or stack and use to spell out child's name or age.

- Frame a large portrait with them.

- Make personalized greeting cards with them.

- Place in windows of paper-pieced schoolhouse or bus.

- Punch with a large shape punch and use for a border or corner design.

- Silhouette-crop photos and tuck into paper-pieced designs.

- Silhouette-crop photos and use for border.

- They are the perfect size for creating "family trees."

- Trim edges with decorative scissors to make a "postage stamp" for a school collage.

- Use to create the School Days page shown on page 504.

DYLAN, 2ND GRADE

Josh

PIN UP A SELF-PORTRAIT

Lori adds a fun element to her son's school portraits by posting a self-portrait that her son drew next to his individual portrait. First, crop and round corners of cardstock "bulletin board." Mount individual portrait and child's drawing; add pushpin stickers (Stickopotamus). Mat and mount class portrait; add pushpin die cut (Ellison) to complete page.

Lori Crain, Kent, Washington

Kendra in Kindergarten

FEATURE FULL-LENGTH PORTRAIT, TOO

Both casual and formal portraits of Dawn's daughter wearing her favorite dress on photo day come together in a simple layout. Begin by cropping photos; double mat on solid paper. Add detail with chalk around edges of second mat; mount on patterned background paper (Karen Foster Design). Tape embroidery floss (DMC Corp.) to backs of matted photos. "Hang" framed photos under silver fasteners (Westrim Crafts) mounted to page. Print title letters on computer; add color with chalk.

Design Brandi Ginn, Lafayette, Colorado

Photos Dawn Mabe, Broomfield, Colorado

Grant

DETAIL A MONOCHROMATIC BORDER

Barbara pieced together a detailed border to highlight a special nephew's school portrait. Begin by triple-matting portrait on solid and patterned (Keeping Memories Alive) papers. Cut photo corners with decorative scissors (Fiskars); mount matted photo on paper (Keeping Memories Alive). Begin border by cutting upper and lower center rectangles; double-mat. Crop rectangles for sides of the border; single- and double-mat. Draw title letters with template (The Crafter's Workshop); outline with pen and color in with pencils. Adhere school theme stickers (Creative Imaginations). Slice ¼" paper strips; tie and mount on page. Freehand draw and cut crayon box; color with pencils and chalk. Finish with journaling block.

Barbara Otten, Durand, Michigan

Adding Eyelets

One of the latest hardware crazes to find its way into our scrapbooks is eyelets—little, one-piece metal fasteners that you apply to the page with an eyelet setter and a craft hammer. Eyelets work well for both masculine and feminine pages, such as this school portrait of a young girl. Eyelets can be left unadorned or laced with ribbon, raffia, metallic cord or natural jute, depending on the look you wish to achieve.

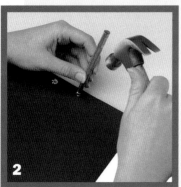

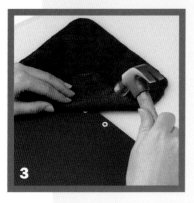

1 *Use a ⅛" round hand punch to punch two holes in cardstock that you will use for photo mat's background (Figure 1).*

2 *Turn cardstock over and push the elongated, tubular end of eyelet into punched hole from the front of the cardstock. Place cardstock, with eyelet tube facing up, on a craft mat. Insert eyelet setter into eyelet's tube and strike the top of the eyelet setter a few times to flatten tube (Figure 2).*

3 *Turn cardstock over to its front. Cover eyelet with a soft cloth to protect it from scratches, then strike the eyelet with a hammer again one or two times to "finish the set" and further flatten out the eyelet (Figure 3).*

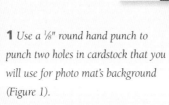

Kindergarten picture ·· Teacher: Mrs. Campaglio ·· Friends: Sage, Lily, Courtney, Savannah, September 2000

Shannon

ADD A DAINTY TOUCH WITH EYELETS

Liz pulls an element from her daughter's red-bowed dress onto a photo mat with the use of eyelets and ribbon. Begin with child's name cut from template (Cut-It-Up) on patterned paper (The Paper Patch), matted and adhered across top of page. Add double-matted journaling block across lower edge of page. Follow the steps at left to attach eyelets to background of photo mat. Double mat photo and accent with punched daisies; draw pen stroke details on daisy petals and add punched circles at daisy centers. Insert ribbon into eyelets; tie in a bow. Mount matted photo to page to finish.

Liz Connolly, Sturbridge, Massachusetts

ENLISTING YOUR CHILD'S HELP TO MAKE PHOTO MATS

Looking for a creative way to spend time with your child and preserve memories at the same time? Enlist your child's help in creating photo mats for his or her school portraits. You will both enjoy these project ideas:

• Punch out or cut many different-sized shapes from bright-colored cardstock and make a collage. See page 472 for using tiny portrait "postage stamps" in your collage.

• Give your budding artists lots of drawing paper and acid-free pens so that they can create their own masterpieces for photo mats or frames.

• Remember how much fun you had sprinkling glitter when you were a child? New, acid-free glitter glues can give your child the same fun without the mess. They are great for making abstract designs on photo mats.

• Everybody loves stickers! Make a fun border using favorite stickers.

• Press your child's hand onto a washable ink pad, and have him make handprints on paper. Keep plenty of moist wipes on hand to clean up any excess ink left on his fingers.

• Children love to collect things. Take them on a nature hike and have them gather leaves, flowers, stones or seashells. Scan a photo of these items into your computer, and print out a mat featuring your child's favorite things!

• Provide your child with large die cuts and let her decorate them with chalk.

• What could be more fun than tearing paper into pieces and not getting scolded for it? Enlist your child's help in creating mats with torn edges by giving him cardstock and letting him tear to his heart's delight.

• Make bubble paper. Mix up some soap water with food coloring, give your child a bubble wand, and let her blow bubbles onto a piece of white cardstock. Cut the cardstock into mats.

• Have your child make patterned paper using rubber stamps, washable ink or markers or crayons.

Nicolas Paul Wilhite

FRAME A PORTRAIT WITH CHILD'S OWN ARTWORK

Charlotte's son was seven years old when he discovered fonts and was intrigued with them. Charlotte framed his school portrait with the "ABCs" written in various "fonts" by Nick.

Charlotte Wilhite, Fort Worth, Texas

Paper Folding

The wide array of school-theme patterned papers available makes paper folding a fun and unique way to accent school portraits. Paper folding, with its origins deep in the ancient art of origami, is easy to do. Just a few folds here, a few creases there and some creative assembly is all you need to do.

You can use many different folds. Here we feature the envelope fold. By assembling folded pieces into a ring, you can easily frame a portrait. Experiment by altering the number of folded pieces used to make squares, rectangles or smaller circles to frame photos.

For the folded frame shown here, you will need twenty-five 2¼" squares of patterned paper (Hot Off The Press). One 8½ x 11" piece of patterned paper will yield twelve squares. Fold each piece following the steps below. Try folding a few practice pieces first.

Nicky

FOLD A SCHOOL PORTRAIT FRAME

Folded school-theme papers add excitement to Andrea's page featuring her son's first-grade portrait. Begin with matted cardstock background. Circle-crop an enlarged photo into an 8" circle; mount at center of page. Add apple die cuts (Colorbök) and school stickers (Frances Meyer) to page. Fold pieces following the steps below and at right; then assemble pieces and mount on page. Add journaling to die cuts to finish page.

Andrea Price, Auburn, New York

Envelope Fold

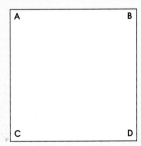

1 *Begin by cutting 2¼ x 2¼" squares from any style of lightweight paper. Cut a few extra for practice. On the backside of your practice square, label the corners with a pencil.*

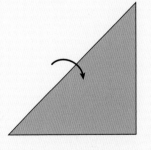

2 *Fold corner A to corner D and crease the diagonal edge.*

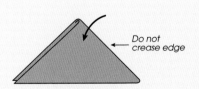

3 *Fold corner B to C. Do not crease the edge.*

Assembly

Line up twenty-five folded paper pieces atop the circle photo's edge with even spacing, overlapping square, non-folded edges as needed to complete the circle. When you are satisfied with the placement and spacing of each piece, secure each piece in place with adhesive.

Paper folding technique by Kris Mason of Folded Memories and Laura Lees of L Paper Designs. For more on paper folding, see Memory Makers® Memory Folding™. *(Ordering information is on page 509.)*

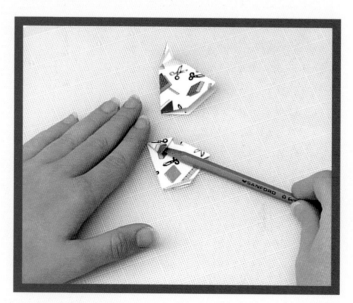

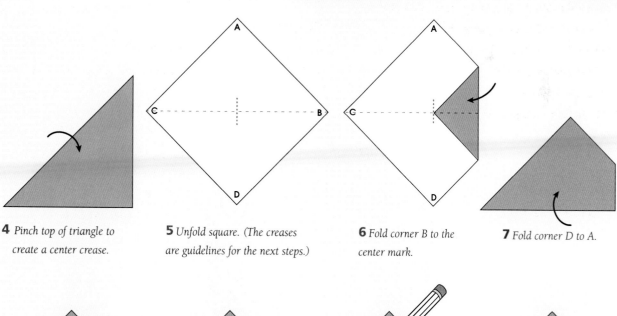

4 *Pinch top of triangle to create a center crease.*

5 *Unfold square. (The creases are guidelines for the next steps.)*

6 *Fold corner B to the center mark.*

7 *Fold corner D to A.*

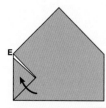

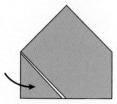

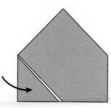

8 *Fold corner C to the center.*

9 *Next fold back corner C to E.*

10 *Insert a pencil into the last fold to create a pocket (Figure 1).*

11 *Flatten the pocket to form a small kite shape.*

School Days

FEATURE CLASSMATE PHOTOS

Carrie, a first-grade teacher, documents her class's individual photos with handmade apples and the three "Rs": reading, 'riting and 'rithmetic. First, circle-crop photos. Adhere photos to various-colored, freehand cut and accented apple die cuts; set aside. Adhere cropped title and apples from patterned paper (Provo Craft) to page as shown. Journal around page edges. Place die-cut photo apples on spread in a carefree arrangement; mount in place. Add student names and small punched apples to finish page.

Carrie Davis, Everett, Washington

Ryan

USE HARDWARE FOR MASCULINE TOUCH

Liz's use of punched rectangles and brass fasteners
lend a masculine touch to her son's school portrait.
First, crop photo, round corners and double mat.
Create photo border with punched rectangles
(Family Treasures) layered on punched 1" squares
(Family Treasures). Mat again; add decorative fasteners
(Impress Rubber Stamps) to corners before mounting
on page. Crop and double-mat paper for title block, add
journaling and decorative fasteners to complete page.

Liz Connolly, Sturbridge, Massachusetts

Sarah's Story, 3rd grade

Sarah—the third-grade scrapbooking sidekick of her
mother, Megan—enjoys creating pages about her first
day of school, field trips and her Halloween parade.
One of her recent pages shows a paper doll dressed
cleverly in the same outfit that Sarah is wearing for
her school portrait.

"I thought it was a great 'picture day' outfit and I
thought by doing the paper doll in a matching outfit, it
would bring out the clothes I was wearing," says Sarah,
who matched even the button details on her paper doll.

"I will pass my scrapbook on to my kids," she says.
"They will be able to see what I looked like as a little
girl and what my clothes and school looked like. My
mom says it's important for my kids to see my handwriting, too."

Sarah Glynis-Margaret Bennett, Denver, Colorado

WORKING WITH HERITAGE PHOTOS

For an archival-quality album environment:

• Handle heritage photos with care; avoid direct light.

• Use non-permanent mounting techniques (photo corners, sleeves, etc.) for easy removal for copying or restoration.

• Keep cropping to a minimum; background objects tell their own stories of place and time.

• Do not trim or hand-tint old photos. Have reprints made first.

Carol Jo Gajewski

Christie created multiple monochromatic pages for her mother's priceless sepia-toned class photos. Mat photos on paper trimmed with decorative scissors (Westrim) with clear photo corners (3L); mount over patterned background paper (NRN Designs). Add vintage school theme stickers (NRN Designs) atop paper squares trimmed with decorative scissors. Create title block with sticker frame (NRN Designs). Finish with double-matted title block.

Christie Scott, Trevor, Wisconsin

Paper Silhouettes

PROFILE YOUR CHILD WITH A SILHOUETTE

Paper silhouettes are easy to make and add to any child's school
days scrapbook album.

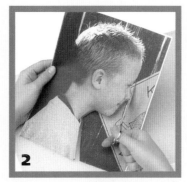

1 *Begin with a "profile" photo-graph that shows just head and shoulders. Photocopy the photo-graph, enlarging to desired size to fit intended space on a scrap-book page (Figure 1).*

2 *Cut out the photocopied profile, staying true to outlines of facial features and hair (Figure 2).*

3 *Place the cut out profile onto black paper and trace around it with a pencil (Figure 3).*

4 *Cut out the black paper silhou-ette and mount on a lighter, double-matted background if desired (Figure 4).*

Photo MaryJo Regier
Littleton, Colorado

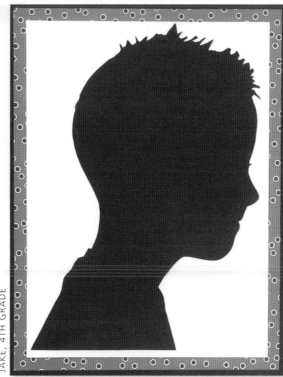

JAKE, 4TH GRADE

May '97

POST SIGNS ALONG THE ROAD TO LEARNING

Pamela looked no further than the background of her son's portrait for inspiration when creating a page border. Begin by slicing four 1½" wide strips of black paper; mount on page. Slice a yellow sticker strip (Mrs. Grossman's) at ¼" intervals and adhere down center of black border for road lines. Adhere road signs and bus stickers (Mrs. Grossman's) and sticker letter outlines (Creative Memories). Mount photo with clear mounting corners (Creative Memories).

Pamela Byrd, Huntsville, Alabama

School Days

FRAME A CLASS PHOTO

Keep the focus on a large class photo with a simple frame and background. Begin by framing a photo with a paper frame (Provo Craft). Add silhouette-cropped title and apples from patterned paper (Provo Craft) to keep the page clean and simple.

Joyce Schweitzer
Greensboro, North Carolina

Smile

SLICE A TITLE WITHIN A TITLE

Liz was inspired by her daughter's bright smile and so she titled the page accordingly! Begin by cropping photo; round corners and mat. Trim mat with decorative corner punch (All Night Media) and mat two more times. Punch smiley faces (Marvy/Uchida); mount on 1½" paper border strip. Add eyelets (Impress Rubber Stamps; see technique on page 474) to corners and detail with white pen. Create title block; cut letters from template (Scrap Pagerz). Slice letters horizontally; adhere to cardstock, leaving ⅜" space between letter pieces. Write title phrase and detail lines around edges.

Liz Connolly, Sturbridge, Massachusetts

Grade 4

FRAME PORTRAIT WITH CLASSMATES

Ardie framed her daughter's fourth-grade portrait with classmate photos cropped to fit a bold border. Begin by slicing two 2⅜" wide paper strips for the sides of the border and slice two 1½" strips for the upper and lower borders. Crop class photos into rectangles; mount as shown. Adhere title letters (Creative Memories) at top of page. Crop portrait; mat on patterned paper (Creative Memories). Complete with student and teacher names.

Ardie Clark, Eugene, Oregon

St. Walter's School of Religion

IDENTIFY CLASSMATES IN A PHOTO

With all of those class photos taken during school, it can be tricky to put names with faces as the years pass by. One simple solution is to create a diagram right on the scrapbook page to reference those in the photo.

Follow the instructions below to create a reference diagram. Then mount matted class photo, accented with handmade letters (see pattern on page 502), to page. Add page title and journaling in pen.

Photo Kimberly Ball, Denver, Colorado

Make a photocopy of the photo, enlarging or reducing as needed to fit intended space on scrapbook page. Place white scrapbook page atop photocopy on a light box or bright window; moving photocopy around beneath page to find proper positioning. Use a pencil to trace outlines of each individual in photo directly onto scrapbook page as shown; retrace in black ink. Assign a number to each person in the diagram and list the numbers and corresponding names directly on the scrapbook page.

Portrait Theme Album

Sometimes it is hard to know what to do with all of those 8 x 10" portraits that come in portrait packages. Joyce creates a page for each enlargement to show a chronological progression of her daughter's school days growth.

Joyce's page design layouts enhance the portraits and are simple enough to keep from stealing attention away from the photos. The combination of bright and muted patterned papers and cardstock work together for a unified look, while different sticker, decorative scissors, punch and die-cut accents make each page unique.

This is a great way to scrapbook these wall-size portraits when they are taken down from the living room wall each year and replaced with a new school year portrait.

Joyce Schweitzer
Greensboro, North Carolina

Documenting the Difficult Times

Life's challenges are rarely the most fun times, but they are often the most meaningful. Kids have a tremendous adaptability to overcome obstacles. Mark their progress to show your support. Remember that challenges are best met together.

Alina's Story, 2nd grade

As a toddler, Wendi's daughter was diagnosed "developmentally delayed" with low muscle tone. Wendi and her husband spent countless hours trying to inspire Alina to use a crayon on paper. "Finally, she did begin... and creating art for herself and for others has been her favorite pastime for years," says Wendi.

By age six, Alina was diagnosed as mildly autistic with continued low muscle tone. Today, with a loving family and a home program called Applied Behavior Analysis or ABA, she thrives beautifully with a little extra support in a regular class. She also participates in Girl Scouts and is on a summer swim team.

Alina says, "I like to scrapbook every day!" She is as familiar with Wendi's scrapbook supplies as her mother is. "Sometimes I remind her of the steps (select pictures, paper, stickers, etc.), which helps her with her independent-type skills," says Wendi. "Then Alina is left to create. The only requirement is that she writes on each page."

Through scrapbooking and living with a special-needs child, Wendi has learned how to tell history and cherish today as it is. "This is our life and even though we believe Alina will overcome her autism, the road she and the family have traveled is important and needs to be embraced in our family history."

For Alina, scrapbooking allows her to express her likes, dislikes and how she perceives her world. "It's a way to communicate through art," says Wendi. "Alina's fine motor skills have improved significantly using cutters, punches, scissors and stickers. You know how hard they are to get just where you want them!"

Alina and Wendi Hitchings
Issaquah, Washington

A New School

SOFTEN THE BLOW OF A NEW SCHOOL

Alex used a photocopy of her daughter's favorite new shirt, complete with "pop-dotted" hula skirts, to document her start at a new school in Hawaii. Begin by adding matted border strips to page edges. Crop and mat photos, adhere as desired. Add child's drawing and matted journaling blocks. Freehand cut and adhere title lettering. Accent pages with chalked punched shapes (EK Success, Family Treasures, McGill) to finish.

Alexandra Bishop, Honolulu, Hawaii

My Son, My Hero

JOURNAL A SPECIAL STORY

(BELOW) Kimberly titled her page to reflect the hard work and dedication her son put forth to overcome his learning disability. Freehand cut large book; mount layers over solid background. Cut title letters with template (source unknown) from solid and patterned (Northern Spy) papers. Circle-crop photo; mat for letter "O" in "son." Assemble paper doll (EK Success); detail with pen. Print journaling; crop and double mat. Reduce report card and certificate; double mat. Mount ribbon to page.

Kimberly Edwards, Jacksonville, Florida

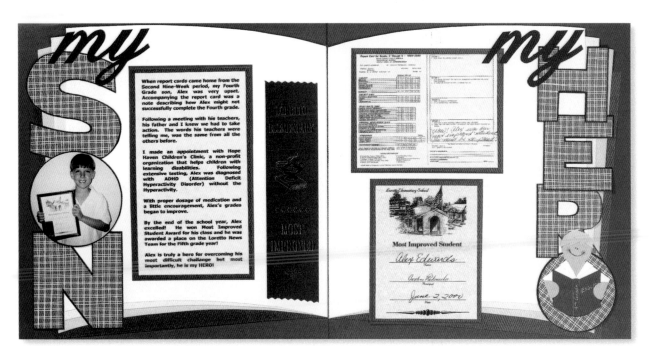

HELPING YOUR CHILD BUILD CONFIDENCE

Self-confidence helps children succeed in school. Self-confident children take risks that are necessary to try new things and be creative. Here are some ways to foster self-esteem:

- Teach children to respect themselves by treating them with respect. Listen to them and acknowledge their feelings.

- Accentuate the positive. Focus on children's unique interests and strengths and help foster them.

- Do not compare children with their siblings or classmates.

- Help children find group activities where they can make friends with other children who share their interests.

- Teach children how to set realistic goals for themselves. Break down goals and tasks into easy steps.

- Mistakes are not failures! They are simply opportunities to learn new skills. Give children the freedom to make mistakes.

- Provide lots of encouragement and celebrate life's little victories.

- When criticism is necessary, provide feedback that is specific to the children's actions.

- Don't criticize the child as a whole person.

- Give choices so that children develop a sense of independence and accountability.

- Allocate responsibility. Give children age-appropriate chores and tasks to foster a sense of responsibility.

- Be consistent. Foster children's sense of trust and safety by setting fair and reasonable boundaries.

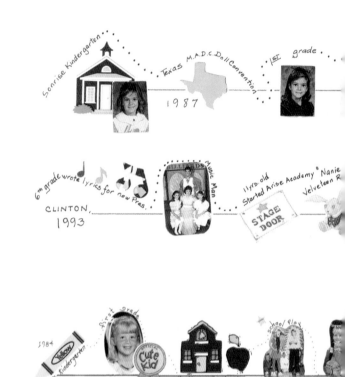

Proud to Be Me

DOCUMENT A CHILD'S CONFIDENCE

Kathy found herself smiling at her son's answers to a class assignment, so she made a copy of his work and created a page reflecting his healthy self-esteem. Begin by cropping school pages and matting with decorative scissors (Fiskars) and corner rounder. Mount extra school photos down side of page; complete page with sticker letters (Making Memories) and monster stickers (Mrs. Grossman's).

Kathy Thomas, Fairfax Station, Virginia

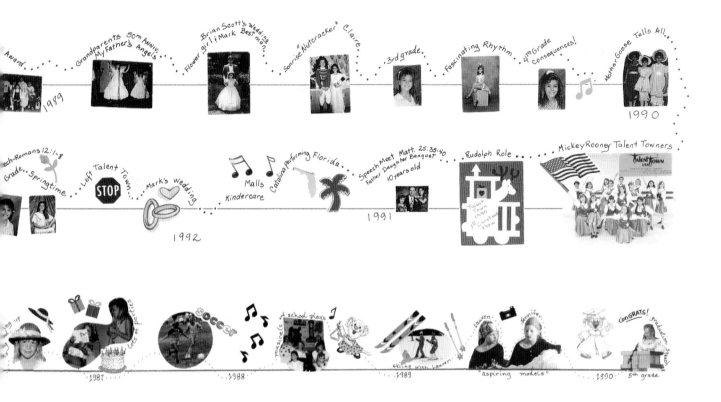

Grade School Timelines

SHOWCASE ELEMENTARY HIGHLIGHTS

Naomi (UPPER) and Barbara (LOWER) capture the growth and activities that their children experienced during their elementary school years with small photo vignettes and a variety of stickers on a comprehensive timeline. Although these timelines are shown as one continuous line, adjust the number of lines across your page to accommodate the amount of your child's "highlights." Begin making a timeline by drawing horizontal lines 1¾" apart.

Silhouette-crop photos and place along freehand-drawn timeline, leaving room for stickers (Bo-Bunny Press, Frances Meyer, Mrs. Grossman's, Sandylion, Suzy's Zoo) and journaling. Assemble and arrange all photos and stickers along timeline before adhering to page to ensure adequate spacing. Finish with journaling.

Naomi Paris, Covina, California

Barbara Wegener, Huntington Beach, California

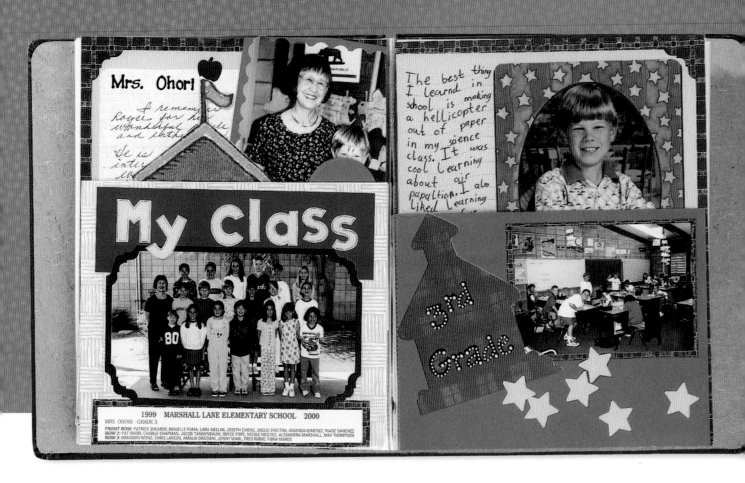

The best thing I learned in school is making a hellicopter out of paper in my science class. It was cool learning about air papaltion. I also liked learning

Mrs. Ohori

My Class

1999 MARSHALL LANE ELEMENTARY SCHOOL 2000
MRS. OHORI - GRADE 3
FRONT ROW: PATRICK SHEARER, DANIELLE PUMA, LARA ABELAR, JOSEPH CHONG, JOELLE SHELTON, AMANDA GIMENEZ, RIANE SANCHEZ
ROW 2: PAT OHORI, CHARLIE CHAPMAN, JACOB TANNENBAUM, ROYCE POPE, NICOLE MESTICE, ALEXANDRA MARSHALL, MAX THOMPSON
ROW 3: BRANDON WONG, CHRIS LARSON, AMALIA GRAZIANI, JONNY WAHL, FRED RUBIO, FIONA MARES

3rd Grade

My Class

FOLD OUT AN INTERACTIVE "YEAR IN REVIEW"

It is almost unbelievable how much happens in just one school year! Nevertheless, with creative page additions and creative cropping, Oksanna managed to feature her son's entire 1999/2000 school year in an amazing two-page spread. Exact instructions for this incredible scrapbooking fete will depend upon what you wish to include, but here is some insight to perhaps inspire you to try this.

Start with a four blank scrapbook pages—two will be the base "spread" and the two in the center are cropped in half horizontally, one forming a fold out pocket. Attach more pages with artist's tape to the outer edges of your base spread to create a "gate fold," if desired. From here, the world is your stage! Read on the next page for all of the little "interactions" that Oksanna built into her "Year in Review."

Oksanna Pope, Los Gatos, California

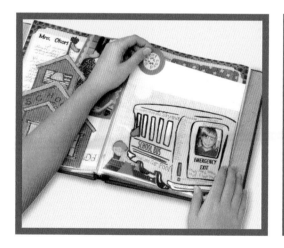

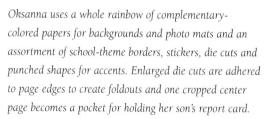

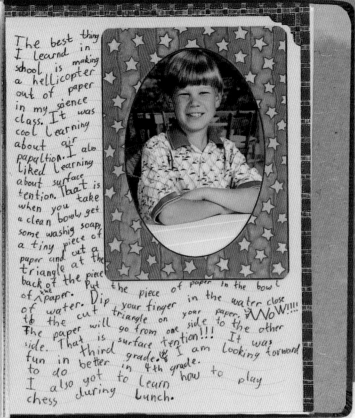

Oksanna uses a whole rainbow of complementary-colored papers for backgrounds and photo mats and an assortment of school-theme borders, stickers, die cuts and punched shapes for accents. Enlarged die cuts are adhered to page edges to create foldouts and one cropped center page becomes a pocket for holding her son's report card.

The photos and journaling work in unison to tell the story of the school year. Topics include projects, a note from Royce's teacher, a carpool schedule, his daily school activities, a class photo with classmate names, and a letter from Royce about what he learned in third grade. This unique spread scores an "A+"!

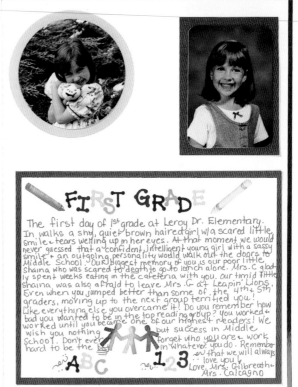

FIRST GRADE

The first day of 1st grade at Leroy Dr. Elementary. In walks a shy, quiet, brown haired girl w/a scared little smile + tears welling up in her eyes. At that moment we would never guessed that a confident, intelligent young girl with a sassy smile + an outgoing personality would walk out the doors to Middle School. Our biggest memory of you is our poor little Shaina who was scared to death to go to lunch alone. Mrs. C gladly spent weeks eating in the cafeteria with you. Our timid little Shaina was also afraid to leave Mrs. G at Leapin' Lions. Even when you jumped better than some of the 4th + 5th graders, moving up to the next group terrified you! Like everything else, you overcame it! Do you remember how bad you wanted to be in the top reading group? You worked + worked until you became one of our highest readers! We wish you nothing but success in Middle School. Don't ever forget who you are - work hard to be the best that you can be in whatever you do. Remember that we will always love you.
Love, Mrs. Gilbreath + Mrs. Calcagno

ABC   123

Student Appreciation Theme Album

PRAISE A JOB WELL DONE

When grade school gave way to middle school, Tracy enlisted the help of her daughter's grade school teachers to create a "continuation" gift album for Shaina. Before she left school for summer break, Shaina and her mom visited with all of her past teachers. Tracy took candid student/teacher photos and secretly left blank white note cards and an acid-free pen with each teacher, along with a little note asking them to write Shaina a letter.

The letters, often quite touching, provide a moving documentation of Shaina's learning experience and growth during the grade school years. Some people got very creative—such as the Before and After School program director

that Shaina would help instead of going outside for recess; she wrote her letter in rebus journaling, shown above. The letters were matted and mounted on scrapbook pages, along with the photos and simple school-theme stickers.

The teachers were happy to oblige and the gift album has become very dear to Shaina as she moves on to the next phase of public education.

Tracy Johnson, Thornton, Colorado

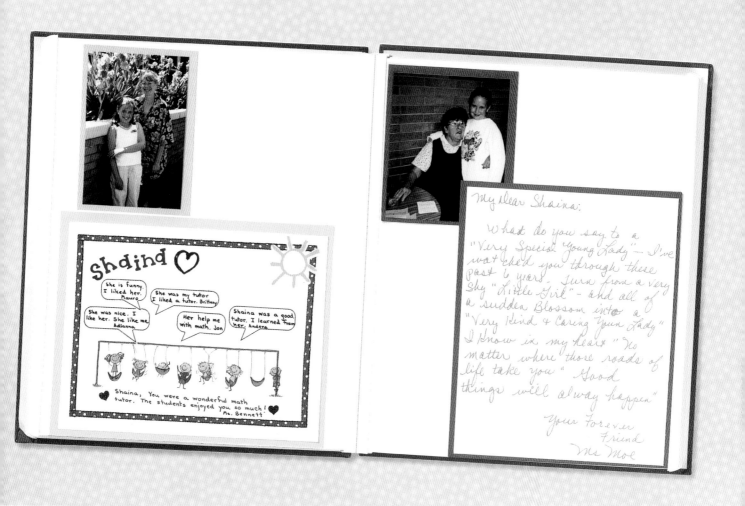

SCRAPBOOKS IN THE CLASSROOM

Scrapbooks can enhance school curriculum because students learn in different ways, and scrapbooking allows for that individuality. Many teachers, like Shelley Balzer, have found fun and innovative ways to use scrapbooks in the classroom. "The kids will say they like the stickers best, but really, looking at the completed project over and over again is the best part," she says.

Some teachers also use scrapbooks in the classroom to encourage writing, preserve a school's history; present a class project (see pages 426-427); document a year of studies, field trips and events; show student pen pals in other countries what school life in America is like; and more.

Shelley Balzer, Bakersfield, California

Teacher Appreciation Theme Album

CRAFT A GIFT FOR A #1 TEACHER

To help celebrate Teacher Appreciation Day in her child's kindergarten class, Nancy enlisted the help of the classmates to create a special ABC album to present to Mrs. Cole.

"I mailed blank scrapbook pages to all the kids in the class to do their own page at home," says Nancy. To compensate for the children who did not return a finished page, she made a basic scrapbook page with each child's name and some colored pen strokes on it. The kids wrote a letter to Mrs. Cole and drew pictures on their pages.

"Mrs. Cole was absolutely thrilled with the book," says Nancy. "She had no idea what we were doing, but she had wondered why I came to school and took some odd pictures—like the one of the kids all hopping like frogs—which was the class mascot."

Nancy's ABC gift album includes a year of memories: the names and photos of all of the classmates, class parties and activities, thank you letters from the children, field trips, certain classes and curriculum—even a personalized pop-up decorated with an assortment of die cuts!

Nancy Picogna, Cullman, Alabama

Gift Bag

PRESENT GIFT ALBUM IN STYLE

Should you decide to help your child's class make a Teacher Appreciation Album for the end of the school year, why not present it in a handmade gift bag—such as Alison's punch art gift bag shown at the left? Begin with a plain or colored, undecorated gift bag large enough to hold the gift album. Computer-print gift tag onto white cardstock and mat. Punch holes in top of large gift tag; insert raffia, tie in knot and adhere to bag. Accent tag with super jumbo punched apples (Marvy/Uchida) from patterned papers (Making Memories); mat with paper and adhere. Add an eyelet (see page 474) to one additional matted apple and dangle from handle on another strip of raffia.

Alison Beachem, San Diego, California

Note: We have included a pop-up pattern on page 502 so that you can make your own school-theme pop-up page. Simply decorate the pop-up with your own silhouette-cropped photos, stickers, die cuts, punch art or embellishments.

School Was Cool
PAPER PIECE A CHALKBOARD

Cindy's kids met the last day of school with the same excitement as the first day. Crop photos; mat on black paper. Print journaling on computer; cut to size and mount. Make chalkboard by mounting ½" strips of patterned paper (Provo Craft) around edges of black rectangle. Write title with chalk (Craft-T Products) using a pointed cotton swab. Cut rest of title letters from template (EK Success); mat and silhouette. Add journaling.

Design Brandi Ginn
Lafayette, Colorado

Photos Cindy Kacynski
Superior, Colorado

School's Out for Summer
USE PAPER SCRAPS FOR TITLE LETTERS

The last day of school always brings a familiar song to Karen's mind, so she built a page around its title. Begin by layering red cardstock over white, leaving ¼" border. Crop photos; single- and double- mat on patterned (Bazzill) and solid papers. Draw title letters (source unknown) with pencil; cut paper scraps to fit wide section of letters from patterned paper. Adhere scraps and outline letters with red pen. Double-mat title block. Journal on apple die cut (Ellison); mat and silhouette. Complete page with sticker numbers (C-Thru Ruler).

Karen Regep Glover
Grosse Pointe Woods, Michigan

Say Bye to Grade Five

PAY TRIBUTE TO A TEACHER

Terri pays tribute to one of her daughter's favorite teachers with last-day-of-school photos. Crop photos into shapes; trim rectangle with corner rounder and mount all on page. Draw grid lines using ruler as guide with pens. Stamp various designs and title letters (Close To My Heart); color with pens. Draw detail lines around photos and journal to complete page.

Terri Howard, Hood, California

End of Year

LAYER A DIE-CUT BORDER

Joyce highlighted her daughter's favorite classmates by layering circle-cropped faces onto a colorful die-cut border that resembles a paper doll chain. Add die-cut paper dolls (Crafty Cutter) across lower edge of page; add circle-cropped photos of children for faces. Crop and mat large photos into ovals with decorative scissors (Fiskars). Freehand draw title block paper "pin ups" and "pushpins," and mount sticker letters (Creative Memories) in squares. Stamp yellow stars (All Night Media). Finish with pen stroke border and journaling.

Joyce Schweitzer, Greensboro, North Carolina

Quotes & Sayings

Give your scrapbook pages an inspirational or comical lift with these quotes and sayings about school days, teachers and learning. For more quotes, see those featured at the beginning of each chapter on pages 397, 417, 437 and 471.

If you ask your mother for one fried egg for breakfast and she gives you two fried eggs and you eat both of them, who is better in arithmetic, you or your mother?

Tracy Johnson, Thornton, Colorado
Quote by Carl Sandberg, 1878-1967

A child's mind is like a shallow brook which ripples and dances merrily over the stony course of its education and reflects here a flower, there a bush, yonder a fleecy cloud...
—*Helen Keller*

A child's life is like a piece of paper on which every person leaves a mark.
—*Chinese proverb*

A good education is the next best thing to a pushy mother.
—*Charles Schultz*

A teacher affects eternity; he can never tell where his influence stops.
—*Henry Brooks Adams*

A teacher can but lead you to the door; learning is up to you.
—*Chinese proverb*

Children are young, but they're not naive. And they're honest. They're not going to keep awake if the story is boring. When they get excited you can see it in their eyes.
—*Chinua Achebe*

Education is not preparation for life; education is life itself.
—*John Dewey*

Good teachers are usually a little crazy.
—*Andy Rooney*

I always tell students that it is what you learn after you know it all that counts.
—*Harry S. Truman*

It is a glorious fever, that desire to know.
—*Edward Butler Lytton*

Learning how to learn is life's most important skill.
—*Michael Gelb and Tony Buzan,* Lessons from the Art of Juggling: How to Achieve Your Full Potential in Business, Learning and Life

Learning is at its best when it is deadly serious and very playful at the same time.
—*Sarah Lawrence Lightfoot*

Let us tenderly and kindly cherish, therefore, the means of knowledge. Let us dare to read, think, speak and write.
—*John Adams,* Dissertation on the Canon and Feudal Law

People seldom see the halting and painful steps by which the most insignificant success is achieved.
—*Annie Sullivan*

The experience gathered from books, though often valuable, is but the nature of learning: whereas the experience gained from actual life is of the nature of wisdom.
—*Samuel Smiles*

The human mind is our fundamental resource.
—*John F. Kennedy*

The important thing is not so much that every child should be taught, as that every child should be given the wish to learn.
—*John Lubbock*

The world exists for the education of each [person].
—*Ralph Waldo Emerson*

To be able to learn is to be young, and whoever keeps the joy of learning in him or her remains forever young.
—*J.G. Bennett*

To me education is a leading out of what is already there in the pupil's soul.
—*Muriel Sparks*

There are two kinds of teachers: the kind that fills you with so much quail shot that you can't move, and the kind that just gives you a little prod behind and you jump to the skies.
—*Robert Frost*

We cannot always build the future for our youth, but we can build our youth for the future.
—*Franklin D. Roosevelt*

Lettering Patterns & Page Title Ideas

Use these convenient lettering patterns to add a fun finishing touch to your grade school pages. Simply photocopy the lettering pattern, scaled to the size you need, and trace onto your page in pencil using a light table or window. Retrace and color in pen color of your choice. Or make your own patterns from the page title ideas listed by theme.

BACK TO SCHOOL

Back-to-school blues
Back-to-school shopping madness
Be true to your school
Bus stop
Catching the bus
First day jitters
First day of school
Getting ready
Getting started
Is summer over already?
My backpack
My school
Our school rocks!
Rise and shine!
School bus
The shopping experience
Special school clothes
The Pledge of Allegiance
Wake up, wake up, wake up!
Waking up

ALL IN A DAY'S WORK

#1 Kid
#1 student
#1 teacher
1st place
A day in review
A few of my favorite things
A typical day
Be true to your school
Best friends
Best friends forever
Lunch
The lunch bunch

My favorite lunch
My favorite teacher
On the playground
Our children, our future
Proud to be me
Recess
Recess fun
School days
School daze
School is cool
School spirit

ACTIVITIES & SPECIAL EVENTS

4-H
The big feast
Celebrate!
Costume parade
Crossing over
Graduate of 2009
Graduate of 2010
Graduate of 2011
Graduate of 2012
Graduate of 2013
Graduate of 2014
Graduate of 2015
Happy Valentine's Day
Holiday brunch
Holiday party
Ice-cream social
It's cookie time!
Jammie day
My funny Valentine
My merit badges
News flash
On my honor
Our Christmas party
Our fundraiser
Pomp and circumstance
School news
School program
Scout's honor
Shamrock shenanigans
Spring fling
Student of the month
Thanksgiving feast
We're so proud!
What a genius!

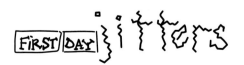

ACADEMICS

Computer whiz
Everything I Need to Know I Learned in…
Field trip
Geography
Gym
Hard at work
Home school is cool!
Homework blues
Homework is fun—NOT!
Honor roll
Honor student
I love reading
Mad science
Making the grade
Mathematical genius
Now that's teamwork
Our little Einstein
Our Picasso
Physical education
Readin', 'ritin', 'rithmetic
Reading rules!
Science fair
Science project
Spelling bee
Spelling champ
Summer school
What a fine artist!
What I learned
The world is our classroom

PORTRAITS & MILESTONES

A new school
Back 2 school
Congratulations!
D.A.R.E. graduation
End-of-year party
Glad grad!
Graduation day
Here's looking at you, kid
Here's to the Graduate!
Hollywood smile
Jr. High, here I come!
Last day of school
Look at me now!
Middle school, here I come!
Middle school rules!
My diploma
No more pencils, no more books
Our shining star
Pomp and Circumstance
Proud to be me
Say "Cheese"
School's out for the summer
School was cool, but now we're out!
See you in September
Watch me grow!
The year in review
You ought to be in pictures

PERFORMANCES

A note-able performance
A sparkling performance
A star is born
A stellar performance
Born to dance
Curtain call
It's show time
Keepin' the beat
Making music
Musical celebration
My recital
The world's a stage
You're a star!

SPORTS

All star
First and ten
Goal!
Little league champs
Put me in coach, I'm ready to play
Take me out to the ballgame
There's no "I" in "teamwork"
You did it!

Project Patterns

Use these helpful patterns to complete specific scrapbook pages featured in this book. Enlarge and photocopy the patterns as needed to fit your photos and/or page size.

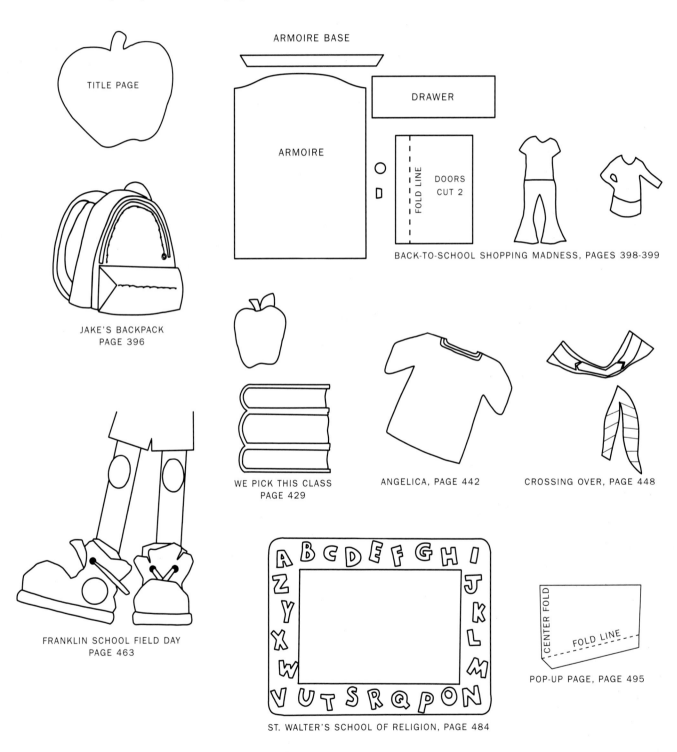

TITLE PAGE

JAKE'S BACKPACK
PAGE 396

ARMOIRE BASE

ARMOIRE

DRAWER

DOORS
CUT 2

FOLD LINE

BACK-TO-SCHOOL SHOPPING MADNESS, PAGES 398-399

WE PICK THIS CLASS
PAGE 429

ANGELICA, PAGE 442

CROSSING OVER, PAGE 448

FRANKLIN SCHOOL FIELD DAY
PAGE 463

ST. WALTER'S SCHOOL OF RELIGION, PAGE 484

CENTER FOLD

FOLD LINE

POP-UP PAGE, PAGE 495

Paper Piecing Patterns

To incorporate your own photos into these original paper-pieced designs, photocopy and enlarge the patterns below to fit your selected photos. Cut the pattern pieces apart, transfer the pieces to colored or printed papers of your choice and cut out. Reassemble all elements, adding a silhouette-cropped photo to complete the design.

TITLE PAGE

PAGE 395

PAGE 419

PAGE 397

PAGE 387

PAGE 417

PAGE 423

PAGE 422

PAGE 422

PAGE 464

PAGE 437

PAGE 471

PAGE 508

Page Patterns

Our ready-made patterns make it easy to begin a portrait, vital statistics or autographs scrapbook page. Simply enlarge to 120% (for an 8½ x 11" page) or 135% (for a 12 x 12" page) and photocopy onto desired paper; then add cropped photos or journaling.

School Days

Kinder garten

2nd grade

1st grade

3rd grade

5th grade

4th grade

6th grade

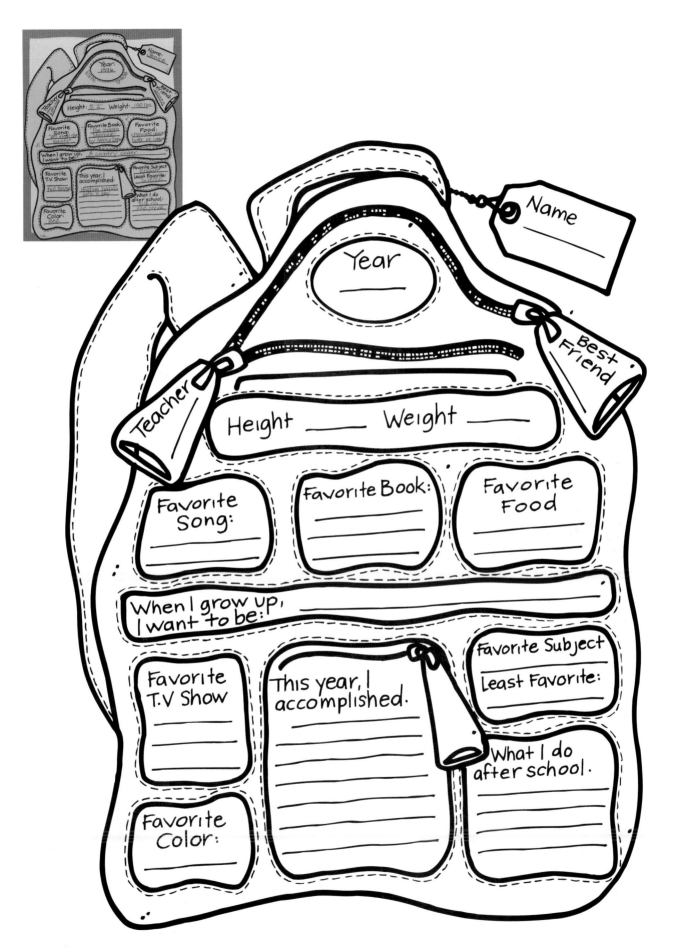

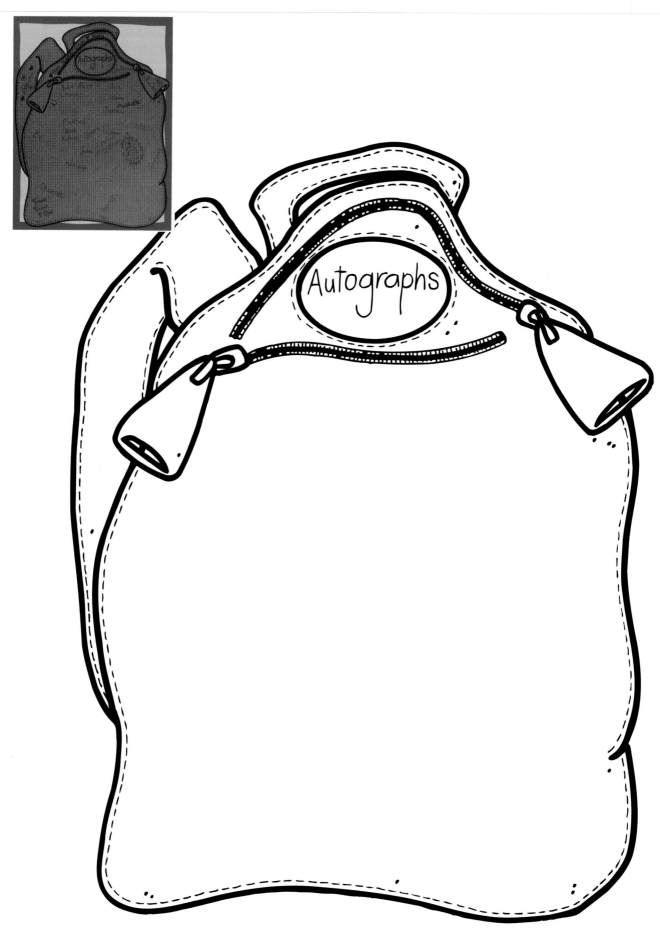

Autographs

Instructions & Credits

cover, page 470

Casey

Irma's flair for detail and design in the clothes that she makes for her daughter is reflected on a page decorated with school day symbols. Begin by mounting large portrait. Slice ½" strip of solid paper; mount below photo. Cut rectangle from vellum for title block; mat on solid paper. Cut letters from templates (C-Thru Ruler, EK Success). Use craft knife to cut letter "a" out of apple die cut (Provo Craft); mount solid paper behind letter before mounting on page. Cut ten 2⅛" squares from solid and patterned papers (Making Memories, Paper Adventures, Provo Craft). For left border, cut vellum to size of square and adhere with eyelets (Impress Rubber Stamps); slip small photo in pocket. Punch medium apples (HyGlo/American Pin); mount over square with self-adhesive foam spacers. Draw letters on next square. Cut apple from template (source unknown) with craft knife; mount over solid paper. Adhere sticker letters (Making Memories) for lower square. For right border, cut letter "C" using template (C-Thru Ruler); layer over patterned paper. Draw letters on next square with white pencil; layer apple die cut (Provo Craft) over squares. Mount die-cut apple on next square with foam spacers. Draw letter "a" with template on patterned paper. Print journaling on vellum; mount over last two squares. Mount all squares on page in topsy-turvy fashion. *Design Pam Klassen; Photos Irma Lozano-Gabbard, San Diego, California*

page 388

Our Little Artists

Creativity and art plays a major role in the lives of her family, so Michele makes sure to feature her kids' artwork whenever possible. Frame the page by drawing a wavy border with decorative ruler (C-Thru); cut out, crimp (Paper Adventures) and slice ends at an angle where corners meet; mount over solid background paper. Crop photos; mount behind paper "frames." Slice strips for frame title plates; mount with eyelets (Impress Rubber Stamps). Mount eyelets to sides of frames; tie craft thread (DMC Corp.) to eyelets.

Mount eyelets to page to "hang" frames, looping thread under eyelet to secure. Create title letters with pen; color with pencils and adhere sticker letters (Mrs. Grossman's). Complete page with journaling. *Design Ann Kitayama, Broomfield, Colorado; Photos Michele Gerbrandt*

page 396

Jake's Backpack

MaryJo captured in photos the best part of starting the school year to her son—buying new school supplies and a new backpack to carry them in—and saved her least favorite part: the receipt! Paper tear a 2 x 2½" strip from the top and bottom of a 12 x 12" cardstock; layer over solid background paper as shown, leaving space between torn strips. Double mat photos; mount on page. Print journaling from computer; mount on page. Punch large rectangles (Family Treasures) in various colors; layer at top of page, over photos and on text block as shown. Cut title letters from template (C-Thru Ruler); mat and silhouette. Layer first letter of each word on large rectangle. Paper piece backpack (see page 502 for pattern). Add detail with metallic thread (Kreinik), ribbon (C.M. Offray & Son), eyelets (Creative Impressions) and cording (source unknown). Complete page with hidden school supply receipt; fold "accordion-style" under triple-matted text block. *Design Pam Metzger, Boulder, Colorado; Photos MaryJo Regier, Littleton, Colorado*

page 416

The Science Fair

Pennie's son enjoyed the success of a science experiment that led him to a district science fair. Crop and partially silhouette photos; mat two photos on solid and patterned (Paper Adventures) papers. Cut large circle and ring from solid and patterned paper; layer over patterned background paper (Paper Adventures). Freehand draw and cut title banner from vellum and mat. Adhere sticker letters (Stickopotamus); write subtitle. Complete page with journaling; mat and mount on page. *Pennie Stutzman, Broomfield, Colorado*

page 436

Lady Storm

A colorful combination of patterned paper sets the stage for Narda's action photos. Begin by cutting patterned papers (Paper Fever) along design lines; mount at upper and lower edges of page over red patterned paper (Scrapbook Wizard). Crop photos and mat on solid paper. Cut title and journaling block; add freehand-drawn decorative lettering, pen stroke stitching and freehand-drawn soccer ball. Freehand cut lightning bolt from patterned paper (Scrapbook Wizard). Detail with chalk to complete page. *Narda Poe, Midland, Texas*

PHOTOGRAPHING MEMORABILIA

A picture of your child's sports, club and activities memorabilia gets those items into the scrapbook without adding bulk. Try these great tips:

• Memorabilia can include uniforms, equipment, trophies—even shoes!

• Outdoors, use 200-speed film and flash; shoot in open shade or soft sunlight.

• Indoors, use 400-speed film and flash; shoot in well-lit location or late in the day for a nostalgic effect.

• Arrange memorabilia on floor or tabletop in an eye-pleasing display.

• Fill the frame with your arrangement when you look through the camera's viewfinder.

• Get in as close as possible to accurately record words and numbers.

• Snap many photos from different angles, rearranging memorabilia as needed for greater visual appeal.

• For a photography alternative for flat memorabilia such as ribbons and certificates, scan the item(s) into your computer, either alone or in collage-style, reduce the size, and print on acid-free paper of choice.

KARI, 6TH GRADE

Sources

The following companies manufacture products featured in this book. Please check your local retailers to find these materials. In addition, we have made every attempt to properly credit the trademarks and brand names of the items mentioned in this book. We apologize to any company that we have listed incorrectly or the sources were unknown, and we would appreciate hearing from you.

3L Corp.
(800) 828-3130 (wholesale only)

Accu-Cut
(800) 288-1670
www.accucut.com

All Night Media, Inc.
(800) 782-6733

Bazzill Basics Paper
(480) 558-8557

Beary Patch, The
(877) 327-2111 (wholesale only)

Bo-Bunny Press
(801) 771-4010 (wholesale only)
www.bobunny.com

Boy Scouts of America National Council
(972) 580-2000

Broderbund Software
(319) 247-3325
www.broderbund.com

Canson, Inc.
(800) 628-9283

Clearsnap, Inc.
(800) 448-4862
www.clearsnap.com

Close to My Heart
(888) 655-6552
www.closetomyheart.com

C.M. Offray & Son, Inc.
(800) 344-5533
www.offray.com

Cock-A-Doodle Design, Inc.
(800) 262-9727
www.cockadoodledesign.com

Colorbök
(800) 366-4660 (wholesale only)

Crafter's Workshop, The
(877) CRAFTER
www.thecraftersworkshop.com

Craf-T Products
(507) 235-3996

Crafty Cutter
(805) 237-7833
www.crftycttr.com

Creative Imaginations
(800) 942-6487

Creative Memories
(800) 468-9335
www.creative-memories.com

C-Thru Ruler Company, The
(800) 243-8419
www.cthruruler.com

Cut-It-Up
(530) 389-2233
www.cut-it-up.com

Darice, Inc.
(800) 321-1494

Design Originals
(800) 877-7820
www.d-originals.com

D.J. Inkers
(800) 325-4890

DMC Corp.
(973) 589-0606
www.dmc.usa.com

DMD Industries, Inc.
(800) 805-9890
www.dmdind.com

Doodlebug Design, Inc.
(801) 524-0050

Duncan Enterprises
(559) 291-4444

EK Success
(800) 524-1349
www.eksuccess.com

Ellison Craft & Design
(800) 253-2238
www.ellison.com

Emagination Crafts, Inc.
(630) 833-9521
www.emaginationcrafts.com

Family Treasures, Inc.
(800) 413-2645
www.familytreasures.com

Fiskars, Inc.
(800) 950-0203
www.fiskars.com

Frances Meyer, Inc.
(800) 372-6237
www.francesmeyer.com

Hambly Studios
(800) 451-3999
www.hamblystudios.net

Hot Off The Press
(800) 227-9595
www.paperpizzaz.com

Hyglo/American Pin
(800) 821-7125
www.ameripin.com

Impress Rubber Stamps
(206) 901-9101

Inkadinkado Rubber Stamps
(800) 888-4652
www.inkadinkado.com

It Takes Two
(800) 331-9843

Joyful Heart Stamps
(949) 770-7959
www.joyfulheartstamps.com

Judi-Kins
(800) 398-5834
www.judikins.com

Karen Foster Design
(801) 451-9779
www.karenfosterdesign.com

Keeping Memories Alive
(800) 419-4949

Kreinik Manufacturing Co.
(800) 537-2166

Magic Scraps
(972) 385-1838

Making Memories
(800) 286-5263
www.makingmemories.com

Marvy Uchida
(800) 541-5877
www.uchida.com

Mary Engelbreit Studios
(800) 443-6379

Masterpiece Studios
(800) 447-0219
www.masterpiecestudios.com

McGill Inc.
(800) 982-9884
www.mcgillinc.com

Me and My BIG Ideas
(949) 589-4607 (wholesale only)
www.meandmybigideas.com

MPR Associates, Inc.
(336) 861-6343

Mrs. Grossman's Paper Co
(800) 429-4549
www.mrsgrossmans.com

My Mind's Eye, Inc.
(801) 298-3709

Nankong Enterprises, Inc.
(wholesale only)
(302) 731-2995

Northern Spy
(530) 620-7430
www.nspycom

NRN Designs (wholesale only)
(800) 421-6958

Paper Adventures
(800) 727-0699
www.paperadventures.com

Paper Cuts
(800) 661-4399
www.papercuts.com

Paper Fever Inc.
(801) 412-0495

Paper Patch, The
(800) 397-2737 (wholesale only)

Pebbles In My Pocket
(800) 438-8153
www.pebblesimypocket.com

Plaid Enterprises, Inc.
(800) 842-4197
www.plaidenterprises.com

Posh Impressions
(800) 421-7674

Preservation Technologies
(800) 416-2665

Provo Craft
(888) 588-3545

Pulsar Paper Products
(877) 861-0031

Punch Bunch, The
(254) 791-4209 (wholesale only)

Puzzle Mates
(888) 595-2887
www.puzzlemates.com

Ranger Industries, Inc.
(800) 244-2211
www.rangerink.com

Robin's Nest Press, The
(435) 789-5387

Rubber Stampede
(800) 423-4135
www.rubberstampede.com

Sandylion Sticker Designs
(800) 387-4215
www.sandylion.com

Scrapbook Wizard, The
(801) 947-0019

Scrapable Scribbles
(801) 255-5465

Scrap Pagerz
(435) 645-0696
www.scrappagerz.com

Sonburn, Inc.
(800) 527-7505
www.sonburn.com

Stampabilities
(800) 888-0321

Stampendous! (wholesale only)
(800) 869-0474

Stampin' Up!
(800) 782-6787
www.stampinup.com

Stamping Station Inc.
(801) 444-3828

Stamps N Memories
(909) 381-6063

Stickopotamus
(888) 270-4443
www.stickopotamus.com

Suzy's Zoo
(800) 777-4846
www.suzyszoo.com

Therm O Web, Inc.
(800) 323-0799

Too Much Fun Rubber Stamps
(517) 351-2030

Tsukineko, Inc.
(800) 769-6633
www.tsukineko.com

Westrim Crafts
(800) 727-2727

Windows Of Time
(801) 732-1053
www.windowsoftime.com

Bibliography & Web Sites

Burns, Robert B. *Child Development: A Text for the Caring Professions.* New York: Nichols Publishing Company. 1986

Furgeson, Lael C. and Stephanie F. Taylor. *Family Scrapbooking.* New York: Sterling Publishing Company. 2000

Ramey, Craig T. *Going to School: How to Help Your Child Succeed.* New York: Goddard Press. 1999

WEB SITES

www.healthleader.uthouston.edu/archive/children/010813 (University of Texas Health Science Center at Houston, *"Plain Sense: Self Esteem"*)

www.plainsense.com/Health/Children/self_esteem.htm

http://ohioline.osu.edu/hyg-fact/5000/5263.html (Ohio State University Fact Sheet, *"Building Children's Self Esteem"*)

The material in this compilation appeared in the following previously published Memory Makers Books and appears here by permission of the authors. (The initial page numbers given refer to pages in the original work; page numbers in parentheses refer to pages in this book.)

Editors of Memory Makers.   Scrapbook Basics © 2002.   Pages 1, 4-127 (7-131)
Editors of Memory Makers.   Creative Photo Cropping for Scrapbooks   Pages 1, 4-127 (132-257)
                            © 2001.
Editors of Memory Makers.   Baby Scrapbooks © 2000.   Pages 3, 5-127 (258-383)
Editors of Memory Makers.   School Days Scrapbooks © 2002.   Pages 1, 4-127 (384-509)

Other fine Memory Makers Books are available from your local bookstore, scrapbooking store or direct from the publisher.

07 06 05 04 5 4 3 2

Library of Congress Cataloging in Publication Data

Scrapbooking Your Favorite Family Memories / edited by editors of Memory Makers Books-1st ed.
          p. cm.
     ISBN 1-892127-33-4 (hc. : alk. paper)

Cover Designer: Marissa Bowers
Production Coordinator: Sara Dumford

Explore the world of scrapbooking!

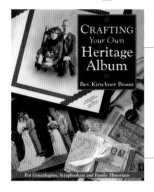

This guide helps you capture and preserve the precious keepsakes of your family history. You'll learn to create an elegant album that weaves family history, lore and tradition with cherished photos, documents and memorabilia and preserves them for generations to come!

ISBN 1-55870-534-1, paperback, 128 pages, #70457-K

Enrich your pages and by combining two pastimes both personal and long lasting—writing and scrapbooking. Inside are stunning color photos that instruct and inspire scrapbookers to create pages which will speak to generations to come. Tips on what to say and how to say it, lists of powerful, descriptive words, advice for overcoming journaling jitters and much more also included.

ISBN 1-892127-23-7, paperback, 96 pages, #32459-K

Learn to preserve precious family memories in a one-of-a-kind heritage album. This books guides you through the process of researching family history, protecting old photos & memorabilia, and creating stunning scrapbooks that are sure to become family treasures.

ISBN 1-892127-22-9, paperback, 128 pages, #32473-K

Get inspired by this fresh, fun selection of page borders, corners and title designs perfect for any theme—including holidays! More than 70 custom-coordinated page elements can be combined with your photos for the best-dressed pages around. Patterns and step-by-step illustrations are also included which help create easy-to-make accents with designer appeal.

ISBN 1-892127-13-X, paperback, 96 pages, #32683-K

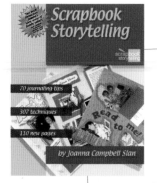

Go beyond typical scrapbooking techniques! This inspiring book offers dozens of great ideas for documenting family stories and events with words and images. You'll find step-by-step techniques for creating clever scrapbook layouts and unique booklets—even web pages! You'll also learn new ways to combine cherished family stories with photos, collages and illustrations.

ISBN 0-9630222-8-8, paperback, 144 pages, #70450-K

More books for scrapbookers!

This book provides you with 50 new alphabets created by the nation's top scrapbook lettering artists, along with the most popular Memory Makers letter styles from the past. Also included are easy-to-photocopy alphabet patterns, styles from classic elegance to cutting-edge creative, plus a variety of ways to personalize each style.

ISBN 1-892127-15-6, paperback, 96 pages, #32682-K

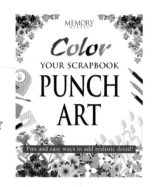

Inside you'll find more than 50 brand new, full-color punch art pages along with how to add texture and dimension to punch art using 20 basic-level pen, pencil, ink, paint and chalk techniques. With this "no fear and no experience needed" approach, easy-to-follow instructions and illustrations and a variety of color combinations, adding color to your punch art pages has never been simpler and more fun!

ISBN 1-892127-03-2, paperback, 96 pages, #32472-K

This book combines dazzling ideas with simple techniques for creating a gorgeous wedding scrapbook album. More than 200 full-color sample pages provide the inspiration you need to record the fun details of every event—from engagement to honeymoon. Find guidelines for every step, including organizing photos, choosing a theme and tips for enhancing your album pages with stories, scriptures, and personal memories.

ISBN 1-89212-708-3, paperback, 128 pages, #31788-K

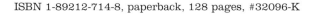

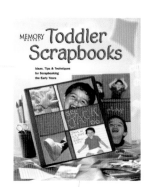

Treasure the special, happy memories from a child's toddlerhood, including playtime, sleepy time, bath time, mealtime, favorite things, preschool, pets and more. 200 never-before-seen page layouts, user-friendly instructions and unique idea galleries for theme and storybook albums are included. Make a lasting memento that you and your child will cherish for a lifetime!

ISBN 1-89212-714-8, paperback, 128 pages, #32096-K

This book shows you how to play "catch-up" in organizing your photos while creating your scrapbook. You'll find tips for organizing supplies and photos, hundreds of page ideas, stamping, photo montage, punch art techniques and more! Dozens of extras, including inspirational quotes, a quick color-mood psychology tutorial and variations for punches, embellishments, sticker borders title treatments and more are also inside.

ISBN 1-892127-20-2, paperback, 128 pages, #32471-K

These books and other fine titles are available from your local art & craft retailer, bookstore, online supplier or by calling 1-800-448-0915.